# OECD AGRICULTURAL STATISTICS
# 1991/1992

OECD agricultural statistics for up to 25 countries are available in printed publications, computer diskettes and on magnetic tape. They provide a unique source of information about levels, trends and structures in agriculture

## TRIENNIAL PUBLICATION

**Food Consumption Statistics  (October 1991)**

This voluminous publication (over 500 pages) shows full supply-utilization balances, including per capita data, for almost 90 commodities and commodity groups, plus a summary table on the daily intake per head of calories and nutrients. It covers all OECD countries, except Iceland, and also shows summary graphs. Because of its volume it is published approximately every three years.

**Prices: Publication   FF 425   £ 60   US$ 100   DM 175**

    **Diskette and Publication (special promotional offer)   FF 720   £85   US$150   DM250**

## ANNUAL PUBLICATIONS

**Meat Balances in OECD Countries   (May 1992)**

Tables presenting international comparisons of production, trade and consumption for each category of meat, plus national tables showing full balances, i.e. the flow of meat by category from the production to the consumption, and graphs.

**Prices: Publication   FF 140   £ 19   US$ 34   DM 57**

    **Diskette and Publication (special promotional offer):   FF 300   £ 32   US$ 62   DM 117**

**Economic Accounts for Agriculture  (December 1991)**

Tables and graphs showing a detailed and comparable OECD-wide data base on farm accounts, providing data on output and its components, intermediate consumption and the different measures of gross value added down to net income. It also includes the capital formation account.

**Prices: Publication FF170   £23   US$40   DM70**

    **Diskette and Publication (special promotional offer):   FF 450   £ 55   US$ 95   DM 175**

## COMPUTER DISKETTES

All statistical publications listed above are also available on 3 1/2 and 5 1/4 inches diskettes. The data are in compressed format on double-density diskettes  with a translation programme provided for easy decompression and translation into a suitable format.

## MAGNETIC TAPE

A magnetic tape version of the above publications, plus other agricultural statistics not regularly published (such as trade in US $), is available for longer time periods.

## SELECTED EXTRACTS

Selected parts of the agricultural data base may be purchased upon request on listings, diskettes and magnetic tape.

---

### ORDER FORM

Institutions must attach a purchase order to this card.

Enter my order for the printed version:
( ) Meat Balances in OECD Countries   FF/£/$/DM_____
( ) Economic Accounts for Agriculture   FF/£/$/DM_____
( ) Food Consumption Statistics          FF/£/$/DM_____
                              Total _____

Enter my order for the diskette version:
( ) Meat Balances in OECD Countries   FF/£/$/DM_____
( ) Economic Accounts for Agriculture   FF/£/$/DM_____
( ) Food Consumption Statistics          FF/£/$/DM_____
                              Total _____

I wish to receive:
( )  5 1/4 inch diskettes     ( )  3 1/2 inch diskettes

VISA card number_____Exp. date_____

Signature_____

Name_____

Address_____

_____Country_____

Diskettes are sent air mail free of charge. Individual orders must be prepaid with cheque, money order or VISA card.

If you pay by VISA you will be charged the French franc price.

---

*Send your order to :*

OECD Publications
2, rue André-Pascal
F- 75775 PARIS Cedex 16, France

# STATISTIQUES AGRICOLES DE L'OCDE
## 1991/1992

Les statistiques agricoles de l'OCDE portent sur près de 25 pays et sont disponibles sous forme de publications, de disquettes et de bande magnétique. Elles constituent une source unique d'information sur les structures, les niveaux et les tendances dans le domaine agricole.

## PUBLICATION TRIENNALE

**Statistiques de la Consommation des Denrées Alimentaires (octobre 1991)**

Cette publication volumineuse (plus de 500 pages) contient des bilans alimentaires complets, y compris la consommation par tête, pour près de 90 produits et groupes de produits. Sont également montrés la consommation par tête en calories et éléments nutritifs. Tous les pays de l'OCDE, à l'exception de l'Islande, sont présentés ainsi que des graphiques récapitulatifs. Cette publication n'est publiée qu'approximativement tous les trois ans à cause de son volume.

**Prix: Publication  FF 425  £ 60  US $ 100  DM 175**
**Disquette et publication (offre spéciale de promotion) FF720  £85  US$150  DM250**

## PUBLICATIONS ANNUELLES

**Bilans de la Viande dans les Pays de l'OCDE (mai 1992)**

Tableaux présentant des comparaisons internationales de la production, des échanges et de la consommation dans chacune des catégories de la viande. En outre, des bilans complets, c.a.d. le flux de viande par catégorie du stade de la production à celle de la consommation, sont montrés sur des tableaux nationaux et des graphiques.

**Prix: Publication  FF 140  £ 19  US $ 34  DM 57**
**Disquette et publication  (offre spéciale de promotion): FF 300  £ 32  US $ 62  DM 117**

**Comptes Économiques de l'Agriculture (décembre 1991)**

Tableaux et graphiques présentant une base de données détaillée et comparable sur les pays de l'OCDE. Des données sur la production finale et ses composantes, allant de la consommation intermédiaire et des différentes mesures de la valeur ajoutée aux revenus nets. Comprend également le compte de la formation de capital.

**Prix: Publication  FF170  £23  US$40  DM70**
**Disquette et publication  (offre spéciale de promotion): FF 450  £ 55  US$ 95  DM 175**

## DISQUETTES

Toutes les publications citées ci-dessus sont également disponibles sur des disquettes de format 3 1/2 et 5 1/4. Les données sont compressées sur des disquettes à double densité et un programme de décompression et traduction vers d'autres formats est fourni.

## BANDE MAGNÉTIQUE

Une version sur bande magnétique, contenant les publications ci-dessus et d'autres statistiques agricoles non publiées régulièrement (comme les échanges agricoles en $ E-U) pour des périodes plus longues, est également disponible.

## EXTRACTIONS SPÉCIALES

Des extractions spécifiques de la base de données agricole peuvent être obtenues contre paiement sous forme de listings, de disquettes.

---

**BON DE COMMANDE**

Les organismes doivent attacher un bon d'achat à ce coupon.

N° carte VISA _____  Date d'expiration _____

Signature _____

Nom _____

Adresse _____

Pays _____

Je souhaite recevoir la version imprimée:
( ) Bilans de la Viande dans les Pays de l'OCDE  FF/£/$/DM
( ) Comptes Économiques de l'Agriculture  FF/£/$/DM
( ) Statistiques de la Consommation des Denrées Alimentaires  FF/£/$/DM
Total _____

Je souhaite recevoir la version sur disquette:
( ) Bilans de la Viande dans les Pays de l'OCDE  FF/£/$/DM
( ) Comptes Économiques de l'Agriculture  FF/£/$/DM
( ) Statistiques de la Consommation des Denrées Alimentaires  FF/£/$/DM
Total _____

Je souhaiterais recevoir:
( ) des disquettes 5 1/4    ( ) des disquettes 3 1/2

Les disquettes seront envoyées gratuitement par courrier avion.
Les commandes sont payables d'avance par chèque, par mandat ou par carte de crédit VISA.
Dans ce dernier cas, le prix payé sera celui en Francs français.

---

*Veuillez adresser votre commande à:*

OCDE Publications
2, rue André-Pascal
F-75775 PARIS Cédex 16, France

# MEAT BALANCES IN OECD COUNTRIES

# BILANS DE LA VIANDE DANS LES PAYS DE L'OCDE

# 1984-1990

ORGANISATION FOR ECONOMIC CO-OPERATION AND DEVELOPMENT
ORGANISATION DE COOPÉRATION ET DE DÉVELOPPEMENT ÉCONOMIQUES

# ORGANISATION FOR ECONOMIC CO-OPERATION AND DEVELOPMENT

## ORGANISATION DE COOPÉRATION ET DE DÉVELOPPEMENT ÉCONOMIQUES

Pursuant to Article 1 of the Convention signed in Paris on 14th December 1960, and which came into force on 30th September 1961, the Organisation for Economic Co-operation and Development (OECD) shall promote policies designed:

— to achieve the highest sustainable economic growth and employment and a rising standard of living in Member countries, while maintaining financial stability, and thus to contribute to the development of the world economy;

— to contribute to sound economic expansion in Member as well as non-member countries in the process of economic development; and

— to contribute to the expansion of world trade on a multilateral, non-discriminatory basis in accordance with international obligations.

The original Member countries of the OECD are Austria, Belgium, Canada, Denmark, France, Germany, Greece, Iceland, Ireland, Italy, Luxembourg, the Netherlands, Norway, Portugal, Spain, Sweden, Switzerland, Turkey, the United Kingdom and the United States. The following countries became Members subsequently through accession at the dates indicated hereafter: Japan (28th April 1964), Finland (28th January 1969), Australia (7th June 1971) and New Zealand (29th May 1973). The Commission of the European Communities takes part in the work of the OECD (Article 13 of the OECD Convention). Yugoslavia has a special status at OECD (agreement of 28th October 1961).

En vertu de l'article 1er de la Convention signée le 14 décembre 1960, à Paris, et entrée en vigueur le 30 septembre 1961, l'Organisation de Coopération et de Développement Economiques (OCDE) a pour objectif de promouvoir des politiques visant :

— à réaliser la plus forte expansion de l'économie et de l'emploi et une progression du niveau de vie dans les pays Membres, tout en maintenant la stabilité financière, et à contribuer ainsi au développement de l'économie mondiale ;

— à contribuer à une saine expansion économique dans les pays Membres, ainsi que les pays non membres, en voie de développement économique ;

— à contribuer à l'expansion du commerce mondial sur une base multilatérale et non discriminatoire conformément aux obligations internationales.

Les pays Membres originaires de l'OCDE sont : l'Allemagne, l'Autriche, la Belgique, le Canada, le Danemark, l'Espagne, les Etats-Unis, la France, la Grèce, l'Irlande, l'Islande, l'Italie, le Luxembourg, la Norvège, les Pays-Bas, le Portugal, le Royaume-Uni, la Suède, la Suisse et la Turquie. Les pays suivants sont ultérieurement devenus Membres par adhésion aux dates indiquées ci-après : le Japon (28 avril 1964), la Finlande (28 janvier 1969), l'Australie (7 juin 1971) et la Nouvelle-Zélande (29 mai 1973). La Commission des Communautés européennes participe aux travaux de l'OCDE (article 13 de la Convention de l'OCDE). La Yougoslavie a un statut spécial à l'OCDE (accord du 28 octobre 1961).

# TABLE OF CONTENTS – TABLE DES MATIÈRES

## COUNTRY TABLES – TABLEAUX PAR PAYS

# INTRODUCTION

This volume is the 20th issue of the Meat balances in OECD Member countries. It covers the years 1984-1990 (with the exception of the General Tables covering the period 1983-1990 and an average for 1980-1982).

The Agricultural Statistics Section, which is responsible for this volume, would welcome any observations or suggestions which may lead to improvements in the future. The Statistical Section will, as far as it is able, meet any request for further information.

Agricultural Statistics Section
OECD Directorate for Agriculture
March 1992

Le présent volume constitue la 20e édition des Bilans de la viande dans les pays Membres de l'OCDE. Il couvre les années 1984-1990 (sauf les tableaux généraux qui couvrent la période 1983-1990 et une moyenne pour les années 1980 à 1982).

La Section de statistique agricole responsable du présent volume serait heureuse de recevoir des utilisateurs les observations et suggestions qui permettront, dans le futur, de nouveaux progrès. Elle répondra, dans toute la mesure de ses possibilités, aux demandes de renseignements complémentaires.

Section de Statistique Agricole
Direction de l'Agriculture de l'OCDE
Mars 1992

# GENERAL NOTES – NOTES GÉNÉRALES

# I.  PRESENTATION – PRÉSENTATION

This volume is divided into two parts, preceded by explanatory notes indicating the methods of compilation.

The first part consists of **"General Tables"**, in which, after a summary table on human population, all major items of the country tables are given for each OECD Member country, except Iceland, as well as for groups of countries.

The second part consists of **"Country tables"**, in which a more detailed breakdown is given.

Le présent volume comprend deux parties, précédées de notes explicatives indiquant la méthodologie suivie pour les établir.

La première partie comprend, les **« Tableaux généraux »**, dans lesquels, après un premier tableau sur la population humaine, tous les principaux sujets des tableaux par pays sont repris pour chaque pays, à l'exception de l'Islande, ainsi que pour des groupements de pays.

La deuxième partie se compose des **« Tableaux par pays »**, qui proposent des informations plus détaillées.

# II.  CONTENTS OF THE TABLES – CONTENU DES TABLEAUX

Unless otherwise stated, the data relate to calendar years. The general tables cover a 1980-1982 average and each calendar year from 1983 to 1990. The country tables cover the 1984-1990 period. Both sets of tables include 1989/1990 percentage changes.

Sauf indication contraire, les données concernent les années civiles. Les tableaux généraux couvrent la période moyenne 1980-1982, et les années civiles 1983 à 1990. Les tableaux par pays couvrent la période 1984 à 1990. Les deux séries de tableaux indiquent les variations en pourcentage entre 1989 et 1990.

## A.  GENERAL TABLES

The general tables are in seven "series", dealing respectively with the following:

1. Human population
2. Livestock numbers
3. Gross indigenous production of meat
4. Meat production from slaughtered animals
5. Foreign trade
6. Consumption
7. Meat consumption per head

Each of the series 3 to 7 consists of separate tables dealing respectively with the following meat categories:

1. Total meat
2. Beef and veal
3. Pigmeat (including bacon and ham)
4. Poultry meat
5. Mutton, lamb and goat meat
6. Horse meat
7. Other meat
8. Edible offals

## A.  TABLEAUX GÉNÉRAUX

Les tableaux généraux appartiennent à sept « séries » consacrées respectivement aux sujets suivants :

1. Population humaine
2. Effectifs du cheptel
3. Production indigène brute de viande
4. Production de viande provenant des abattages
5. Commerce extérieur
6. Consommation
7. Consommation de viande par tête.

Chacune des séries 3 à 7 est composée de tableaux distincts consacrés respectivement aux catégories de viandes suivantes :

1. Total viande.
2. Viande bovine (viande de bœuf + viande de veau)
3. Viande porc (y compris jambon et bacon)
4. Viande de volaille
5. Viande de mouton et de chèvre
6. Viande d'équidés
7. Autres viandes
8. Abats comestibles

All the figures in the general tables have been drawn from the "country tables" (except for the tables on human population and livestock numbers). Yugoslavia is excluded from the respective totals.

Each general table provides data for every OECD Member or Associate country, and totals for the following groups of countries:
OECD – Total;
OECD – North America;
OECD – Oceania;
OECD – Europe;
European Economic Community (12 countries);
Other OECD Europe.

## B.  COUNTRY TABLES

The country tables consist of 10 tables dealing respectively with the following meat categories:

1. Beef
2. Veal
3. (= 1 + 2): total beef and veal
4. Pigmeat (including bacon and ham)
5. Poultry meat (a)
6. Mutton, lamb and goat meat
7. Horse meat
8. Other meat
9. Edible offals (b)
10. (= sum 3 to 9). Total all categories of meat.

a) Ready-to-cook weight. Eviscerated weight for Canada and Sweden.

b) Product weight.

Each table contains the following items:

| 1. | | Number of animals slaughtered | (in thousands) |
|---|---|---|---|
| 2. | | Average dressed carcass weight | (in kilogrammes) |
| 3. | | GROSS INDIGENOUS PRODUCTION | |
| 4. | LESS: | Meat equivalent of exported live animals | |
| 5. | PLUS: | Meat from slaughterings of imported animals | |
| 6. (=3–4+5 =1x2) | | TOTAL MEAT PRODUCTION FROM SLAUGHTERED ANIMALS | (in thousand metric tons) Dressed carcass weight |
| 7. | LESS: | Exports of meat | |
| 8. | PLUS: | Imports of meat | |
| 9. | MINUS: | Stock variations | |
| 10.=(6–7+8–9) | | MEAT CONSUMPTION | |
| 11. | | CONSUMPTION PER HEAD | (in kilogrammes per year) |

La totalité des données figurant dans les tableaux généraux est extraite des «tableaux par pays» (exception faite pour les tableaux concernant la population humaine et les effectifs du cheptel). La Yougoslavie est exclue des totaux respectifs.

Chaque tableau général fournit les données relatives à chacun des pays Membres, ou associés de l'OCDE, ainsi que les totaux relatifs aux groupes de pays suivants :
Ensemble des pays Membres de l'OCDE ;
OCDE – Amérique du Nord ;
OCDE – Océanie ;
OCDE – Europe ;
Communauté Economique Européenne (12 pays) ;
Autres pays européens de l'OCDE.

## B.  TABLEAUX PAR PAYS

Les tableaux par pays comprennent 10 tableaux consacrés respectivement aux catégories de viandes suivantes :

1. Viande de bœuf
2. Viande de veau
3. (= 1 + 2) : total viande bovine
4. Viande de porc (y compris jambon et bacon)
5. Viande de volaille (a)
6. Viande de mouton et de chèvre
7. Viande d'équidés
8. Autres viandes
9. Abats comestibles (b)
10. (= somme de 3 à 9). Total de toutes catégories de viande.

a) Poids «prêt à cuire». Poids éviscéré pour le Canada et la Suède.

b) Poids de produits.

Chaque tableau comporte les rubriques suivantes :

| 1. | | Nombre d'animaux abattus | (en milliers) |
|---|---|---|---|
| 2. | | Poids moyen en carcasse parée | (en kilogrammes) |
| 3. | | PRODUCTION INDIGÈNE BRUTE | |
| 4. | MOINS : | Equivalent en viande des animaux exportés vivants | |
| 5. | PLUS : | Viande provenant des abattages d'animaux importés vivants | |
| 6. (=3–4+5 =1x2) | | PRODUCTION TOTALE DE VIANDE PROVENANT DES ABATTAGES | (en milliers de tonnes métriques) Poids en carcasse parée |
| 7. | MOINS : | Exportations de viande | |
| 8. | PLUS : | Importations de viande | |
| 9. | MOINS : | Variations des stocks | |
| 10.=(6–7+8–9) | | CONSOMMATION DE VIANDE | |
| 11. | | CONSOMMATION PAR TÊTE | (en kilogrammes par an) |

10

A standard lay-out is used for the tables, enabling the product flows for each meat category to be followed from the production to the consumption stage. This lay-out is largely that adopted by the Statistical Office of the European Communities in its "Agricultural Statistics", implementing the substance of the recommendations made by the Study group on Food and Agricultural Statistics for Europe (meeting in Geneva under the joint auspices of the Economic Commission for Europe and the FAO[1]).

La présentation des tableaux est standardisée; elle a pour objet de permettre, pour chaque catégorie de viande, de suivre le flux des produits depuis la production jusqu'à la consommation. Cette présentation s'inspire pour une large part du cadre adopté par l'Office Statistique des Communautés Européennes dans sa « Statistique Agricole » cadre qui, pour l'essentiel résulte de la mise en pratique des recommandations élaborées par le Groupe d'Etudes des Statistiques alimentaires et agricoles en Europe (siégeant à Genève sous la double égide de la Commission Economique pour l'Europe et de la FAO[1]).

# III. DEFINITIONS AND CONCEPTS – DÉFINITIONS ET CONCEPTS
## COMPARABILITY – COMPARABILITÉ

## A. MEAT CATEGORIES

## A. CATÉGORIES DE VIANDES

The definition of "meat categories", based on a simple classification by animal species, needs little explanation.

La définition des « catégories de viandes » basée sur une simple répartition des animaux selon les espèces, n'appelle guère d'explications générales.

A few special points call for comment however.

Par contre, quelques points particuliers nécessitent des remarques.

### Buffalo meat

### Viande de buffle

In those countries (Italy, Turkey, etc.) where buffaloes play a significant part in meat production, the relevant data are included under beef and veal.

Dans les pays (Italie, Turquie, etc.) où les buffles jouent un rôle dans la production de viande, les données correspondantes sont incluses dans les rubriques relatives à la viande bovine.

### Distinction between beef and veal

### Distinction entre la viande de bœuf et la viande de veau

Almost all countries' national statistics distinguish between beef and veal production, but where the line is drawn between the two depends on national practice; the corresponding livestock ages may differ appreciably from country to country.

Dans presque tous les pays, les statistiques nationales fournissent une ventilation de la production de viande bovine entre la viande de bœuf d'une part, la viande de veau d'autre part. Mais la place de la « frontière » entre le bœuf et le veau reflète des habitudes nationales et se situe donc à des niveaux d'âge du bétail qui peuvent différer très sensiblement selon les pays.

### "Other meat"

### « Autres viandes »

The coverage of this category in each country is indicated in detail in the notes of the 8th issue of this publication (April 1979).

Pour chaque pays, les notes publiées dans la 8ᵉ édition (avril 1979) précisent en détail le champ couvert par cette catégorie.

### Edible offals

### Abats comestibles

This item probably has a rather different coverage in different countries.

Le contenu de cette rubrique est probablement assez différent selon les pays.

11

## B. ITEMS

### Number of animals slaughtered

Data are not given for poultry, edible offals and "other meat".

The figures cover – except othewise indicated – all killings within the frontiers of the country considered in the year concerned, whether in slaughterhouses, in local butchers' yards, or on the farm, whether or not subject to control, whether or not declared, whether to supply the meat market or for consumption by the producer and his family alone.

When the data given for any country in the tables do not cover total slaughterings, the coverage is indicated in the notes.

It should first be noted that, in most countries, the statistics do not take into account killings of animals found, before or after slaughter, to be unfit for human consumption[2].

In countries where the data actually cover all slaughterings, these data are obtained by adding together two different sets of figures:

1. The first set covers all "controlled" slaughterings (i.e. submitted to statistical control, often linked with a veterinary control, ascertaining whether the meat from the animal concerned can be used for human consumption under the national sanitary regulations). The number of "controlled slaughterings" is thus often the same as the number of "inspected slaughterings". According to the country concerned, control may depend on the place of slaughter (slaughterhouses are generally controlled, whereas local shambles and killings on farms are not always so), the use for which the meat is intended (for the meat market or for consumption on the farm), kind of livestock (there may be complete control for certain meat categories, e.g. beef and veal, while control is less thorough, and sometimes non-existent, for other categories).

2. The second set of figures refers to "non-controlled slaughterings". These figures, even when drawn from "official" sources, always include an element of estimation, and may be arrived at by very different methods: sample surveys, annual surveys, estimates based on censuses of livestock numbers (and fertility assumptions), consumption estimates, etc.

### Average dressed carcass weight

Data are only given in the tables for beef, veal, pigmeat, mutton, lamb and goat meat and horse meat.

Reference should first be made to the definitions worked out by the Study Group on Food and Agricultural Statistics in Europe and the Statistical Office of the European Communities.

*Live weight:* weight of animal intended for slaughter, measured immediately before slaughter.

## B. RUBRIQUES

### Nombre d'animaux abattus

Ces données ne figurent pas dans les tableaux pour les viandes de volaille, les abats comestibles et « autres viandes ».

Les données couvrent – sauf indication contraire – la totalité des abattages effectués à l'intérieur des frontières du pays considéré au cours de l'année indiquée, que ces abattages soient réalisés en abattoirs, chez les bouchers locaux ou chez le producteur, qu'ils soient ou non soumis à un contrôle, qu'ils donnent, ou non, lieu à une déclaration, qu'ils aient pour objet la fourniture de viande à un circuit commercial, ou que la viande produite soit seulement destinée à l'autoconsommation du producteur et de sa famille.

Lorsque, pour un pays, les données figurant aux tableaux ne couvrent pas la totalité des abattages, les notes indiquent le champ couvert.

Il faut remarquer que, dans la plupart des pays, les statistiques ne prennent pas en compte les abattages d'animaux reconnus, avant ou après abattage, comme impropres à la consommation humaine[2].

D'autre part, dans les pays dont les données se réfèrent effectivement à la totalité des abattages, l'établissement de ces données se fait par addition de deux catégories différentes de chiffres :

1. La première de ces catégories couvre le nombre des abattages « contrôlés » (ce contrôle est un contrôle statistique, lié très souvent à un contrôle vétérinaire ayant pour but de vérifier si l'animal est apte à fournir de la viande qui, dans le cadre des règlements sanitaires en vigueur dans le pays, puisse être effectivement affectée à la consommation humaine). Le nombre des « abattages contrôlés » est donc souvent synonyme du nombre des « abattages inspectés ». Selon les pays, le contrôle peut être basé sur le lieu d'abattage (les « abattoirs » sont en général « contrôlés » tandis que les « tueries » locales et les abattages chez le producteur ne le sont pas toujours), la destination de la viande (viande destinée au circuit commercial ou à l'autoconsommation), la catégorie d'animaux (le contrôle peut être total pour certaines catégories comme la viande bovine, plus ou moins complet, et parfois inexistant, pour d'autres catégories).

2. La seconde catégorie de chiffres se réfère aux « abattages non contrôlés ». Ces chiffres, même « officiels », comportent toujours une part d'estimation et peuvent être établis selon des méthodes très diverses: enquêtes par sondage, enquêtes annuelles, estimations à partir des recensements du nombre des animaux (et d'hypothèse sur la fécondité), estimations de consommation, etc.

### Poids moyen en carcasse parée

Ces données ne figurent dans les tableaux que pour les viandes de bœuf, de veau, de porc, de mouton et de chèvre et d'équidés.

Il convient de rappeler tout d'abord les définitions résultant des travaux du groupe d'Etudes des Statistiques Alimentaires et Agricoles en Europe et de l'Office Statistique des Communautés Européennes.

*Poids vif :* Poids des animaux destinés à l'abattage, mesuré immédiatement avant l'abattage.

*Killed weight:* weight of animal after slaughter (equals live weight of blood not collectected during slaughter).

*Carcass weight:* weight of the slaughtered animal, after removal of certain parts, measured when cold ("cold carcass"). The carcass weight for the various meat categories is generally defined as the weight of the animal after slaughter and removal of the following parts:

for cattle, sheep, goats and solipeds: head, feet, fect, tail, skin, organs from the thoracic and abdominal cavities, genito-urinary organs, except kidneys.

for pigs: organs and blood vessels from the thoracic and abdominal cavities, genito-urinary organs, except kidneys.

*Dressed carcass weight:* carcass weight as defined above, less slaughter fats i.e. fats removed at the slaughtehouse and thus not marketed with the meat (as opposed to "graisses de découpe", which are sold with the meat and included in the dressed carcass weight).

In practice, the definitions used in the various countries for carcass weight and dressed carcass weight are not always comparable as the portions removed, which represent the difference between killed weight, are not everywhere exactly the same[3]. Complete international homogeneity of the data cannot therefore be expected.

Furthermore, different countries use different methods of compiling data expressed in "dressed carcass weight". Four different weights were mentioned above: live weights, killed weights, carcass weights, dressed carcass weight. Very few countries actually draw up statistical returns for all four weights: most calculate their figures from available basic data (which may correspond to only one of the weights), and compute the other weights by using suitable coefficients (fixed or variable over time) for each meat category. For example, a country whose statistical returns supplied only the carcass weight might assume that, for cattle, the live weight represented 1.85 times the carcass weight, while the dressed carcass weight could be obtained by deducting 4 per cent from the carcass weight.

As its name implies, the "average dressed carcass weight" normally corresponds to the average meat yield (expressed as dressed carcass weight) per animal slaughtered for each category concerned during the period considered. In practice, the determination of this average weight poses certain problems:

1. In any country, the average dressed carcass weight can be accurately ascertained (or determined) only for **controlled** slaughterings , but the statistical control procedures offer two methods of determination.

*i)* If "statistical" control is applied to each animal slaughtered, the "individual" weight of meat corresponding to each killing is known: in this case, the "average" weight will be obtained by taking the average of the weights recorded for all slaughterings;

*Poids mort :* Poids des animaux après l'abattage (égal au poids vif, diminué du poids du sang non récupéré au cours de l'abattage).

*Poids carcasse :* Poids de l'animal abattu et dépouillé, mesuré après refroidissement («carcasse froide»). Pour les diverses catégories de viandes, le poids carcasse est généralement défini comme le poids de l'animal après abattage et prélèvement des parties suivantes :

bovins, ovins, caprins et équidés : la tête, les pieds, la queue, les organes des cavités thoracique et abdominale, les organes génito-urinaires à l'exception des reins.

porcins : les organes et les vaisseaux sanguins des cavités thoracique et abdominale, les organes génito-urinaires, à l'exception des reins.

*Poids en carcasse parée :* Poids carcasse défnini précédemment, diminué des graisses d'abattages, c'est-à-dire des graisses prélevées à l'abattoir et donc non commercialisées avec la viande (par opposition aux graisses de découpe, qui sont commercialisées avec la viande et font partie intégrante du poids en carcasse parée).

Dans la pratique, les définitions utilisées dans les divers pays pour le poids carcasse et le poids en carcasse parée présentent des différences, les portions déduites pour passer du poids mort au poids carcasse n'étant pas partout exactement les mêmes[3]. On ne peut donc s'attendre à une homogénéité complète des données sur le plan international.

Par ailleurs, les divers pays utilisent des méthodes différentes pour établir les données exprimées en «poids en carcasse parée». Les paragraphes précédents ont mentionné l'existence de quatre «poids» différents : poids vif, poids mort, poids en carcasse, poids en carcasse parée. Rares sont les pays qui disposent effectivement de relevés statistiques correspondant à chacun de ces quatre poids : la plupart calculent ces poids à partir de leurs données de base disponibles (données qui peuvent ne correspondre qu'à un seul de ces poids), en admettant l'existence, pour une catégorie de viande donnée, de coefficients (fixes ou variables avec le temps) permettant de passer d'un poids à l'autre. Par exemple, tel pays dont les relevés statistiques ne fournissent que le poids carcasse pourra considérer que, pour les bœufs, le poids vif représente 1,85 fois le poids carcasse et, que le poids en carcasse parée peut s'obtenir en déduisant 4 pour cent du poids en carcasse.

Comme son nom l'indique, le «poids moyen en carcasse parée» correspond en principe à la quantité moyenne de viande (exprimée en poids en carcasse parée) produite par bête abattue dans la catégorie considérée au cours de la période considérée. La détermination pratique de ce poids moyen pose quelques problèmes :

1. Dans un pays, le poids moyen en carcasse parée n'est connu (ou déterminable) avec une certaine précision que pour les abattages **contrôlés**. Mais les modalités statistiques du contrôle conduisent à deux méthodes différentes de détermination.

*i)* Si le contrôle «statistique» s'effectue pour chaque bête abattue, le poids «individuel» de viande correspondant à chaque abattage est connu : dans ce cas, le poids «moyen» sera obtenu en faisant la moyenne des poids enregistrés pour tous les abattages ;

*ii)* if the "statistical" control merely records, on the one hand, the number of animals slaughtered, and on the other, the total output of meat, the average weight will be obtained by dividing the output of meat by the number of animals slaughtered.

2. Once the average dressed carcass weight for controlled slaughterings has been worked out, the average dressed carcass weight for all slaughterings must be determined. Here again, different practices are followed in different countries.

*i)* Certain countries consider that the average dressed carcass weight for controlled slaughterings is aapplicable to all slaughterings is applicable to all slaughterings (controlled and non-controlled).

*ii)* Other countries consider that the average weight for non-controlled slaughterings is significantly different from that for controlled slaughterings (largely owing to the fact that a considerable proportion of non-controlled slaughterings represent animals killed on farms, whose weight differs considerably from the weight differs considerably from the weight of animals killed in commercial slaughterhouses). The countries concerned estimate this average weight explicity or implicity[4].

The average dressed carcass weight for all slaughterings can then be calculated by combining the average weights corresponding to controlled and non-controlled slaughterings respectively

Some countries do not calculate average dressed carcass weights, or do not publish them. They do, however, publish data for the number for slaughterings and the corresponding output of meat, and the OECD Secretariat therefore thought it legitimate to calculate the corresponding average weight by simple division, and to publish the results obtained.

In a given country, the average weights recorded for a specific livestock category generally vary over time. When interpreting the evolution of data, account should always be taken of the fact that the categories specified in the tables are in fact heterogeneous, being the sum of sub-categories: for example, "beef meat" in fact embraces meat obtained from the slaughter of bulls, steers, culled cows, bullocks, heifers, etc., all "sub-categories" which obviously have very different average weights; similarly, "mutton, lamb and goat meat", embraces the meat obtained from the slaughter of sheep, lambs, goats, kids, etc. Accordingly, the changes in the average weights recorded results from the combination of two sets of factors:

1. Change over time in the proportions of the total category represented by the different "sub-categories";

2. Any changes in average weight for each sub-category.

Data in this volume are expressed in "dressed carcass weights" for beef, veal, pigmeat, mutton, lamb and goat meat, horse meat and for the item "other meat".

---

*ii)* si le « statistique » est organisé de telle sorte qu'il fournisse seulement d'une part le nombre des abattages et d'autre part le poids de viande correspondant au total de ces abattages, le poids moyen sera obtenu en divisant la production de viande par le nombre des abattages.

2. Une fois établi, le poids moyen en carcasse parée pour les abattages contrôlés, il faut déterminer le poids moyen en carcasse parée valable pour l'ensemble des abattages. Ici aussi, les pratiques suivies par les pays sont diverses.

*i)* Certains pays considèrent que le poids moyen en abattages contrôlés est valable pour l'ensemble des abattages (contrôlés et non contrôlés);

*ii)* D'autres considèrent au contraire que le poids moyen des abattages non contrôlés est significativement différent de celui des abattages contrôlés (ceci est d'autant plus explicable que les abattages non contrôlés (ceci est d'autant plus explicable que les abattages non contrôlés sont constitués pour une large part par les abattages à la ferme, et que ces abattages portent sur des animaux dont le poids diffère fortement de celui des animaux abattus dans les abattoirs commerciaux). Ils estiment explicitement ou implicitement[4] ce poids moyen.

La combinaison des poids moyens correspon ant respectivement aux abattages contrôlés et aux abattages non contrôlés permet d'évaluer le poids moyen correspondant à l'ensemble des abattages.

Certains pays ne calculent pas, ou ne publient pas de données relatives aux poids moyens en carcasse parée. Ces pays publient néanmoins les données relatives au nombre des abattages et à la production de viande correspondante; le Secrétariat de l'OCDE a considéré qu'il était légitime de calculer par simple division le poids moyen correspondant et de publier les résultats obtenus.

Dans un pays, les poids moyens enregistrés pour une catégorie d'animaux varient en général avec le temps. L'interprétation de cette évolution doit toujours tenir compte du fait que les catégories individualisées dans les tableaux sont en fait hétérogènes, résultant du regroupement de sous-catégories : par exemple, la « viande de bœuf » regroupe en fait la viande obtenue par abattage de taureaux, de bœufs, de vaches de réforme, de taurillons, de génisses, etc., toutes « sous-catégories » ayant évidemment des poids moyens fortement différents ; de même, la « viande de mouton et de chèvre » regroupe la viande obtenue par abattage de moutons, d'agneaux, de chèvres, de cabris, etc. Dans ces conditions, les modifications des poids moyens enregistrés résultent de la combinaison de deux ordres de facteurs :

1. Les modifications dans le temps de la part des différentes « sous-catégories » à l'intérieur du total de la catégorie;

2. Les modifications éventuelles du poids moyen correspondant à chacune des sous-catégories.

Le «poids en carcasse parée» s'applique dans le présent volume aux viandes de bœuf, veau, porc, mouton et chèvre, équidés et à la rubrique «autres viandes».

Data for edible offals are expressed in product weight. Data for poultry meat are expressed in "ready to cook" weight (or "eviscerated weight"), roughly corresponding for poultry, to the "dressed carcass" concept. (In the case of poultry, the "dressed carcass" weight would correspond to the weight of the dead bird, excluding the feathers, head and feet, but including all the offals edible or not.)

## Gross indigenous production

The "gross indigenous production" of meat in a given country equals the meat yield from the slaughter of indigenous animals in the country concerned (thus excluding meat obtained from slaughterings of imported livestock), plus the meat equivalent of live animals exported for slaughter[5].

## Meat equivalent of exported live animals
## Meat from slaughterings of live imported animals

The calculation, for the purposes of a meat balance sheet, of the meat equivalent of foreign trade in live animals is logical: the country exporting live animals is in fact exporting meat, and the quantity involved must be taken into account in any measurement of the country's production effort; conversely, the meat yield from the slaughter of imported animals in a given country corresponds in fact to imported meat, and should not be credited to that country.

The above requirements raise certain logical and practical difficulties:

1. It does not seem logical to take into account all the live animals (in the livestock categories considered) figuring in foreign trade:
   i) Animals not imported or exported for any alimentary or agricultural purpose (e.g. racehorses) should be excluded;

   ii) animals imported or exported for an agricultural purpose which has no direct connection with meat production (breeding stock, milking cows, etc.) should be excluded. (Admittedly, these animals, too, will eventually be turned into meat, after culling, but only in the relatively distant and indefinite future);

   ii) the inclusion of store animals, i.e. livestock to be fattened in the importing country before slaughter in that country (after a lapse of time which may vary from a few weeks to several months) raises a somewhat difficult point of logic: an imported animal slaughtered after fattening in a given country is considered, for statistical purposes, as an "indigenous" animal, whereas in actual fact, only that fraction of its weight in meat gained between import and slaughter is "indigenous". It is, however, practically impossible to accurately determine that fraction.

Les données relatives aux abats comestibles sont exprimées en poids de produit. Les données relatives à la viande de volaille sont exprimées en poids «près à cuire» (synonyme de «poids éviscéré» qui, pour la volaille, correspond à peu près au concept de «en carcasse parée». En effet, le concept «en carcasse parée» correspond dans le cas de la volaille, au poids de la bête morte, non compris les plumes, la tête, et les pattes, mais y compris la totalité des viscères (comestibles et non comestibles).

## Production indigène brute

La «production indigène brute» de viande d'un pays est égale à la quantité de viande provenant de l'abattage dans le pays considéré des animaux d'origine indigène (donc à l'exclusion des animaux importés), augmentée de l'équivalent en viande des animaux de boucherie exportés vivants[5].

## Equivalent en viande des exportations d'animaux vivants
## Viande provenant des abattages des animaux importés vivants

La prise en considération, dans le cadre d'un bilan viande, de l'équivalent en viande du commerce des animaux vivants répond à une logique évidente: le pays qui exporte des animaux vivants exporte en fait de la viande, et cette quantité de viande doit être prise en considération dans toute mesure de l'effort de production réalisé par ce pays; inversement, la viande provenant de l'abattage dans un pays d'animaux importés est en fait une viande importée qui ne doit pas aller au crédit du pays dans lequel a lieu l'abattage.

Les nécessités précitées posent certains problèmes logiques et pratiques :

1. Il ne paraît pas logique de prendre en ligne de compte la totalité des animaux vivants (dans les catégories d'animaux considérés) rentrant dans le commerce extérieur:
   i) Il convient d'exclure les animaux dont le commerce ne correspond à aucun but alimentaire ou agricole (par exemple les chevaux de course);

   ii) il convient d'exclure les animaux dont le commerce correspond à un objet agricole sans rapport direct avec la production de viande (animaux reproducteurs, vaches laitières, etc. Certes, même ces animaux finiront un jour par être transformés en viande – après «réforme» – mais cet aboutissement se situe dans un avenir assez lointain et indéterminé);

   iii) la prise en considération des «animaux d'embouche» c'est-à-dire des animaux destinés à être engraissés dans le pays importateur avant leur abattage dans ce pays (cet abattage survenant après un délai allant de quelques semaines à plusieurs mois) est, sur le plan de la logique, assez délicat : un animal importé abattu après engraissement sur le territoire d'un pays est considéré par la statistique comme un animal «indigène» alors qu'en fait, il n'est «indigène» que pour la fraction de son poids en viande gagné entre son importation et son abattage. Mais la détermination de cette «fraction» avec précision est pratiquement impossible.

*iv)* on the other hand, "animals for slaughter" are to be killed in the importing country almost immediately (within a few days at most, to cover the time needed for transport to the slaughterhouses) and are to be taken into account at their total meat equivalent.

2. In practice, the data presently available limit the feasibility of taking logical considerations into account.

*i)* The foreign trade statistics generally allow animals imported or exported for no alimentary or agricultural purpose to be easily identified (but only small numbers are involved), and also (sometimes less easily) animals imported or exported for reasons not directly connected with meat production.

On the other hand the distinction between "slaughter animals" and "store animals" is often unclear. In addition, although the Customs nomenclature may be detailed enough, some countries prefer, for the sake of simplicity, to use the total figures for imports and exports of live animals in their estimates.

*ii)* The figures for the output of meat from the slaughter of imported animals in a given country are usually obtained from the slaughterhouses, and have direct reference to the weight of meat. Their accuracy depends on the criteria applied for the identification of "imported animals" in the slaughterhouses.

### Total meat production from slaughtered animals

Total meat production from slaughterings (or "net production") is the basic figure most easily available in the countries concerned, and the starting-point for estimates of the other production concepts.

The data are drawn from slaughtering statistics, and should, in a consistent system, equal the total number of animals slaughtered multiplied by the average meat yield per animal.

As a rule, data for total meat production from slaughterings, are obtained by combining data for controlled slaughterings with estimates for non-controlled slaughterings.

In most countries, the data allow the total figures to be broken down into the meat yield from slaughterings of indigenous animals (= net indigenous production) and meat obtained from the slaughterings of imported slaughter animals.

### Meat imports and exports

Foreign trade data for meat normally cover, for each meat category, the total quantities imported or exported in any form (except in the form of live animals), including canned meat and meat preparations, expressed in dressed carcass weight equivalent.

*iv)* par contre, les « animaux de boucherie » destinés à être abattus à l'intérieur du pays importateur dans un délai très bref (quelques jours au maximum, correspondant aux délais de transport vers les abattoirs) sont à prendre en considération pour la totalité de leur équivalent en viande.

2. Sur le plan pratique, la disponibilité effective des données limite les possibilités de tenir compte des considérations logiques.

*i)* Les statistiques de commerce extérieur permettent en général d'identifier facilement les animaux dont le commerce ne correspond à aucun but alimentaire ou agricole (mais les quantités en cause sont peu importantes) ainsi que (moins facilement parfois) les animaux dont le commerce est sans rapport direct avec la production de la viande.
Par contre, la distinction entre « animaux de boucherie » et « animaux d'embouche » est souvent difficile. De plus, même si la nomenclature douanière est détaillée, certains pays préfèrent, pour des raisons de simplicité, prendre en considération pour leurs évaluations l'ensemble du commerce des animaux vivants.

*ii)* Les données relatives à la viande produite dans un pays par abattage d'animaux importés sont obtenues le plus souvent au niveau des abattages et se réfèrent directement au poids de viande. Leur précision dépend des critères d'identification des « animaux importés » dans les abattoirs.

### Production totale de viande provenant des abattages

La production totale de viande provenant des abattages (ou « production nette ») est la donnée de base dont disposent le plus aisément les pays et celle autour de laquelle s'ordonnent les évaluations des autres « optique » de la production.

Les données sont obtenues à partir des statistiques d'abattages et doivent, dans un système cohérent, être égales au produit du nombre total des animaux abattus par le poids moyen en viande de ces animaux.

En règle générale, les données de production totale de viande provenant des abattages sont obtenues par combinaison des données relatives aux abattages contrôlés et des estimations.

Dans la plupart des pays, les données permettent la ventilation du chiffre total entre la viande obtenue par abattage d'animaux « indigènes » (= production indigène nette) et la viande provenant de l'abattage d'animaux de boucherie importés vivants.

### Importations et exportations de viande

Les données relatives au commerce extérieur de viande couvrent en principe, pour chaque catégorie de viande, l'ensemble des quantités importées ou exportées sous toutes les formes (sauf sous la forme d'animaux vivants), y compris, les conserves de viande et les préparations à base de viande, exprimé en équivalent de poids de viande en carcasse parée.

The prerequisite for the compilation of data corresponding to the above general definition is the availability (in the Customs statistics of the country concerned) of sufficiently detailed foreign trade figures for meat giving for all items a breakdown among the various meat categories (e.g. it should be possible to break down "canned meat" into canned beef, canned pork, etc.). In addition, it should be possible for each detailed figure to be converted into dressed carcass weight equivalent by applying an appropriate coefficient.

In practice, only a few countries compute data corresponding to the general definition. For the others, various more or less approximate solutions have been used (by the country itself or by the OECD Secretariat): dressed carcass weight equivalent of imports and exports of meat (excluding canned meat and meat preparations) aggregations in "product weight" (ton for ton, with no attempt to calculate the dressed carcass weight equivalent) of certain items in the Customs statistics, etc.

## Stock variations

Owing to the method of drawing up the balance-sheets, an increase in stocks is deducted from total availabilities as this increase in stocks corresponds to a decrease in the quantities available for consumption. Conversely, a decrease in stocks is added to total availabilities.

## Meat consumption

The "consumption" data shown are consistent with the figures given for the preceding items, i.e. for each meat category they are equal to meat production from slaughterings, less meat exports, plus meat imports, plus or minus stock variations.

These consumption data are thus expressed in dressed carcass weight equivalent, but this by no means implies that final consumption is in the form of dressed carcass weight. The meat may, indeed, before reaching the consumer, undergo various processing operations, up to and including meat canning, preparation of ready-to-serve dishes, "charcuterie", etc.

## Intermediate items between "consumption" and "human consumption"

In most cases, the figures for meat consumption referred to the preceding in paragraph above coincide with human consumption of food.

This is not, however, the case in the following instances:

1. For countries where the slaughter statistics include animals whose meat is found unfit for human consumption, the corresponding quantities must be deducted.

2. For certain countries, the data for human consumption may correspond to a specific definition involving certain adjustments.

L'élaboration de données correspondant à la définition de principe ci-dessus implique d'abord que les données de commerce extérieur de viande – telles qu'elles figurent dans les statistiques douanières du pays intéressé – sont suffisamment détaillées pour permettre une ventilation complète de toutes les rubriques entres les diverses catégories de viandes (par exemple, les « conserves de viande » doivent pouvoir être ventilées en conserves de bœuf, de porc, etc.). Elle implique aussi que chaque chiffre détaillé soit transformé en équivalent de poids de viande en carcasse parée, par application d'un coefficient approprié.

Dans la pratique, quelques pays seulement calculent des données correspondant à la définition de principe. Pour les autres pays, diverses solutions plus ou moins « approchées » ont été utilisées (par le pays lui-même ou par le Secrétariat de l'OCDE): équivalent en poids en carcasse parée du commerce extérieur de viande (à l'exclusion des conserves et préparations à base de viande) totalisation en « poids de produit » (c'est-à-dire tonne pour tonne, sans essai de calcul d'équivalent en poids carcasse parée) de certaines rubriques de la statistique douanière, etc.

## Variations de stocks

Du fait de la méthode de construction des bilans, un accroissement des stocks a été déduit des disponibilités totales car cet accroissement de stocks correspond à une diminution des quantités disponibles pour la consommation. Inversement, une diminution des stocks a été ajouté aux disponibilités totales.

## Consommation de viande

Les données de « consommation » indiquées sont « cohérentes » avec les chiffres de rubriques précédentes, c'est-à-dire qu'elles sont égales, pour chaque catégorie de viande, à la production provenant des abattages, diminuée des exportations de viande, augmentée des importations de viande et corrigée (en plus ou en moins) des variations de stocks.

Ces données de consommation sont donc exprimées en poids de viande en carcasse parée. Elles n'impliquent nullement que c'est sous forme de viande en carcasse parée qu'a lieu la consommation finale. En effet, cette viande peut, avant d'aboutir au consommateur, subir diverses transformations, jusqu'à et y compris la fabrication de conserves, de plats préparés, de charcuterie, etc.

## Rubriques éventuelles intermédiaires entre « consommation » et « consommation pour l'alimentation humaine »

Dans la plupart des cas, les données de consommation de viande faisant l'objet du paragraphe) précédent, coïncident avec la consommation destinée à l'alimentation humaine.

Il n'en est toutefois pas ainsi dans les cas suivants :

1. Pour les pays où la statistique des abattages inclut les animaux dont la viande est reconnue impropre à la consommation humaine, il est nécessaire de déduire les quantités correspondantes.

2. Pour certains pays enfin, les chiffres de consommation humaine peuvent correspondre à une définition particulière entraînant certains ajustements.

## Consumption per head

This is obtained by dividing the figures for human consumption (equal in most cases to the total consumption figures) by the relevant population figure.

The population figures used are those shown in the special table in the front of this publication. They generally correspond to estimates of the average population present in the area during the year (or estimates of the present in area population at the middle of the year concerned).

The figures for consumption per head are naturally expressed in weight of dressed carcass meat (except for offal): they therefore include the "graisses de découpe" and bones included in the carcass weight: these non-edible portions constitute an appreciable fraction of the carcass weight (about 25 per cent for beef, 17 per cent for veal, 11 per cent for mutton, 7 per cent for pigmeat).

## C. COMPARABILITY OF DATA

The comparability of data is to be considered from two aspects:

### Comparability through time

Comparability through time exists when the data for a given country and series have been computed throughout the period covered using the same definitions and methods. These conditions are fulfilled in most cases. When a "break" (i.e. precisely a lack of homogeneity through time) exists for one series, the place of the break is indicated by the letter (b).

### Comparability through space

a) In order to have comparable data, the various countries should use, for each item, the same concepts and the same definition[6]. It is difficult from the documentation now available, to form a judgment on the situation, but it is clear that not all countries use exactly the same definitions and concepts. These differences may be particularly apparent for certain items: for instance, the distinction between beef and veal meat or the coverage of foreign trade data are fields where national practices can differ widely, and adjustments made subsequently – generally at the request of international organisations – in order to increase the comparability of data are always open to question.

b) Comparability through space can exist only between data of similar quality (i.e. having a similar margin of error). It is clear that data relating to different countries (and even data of different series relating to the same country) are far from possessing a homogeneous quality.

## Consommation par tête

Les données sont calculées en divisant les chiffres de consommation pour l'alimentation humaine (égaux dans la plupart des cas aux chiffres de consommation totale) par le chiffre de population approprié.

Les chiffres de population utilisés figurent au début de cette publication. Ils correspondent en général à des estimations de population présente moyenne dans le pays considéré au cours de l'année considéré (ou à des estimations de population présente au milieu de l'année considérée).

Bien entendu, les chiffres de consommation par tête restent exprimés (sauf pour les abats) en poids de viande en carcasse parée: ils incluent donc les graisses de découpe et les os compris dans le poids carcasse: ces portions non comestibles constituent une fraction importante du poids carcasse (de l'ordre de 25 pour cent pour la viande de bœuf, 17 pour cent pour la viande de veau, 11 pour cent pour la viande de mouton, 7 pour cent pour la viande de porc).

## C. COMPARABILITÉ DES DONNÉES

La comparabilité des données est à envisager sous deux aspects:

### Comparabilité dans le temps

Les données sont comparables dans le temps quand elles ont été calculées, pour le même pays et une même série, avec les mêmes définitions et méthodes pour la période indiquée. Ces conditions sont remplies dans la grande majorité des cas. Dans ceux où il existe une «rupture» de série (c'est-à-dire précisément une absence d'homogénéité dans le temps), une lettre (b) précise la place de cette rupture.

### Comparabilité dans l'espace

a) Pour que leurs données soient comparables, les divers pays devraient pour chaque rubrique utiliser les mêmes concepts et les mêmes définitions[6]. Bien qu'il soit difficile, dans l'état de la documentation actuelle disponible, de porter des jugements, il est certain que tous les pays n'utilisent pas exactement les mêmes concepts et définitions. Les différences peuvent être particulièrement sensibles sur certains points : par exemple, la limite entre la viande de bœuf et la viande de veau, où le champ couvert par les données de commerce extérieur sont des domaines où les pratiques nationales peuvent différer sensiblement, et les ajustements opérés ultérieurement pour répondre au désir des organismes internationaux d'accroître la comparabilité des données sont toujours quelque peu sujets à caution.

b) La comparabilité des données dans l'espace postule que ces données soient de même qualité (c'est-à-dire que leur marge d'erreur soit du même ordre). Or il est évident que les données des divers pays (et même les données des diverses séries pour un même pays) sont loin de présenter une qualité homogène.

Conclusions to be drawn from comparisons of data relating to different countries must take into account the above considerations. The same applies to the use of totals for groups of countries, totals obtained by the addition of data relating to each country of the group. Moreover, computation of these totals necessarily implies that important lacks of comparability of the data have been ignored.

Les conclusions à tirer des comparaisons entre les données relatives à divers pays doivent tenir compte des considérations précédentes. La même remarque s'applique à l'utilisation des totaux relatifs à des groupes de pays, totaux obtenus par addition des données relatives à chacun des pays composants. Au surplus, le calcul de ces totaux implique nécessairement de passer sur certains manques importants à l'homogénéité des données.

## IV. COUNTRY NOTES – NOTES PAR PAYS

Detailed country notes on sources, definitions, concepts and methods of computation were published in the 8th issue of Meat Balances (April 1979). Because of their length they will not be reproduced in this volume but can be obtained upon request from the Secretariat.

Des notes détaillées par pays sur les sources, définitions, concepts et méthodes de calcul ont été publiées dans la 8ᵉ édition des Bilans de la Viande (avril 1979). En raison de leur volume elles ne seront pas reproduites dans l'édition présente, mais seront disponibles sur demande auprès du Secrétariat.

## V. ABBREVIATIONS AND SYMBOLS – ABRÉVIATIONS ET SIGNES CONVENTIONNELS

| | | | |
|---|---|---|---|
| . | Included in another meat categorie. | . | Compris dans une autre catégorie de viande. |
| .. | Not available. | .. | Non disponible. |
| – | Nil, or less than half the last digit shown. | – | Zéro ou moins de la moitié du dernier chiffre significatif. |
| e | Estimated by the Secretariat or provisional. | e | Estimation du Secrétariat ou provisoire. |
| b | Break. | b | Rupture. |

## NOTES

1. Recommendations adopted at the second session (January 1962) of the Study Group on Problems of Methodology in Agricultural Statistics in European countries.
2. In countries where the statistics include animals found unfit for human consumption, the corresponding meat yield is included in the meat production figures. To obtain the data on human consumption of meat, a separate item has to be shown for the meat ©seized' by the veterinary control services and subtracted from the total consumption in order to arrive at human consumption.

3. Accurate comparisons could only be made in the form of a synoptic table prepared for each meat category, showing precisely what portions were removed in each country. The preparation of such a table would be a task for a specialist, and would entail a minute investigation.
4. "Implicitly" when the number of non-controlled slaughterings and the corresponding output of meat are estimated without indicating the average weight.
5. A more refined concept than "gross indigenous production" is that of "total indigenous production", which takes account of variations in the weight of livestock in the country concerned (representing both changes in the number of animals and changes in their average weight). The number of countries possessing the necessary statistical data is so small that it was not deemed possible to include the relevant data in the tables.
6. Independently of the methods used to compile the data. Countries using common concepts and definitions can make the relevant statistical surveys according to whatever methods they judge most appropriate.

1. Recommandations adoptées à la deuxième session (janvier 1962) du groupe d'Etudes des problèmes de méthodologie des Statistiques Agricoles dans les pays européens.
2. Dans les pays où la statistique inclut les animaux reconnus comme impropres à la consommation humaine, la viande produite lors des abattages de ces animaux se trouve comprise dans la production de viande et il est nécessaire, pour aboutir aux données de consommation humaine, de prévoir une rubrique spéciale qui permette de soustraire cette viande «saisie» par les services de contrôle vétérinaire retirée des circuits de consommation humaine.
3. Une comparaison précise ne pourrait se faire que sous forme d'un tableau synoptique établi pour chaque catégorie de viande et indiquant avec précision les portions déduites dans chaque pays. L'établissement d'un tel tableau représenterait un travail de spécialiste et nécessiterait une enquête minutieuse.
4. «Implicitement» lorsque, sans indiquer de poids moyens, le pays estime le nombre des abattages non contrôlés et la production de viande correspondante.
5. Au-delà de la «production indigène brute» existe le concept de «production indigène totale», qui tient compte des variations du poids de viande du cheptel sur pied du pays considéré (ces variations traduisant à la fois les changements survenus dans le poids moyen de ces animaux). Le nombre de pays disposant des éléments statistiques nécessaires est si limité qu'il n'a pas été jugé possible d'inclure dans les tableaux les rubriques correspondantes.
6. Ceci indépendamment des méthodes utilisées pour établir les données. Des pays ayant adopté des concepts et définitions communs peuvent procéder aux mesures statistiques correspondantes selon la méthode qu'ils jugent la plus appropriée à leur situation respective.

# GENERAL TABLES - TABLEAUX GÉNÉRAUX

# POPULATION

| | 1980/82 average | 1983 | 1984 | 1985 | 1986 | 1987 | 1988 | 1989 | 1990 | 1989/90 % change |
|---|---|---|---|---|---|---|---|---|---|---|
| OECD - Total | 786132 | 797590 | 802866 | 808291 | 813885 | 819211 | 825199 | 831575 | 839482 | 1.0 |
| OECD - North America | 254503 | 259602 | 262006 | 264460 | 266999 | 269578 | 272246 | 275016 | 278014 | 1.1 |
| Canada | 24364 | 24803 | 24995 | 25181 | 25374 | 25644 | 25939 | 26254 | 26620 | 1.4 |
| United States | 230138 | 234799 | 237011 | 239279 | 241625 | 243934 | 246307 | 248762 | 251394 | 1.1 |
| Japan | 117633 | 119260 | 120020 | 120750 | 121490 | 122090 | 122610 | 123116 | 123540 | 0.3 |
| OECD - Oceania | 18108 | 18623 | 18839 | 19072 | 19297 | 19573 | 19864 | 20176 | 20465 | 1.4 |
| Australia | 14934 | 15393 | 15579 | 15788 | 16018 | 16264 | 16538 | 16833 | 17086 | 1.5 |
| New Zealand | 3174 | 3230 | 3260 | 3284 | 3279 | 3309 | 3326 | 3343 | 3379 | 1.1 |
| OECD - Europe | 395888 | 400105 | 402001 | 404009 | 406099 | 407970 | 410479 | 413267 | 417463 | 1.0 |
| EC-12 Total | 318917 | 320553 | 321164 | 321849 | 322773 | 323512 | 324652 | 325981 | 328002 | 0.6 |
| Belgium / Luxembourg | 10217 | 10221 | 10221 | 10225 | 10232 | 10240 | 10259 | 10316 | 10374 | 0.6 |
| Denmark | 5122 | 5114 | 5112 | 5114 | 5121 | 5127 | 5130 | 5132 | 5140 | 0.2 |
| France | 54181 | 54729 | 54946 | 55170 | 55393 | 55630 | 55884 | 56160 | 56437 | 0.5 |
| Germany | 61629 | 61423 | 61175 | 61024 | 61066 | 61077 | 61451 | 61990 | 63074 | 1.7 |
| Greece | 9721 | 9847 | 9900 | 9934 | 9966 | 9984 | 10010 | 10033 | 10140 | 1.1 |
| Ireland | 3441 | 3505 | 3529 | 3540 | 3541 | 3542 | 3538 | 3515 | 3503 | -0.3 |
| Italy | 56519 | 56825 | 56983 | 57128 | 57221 | 57331 | 57441 | 57525 | 57647 | 0.2 |
| Netherlands | 14237 | 14367 | 14424 | 14491 | 14572 | 14665 | 14760 | 14849 | 14944 | 0.6 |
| Portugal | 9893 | 10050 | 10129 | 10185 | 10230 | 10270 | 10305 | 10337 | 10369 | 0.3 |
| Spain | 37614 | 38095 | 38257 | 38420 | 38668 | 38716 | 38809 | 38888 | 38966 | 0.2 |
| United Kingdom | 56343 | 56377 | 56488 | 56618 | 56763 | 56930 | 57065 | 57236 | 57408 | 0.3 |
| Other OECD - Europe | 76971 | 79552 | 80837 | 82160 | 83326 | 84458 | 85827 | 87286 | 89461 | 2.5 |
| Austria | 7562 | 7552 | 7552 | 7558 | 7565 | 7575 | 7595 | 7624 | 7712 | 1.2 |
| Finland | 4802 | 4856 | 4882 | 4902 | 4918 | 4932 | 4946 | 4964 | 4982 | 0.4 |
| Norway | 4101 | 4128 | 4141 | 4153 | 4169 | 4187 | 4209 | 4227 | 4242 | 0.4 |
| Sweden | 8321 | 8329 | 8337 | 8350 | 8370 | 8398 | 8436 | 8493 | 8566 | 0.9 |
| Switzerland | 6427 | 6482 | 6505 | 6533 | 6573 | 6619 | 6672 | 6723 | 6796 | 1.1 |
| Turkey | 45758 | 48205 | 49420 | 50664 | 51731 | 52747 | 53969 | 55255 | 57163 | 3.5 |
| Yugoslavia | 22468 | 22800 | 22960 | 23120 | 23270 | 23410 | 23560 | 23690 | 23798 | 0.5 |

# LIVESTOCK NUMBERS

## TOTAL CATTLE (including buffaloes) / ENSEMBLE DES BOVINS (y compris les buffles)

| | 1980/82 average | 1983 | 1984 | 1985 | 1986 | 1987 | 1988 | 1989 | 1990 | 1989/90 % change |
|---|---|---|---|---|---|---|---|---|---|---|
| OECD - Total | 273223 [e] | 270573 [e] | 267087 [e] | 260446 [e] | 256711 [e] | 250745 [b] | 248010 [e] | 246616 | 247460 [e] | 0.4 |
| OECD - North America | 125742 | 126630 | 124690 | 120538 | 116180 | 112981 | 110564 | 109211 | 109360 | 0.3 |
| Canada | 12063 | 11629 | 11330 | 10956 | 10802 | 10863 | 10942 | 11146 | 11198 | 1.9 |
| United States | 113679 | 115001 | 113360 | 109582 | 105378 | 102118 | 99622 | 98065 | 98162 | 0.1 |
| Japan | 4487 | 4682 | 4698 [e] | 4742 | 4694 | 4667 | 4682 | 4760 | 4903 [e] | 3.0 |
| OECD - Oceania | 33334 | 30109 | 29937 | 30705 | 31715 | 31666 | 31579 | 31815 | 32635 | 2.6 |
| Australia | 25308 | 22478 | 22161 | 22784 | 23436 | 23667 | 23521 | 23987 | 24570 | 2.4 |
| New Zealand | 8026 | 7631 | 7776 | 7921 | 8279 | 7999 | 8058 | 7828 | 8065 | 3.0 |
| OECD - Europe | 109660 [e] | 109152 [e] | 107762 [e] | 104461 [e] | 104122 [e] | 101431 [b] | 101185 [e] | 100825 | 100562 [e] | -0.3 |
| EC-12 Total | 84068 [e] | 85529 [e] | 84539 [e] | 83059 [e] | 81544 [e] | 79451 [b] | 79479 | 80224 | 79673 [e] | -0.7 |
| Belgium / Luxembourg | 3101 | 3178 | 3210 | 3163 | 3179 | 3159 | 3174 | 3277 | 3376 | 3.0 |
| Denmark | 2889 | 2876 | 2704 | 2623 | 2490 | 2323 | 2230 | 2232 | 2241 | 0.4 |
| France | 23585 | 23519 | 23102 | 22802 | 22171 | 21052 | 21340 | 21394 | 21500 | 0.5 |
| Germany | 15053 | 15552 | 15688 | 15627 | 15305 | 14887 | 14659 | 14563 | 14587 | 0.2 |
| Greece | 819 | 770 | 757 | 776 | 761 | 741 | 696 | 690 | 687 | -0.4 |
| Ireland | 5789 | 5812 | 5836 | 5781 | 5627 | 5580 | 5637 | 5899 | 6029 | 2.2 |
| Italy | 8956 | 9507 | 9207 | 9009 | 8921 | 8898 | 8843 | 8858 | 8235 | -7.0 |
| Netherlands | 5083 | 5359 | 5280 | 5076 | 4922 | 4549 | 4606 | 4731 | 4830 | 2.1 |
| Portugal | 1030 [e] | 835 [e] | 850 [e] | 600 [e] | 760 [e] | 1332 [b] | 1356 | 1335 | 1341 [e] | 0.4 |
| Spain | 4698 | 4964 | 4920 | 4907 | 4932 | 5075 | 5036 | 5312 | 5001 | -5.9 |
| United Kingdom | 13066 | 13157 | 12985 | 12695 | 12476 | 11855 | 11902 | 11933 | 11846 | -0.7 |
| Other OECD - Europe | 25593 | 23623 | 23223 | 21402 | 22578 [e] | 21980 [e] | 21706 [e] | 20601 | 20889 | 1.4 |
| Austria | 2531 | 2633 | 2669 | 2651 | 2637 | 2590 | 2541 | 2563 | 2584 | 0.8 |
| Finland | 1741 | 1682 | 1658 | 1608 | 1567 | 1498 | 1443 | 1347 | 1357 | 0.7 |
| Norway | 1007 | 989 | 976 | 970 | 967 | 945 | 979 | 979 | 998 | 1.9 |
| Sweden | 1937 | 1902 | 1878 | 1837 | 1716 | 1656 | 1662 | 1688 | 1718 | 1.8 |
| Switzerland | 1977 | 1933 | 1943 | 1926 | 1902 | 1858 | 1870 | 1851 | 1855 | 0.2 |
| Turkey | 16400 | 14484 | 14099 | 12410 | 13789 [e] | 13433 [e] | 13211 [e] | 12173 | 12377 | 1.7 |
| Yugoslavia | 5430 | 5341 | 5199 | 5034 | 5030 | 4881 | 4759 | 4705 | 4527 | -3.8 |

All totals exclude Yugoslavia / Tous les totaux excluent la Yougoslavie

# EFFECTIFS DU CHEPTEL
## ENSEMBLE DES PORCINS / TOTAL PIGS

Milliers — Thousands

| | 1980/82 moyenne | 1983 | 1984 | 1985 | 1986 | 1987 | 1988 | 1989 | 1990 | 1989/90 % var. |
|---|---|---|---|---|---|---|---|---|---|---|
| **OCDE - Total** | 190845 [e] | 184265 [e] | 186375 [e] | 184694 [e] | 190498 [e] | 190764 [b] | 192167 | 192928 | 189655 [e] | -1.8 |
| **OCDE - Amérique du Nord** | 73509 | 64880 | 67267 | 64040 | 62310 | 61749 | 65402 | 66190 | 64429 | -2.9 |
| Canada | 10017 | 10346 | 10573 | 9967 | 9996 | 10748 | 11018 | 10721 | 10608 | -2.7 |
| États-Unis | 63493 | 54534 | 56694 | 54073 | 52314 | 51001 | 54384 | 55469 | 53821 | -3.0 |
| **Japon** | 10126 | 10423 | 10718 [e] | 11061 | 11354 | 11725 | 11866 | 11816 | 11802 [e] | -0.1 |
| **OCDE - Océanie** | 2860 | 2898 | 2963 | 2966 | 2988 | 3098 | 3180 | 3059 | 2926 | -4.3 |
| Australie | 2440 | 2490 | 2527 | 2512 | 2553 | 2672 | 2766 | 2648 | 2531 | -4.4 |
| Nouvelle Zélande | 420 | 408 | 436 | 454 | 435 | 426 | 414 | 411 | 395 | -3.9 |
| **OCDE - Europe** | 104350 [e] | 106064 [e] | 105427 [e] | 106627 [e] | 113846 [e] | 114192 [b] | 111719 | 111863 | 110498 [e] | -1.2 |
| **CE-12 Total** | 93464 [e] | 95156 [e] | 94622 [e] | 96143 [e] | 103579 [e] | 103977 [b] | 101571 | 101989 | 100707 | -1.3 |
| Belgique / Luxembourg | 5145 | 5253 | 5340 | 5484 | 5837 | 6047 | 6234 | 6551 | 6342 | -3.2 |
| Danemark | 9662 | 9016 | 8960 | 9104 | 9422 | 9048 | 9105 | 9120 | 9282 | 1.8 |
| France | 11698 | 11251 | 10975 | 10956 | 12063 | 11915 | 11706 | 12275 | 12219 | -0.5 |
| Allemagne | 22447 | 23449 | 23617 | 24282 | 24180 | 23670 | 22589 | 22165 | 22035 | -0.6 |
| Grèce | 1179 | 1168 | 1115 | 1095 | 1130 | 1139 | 1226 | 1160 | 1143 | -1.5 |
| Irlande | 1046 | 1053 | 1020 | 994 | 980 | 960 | 961 | 999 | 1069 | 7.0 |
| Italie | 9025 | 9252 | 9041 | 9169 | 9278 | 9383 | 9360 | 9254 | 8837 | -4.5 |
| Pays-Bas | 10326 | 11008 | 11799 | 12908 | 14063 | 14226 | 13820 | 13634 | 13788 | 1.1 |
| Portugal | 3597 [e] | 3560 [e] | 3000 [e] | 2261 [e] | 2940 [e] | 2452 [b] | 2331 | 2598 | 2664 | 2.5 |
| Espagne | 11378 | 12364 | 11962 | 11960 | 15731 | 17222 | 16613 | 16850 | 15949 | -5.3 |
| Royaume-Uni | 7962 | 7782 | 7793 | 7930 | 7955 | 7915 | 7626 | 7383 | 7379 | -0.1 |
| **Autre pays européens de l'OCDE** | 10886 | 10908 | 10805 | 10484 | 10267 | 10215 | 10148 | 9874 | 9791 [e] | -0.8 |
| Autriche | 3899 | 3881 | 4027 | 3926 | 3801 | 3947 | 3874 | 3773 | 3688 | -2.3 |
| Finlande | 1451 | 1440 | 1358 | 1276 | 1304 | 1326 | 1291 | 1277 | 1298 [e] | 1.6 |
| Norvège | 679 | 705 | 720 | 693 | 738 | 779 | 756 | 683 | 743 | 8.8 |
| Suède | 2721 | 2677 | 2685 | 2589 | 2439 | 2234 | 2274 | 2264 | 2264 | 0.0 |
| Suisse | 2123 | 2191 | 2004 | 1988 | 1973 | 1917 | 1941 | 1869 | 1787 | -4.4 |
| Turquie | 13 | 14 | 11 | 12 | 12 | 12 | 12 | 8 | 11 [e] | 37.5 |
| Yougoslavie | 8223 | 9337 | 8673 | 7820 | 8459 | 8323 | 7396 | 7321 | 7358 | 0.5 |

## ENSEMBLE DES OVINS / TOTAL SHEEP

| | 1980/82 moyenne | 1983 | 1984 | 1985 | 1986 | 1987 | 1988 | 1989 | 1990 | 1989/90 % var. |
|---|---|---|---|---|---|---|---|---|---|---|
| **OCDE - Total** | 348557 [e] | 351939 [e] | 357560 [e] | 357180 [e] | 365593 [b] | 373883 [e] | 381710 [e] | 388184 | 377800 [e] | -2.7 |
| **OCDE - Amérique du Nord** | 13437 | 12690 | 12072 | 11205 | 10626 | 11047 | 11426 | 11363 | 11863 [e] | 4.8 |
| Canada | 556 | 550 | 513 | 489 | 481 | 475 | 481 | 515 | 500 [e] | 7.1 |
| États-Unis | 12881 | 12140 | 11559 | 10716 | 10145 | 10572 | 10945 | 10858 | 11363 | 4.7 |
| Japon | 19 | 22 | 24 [e] | 26 | 27 | 29 | 30 | 31 | 30 [e] | -3.2 |
| **OCDE - Océanie** | 205775 | 203500 | 208985 | 217601 | 223031 | 223314 | 229600 | 231569 | 222875 [e] | -3.8 |
| Australie | 136123 | 133237 | 139246 | 149747 | 155561 | 159070 | 165000 | 171000 | 165023 [e] | -3.5 |
| Nouvelle Zélande | 69652 | 70263 | 69739 | 67854 | 67470 | 64244 | 64600 | 60569 | 57852 | -4.5 |
| **OCDE - Europe** | 129326 [e] | 135727 [e] | 136479 [e] | 128348 [e] | 131909 [b] | 139493 [e] | 140654 [e] | 145211 | 143032 | -1.5 |
| **CE-12 Total** | 78067 [e] | 82702 [e] | 84293 [e] | 84402 [e] | 88025 [b] | 95469 | 96831 | 98009 | 99031 | 1.0 |
| Belgique / Luxembourg | 87 | 103 | 114 | 128 | 132 | 140 | 136 | 141 | 143 | 1.4 |
| Danemark | 43 | 39 | 40 | 52 | 70 | 73 | 86 | 100 | 111 | 11.0 |
| France | 13099 | 13035 | 12676 | 12001 | 12315 | 12105 | 11495 | 11208 | 10958 | -2.2 |
| Allemagne | 1153 | 1218 | 1300 | 1296 | 1383 | 1414 | 1430 | 1533 | 1784 | 16.4 |
| Grèce | 8670 | 9962 | 10029 | 9989 | 11032 | 10816 | 10376 | 10353 | 10150 | -2.0 |
| Irlande | 2467 | 2813 | 3082 | 3304 | 3672 | 4301 | 4991 | 5782 | 6001 | 3.8 |
| Italie | 10143 | 10745 | 11293 | 11293 | 11451 | 11457 | 11623 | 11569 | 10848 | -6.2 |
| Pays-Bas | 910 | 875 | 920 | 985 | 1115 | 1320 | 1405 | 1725 | 1870 | 8.4 |
| Portugal | 3835 [e] | 3840 [e] | 3840 [e] | 3860 [e] | 3000 [b] | 3035 | 3187 | 3347 | 3190 | -4.7 |
| Espagne | 15416 | 16755 | 17053 | 16954 | 17879 | 22988 | 23057 | 22730 | 24022 | 5.7 |
| Royaume-Uni | 22245 | 23317 | 23946 | 24540 | 25976 | 27820 | 29045 | 29521 | 29954 | 1.5 |
| **Autre pays européens de l'OCDE** | 51259 | 53025 | 52186 | 43946 | 43884 [e] | 44024 [e] | 43823 [e] | 47202 | 44001 | -6.8 |
| Autriche | 195 | 216 | 220 | 245 | 256 | 261 | 256 | 289 | 309 | 6.9 |
| Finlande | 104 | 104 | 110 | 112 | 116 | 126 | 119 | 108 | 107 | -0.9 |
| Norvège | 2124 | 2272 | 2351 | 2415 | 2340 | 2248 | 2210 | 2183 | 2231 | 2.2 |
| Suède | 410 | 442 | 437 | 426 | 407 | 397 | 395 | 401 | 406 | 1.2 |
| Suisse | 341 | 355 | 361 | 357 | 365 | 355 | 367 | 374 | 395 | 5.6 |
| Turquie | 48085 | 49636 | 48707 | 40391 | 40400 [e] | 40637 [e] | 40476 [e] | 43847 | 40553 | -7.5 |
| Yougoslavie | 7411 | 7458 | 7680 | 7693 | 7819 | 7824 | 7564 | 7596 | 7431 | -2.2 |

All totals exclude Yugoslavia / Tous les totaux excluent la Yougoslavie

# GROSS INDIGENOUS PRODUCTION
## TOTAL MEAT / TOTAL VIANDE

*Thousand metric tons - Dressed carcass weight* — *Milliers de tonnes métriques - Poids en carcasse parée*

| | 1980/82 average | 1983 | 1984 | 1985 | 1986 | 1987 | 1988 | 1989 | 1990 | 1989/90 % change |
|---|---|---|---|---|---|---|---|---|---|---|
| **OECD - Total** | 66417 | 68037 | 69164 | 70322 [b] | 71016 | 72851 | 74462 | 74566 [e] | 75664 [e] | 1.5 |
| **OECD - North America** | 28313 | 28984 | 29315 | 29952 | 30202 | 30817 | 31964 | 32373 | 32622 [e] | 0.8 |
| Canada | 2699 | 2761 | 2854 | 2976 | 2924 | 2948 | 3124 | 3139 | 3122 [e] | -0.5 |
| United States | 25614 | 26223 | 26461 | 26976 | 27278 | 27869 | 28840 | 29234 | 29500 | 0.9 |
| **Japan** | 3321 | 3461 | 3566 | 3747 | 3805 | 3879 | 3858 | 3829 | 3747 | -2.1 |
| **OECD - Oceania** | 4029 | 3912 | 3764 | 4056 | 4073 | 4336 | 4299 | 4373 | 4461 | 2.0 |
| Australia | 2791 | 2580 | 2513 | 2678 | 2841 | 3012 | 2958 | 3051 | 3287 | 7.7 |
| New Zealand | 1238 | 1332 | 1251 | 1378 | 1232 | 1324 | 1341 | 1322 | 1174 | -11.2 |
| **OECD - Europe** | 30754 | 31680 | 32519 | 32567 [b] | 32936 | 33819 | 34341 | 33991 [e] | 34834 [e] | 2.5 |
| **EC-12 Total** | 27225 | 28057 | 28817 | 28751 [b] | 29277 | 30254 | 30559 | 30203 | 31188 | 3.3 |
| Belgium / Luxembourg | 1185 | 1194 | 1250 | 1260 | 1295 | 1351 | 1401 | 1415 | 1344 | -5.0 |
| Denmark | 1395 | 1467 | 1461 | 1503 | 1578 | 1572 | 1576 | 1567 | 1616 | 3.1 |
| France | 5702 | 5705 | 5878 | 5776 | 5884 | 6093 | 6150 | 6087 | 6331 | 4.0 |
| Germany | 5392 | 5395 | 5535 | 5481 | 5803 | 5778 | 5658 | 5494 | 5652 | 2.9 |
| Greece | 545 | 555 | 552 | 552 | 529 | 565 | 566 | 555 | 556 | 0.2 |
| Ireland | 795 | 800 | 838 | 876 [b] | 894 | 864 | 891 | 856 | 1009 | 17.9 |
| Italy | 3359 | 3522 | 3627 | 3519 | 3413 | 3517 | 3594 | 3620 | 3687 | 1.9 |
| Netherlands | 2367 | 2460 | 2617 | 2711 | 2848 | 3011 | 3040 | 2953 | 3068 | 3.9 |
| Portugal | 521 | 567 | 540 | 520 | 573 | 624 | 612 | 671 | 683 | 1.8 |
| Spain | 2740 | 3084 | 3134 | 3114 | 3045 | 3226 | 3528 | 3490 | 3683 | 5.5 |
| United Kingdom | 3224 | 3308 | 3385 | 3439 | 3415 | 3653 | 3543 | 3495 | 3559 | 1.8 |
| **Other OECD - Europe** | 3528 | 3623 | 3702 | 3816 | 3659 | 3565 | 3782 | 3788 [e] | 3646 [e] | -3.7 |
| Austria | 663 | 689 | 707 | 741 | 734 | 729 | 751 | 741 | 774 | 4.5 |
| Finland | 359 | 364 | 366 | 369 | 371 | 377 | 356 | 338 | 365 | 8.0 |
| Norway | 211 | 212 | 211 | 218 | 221 | 233 | 232 | 228 | 235 | 3.1 |
| Sweden | 579 | 584 | 578 | 593 | 550 | 514 | 515 | 540 | 540 | 0.0 |
| Switzerland | 496 | 497 | 498 | 512 | 514 | 509 | 496 | 500 | 496 | -0.8 |
| Turkey | 1220 | 1277 | 1342 | 1383 | 1269 | 1203 | 1432 | 1441 [e] | 1236 [e] | -14.2 |
| Yugoslavia | 1550 | 1571 | 1716 | 1617 | 1587 | 1720 | 1710 | 1611 [e] | 1581 [e] | -1.9 |

## TOTAL BEEF AND VEAL / TOTAL VIANDE BOVINE

| | 1980/82 average | 1983 | 1984 | 1985 | 1986 | 1987 | 1988 | 1989 | 1990 | 1989/90 % change |
|---|---|---|---|---|---|---|---|---|---|---|
| **OECD - Total** | 22356 | 22787 | 23385 | 23538 [b] | 23899 | 23598 | 23315 | 22733 | 22951 | 1.0 |
| **OECD - North America** | 11228 | 11707 | 11883 | 12001 | 12172 | 11748 | 11851 | 11545 | 11296 | -2.2 |
| Canada | 1061 | 1090 | 1066 | 1110 | 1081 | 1027 | 1103 | 1111 | 1162 | 4.6 |
| United States | 10167 | 10617 | 10817 | 10891 | 11091 | 10721 | 10748 | 10434 | 10134 | -2.9 |
| **Japan** | 464 | 505 | 539 | 556 | 563 | 568 | 569 | 539 | 554 | 2.8 |
| **OECD - Oceania** | 2048 | 1926 | 1705 | 1825 | 1943 | 2119 | 2123 | 2115 | 2196 | 3.8 |
| Australia | 1545 | 1414 | 1272 | 1338 | 1477 | 1564 | 1551 | 1574 | 1717 | 9.1 |
| New Zealand | 504 | 512 | 433 | 487 | 466 | 555 | 572 | 541 | 479 | -11.5 |
| **OECD - Europe** | 8615 | 8649 | 9258 | 9156 [b] | 9221 | 9163 | 8772 | 8534 | 8905 | 4.3 |
| **EC-12 Total** | 7490 | 7472 | 8026 | 7876 [b] | 8014 | 8066 | 7617 | 7340 | 7741 | 5.5 |
| Belgium / Luxembourg | 300 | 292 | 330 | 342 | 345 | 336 | 336 | 323 | 326 | 0.9 |
| Denmark | 238 | 240 | 247 | 236 | 243 | 235 | 217 | 204 | 202 | -1.0 |
| France | 1947 | 1937 | 2121 | 2039 | 2068 | 2129 | 2003 | 1843 | 1912 | 3.7 |
| Germany | 1549 | 1528 | 1637 | 1596 | 1739 | 1704 | 1613 | 1601 | 1676 | 4.7 |
| Greece | 95 | 79 | 80 | 75 | 74 | 70 | 73 | 66 | 66 | 0.0 |
| Ireland | 472 | 465 | 505 | 533 [b] | 558 | 512 | 520 | 480 | 569 | 18.5 |
| Italy | 882 | 931 | 987 | 967 | 919 | 912 | 908 | 859 | 919 | 7.0 |
| Netherlands | 440 | 452 | 524 | 509 | 523 | 526 | 481 | 451 | 474 | 5.1 |
| Portugal | 109 | 112 | 101 | 98 | 102 | 99 | 112 | 120 | 112 | -6.7 |
| Spain | 420 | 417 | 390 | 384 | 423 | 438 | 427 | 435 | 499 | 14.7 |
| United Kingdom | 1038 | 1019 | 1104 | 1097 | 1020 | 1105 | 927 | 958 | 986 | 2.9 |
| **Other OECD - Europe** | 1126 | 1177 | 1232 | 1280 | 1207 | 1097 | 1155 | 1194 | 1164 | -2.5 |
| Austria | 212 | 212 | 227 | 242 | 247 | 231 | 223 | 210 | 239 | 13.8 |
| Finland | 117 | 119 | 124 | 126 | 125 | 124 | 111 | 107 | 118 | 10.3 |
| Norway | 75 | 74 | 69 | 73 | 74 | 76 | 76 | 76 | 82 | 7.9 |
| Sweden | 159 | 161 | 155 | 158 | 147 | 135 | 127 | 138 | 147 | 6.5 |
| Switzerland | 162 | 153 | 166 | 171 | 170 | 173 | 157 | 157 | 165 | 5.1 |
| Turkey | 400 | 458 | 491 | 510 | 444 | 358 | 461 | 506 | 413 | -18.4 |
| Yugoslavia | 349 | 357 | 371 | 333 | 317 | 359 | 346 | 357 [e] | 356 [e] | -0.3 |

All totals exclude Yugoslavia / Tous les totaux excluent la Yougoslavie

24

# PRODUCTION INDIGÈNE BRUTE
## VIANDE DE PORC / PIG MEAT

*Milliers de tonnes métriques - Poids en carcasse parée*       *Thousand metric tons - Dressed carcass weight*

| | 1980/82 moyenne | 1983 | 1984 | 1985 | 1986 | 1987 | 1988 | 1989 | 1990 | 1989/90 % var. |
|---|---|---|---|---|---|---|---|---|---|---|
| **OCDE - Total** | 22204 | 22747 | 22793 | 22986 | 22914 | 23603 | 24798 | 24659 | 24596 | -0.3 |
| **OCDE - Amérique du Nord** | 8084 | 7926 | 7764 | 7798 | 7478 | 7650 | 8312 | 8359 | 8114 | -2.9 |
| Canada | 1036 | 1065 | 1145 | 1175 | 1136 | 1163 | 1256 | 1260 | 1198 | -4.9 |
| États-Unis | 7048 | 6861 | 6619 | 6623 | 6342 | 6487 | 7056 | 7099 | 6916 | -2.6 |
| **Japon** | 1437 | 1430 | 1433 | 1550 | 1558 | 1592 | 1577 | 1597 | 1536 | -3.8 |
| **OCDE - Océanie** | 267 | 287 | 346 | 316 | 299 | 333 | 349 | 355 | 362 | 2.0 |
| Australie | 231 | 247 | 303 | 268 | 251 | 288 | 303 | 310 | 319 | 2.9 |
| Nouvelle Zélande | 36 | 40 | 43 | 48 | 48 | 45 | 46 | 45 | 43 | -4.4 |
| **OCDE - Europe** | 12417 | 13104 | 13250 | 13322 | 13579 | 14028 | 14560 | 14348 | 14584 | 1.6 |
| **CE-12 Total** | 11222 | 11880 | 12042 | 12075 | 12365 | 12828 | 13319 | 13103 | 13350 | 1.9 |
| Belgique / Luxembourg | 656 | 670 | 684 | 676 | 701 | 753 | 806 | 830 | 747 | -10.0 |
| Danemark | 990 | 1051 | 1039 | 1086 | 1146 | 1150 | 1169 | 1164 | 1208 | 3.8 |
| France | 1580 | 1564 | 1575 | 1571 | 1591 | 1646 | 1779 | 1779 | 1816 | 2.1 |
| Allemagne | 3089 | 3146 | 3161 | 3151 | 3288 | 3286 | 3250 | 3094 | 3142 | 1.6 |
| Grèce | 148 | 149 | 146 | 147 | 153 | 164 | 160 | 151 | 147 | -2.6 |
| Irlande | 142 | 148 | 141 | 136 | 139 | 140 | 142 | 146 | 160 | 9.6 |
| Italie | 1036 | 1115 | 1167 | 1112 | 1053 | 1121 | 1154 | 1207 | 1211 | 0.3 |
| Pays-Bas | 1395 | 1476 | 1544 | 1635 | 1736 | 1846 | 1910 | 1852 | 1909 | 3.1 |
| Portugal | 171 | 200 | 208 | 197 | 223 | 259 | 226 | 261 | 278 | 6.5 |
| Espagne | 1041 | 1342 | 1429 | 1388 | 1342 | 1448 | 1702 | 1674 | 1772 | 5.9 |
| Royaume-Uni | 974 | 1019 | 948 | 976 | 993 | 1015 | 1021 | 945 | 960 | 1.6 |
| **Autre pays européens de l'OCDE** | 1195 | 1224 | 1208 | 1247 | 1214 | 1200 | 1241 | 1245 | 1234 | -0.9 |
| Autriche | 334 | 357 | 355 | 374 | 360 | 366 | 404 | 400 | 401 | 0.3 |
| Finlande | 177 | 177 | 170 | 172 | 174 | 176 | 169 | 174 | 187 | 7.5 |
| Norvège | 82 | 81 | 84 | 84 | 85 | 92 | 90 | 84 | 83 | -1.2 |
| Suède | 321 | 318 | 323 | 332 | 309 | 288 | 299 | 307 | 293 | -4.6 |
| Suisse | 281 | 291 | 276 | 285 | 286 | 278 | 279 | 280 | 270 | -3.6 |
| Turquie | - | - | - | - | - | - | - | - | - | .. |
| Yougoslavie | 770 | 772 | 876 | 833 | 795 | 871 | 853 | 789 | 781 | -1.0 |

## VIANDE DE VOLAILLE / POULTRY MEAT [1]

| | 1980/82 moyenne | 1983 | 1984 | 1985 | 1986 | 1987 | 1988 | 1989 | 1990 | 1989/90 % var. |
|---|---|---|---|---|---|---|---|---|---|---|
| **OCDE - Total** | 14510 | 14983 | 15401 | 16041 | 16653 | 17992 | 18577 | 19427 | 20433 [e] | 5.2 |
| **OCDE - Amérique du Nord** | 7370 | 7679 | 7985 | 8473 | 8891 | 9783 | 10111 | 10791 | 11563 [e] | 7.2 |
| Canada | 525 | 527 | 558 | 608 | 628 | 683 | 685 | 686 | 685 [e] | -0.1 |
| États-Unis | 6845 | 7152 | 7427 | 7865 | 8263 | 9100 | 9426 | 10105 | 10878 | 7.6 |
| **Japon** | 1156 | 1257 | 1325 | 1354 | 1398 | 1437 | 1436 | 1417 | 1387 | -2.1 |
| **OCDE - Océanie** | 339 | 335 | 361 | 413 | 416 | 442 | 454 | 490 | 505 | 3.1 |
| Australie | 304 | 302 | 315 | 365 | 370 | 394 | 402 | 432 | 445 | 3.0 |
| Nouvelle Zélande | 34 | 33 | 46 | 48 | 46 | 48 | 52 | 58 | 60 | 3.4 |
| **OCDE - Europe** | 5645 | 5712 | 5730 | 5801 | 5948 | 6330 | 6576 | 6729 | 6978 | 3.7 |
| **CE-12 Total** | 5201 | 5289 | 5261 | 5331 | 5443 | 5783 | 5996 | 6122 | 6336 | 3.5 |
| Belgique / Luxembourg | 123 | 126 | 126 | 131 | 134 | 141 | 152 | 154 | 167 | 8.4 |
| Danemark | 104 | 112 | 110 | 115 | 116 | 113 | 117 | 128 | 132 | 3.1 |
| France | 1236 | 1284 | 1251 | 1267 | 1328 | 1408 | 1449 | 1557 | 1665 | 6.9 |
| Allemagne | 377 | 345 | 352 | 357 | 377 | 390 | 411 | 425 | 449 | 5.6 |
| Grèce | 130 | 153 | 152 | 155 | 145 | 149 | 149 | 153 | 160 | 4.6 |
| Irlande | 48 | 53 | 52 | 55 | 59 | 66 | 75 | 69 | 81 | 17.4 |
| Italie | 1019 | 1043 | 1020 | 998 | 1001 | 1046 | 1072 | 1094 | 1100 | 0.5 |
| Pays-Bas | 402 | 398 | 410 | 425 | 442 | 484 | 492 | 498 | 520 | 4.4 |
| Portugal | 159 | 164 | 140 | 137 | 157 | 171 | 175 | 183 | 185 | 1.1 |
| Espagne | 836 | 813 | 790 | 815 | 754 | 786 | 819 | 828 | 834 | 0.7 |
| Royaume-Uni | 768 | 798 | 858 | 876 | 930 | 1029 | 1085 | 1033 | 1043 | 1.0 |
| **Autre pays européens de l'OCDE** | 444 | 423 | 469 | 470 | 505 | 547 | 580 | 607 | 642 | 5.8 |
| Autriche | 73 | 76 | 80 | 79 | 83 | 86 | 82 | 89 | 90 | 1.1 |
| Finlande | 16 | 18 | 20 | 21 | 22 | 27 | 28 | 30 | 33 | 10.0 |
| Norvège | 11 | 11 | 11 | 12 | 13 | 15 | 18 | 20 | 20 | 0.0 |
| Suède | 46 | 47 | 46 | 46 | 45 | 43 | 41 | 45 | 51 | 13.3 |
| Suisse | 24 | 25 | 26 | 27 | 27 | 26 | 31 | 33 | 33 | 0.0 |
| Turquie | 275 | 246 | 286 | 285 | 315 | 350 | 380 | 390 | 415 | 6.4 |
| Yougoslavie | 282 | 287 | 313 | 297 | 328 | 323 | 351 | 310 | 295 | -4.8 |

1. Poids éviscéré ou «prêt à cuire» / Eviscerated or ready-to-cook weight      All totals exclude Yugoslavia / Tous les totaux excluent la Yougoslavie

# GROSS INDIGENOUS PRODUCTION
## *MUTTON, LAMB AND GOAT MEAT / VIANDE DE MOUTON ET DE CHÈVRE*

*Thousand metric tons - Dressed carcass weight*                                                                      *Milliers de tonnes métriques - Poids en carcasse parée*

| | 1980/82 average | 1983 | 1984 | 1985 | 1986 | 1987 | 1988 | 1989 | 1990 | 1989/90 % change |
|---|---|---|---|---|---|---|---|---|---|---|
| **OECD - Total** | 2671 | 2797 | 2783 | 2961 | 2766 | 2820 | 2899 | 2946 | 2880 | -2.2 |
| **OECD - North America** | 165 | 177 | 180 | 170 | 160 | 150 | 160 | 165 | 174 | 5.5 |
| Canada | 6 | 7 | 8 | 7 | 7 | 7 | 8 | 8 | 9 | 12.5 |
| United States | 159 | 170 | 172 | 163 | 153 | 143 | 152 | 157 | 165 | 5.1 |
| **Japan** | - | - | - | - | - | - | - | - | - | .. |
| **OECD - Oceania** | 1147 | 1150 | 1143 | 1284 | 1196 | 1209 | 1155 | 1195 | 1184 | -0.9 |
| Australia | 544 | 470 | 475 | 556 | 585 | 599 | 551 | 583 | 649 | 11.3 |
| New Zealand | 603 | 680 | 668 | 728 | 611 | 610 | 604 | 612 | 535 | -12.6 |
| **OECD - Europe** | 1359 | 1470 | 1460 | 1507 | 1410 | 1461 | 1584 | 1586 | 1522 | -4.0 |
| **EC-12 Total** | 876 | 962 | 963 | 980 | 946 | 1003 | 1031 | 1083 | 1153 | 6.5 |
| Belgium / Luxembourg | 4 | 4 | 4 | 3 | 4 | 4 | 4 | 4 | 3 | -25.0 |
| Denmark | - | - | 1 | 1 | 1 | 1 | 1 | 1 | 1 | 0.0 |
| France | 179 | 178 | 174 | 173 | 162 | 159 | 151 | 151 | 177 | 17.2 |
| Germany | 21 | 23 | 23 | 23 | 23 | 26 | 25 | 25 | 29 | 16.0 |
| Greece | 120 | 119 | 120 | 121 | 106 | 124 | 127 | 128 | 128 | 0.0 |
| Ireland | 40 | 40 | 41 | 49 | 47 | 49 | 50 | 64 | 85 | 32.8 |
| Italy | 54 | 51 | 54 | 49 | 49 | 47 | 51 | 56 | 56 | 0.0 |
| Netherlands | 22 | 21 | 18 | 18 | 18 | 21 | 20 | 23 | 32 | 39.1 |
| Portugal | 24 | 27 | 26 | 25 | 25 | 27 | 28 | 28 | 28 | 0.0 |
| Spain | 140 | 202 | 207 | 210 | 210 | 225 | 232 | 218 | 223 | 2.3 |
| United Kingdom | 272 | 297 | 295 | 308 | 301 | 320 | 342 | 385 | 391 | 1.6 |
| **Other OECD - Europe** | 483 | 508 | 497 | 527 | 464 | 458 | 553 | 503 | 369 | -26.6 |
| Austria | 3 | 4 | 4 | 4 | 4 | 5 | 5 | 5 | 6 | 20.0 |
| Finland | 1 | 1 | 1 | 1 | 1 | 1 | 1 | 1 | 1 | 0.0 |
| Norway | 21 | 24 | 25 | 25 | 26 | 26 | 25 | 24 | 25 | 4.2 |
| Sweden | 5 | 5 | 5 | 5 | 5 | 5 | 5 | 5 | 5 | 0.0 |
| Switzerland | 4 | 4 | 4 | 5 | 5 | 5 | 5 | 5 | 5 | 0.0 |
| Turkey | 449 | 470 | 458 | 487 | 423 | 416 | 512 | 463 | 327 | -29.4 |
| Yugoslavia | 59 | 62 | 59 | 62 | 63 | 65 | 70 | 69 | 67 | -2.9 |

## *HORSE MEAT / VIANDE D'ÉQUIDÉS [1]*

| | 1980/82 average | 1983 | 1984 | 1985 | 1986 | 1987 | 1988 | 1989 | 1990 | 1989/90 % change |
|---|---|---|---|---|---|---|---|---|---|---|
| **OECD - Total** | 92 | 81 | 80 | 74 | 69 | 67 | 64 | 61 | 54 | -11.5 |
| **OECD - North America** | - | - | - | - | - | - | - | - | - | .. |
| Canada | - | - | - | - | - | - | - | - | - | .. |
| United States | - | - | - | - | - | - | - | - | - | .. |
| **Japan** | 4 | 5 | 6 | 6 | 5 | 5 | 4 | 5 | 5 | 0.0 |
| **OECD - Oceania** | - | - | - | - | - | - | - | - | - | .. |
| Australia | - | - | - | - | - | - | - | - | - | .. |
| New Zealand | - | - | - | - | - | - | - | - | - | .. |
| **OECD - Europe** | 88 | 76 | 74 | 68 | 64 | 62 | 60 | 56 | 49 | -12.5 |
| **EC-12 Total** | 78 | 69 | 66 | 61 | 58 | 55 | 52 | 49 | 42 | -14.3 |
| Belgium / Luxembourg | 4 | 3 | 3 | 3 | 2 | 2 | 3 | 2 | 1 | -50.0 |
| Denmark | 2 | 1 | 1 | 1 | 1 | 1 | 1 | 1 | 1 | 0.0 |
| France | 18 | 15 | 15 | 14 | 13 | 14 | 15 | 13 | 10 | -23.1 |
| Germany | 9 | 9 | 8 | 9 | 7 | 7 | 5 | 5 | 4 | -20.0 |
| Greece | 2 | 1 | - | - | 1 | 1 | 1 | 1 | - | -100.0 |
| Ireland | 3 | 2 | 2 | 2 | 1 | 1 | - | 1 | - | -100.0 |
| Italy | 15 | 15 | 16 | 12 | 17 | 13 | 14 | 15 | 15 | 0.0 |
| Netherlands | 7 | 6 | 5 | 5 | 4 | 4 | 4 | 3 | 2 | -33.3 |
| Portugal | 1 | 1 | 2 | 1 | 1 | 1 | 1 | 1 | 1 | 0.0 |
| Spain | 11 | 9 | 8 | 8 | 7 | 7 | 6 | 6 | 7 | 16.7 |
| United Kingdom | 7 | 7 | 6 | 6 | 4 | 4 | 2 | 1 | 1 | 0.0 |
| **Other OECD - Europe** | 10 | 7 | 8 | 7 | 6 | 7 | 8 | 7 | 7 | 0.0 |
| Austria | - | - | - | - | - | - | 1 | 1 | 1 | 0.0 |
| Finland | 1 | 1 | 1 | 1 | 1 | 1 | 1 | 1 | 1 | 0.0 |
| Norway | 1 | 1 | 1 | 1 | 1 | 1 | 1 | 1 | 1 | 0.0 |
| Sweden | 3 | 3 | 2 | 3 | 2 | 2 | 2 | 2 | 2 | 0.0 |
| Switzerland | 1 | 1 | 2 | 1 | 1 | 2 | 2 | 1 | 1 | 0.0 |
| Turkey | 3 | 1 | 2 | 1 | 1 | 1 | 1 | 1 | 1 | 0.0 |
| Yugoslavia | 10 | 14 | 7 | 10 | 6 | 21 | 10 | 8 | 3 | -62.5 |

1. Including mules and asses / Y compris les mulets et les anes            All totals exclude Yugoslavia / Tous les totaux excluent la Yougoslavie

# PRODUCTION INDIGÈNE BRUTE
## AUTRES VIANDES / OTHER MEAT

*Milliers de tonnes métriques - Poids en carcasse parée*　　　　　　　　　　　*Thousand metric tons - Dressed carcass weight*

| | 1980/82 moyenne | 1983 | 1984 | 1985 | 1986 | 1987 | 1988 | 1989 | 1990 | 1989/90 % var. |
|---|---|---|---|---|---|---|---|---|---|---|
| **OCDE - Total** | 1038 | 997 | 1009 | 1015 | 1000 | 1005 | 1032 | 1029 | 1017 | -1.2 |
| **OCDE - Amérique du Nord** | 230 | 235 | 240 | 243 | 244 | 250 | 250 | 250 | 250 | 0.0 |
| Canada | - | - | - | - | - | - | - | - | - | .. |
| États-Unis | 230 | 235 | 240 | 243 | 244 | 250 | 250 | 250 | 250 | 0.0 |
| Japon | 19 | 21 | 16 | 15 | 14 | 5 | 2 | 1 | 2 | 100.0 |
| **OCDE - Océanie** | 46 | 47 | 47 | 42 | 43 | 38 | 25 | 26 | 16 | -38.5 |
| Australie | 44 | 45 | 45 | 40 | 41 | 36 | 23 | 24 | 14 | -41.7 |
| Nouvelle Zélande | 2 | 2 | 2 | 2 | 2 | 2 | 2 | 2 | 2 | 0.0 |
| **OCDE - Europe** | 742 | 694 | 706 | 715 | 699 | 712 | 755 | 752 | 749 | -0.4 |
| **CE-12 Total** | 691 | 638 | 651 | 658 | 651 | 662 | 705 | 699 | 697 | -0.3 |
| Belgique / Luxembourg | 13 | 15 | 15 | 17 | 18 | 19 | 20 | 22 | 25 | 13.6 |
| Danemark | 3 | 3 | 3 | 3 | 3 | 3 | 3 | 3 | 3 | 0.0 |
| France | 284 | 269 | 269 | 270 | 269 | 272 | 290 | 300 | 300 | 0.0 |
| Allemagne | 42 | 39 | 38 | 38 | 37 | 37 | 37 | 37 | 37 | 0.0 |
| Grèce | 6 | 5 | 5 | 5 | 4 | 5 | 5 | 5 | 5 | 0.0 |
| Irlande | - | - | - | - | - | - | 3 | 1 | 2 | 100.0 |
| Italie | 188 | 191 | 197 | 200 | 201 | 203 | 218 | 212 | 201 | -5.2 |
| Pays-Bas | - | 1 | 1 | 1 | 2 | 2 | 6 | 3 | 4 | 33.3 |
| Portugal | 8 | 14 | 16 | 16 | 16 | 16 | 17 | 22 | 23 | 4.5 |
| Espagne | 139 | 94 | 99 | 100 | 94 | 97 | 98 | 85 | 87 | 2.4 |
| Royaume-Uni | 8 | 7 | 8 | 8 | 7 | 8 | 8 | 9 | 10 | 11.1 |
| **Autre pays européens de l'OCDE** | 51 | 56 | 55 | 57 | 48 | 50 | 50 | 53 | 52 | -1.9 |
| Autriche | 9 | 7 | 7 | 7 | 5 | 6 | 6 | 7 | 7 | 0.0 |
| Finlande | 10 | 11 | 13 | 11 | 11 | 11 | 11 | 12 | 11 | -8.3 |
| Norvège | 7 | 8 | 8 | 10 | 9 | 9 | 9 | 9 | 10 | 11.1 |
| Suède | 21 | 26 | 23 | 25 | 19 | 20 | 21 | 22 | 21 | -4.5 |
| Suisse | 4 | 4 | 4 | 4 | 4 | 4 | 3 | 3 | 3 | 0.0 |
| Turquie | - | - | - | - | - | - | - | - | - | .. |
| Yougoslavie | 6 | 6 | 8 | 8 | 8 | 8 | 8 | 7 | 7 | 0.0 |

## ABATS COMESTIBLES / EDIBLES OFFALS [1]

| | 1980/82 moyenne | 1983 | 1984 | 1985 | 1986 | 1987 | 1988 | 1989 | 1990 | 1989/90 % var. |
|---|---|---|---|---|---|---|---|---|---|---|
| **OCDE - Total** | 3547 | 3645 | 3713 | 3707 | 3715 | 3766 | 3777 | 3711 [e] | 3733 [e] | 0.6 |
| **OCDE - Amérique du Nord** | 1237 | 1260 | 1263 | 1267 | 1257 | 1236 | 1280 | 1263 | 1225 [e] | -3.0 |
| Canada | 71 | 72 | 77 | 76 | 72 | 68 | 72 | 74 | 68 [e] | -8.1 |
| États-Unis | 1166 | 1188 | 1186 | 1191 | 1185 | 1168 | 1208 | 1189 | 1157 | -2.7 |
| Japon | 241 | 243 | 247 | 266 | 267 | 272 | 270 | 270 | 263 | -2.6 |
| **OCDE - Océanie** | 182 | 167 | 162 | 176 | 176 | 195 | 193 | 192 | 198 | 3.1 |
| Australie | 123 | 102 | 103 | 111 | 117 | 131 | 128 | 128 | 143 | 11.7 |
| Nouvelle Zélande | 59 | 65 | 59 | 65 | 59 | 64 | 65 | 64 | 55 | -14.1 |
| **OCDE - Europe** | 1887 | 1975 | 2041 | 1998 | 2015 | 2063 | 2034 | 1986 [e] | 2047 [e] | 3.1 |
| **CE-12 Total** | 1667 | 1747 | 1808 | 1770 | 1800 | 1857 | 1839 | 1807 | 1869 | 3.4 |
| Belgique / Luxembourg | 85 | 84 | 88 | 88 | 91 | 96 | 80 | 80 | 75 | -6.2 |
| Danemark | 58 | 60 | 60 | 61 | 68 | 69 | 68 | 66 | 69 | 4.5 |
| France | 458 | 458 | 473 | 442 | 453 | 465 | 463 | 444 | 451 | 1.6 |
| Allemagne | 304 | 305 | 316 | 307 | 332 | 328 | 317 | 307 | 315 | 2.6 |
| Grèce | 44 | 49 | 49 | 49 | 46 | 52 | 51 | 51 | 50 | -2.0 |
| Irlande | 90 | 92 | 97 | 101 | 90 | 96 | 101 | 95 | 112 | 17.9 |
| Italie | 166 | 176 | 186 | 181 | 173 | 175 | 177 | 177 | 185 | 4.5 |
| Pays-Bas | 101 | 106 | 115 | 118 | 123 | 128 | 127 | 123 | 127 | 3.3 |
| Portugal | 49 | 49 | 47 | 46 | 49 | 51 | 53 | 56 | 56 | 0.0 |
| Espagne | 153 | 207 | 211 | 209 | 215 | 225 | 244 | 244 | 261 | 7.0 |
| Royaume-Uni | 158 | 161 | 166 | 168 | 160 | 172 | 158 | 164 | 168 | 2.4 |
| **Autre pays européens de l'OCDE** | 219 | 228 | 233 | 228 | 215 | 206 | 195 | 179 [e] | 178 [e] | -0.6 |
| Autriche | 33 | 33 | 34 | 35 | 35 | 35 | 30 | 29 | 30 | 3.4 |
| Finlande | 37 | 37 | 37 | 37 | 37 | 37 | 35 | 13 | 14 | 7.7 |
| Norvège | 13 | 13 | 13 | 13 | 13 | 14 | 13 | 14 | 14 | 0.0 |
| Suède | 24 | 24 | 24 | 24 | 23 | 21 | 20 | 21 | 21 | 0.0 |
| Suisse | 20 | 19 | 20 | 19 | 21 | 21 | 19 | 21 | 19 | -9.5 |
| Turquie | 93 | 102 | 105 | 100 | 86 | 78 | 78 | 81 [e] | 80 [e] | -1.2 |
| Yougoslavie | 74 | 73 | 82 | 74 | 70 | 73 | 72 | 71 | 72 | 1.4 |

1. Poids de produit / Product weight　　　　　　　　　　All totals exclude Yugoslavia / Tous les totaux excluent la Yougoslavie

# MEET PRODUCTION FROM SLAUGHTERED ANIMALS
## TOTAL MEAT / TOTAL VIANDE

*Thousand metric tons - Dressed carcass weight*      *Milliers de tonnes métriques - Poids en carcasse parée*

| | 1980/82 average | 1983 | 1984 | 1985 | 1986 | 1987 | 1988 | 1989 | 1990 | 1989/90 % change |
|---|---|---|---|---|---|---|---|---|---|---|
| OECD - Total | 66418 | 68051 | 69135 | 70374 [b] | 71187 | 72977 | 74473 | 74747 [e] | 76224 [e] | 2.0 |
| OECD - North America | 28347 | 29061 | 29355 | 29991 | 30362 | 30937 | 31967 | 32451 | 32712 [e] | 0.8 |
| Canada | 2621 | 2666 | 2668 | 2801 | 2837 | 2866 | 2922 | 2923 | 2814 [e] | -3.7 |
| United States | 25726 | 26395 | 26687 | 27190 | 27525 | 28071 | 29045 | 29528 | 29898 [e] | 1.3 |
| Japan | 3321 | 3461 | 3566 | 3747 | 3805 | 3879 | 3858 | 3829 | 3747 | -2.1 |
| OECD - Oceania | 3905 | 3768 | 3619 | 3918 | 3931 | 4193 | 4152 | 4257 | 4378 | 2.8 |
| Australia | 2667 | 2436 | 2368 | 2540 | 2699 | 2869 | 2811 | 2935 | 3204 | 9.2 |
| New Zealand | 1238 | 1332 | 1251 | 1378 | 1232 | 1324 | 1341 | 1322 | 1174 | -11.2 |
| OECD - Europe | 30844 | 31761 | 32595 | 32718 [b] | 33089 | 33968 | 34496 | 34210 [e] | 35387 [e] | 3.4 |
| EC-12 Total | 27325 | 28144 | 28899 | 28922 [b] | 29452 | 30426 | 30729 | 30428 | 31742 | 4.3 |
| Belgium / Luxembourg | 1231 | 1257 | 1320 | 1335 | 1366 | 1415 | 1424 | 1426 | 1415 | -0.8 |
| Denmark | 1382 | 1458 | 1457 | 1500 | 1576 | 1571 | 1575 | 1566 | 1615 | 3.1 |
| France | 5690 | 5710 | 5876 | 5734 | 5817 | 6013 | 6051 | 5984 | 6234 | 4.2 |
| Germany | 5477 | 5445 | 5587 | 5568 | 5814 | 5850 | 5764 | 5550 | 6023 | 8.5 |
| Greece | 546 | 562 | 559 | 561 | 536 | 582 | 576 | 572 | 573 | 0.2 |
| Ireland | 701 | 690 | 726 | 782 [b] | 831 | 832 | 829 | 802 | 944 | 17.7 |
| Italy | 3759 | 3883 | 3962 | 3938 | 3892 | 3998 | 4070 | 4120 | 4164 | 1.1 |
| Netherlands | 2083 | 2168 | 2312 | 2379 | 2505 | 2644 | 2728 | 2694 | 2818 | 4.6 |
| Portugal | 523 | 568 | 542 | 525 | 577 | 630 | 617 | 677 | 688 | 1.6 |
| Spain | 2740 | 3088 | 3142 | 3131 | 3110 | 3265 | 3557 | 3550 | 3728 | 5.0 |
| United Kingdom | 3194 | 3315 | 3416 | 3469 | 3428 | 3626 | 3538 | 3487 | 3540 | 1.5 |
| Other OECD - Europe | 3519 | 3617 | 3696 | 3796 | 3637 | 3542 | 3767 | 3782 [e] | 3645 [e] | -3.6 |
| Austria | 657 | 684 | 702 | 722 | 713 | 707 | 734 | 736 | 774 | 5.2 |
| Finland | 359 | 364 | 366 | 369 | 371 | 377 | 356 | 338 | 365 | 8.0 |
| Norway | 211 | 212 | 211 | 218 | 221 | 233 | 232 | 228 | 235 | 3.1 |
| Sweden | 579 | 584 | 578 | 593 | 550 | 514 | 515 | 540 | 540 | 0.0 |
| Switzerland | 496 | 497 | 499 | 512 | 514 | 509 | 499 | 500 | 496 | -0.8 |
| Turkey | 1217 | 1276 | 1340 | 1382 | 1268 | 1202 | 1431 | 1440 [e] | 1235 [e] | -14.2 |
| Yugoslavia | 1523 | 1541 | 1688 | 1587 | 1559 | 1653 | 1655 | 1555 | 1574 | 1.2 |

## TOTAL BEEF AND VEAL / TOTAL VIANDE BOVINE

| | 1980/82 average | 1983 | 1984 | 1985 | 1986 | 1987 | 1988 | 1989 | 1990 | 1989/90 % change |
|---|---|---|---|---|---|---|---|---|---|---|
| OECD - Total | 22341 | 22827 | 23373 | 23580 [b] | 24065 | 23745 | 23359 | 22910 | 23268 [e] | 1.6 |
| OECD - North America | 11261 | 11779 | 11919 | 12026 | 12321 | 11857 | 11853 | 11611 | 11388 | -1.9 |
| Canada | 1003 | 1033 | 990 | 1029 | 1035 | 979 | 973 | 978 | 924 | -5.5 |
| United States | 10258 | 10746 | 10929 | 10997 | 11286 | 10878 | 10880 | 10633 | 10464 | -1.6 |
| Japan | 464 | 505 | 539 | 556 | 563 | 568 | 569 | 539 | 554 | 2.8 |
| OECD - Oceania | 2031 | 1913 | 1686 | 1812 | 1929 | 2105 | 2107 | 2101 | 2181 [e] | 3.8 |
| Australia | 1527 | 1401 | 1253 | 1325 | 1463 | 1550 | 1535 | 1560 | 1702 [e] | 9.1 |
| New Zealand | 504 | 512 | 433 | 487 | 466 | 555 | 572 | 541 | 479 | -11.5 |
| OECD - Europe | 8585 | 8630 | 9229 | 9186 [b] | 9252 | 9215 | 8830 | 8659 | 9145 | 5.6 |
| EC-12 Total | 7472 | 7461 | 8003 | 7925 [b] | 8066 | 8140 | 7689 | 7470 | 7981 | 6.8 |
| Belgium / Luxembourg | 303 | 290 | 319 | 326 | 326 | 326 | 317 | 305 | 322 | 5.6 |
| Denmark | 237 | 239 | 247 | 236 | 243 | 235 | 217 | 204 | 202 | -1.0 |
| France | 1807 | 1812 | 1991 | 1893 | 1910 | 1960 | 1826 | 1673 | 1753 | 4.8 |
| Germany | 1528 | 1495 | 1614 | 1576 | 1695 | 1681 | 1608 | 1576 | 1793 | 13.8 |
| Greece | 98 | 85 | 85 | 83 | 82 | 86 | 82 | 83 | 82 | -1.2 |
| Ireland | 373 | 353 | 401 | 448 [b] | 504 | 477 | 458 | 432 | 514 | 19.0 |
| Italy | 1121 | 1149 | 1182 | 1205 | 1179 | 1175 | 1164 | 1150 | 1164 | 1.2 |
| Netherlands | 430 | 451 | 515 | 510 | 539 | 546 | 506 | 487 | 519 | 6.6 |
| Portugal | 111 | 113 | 103 | 103 | 106 | 105 | 115 | 124 | 117 | -5.6 |
| Spain | 420 | 423 | 399 | 401 | 435 | 444 | 444 | 459 | 514 | 12.0 |
| United Kingdom | 1044 | 1051 | 1147 | 1144 | 1047 | 1105 | 952 | 977 | 1001 | 2.5 |
| Other OECD - Europe | 1113 | 1169 | 1226 | 1261 | 1186 | 1075 | 1141 | 1189 | 1164 | -2.1 |
| Austria | 199 | 204 | 220 | 223 | 226 | 209 | 206 | 205 | 239 | 16.6 |
| Finland | 117 | 119 | 124 | 126 | 125 | 124 | 111 | 107 | 118 | 10.3 |
| Norway | 75 | 74 | 69 | 73 | 74 | 76 | 76 | 76 | 82 | 7.9 |
| Sweden | 159 | 161 | 155 | 158 | 147 | 135 | 127 | 138 | 147 | 6.5 |
| Switzerland | 162 | 153 | 167 | 171 | 170 | 173 | 160 | 157 | 165 | 5.1 |
| Turkey | 400 | 458 | 491 | 510 | 444 | 358 | 461 | 506 | 413 | -18.4 |
| Yugoslavia | 334 | 345 | 350 | 314 | 295 | 317 | 301 | 309 | 352 | 13.9 |

All totals exclude Yugoslavia / Tous les totaux excluent la Yougoslavie

# PRODUCTION DE VIANDE PROVENANT DES ABATTAGES
## VIANDE DE PORC / PIG MEAT

*Milliers de tonnes métriques - Poids en carcasse parée*  ·  *Thousand metric tons - Dressed carcass weight*

| | 1980/82 moyenne | 1983 | 1984 | 1985 | 1986 | 1987 | 1988 | 1989 | 1990 | 1989/90 % var. |
|---|---|---|---|---|---|---|---|---|---|---|
| OCDE - Total | 22245 | 22780 | 22826 | 23022 | 22966 | 23623 | 24812 | 24673 | 24772 | 0.4 |
| OCDE - Amérique du Nord | 8083 | 7924 | 7763 | 7804 | 7477 | 7650 | 8303 | 8357 | 8098 | -3.1 |
| Canada | 1019 | 1030 | 1044 | 1088 | 1098 | 1130 | 1190 | 1184 | 1133 | -4.3 |
| États-Unis | 7065 | 6894 | 6719 | 6716 | 6379 | 6520 | 7113 | 7173 | 6965 | -2.9 |
| Japon | 1437 | 1430 | 1433 | 1550 | 1558 | 1592 | 1577 | 1597 | 1536 | -3.8 |
| OCDE - Océanie | 267 | 287 | 346 | 316 | 299 | 333 | 349 | 355 | 362 | 2.0 |
| Australie | 231 | 247 | 303 | 268 | 251 | 288 | 303 | 310 | 319 | 2.9 |
| Nouvelle Zélande | 36 | 40 | 43 | 48 | 48 | 45 | 46 | 45 | 43 | -4.4 |
| OCDE - Europe | 12458 | 13139 | 13284 | 13352 | 13632 | 14048 | 14583 | 14364 | 14776 | 2.9 |
| CE-12 Total | 11256 | 11912 | 12074 | 12105 | 12418 | 12848 | 13342 | 13119 | 13542 | 3.2 |
| Belgique / Luxembourg | 676 | 707 | 734 | 725 | 747 | 787 | 814 | 830 | 787 | -5.2 |
| Danemark | 980 | 1043 | 1035 | 1083 | 1144 | 1149 | 1168 | 1163 | 1207 | 3.8 |
| France | 1692 | 1676 | 1684 | 1662 | 1677 | 1729 | 1852 | 1844 | 1871 | 1.5 |
| Allemagne | 3172 | 3211 | 3222 | 3243 | 3336 | 3365 | 3342 | 3161 | 3357 | 6.2 |
| Grèce | 148 | 149 | 146 | 147 | 153 | 164 | 160 | 151 | 147 | -2.6 |
| Irlande | 155 | 163 | 147 | 139 | 139 | 144 | 149 | 146 | 159 | 8.9 |
| Italie | 1100 | 1166 | 1218 | 1187 | 1172 | 1231 | 1268 | 1309 | 1332 | 1.8 |
| Pays-Bas | 1177 | 1248 | 1306 | 1368 | 1444 | 1528 | 1631 | 1607 | 1661 | 3.4 |
| Portugal | 171 | 200 | 208 | 197 | 223 | 259 | 228 | 264 | 279 | 5.7 |
| Espagne | 1041 | 1342 | 1429 | 1388 | 1394 | 1481 | 1714 | 1704 | 1789 | 5.0 |
| Royaume-Uni | 944 | 1007 | 945 | 966 | 989 | 1011 | 1016 | 940 | 953 | 1.4 |
| Autre pays européens de l'OCDE | 1202 | 1227 | 1210 | 1247 | 1214 | 1200 | 1241 | 1245 | 1234 | -0.9 |
| Autriche | 341 | 360 | 357 | 374 | 360 | 366 | 404 | 400 | 401 | 0.3 |
| Finlande | 177 | 177 | 170 | 172 | 174 | 176 | 169 | 174 | 187 | 7.5 |
| Norvège | 82 | 81 | 84 | 84 | 85 | 92 | 90 | 84 | 83 | -1.2 |
| Suède | 321 | 318 | 323 | 332 | 309 | 288 | 299 | 307 | 293 | -4.6 |
| Suisse | 281 | 291 | 276 | 285 | 286 | 278 | 279 | 280 | 270 | -3.6 |
| Turquie | - | - | - | - | - | - | - | - | - | .. |
| Yougoslavie | 770 | 772 | 876 | 833 | 795 | 871 | 853 | 789 | 781 | -1.0 |

## VIANDE DE VOLAILLE / POULTRY MEAT [1]

| | 1980/82 moyenne | 1983 | 1984 | 1985 | 1986 | 1987 | 1988 | 1989 | 1990 | 1989/90 % var. |
|---|---|---|---|---|---|---|---|---|---|---|
| OCDE - Total | 14508 | 14982 | 15401 | 16038 | 16652 | 17989 | 18581 | 19428 | 20437 | 5.2 |
| OCDE - Amérique du Nord | 7370 | 7679 | 7985 | 8473 | 8891 | 9783 | 10111 | 10791 | 11563 | 7.2 |
| Canada | 525 | 527 | 558 | 608 | 628 | 683 | 685 | 686 | 685 | -0.1 |
| États-Unis | 6845 | 7152 | 7427 | 7865 | 8263 | 9100 | 9426 | 10105 | 10878 | 7.6 |
| Japon | 1156 | 1257 | 1325 | 1354 | 1398 | 1437 | 1436 | 1417 | 1387 | -2.1 |
| OCDE - Océanie | 339 | 335 | 361 | 413 | 416 | 442 | 454 | 490 | 505 | 3.1 |
| Australie | 304 | 302 | 315 | 365 | 370 | 394 | 402 | 432 | 445 | 3.0 |
| Nouvelle Zélande | 34 | 33 | 46 | 48 | 46 | 48 | 52 | 58 | 60 | 3.4 |
| OCDE - Europe | 5644 | 5711 | 5730 | 5798 | 5947 | 6327 | 6580 | 6730 | 6982 | 3.7 |
| CE-12 Total | 5200 | 5288 | 5261 | 5328 | 5442 | 5780 | 6000 | 6123 | 6340 | 3.5 |
| Belgique / Luxembourg | 138 | 143 | 144 | 159 | 168 | 172 | 181 | 178 | 191 | 7.3 |
| Danemark | 104 | 112 | 110 | 115 | 116 | 113 | 117 | 128 | 132 | 3.1 |
| France | 1233 | 1284 | 1252 | 1265 | 1325 | 1402 | 1444 | 1552 | 1657 | 6.8 |
| Allemagne | 392 | 358 | 361 | 366 | 384 | 402 | 421 | 431 | 456 | 5.8 |
| Grèce | 130 | 153 | 152 | 155 | 145 | 149 | 149 | 153 | 160 | 4.6 |
| Irlande | 50 | 55 | 53 | 56 | 60 | 68 | 77 | 71 | 84 | 18.3 |
| Italie | 1025 | 1050 | 1027 | 1005 | 1006 | 1050 | 1076 | 1097 | 1102 | 0.5 |
| Pays-Bas | 366 | 361 | 376 | 381 | 398 | 439 | 457 | 470 | 498 | 6.0 |
| Portugal | 159 | 164 | 140 | 137 | 157 | 171 | 175 | 183 | 184 | 0.5 |
| Espagne | 836 | 812 | 790 | 815 | 754 | 787 | 821 | 830 | 837 | 0.8 |
| Royaume-Uni | 767 | 796 | 856 | 874 | 929 | 1027 | 1082 | 1030 | 1039 | 0.9 |
| Autre pays européens de l'OCDE | 444 | 423 | 469 | 470 | 505 | 547 | 580 | 607 | 642 | 5.8 |
| Autriche | 72 | 76 | 80 | 79 | 83 | 86 | 82 | 89 | 90 | 1.1 |
| Finlande | 16 | 18 | 20 | 21 | 22 | 27 | 28 | 30 | 33 | 10.0 |
| Norvège | 11 | 11 | 11 | 12 | 13 | 15 | 18 | 20 | 20 | 0.0 |
| Suède | 46 | 47 | 46 | 46 | 45 | 43 | 41 | 45 | 51 | 13.3 |
| Suisse | 24 | 25 | 26 | 27 | 27 | 26 | 31 | 33 | 33 | 0.0 |
| Turquie | 275 | 246 | 286 | 285 | 315 | 350 | 380 | 390 | 415 | 6.4 |
| Yougoslavie | 282 | 287 | 313 | 297 | 328 | 323 | 351 | 310 | 295 | -4.8 |

1. Poids éviscéré ou «prêt à cuire» / Eviscerated or ready-to-cook weight        All totals exclude Yugoslavia / Tous les totaux excluent la Yougoslavie

# MEAT PRODUCTION FROM SLAUGHTERED ANIMALS
## MUTTON, LAMB AND GOAT MEAT / VIANDE DE MOUTON ET DE CHÈVRE

Thousand metric tons - Dressed carcass weight — Milliers de tonnes métriques - Poids en carcasse parée

| | 1980/82 average | 1983 | 1984 | 1985 | 1986 | 1987 | 1988 | 1989 | 1990 | 1989/90 % change |
|---|---|---|---|---|---|---|---|---|---|---|
| OECD - Total | 2588 | 2680 | 2674 | 2857 | 2654 | 2706 | 2779 | 2864 | 2843 | -0.7 |
| OECD - North America | 161 | 178 | 181 | 171 | 161 | 151 | 160 | 165 | 174 | 5.5 |
| Canada | 6 | 8 | 9 | 8 | 8 | 8 | 8 | 8 | 9 | 12.5 |
| United States | 154 | 170 | 172 | 163 | 153 | 143 | 152 | 157 | 165 | 5.1 |
| Japan | - | - | - | - | - | - | - | - | - | .. |
| OECD - Oceania | 1041 | 1019 | 1017 | 1159 | 1068 | 1080 | 1024 | 1093 | 1116 | 2.1 |
| Australia | 438 | 339 | 349 | 431 | 457 | 470 | 420 | 481 | 581 | 20.8 |
| New Zealand | 603 | 680 | 668 | 728 | 611 | 610 | 604 | 612 | 535 | -12.6 |
| OECD - Europe | 1387 | 1483 | 1476 | 1527 | 1425 | 1475 | 1595 | 1606 | 1553 | -3.3 |
| EC-12 Total | 903 | 975 | 979 | 1000 | 961 | 1017 | 1042 | 1103 | 1184 | 7.3 |
| Belgium / Luxembourg | 7 | 8 | 8 | 8 | 8 | 7 | 7 | 7 | 7 | 0.0 |
| Denmark | - | - | 1 | 1 | 1 | 1 | 1 | 1 | 1 | 0.0 |
| France | 186 | 183 | 179 | 178 | 169 | 170 | 164 | 162 | 194 | 19.8 |
| Germany | 29 | 29 | 28 | 27 | 26 | 29 | 29 | 31 | 37 | 19.4 |
| Greece | 120 | 121 | 122 | 122 | 106 | 125 | 128 | 129 | 129 | 0.0 |
| Ireland | 43 | 40 | 41 | 48 | 46 | 48 | 49 | 63 | 82 | 30.2 |
| Italy | 70 | 67 | 71 | 70 | 67 | 70 | 73 | 80 | 85 | 6.3 |
| Netherlands | 17 | 11 | 10 | 11 | 11 | 13 | 12 | 14 | 18 | 28.6 |
| Portugal | 24 | 27 | 26 | 25 | 25 | 27 | 28 | 27 | 28 | 3.7 |
| Spain | 140 | 202 | 207 | 210 | 211 | 224 | 230 | 222 | 233 | 5.0 |
| United Kingdom | 268 | 287 | 286 | 300 | 291 | 303 | 321 | 367 | 370 | 0.8 |
| Other OECD - Europe | 483 | 508 | 497 | 527 | 464 | 458 | 553 | 503 | 369 | -26.6 |
| Austria | 3 | 4 | 4 | 4 | 4 | 5 | 5 | 5 | 6 | 20.0 |
| Finland | 1 | 1 | 1 | 1 | 1 | 1 | 1 | 1 | 1 | 0.0 |
| Norway | 21 | 24 | 25 | 25 | 26 | 26 | 25 | 24 | 25 | 4.2 |
| Sweden | 5 | 5 | 5 | 5 | 5 | 5 | 5 | 5 | 5 | 0.0 |
| Switzerland | 4 | 4 | 4 | 5 | 5 | 5 | 5 | 5 | 5 | 0.0 |
| Turkey | 449 | 470 | 458 | 487 | 423 | 416 | 512 | 463 | 327 | -29.4 |
| Yugoslavia | 58 | 60 | 59 | 61 | 63 | 65 | 70 | 69 | 67 | -2.9 |

## HORSE MEAT / VIANDE D'ÉQUIDÉS [1]

| | 1980/82 average | 1983 | 1984 | 1985 | 1986 | 1987 | 1988 | 1989 | 1990 | 1989/90 % change |
|---|---|---|---|---|---|---|---|---|---|---|
| OECD - Total | 128 | 119 | 125 | 129 | 109 | 110 | 102 | 98 | 98 | 0.0 |
| OECD - North America | - | - | - | - | - | - | - | - | - | .. |
| Canada | - | - | - | - | - | - | - | - | - | .. |
| United States | - | - | - | - | - | - | - | - | - | .. |
| Japan | 4 | 5 | 6 | 6 | 5 | 5 | 4 | 5 | 5 | 0.0 |
| OECD - Oceania | - | - | - | - | - | - | - | - | - | .. |
| Australia | - | - | - | - | - | - | - | - | - | .. |
| New Zealand | - | - | - | - | - | - | - | - | - | .. |
| OECD - Europe | 124 | 114 | 119 | 123 | 104 | 105 | 98 | 93 | 93 | 0.0 |
| EC-12 Total | 118 | 108 | 113 | 117 | 99 | 99 | 91 | 87 | 87 | 0.0 |
| Belgium / Luxembourg | 6 | 5 | 6 | 6 | 4 | 4 | 4 | 3 | 3 | 0.0 |
| Denmark | 2 | 1 | 1 | 1 | 1 | 1 | 1 | 1 | 1 | 0.0 |
| France | 32 | 28 | 29 | 28 | 20 | 20 | 17 | 14 | 13 | -7.1 |
| Germany | 6 | 7 | 7 | 7 | 5 | 5 | 4 | 4 | 4 | 0.0 |
| Greece | 1 | - | - | - | - | 1 | 1 | - | - | .. |
| Ireland | 3 | 2 | 2 | 2 | 1 | 1 | - | 1 | - | -100.0 |
| Italy | 48 | 48 | 51 | 55 | 54 | 54 | 53 | 54 | 57 | 5.6 |
| Netherlands | 3 | 2 | 2 | 3 | 2 | 2 | 2 | 1 | - | -100.0 |
| Portugal | 1 | 1 | 2 | 1 | 1 | 1 | 1 | 1 | 1 | 0.0 |
| Spain | 11 | 8 | 7 | 8 | 7 | 7 | 6 | 6 | 7 | 16.7 |
| United Kingdom | 6 | 6 | 6 | 6 | 4 | 3 | 2 | 2 | 1 | -50.0 |
| Other OECD - Europe | 6 | 6 | 6 | 6 | 5 | 6 | 7 | 6 | 6 | 0.0 |
| Austria | - | - | - | - | - | - | 1 | 1 | 1 | 0.0 |
| Finland | 1 | 1 | 1 | 1 | 1 | 1 | 1 | 1 | 1 | 0.0 |
| Norway | 1 | 1 | 1 | 1 | 1 | 1 | 1 | 1 | 1 | 0.0 |
| Sweden | 3 | 3 | 2 | 3 | 2 | 2 | 2 | 2 | 2 | 0.0 |
| Switzerland | 1 | 1 | 2 | 1 | 1 | 2 | 2 | 1 | 1 | 0.0 |
| Turkey | - | - | - | - | - | - | - | - | - | .. |
| Yugoslavia | 1 | - | - | - | - | - | - | - | - | .. |

1. Including mules and asses / Y compris les mulets et les anes

All totals exclude Yugoslavia / Tous les totaux excluent la Yougoslavie

# PRODUCTION DE VIANDE PROVENANT DES ABATTAGES
## AUTRES VIANDES / OTHER MEAT

*Milliers de tonnes métriques - Poids en carcasse parée*      *Thousand metric tons - Dressed carcass weight*

| | 1980/82 moyenne | 1983 | 1984 | 1985 | 1986 | 1987 | 1988 | 1989 | 1990 | 1989/90 % var. |
|---|---|---|---|---|---|---|---|---|---|---|
| OCDE - Total | 1047 | 1004 | 1012 | 1019 | 1003 | 1012 | 1037 | 1033 | 1023 | -1.0 |
| OCDE - Amérique du Nord | 230 | 235 | 240 | 243 | 244 | 250 | 250 | 250 | 250 | 0.0 |
| Canada | - | - | - | - | - | - | - | - | - | .. |
| États-Unis | 230 | 235 | 240 | 243 | 244 | 250 | 250 | 250 | 250 | 0.0 |
| Japon | 19 | 21 | 16 | 15 | 14 | 5 | 2 | 1 | 2 | 100.0 |
| OCDE - Océanie | 46 | 47 | 47 | 42 | 43 | 38 | 25 | 26 | 16 | -38.5 |
| Australie | 44 | 45 | 45 | 40 | 41 | 36 | 23 | 24 | 14 | -41.7 |
| Nouvelle Zélande | 2 | 2 | 2 | 2 | 2 | 2 | 2 | 2 | 2 | 0.0 |
| OCDE - Europe | 752 | 701 | 709 | 719 | 702 | 719 | 760 | 756 | 755 | -0.1 |
| CE-12 Total | 700 | 645 | 654 | 662 | 654 | 669 | 710 | 703 | 703 | 0.0 |
| Belgique / Luxembourg | 13 | 16 | 16 | 18 | 19 | 21 | 22 | 24 | 27 | 12.5 |
| Danemark | 3 | 3 | 3 | 3 | 3 | 3 | 3 | 3 | 3 | 0.0 |
| France | 285 | 270 | 270 | 272 | 271 | 275 | 293 | 303 | 303 | 0.0 |
| Allemagne | 42 | 39 | 38 | 38 | 37 | 38 | 38 | 38 | 38 | 0.0 |
| Grèce | 6 | 5 | 5 | 5 | 4 | 5 | 5 | 5 | 5 | 0.0 |
| Irlande | - | - | - | - | - | - | 3 | 1 | 2 | 100.0 |
| Italie | 197 | 197 | 199 | 202 | 203 | 206 | 220 | 213 | 203 | -4.7 |
| Pays-Bas | - | - | - | - | - | - | 3 | - | 2 | .. |
| Portugal | 8 | 14 | 16 | 16 | 16 | 16 | 17 | 22 | 23 | 4.5 |
| Espagne | 139 | 94 | 99 | 100 | 94 | 97 | 98 | 85 | 87 | 2.4 |
| Royaume-Uni | 8 | 7 | 8 | 8 | 7 | 8 | 8 | 9 | 10 | 11.1 |
| Autre pays européens de l'OCDE | 51 | 56 | 55 | 57 | 48 | 50 | 50 | 53 | 52 | -1.9 |
| Autriche | 9 | 7 | 7 | 7 | 5 | 6 | 6 | 7 | 7 | 0.0 |
| Finlande | 10 | 11 | 13 | 11 | 11 | 11 | 11 | 12 | 11 | -8.3 |
| Norvège | 7 | 8 | 8 | 10 | 9 | 9 | 9 | 9 | 10 | 11.1 |
| Suède | 21 | 26 | 23 | 25 | 19 | 20 | 21 | 22 | 21 | -4.5 |
| Suisse | 4 | 4 | 4 | 4 | 4 | 4 | 3 | 3 | 3 | 0.0 |
| Turquie | - | - | - | - | - | - | - | - | - | .. |
| Yougoslavie | 6 | 6 | 8 | 8 | 8 | 8 | 8 | 7 | 7 | 0.0 |

## ABATS COMESTIBLES / EDIBLES OFFALS [1]

| | 1980/82 moyenne | 1983 | 1984 | 1985 | 1986 | 1987 | 1988 | 1989 | 1990 | 1989/90 % var. |
|---|---|---|---|---|---|---|---|---|---|---|
| OCDE - Total | 3560 | 3659 | 3724 | 3729 | 3738 | 3792 | 3803 | 3741 [e] | 3783 [e] | 1.1 |
| OCDE - Amérique du Nord | 1242 | 1266 | 1267 | 1274 | 1268 | 1246 | 1290 | 1277 | 1239 [e] | -3.0 |
| Canada | 67 | 68 | 67 | 68 | 68 | 66 | 66 | 67 | 63 | -6.0 |
| États-Unis | 1174 | 1198 | 1200 | 1206 | 1200 | 1180 | 1224 | 1210 | 1176 [e] | -2.8 |
| Japon | 241 | 243 | 247 | 266 | 267 | 272 | 270 | 270 | 263 | -2.6 |
| OCDE - Océanie | 182 | 167 | 162 | 176 | 176 | 195 | 193 | 192 | 198 | 3.1 |
| Australie | 123 | 102 | 103 | 111 | 117 | 131 | 128 | 128 | 143 | 11.7 |
| Nouvelle Zélande | 59 | 65 | 59 | 65 | 59 | 64 | 65 | 64 | 55 | -14.1 |
| OCDE - Europe | 1895 | 1983 | 2048 | 2013 | 2027 | 2079 | 2050 | 2002 [e] | 2083 [e] | 4.0 |
| CE-12 Total | 1676 | 1755 | 1815 | 1785 | 1812 | 1873 | 1855 | 1823 | 1905 | 4.5 |
| Belgique / Luxembourg | 88 | 88 | 93 | 93 | 94 | 98 | 79 | 79 | 78 | -1.3 |
| Danemark | 57 | 60 | 60 | 61 | 68 | 69 | 68 | 66 | 69 | 4.5 |
| France | 456 | 457 | 471 | 436 | 445 | 457 | 455 | 436 | 443 | 1.6 |
| Allemagne | 306 | 306 | 317 | 311 | 331 | 330 | 322 | 309 | 338 | 9.4 |
| Grèce | 44 | 49 | 49 | 49 | 46 | 52 | 51 | 51 | 50 | -2.0 |
| Irlande | 77 | 77 | 82 | 89 | 81 | 94 | 93 | 88 | 103 | 17.0 |
| Italie | 198 | 206 | 214 | 214 | 211 | 212 | 216 | 217 | 221 | 1.8 |
| Pays-Bas | 90 | 95 | 103 | 106 | 111 | 116 | 117 | 115 | 120 | 4.3 |
| Portugal | 49 | 49 | 47 | 46 | 49 | 51 | 53 | 56 | 56 | 0.0 |
| Espagne | 153 | 207 | 211 | 209 | 215 | 225 | 244 | 244 | 261 | 7.0 |
| Royaume-Uni | 156 | 161 | 168 | 171 | 161 | 169 | 157 | 162 | 166 | 2.5 |
| Autre pays européens de l'OCDE | 219 | 228 | 233 | 228 | 215 | 206 | 195 | 179 [e] | 178 [e] | -0.6 |
| Autriche | 33 | 33 | 34 | 35 | 35 | 35 | 30 | 29 | 30 | 3.4 |
| Finlande | 37 | 37 | 37 | 37 | 37 | 37 | 35 | 13 | 14 | 7.7 |
| Norvège | 13 | 13 | 13 | 13 | 13 | 14 | 13 | 14 | 14 | 0.0 |
| Suède | 24 | 24 | 24 | 24 | 23 | 21 | 20 | 21 | 21 | 0.0 |
| Suisse | 20 | 19 | 20 | 19 | 21 | 21 | 19 | 21 | 19 | -9.5 |
| Turquie | 93 | 102 | 105 | 100 | 86 | 78 | 78 | 81 [e] | 80 [e] | -1.2 |
| Yougoslavie | 73 | 71 | 82 | 74 | 70 | 69 | 72 | 71 | 72 | 1.4 |

1. Poids de produit / Product weight      All totals exclude Yugoslavia / Tous les totaux excluent la Yougoslavie

# FOREIGN TRADE
## TOTAL MEAT / TOTAL VIANDE

## IMPORTS / IMPORTATIONS

Thousand metric tons - Dressed carcass weight                                         Milliers de tonnes métriques - Poids en carcasse parée

| | 1980/82 average | 1983 | 1984 | 1985 | 1986 | 1987 | 1988 | 1989 | 1990 | 1989/90 % change |
|---|---|---|---|---|---|---|---|---|---|---|
| OECD - Total | 8089 | 8541 | 8575 | 9425 | 9796 | 10378 [e] | 10686 [e] | 10938 [e] | 11800 [e] | 7.9 |
| OECD - North America | 1446 | 1626 | 1748 | 1951 | 2004 | 2114 | 2209 | 2040 | 2265 [e] | 11.0 |
| Canada | 161 | 195 | 207 | 209 | 206 | 254 | 253 | 244 | 289 [e] | 18.4 |
| United States | 1285 | 1431 | 1541 | 1742 | 1798 | 1860 | 1956 | 1796 | 1976 [e] | 10.0 |
| Japan | 799 | 893 | 886 | 930 | 1060 | 1255 [e] | 1443 [e] | 1639 [e] | 1629 [e] | -0.6 |
| OECD - Oceania | 3 | 4 | 8 | 4 | 4 | 5 [e] | 5 [e] | 5 [e] | 5 [e] | 0.0 |
| Australia | 3 | 3 | 7 | 4 | 4 | 5 [e] | 5 [e] | 5 [e] | 5 [e] | 0.0 |
| New Zealand | 1 | 1 | 1 | - | - | - | - | - | - | .. |
| OECD - Europe | 5840 | 6018 | 5933 | 6540 | 6728 | 7004 | 7029 | 7254 | 7901 | 8.9 |
| EC-12 Total | 5711 | 5912 | 5818 | 6400 | 6587 | 6836 | 6847 | 7088 | 7740 | 9.2 |
| Belgium / Luxembourg | 338 | 364 | 369 | 368 | 401 | 409 | 380 | 391 | 448 | 14.6 |
| Denmark | 4 | 7 | 9 | 19 | 27 | 36 | 43 | 55 | 68 | 23.6 |
| France | 1052 | 1118 | 1102 | 1173 | 1222 | 1284 | 1314 | 1319 | 1395 | 5.8 |
| Germany | 1303 | 1309 | 1327 | 1408 | 1340 | 1432 | 1547 | 1560 | 2070 | 32.7 |
| Greece | 135 | 226 | 218 | 235 | 249 | 308 | 209 | 297 | 269 | -9.4 |
| Ireland | 72 | 64 | 58 | 54 | 85 | 88 | 71 | 76 | 55 | -27.6 |
| Italy | 1208 | 1266 | 1204 | 1493 | 1533 | 1538 | 1502 | 1557 | 1538 | -1.2 |
| Netherlands | 262 | 225 | 219 | 237 | 257 | 262 | 316 | 322 | 372 | 15.5 |
| Portugal | 14 | 19 | 15 | 46 | 45 | 53 | 67 | 73 | 97 | 32.9 |
| Spain | 45 | 81 | 102 | 128 | 171 | 160 | 151 | 215 | 212 | -1.4 |
| United Kingdom | 1277 | 1233 | 1195 | 1239 | 1257 | 1266 | 1247 | 1223 | 1216 | -0.6 |
| Other OECD - Europe | 130 | 106 | 115 | 140 | 141 | 168 | 182 | 166 | 161 | -3.0 |
| Austria | 41 | 27 | 29 | 20 | 24 | 26 | 31 | 37 | 32 | -13.5 |
| Finland | 3 | - | - | - | - | - | 5 | 2 | 1 | -50.0 |
| Norway | 14 | 5 | 8 | 9 | 11 | 7 | 7 | 4 | 4 | 0.0 |
| Sweden | 15 | 16 | 14 | 16 | 19 | 36 | 42 | 36 | 34 | -5.6 |
| Switzerland | 57 | 58 | 64 | 58 | 63 | 76 | 87 | 80 | 80 | 0.0 |
| Turkey | - | - | - | 37 | 24 | 23 | 10 | 7 | 10 | 42.9 |
| Yugoslavia | 50 | 72 | 32 | 35 | 98 | 80 | 100 | 174 | 176 | 1.1 |

## EXPORTS / EXPORTATIONS

| | 1980/82 average | 1983 | 1984 | 1985 | 1986 | 1987 | 1988 | 1989 | 1990 | 1989/90 % change |
|---|---|---|---|---|---|---|---|---|---|---|
| OECD - Total | 9278 | 9463 [b] | 9588 | 10051 [b] | 10979 | 11351 | 11708 | 12211 | 12846 [e] | 5.2 |
| OECD - North America | 1285 | 1108 [b] | 1262 | 1312 | 1366 | 1519 | 1820 | 1970 | 2211 [e] | 12.2 |
| Canada | 346 | 402 | 567 | 598 | 523 | 550 | 680 | 683 | 791 [e] | 15.8 |
| United States | 940 | 706 [b] | 695 | 714 | 843 | 969 | 1140 | 1287 | 1420 [e] | 10.3 |
| Japan | 3 | 2 | 2 | 3 | 3 | 4 | 5 | 6 | 8 | 33.3 |
| OECD - Oceania | 2136 | 2108 | 1787 | 2000 | 2128 | 2331 | 2224 | 2192 | 2259 | 3.1 |
| Australia | 1246 | 1110 | 913 | 1058 | 1229 | 1315 | 1297 | 1233 | 1469 | 19.1 |
| New Zealand | 889 | 998 | 874 | 942 | 899 | 1016 | 927 | 959 | 790 | -17.6 |
| OECD - Europe | 5854 | 6245 | 6537 | 6736 [b] | 7482 | 7497 | 7659 | 8043 | 8368 | 4.0 |
| EC-12 Total | 5615 | 5949 | 6242 | 6436 [b] | 7238 | 7271 | 7398 | 7792 | 8100 | 4.0 |
| Belgium / Luxembourg | 534 | 554 | 590 | 557 | 659 | 723 | 761 | 810 | 794 | -2.0 |
| Denmark | 982 | 1042 | 1042 | 1064 | 1087 | 1066 | 1102 | 1094 | 1111 | 1.6 |
| France | 937 | 1003 | 1027 | 1095 | 1287 | 1285 | 1359 | 1482 | 1400 | -5.5 |
| Germany | 624 | 648 | 743 | 731 | 928 | 801 | 815 | 981 | 1353 | 37.9 |
| Greece | 4 | 2 | 2 | 1 | 2 | 2 | 6 | 6 | 6 | 0.0 |
| Ireland | 535 | 510 | 502 | 546 [b] | 652 | 651 | 591 | 672 | 631 | -6.1 |
| Italy | 129 | 129 | 177 | 218 | 213 | 199 | 188 | 166 | 173 | 4.2 |
| Netherlands | 1518 | 1615 | 1711 | 1803 | 1937 | 2014 | 2071 | 2045 | 2127 | 4.0 |
| Portugal | - | 9 | 9 | 10 | 10 | 10 | 5 | 9 | 10 | 11.1 |
| Spain | 25 | 29 | 33 | 19 | 26 | 46 | 71 | 65 | 73 | 12.3 |
| United Kingdom | 329 | 408 | 406 | 392 | 437 | 474 | 429 | 462 | 422 | -8.7 |
| Other OECD - Europe | 239 | 296 | 295 | 300 | 244 | 226 | 261 | 251 | 268 | 6.8 |
| Austria | 44 | 42 | 57 | 88 | 87 | 80 | 75 | 58 | 79 | 36.2 |
| Finland | 43 | 43 | 39 | 40 | 31 | 39 | 20 | 19 | 34 | 78.9 |
| Norway | 9 | 11 | 9 | 7 | 2 | 6 | 10 | 9 | 19 | 111.1 |
| Sweden | 69 | 81 | 106 | 114 | 79 | 58 | 52 | 64 | 62 | -3.1 |
| Switzerland | 3 | 5 | 2 | 4 | 4 | 14 | 2 | 1 | 2 | 100.0 |
| Turkey | 71 | 114 | 82 | 47 | 41 | 29 | 102 | 100 | 72 | -28.0 |
| Yugoslavia | 126 | 176 | 183 | 185 | 115 | 162 | 160 | 130 [e] | 69 [e] | -46.9 |

All totals exclude Yugoslavia / Tous les totaux excluent la Yougoslavie

# COMMERCE EXTÉRIEUR
## TOTAL VIANDE BOVINE / TOTAL BEEF AND VEAL

### IMPORTATIONS / IMPORTS
*Milliers de tonnes métriques - Poids en carcasse parée*          *Thousand metric tons - Dressed carcass weight*

| | 1980/82 moyenne | 1983 | 1984 | 1985 | 1986 | 1987 | 1988 | 1989 | 1990 | 1989/90 % var |
|---|---|---|---|---|---|---|---|---|---|---|
| **OCDE - Total** | 3226 | 3399 | 3309 | 3734 | 3938 | 4089 [e] | 4188 [e] | 4296 [e] | 4703 [e] | 9.5 |
| **OCDE - Amérique du Nord** | 1083 | 1166 | 1102 | 1226 | 1339 | 1397 | 1489 | 1411 | 1649 [e] | 16.9 |
| Canada | 99 | 114 | 125 | 130 | 130 | 157 | 164 | 162 | 203 | 25.3 |
| États-Unis | 984 | 1052 | 977 | 1096 | 1209 | 1240 | 1325 | 1249 | 1446 [e] | 15.8 |
| **Japon** | 182 | 208 | 213 | 225 | 268 | 319 | 408 | 520 | 549 | 5.6 |
| **OCDE - Océanie** | 2 | 2 | 4 | 2 | 3 | 3 [e] | 3 [e] | 3 [e] | 3 [e] | 0.0 |
| Australie | 2 | 2 | 4 | 2 | 3 | 3 [e] | 3 [e] | 3 [e] | 3 [e] | 0.0 |
| Nouvelle Zélande | - | - | - | - | - | - | - | - | - | .. |
| **OCDE - Europe** | 1958 | 2023 | 1990 | 2281 | 2328 | 2370 | 2288 | 2362 | 2502 | 5.9 |
| **CE-12 Total** | 1922 | 1995 | 1966 | 2225 | 2281 | 2314 | 2231 | 2318 | 2462 | 6.2 |
| Belgique / Luxembourg | 58 | 53 | 47 | 43 | 43 | 46 | 40 | 47 | 50 | 6.4 |
| Danemark | 2 | 4 | 6 | 12 | 18 | 24 | 26 | 30 | 41 | 36.7 |
| France | 272 | 303 | 302 | 343 | 354 | 330 | 342 | 385 | 433 | 12.5 |
| Allemagne | 308 | 304 | 335 | 349 | 336 | 353 | 359 | 363 | 545 | 50.1 |
| Grèce | 92 | 136 | 133 | 140 | 147 | 189 | 122 | 174 | 164 | -5.7 |
| Irlande | 29 | 18 | 17 | 12 | 40 | 37 | 21 | 26 | 15 | -42.3 |
| Italie | 646 | 683 | 634 | 776 | 746 | 740 | 697 | 727 | 670 | -7.8 |
| Pays-Bas | 109 | 83 | 74 | 92 | 114 | 118 | 126 | 126 | 141 | 11.9 |
| Portugal | 10 | 6 | 7 | 18 | 21 | 29 | 29 | 28 | 51 | 82.1 |
| Espagne | 19 | 32 | 40 | 56 | 20 | 16 | 32 | 41 | 37 | -9.8 |
| Royaume-Uni | 376 | 373 | 371 | 384 | 442 | 432 | 437 | 371 | 315 | -15.1 |
| **Autre pays européens de l'OCDE** | 36 | 28 | 24 | 56 | 47 | 56 | 57 | 44 | 40 | -9.1 |
| Autriche | 11 | 6 | 4 | 2 | 2 | 3 | 4 | 6 | 3 | -50.0 |
| Finlande | 1 | - | - | - | - | - | 3 | 2 | 1 | -50.0 |
| Norvège | 6 | 1 | 2 | 2 | 4 | 2 | 2 | 2 | 2 | 0.0 |
| Suède | 7 | 7 | 5 | 7 | 8 | 16 | 20 | 14 | 12 | -14.3 |
| Suisse | 12 | 14 | 13 | 8 | 9 | 12 | 18 | 13 | 12 | -7.7 |
| Turquie | - | - | - | 37 | 24 | 23 | 10 | 7 | 10 | 42.9 |
| Yougoslavie | 39 | 44 | 24 | 18 | 32 | 45 | 53 | 81 | 74 | -8.6 |

### EXPORTATIONS / EXPORTS

| | 1980/82 moyenne | 1983 | 1984 | 1985 | 1986 | 1987 | 1988 | 1989 | 1990 | 1989/90 % var |
|---|---|---|---|---|---|---|---|---|---|---|
| **OCDE - Total** | 3637 | 3632 | 3752 | 4053 [b] | 4664 | 4627 | 4601 | 4966 | 5107 [e] | 2.8 |
| **OCDE - Amérique du Nord** | 284 | 305 | 368 | 403 | 440 | 482 | 642 | 765 | 857 [e] | 12.0 |
| Canada | 149 | 161 | 191 | 212 | 168 | 163 | 227 | 246 | 361 | 46.7 |
| États-Unis | 135 | 144 | 177 | 191 | 272 | 319 | 415 | 519 | 496 [e] | -4.4 |
| **Japon** | - | - | - | - | - | - | - | - | - | .. |
| **OCDE - Océanie** | 1175 | 1106 | 872 | 1026 | 1114 | 1321 | 1319 | 1305 | 1443 | 10.6 |
| Australie | 822 | 739 | 590 | 666 | 785 | 887 | 884 | 864 | 1066 | 23.4 |
| Nouvelle Zélande | 354 | 367 | 282 | 360 | 329 | 434 | 435 | 441 | 377 | -14.5 |
| **OCDE - Europe** | 2178 | 2221 | 2512 | 2624 [b] | 3110 | 2824 | 2640 | 2896 | 2807 | -3.1 |
| **CE-12 Total** | 2100 | 2113 | 2404 | 2485 [b] | 2980 | 2717 | 2563 | 2834 | 2705 | -4.6 |
| Belgique / Luxembourg | 85 | 84 | 112 | 113 | 131 | 134 | 156 | 160 | 173 | 8.1 |
| Danemark | 175 | 172 | 176 | 165 | 189 | 175 | 168 | 156 | 133 | -14.7 |
| France | 492 | 474 | 556 | 627 | 734 | 664 | 650 | 730 | 618 | -15.3 |
| Allemagne | 429 | 437 | 522 | 505 | 659 | 530 | 528 | 680 | 766 | 12.6 |
| Grèce | - | - | - | - | - | - | 2 | 1 | 1 | 0.0 |
| Irlande | 412 | 388 | 367 | 404 [b] | 500 | 490 | 431 | 488 | 425 | -12.9 |
| Italie | 67 | 66 | 112 | 144 | 149 | 123 | 116 | 96 | 85 | -11.5 |
| Pays-Bas | 260 | 267 | 315 | 323 | 387 | 351 | 328 | 320 | 323 | 0.9 |
| Portugal | - | 2 | 2 | 2 | 3 | 2 | - | 1 | 1 | 0.0 |
| Espagne | 6 | 9 | 14 | 1 | 1 | 13 | 24 | 31 | 38 | 22.6 |
| Royaume-Uni | 175 | 214 | 228 | 201 | 227 | 235 | 160 | 171 | 142 | -17.0 |
| **Autre pays européens de l'OCDE** | 79 | 108 | 108 | 139 | 130 | 107 | 77 | 62 | 102 | 64.5 |
| Autriche | 34 | 36 | 50 | 75 | 81 | 71 | 61 | 49 | 72 | 46.9 |
| Finlande | 8 | 18 | 19 | 22 | 21 | 22 | 11 | 5 | 10 | 100.0 |
| Norvège | 3 | 8 | 3 | 1 | 1 | 1 | - | 1 | 8 | 700.0 |
| Suède | 20 | 23 | 23 | 33 | 23 | 7 | 5 | 7 | 12 | 71.4 |
| Suisse | 2 | 1 | - | 2 | 3 | 5 | - | - | - | .. |
| Turquie | 12 | 22 | 13 | 6 | 1 | 1 | - | - | - | .. |
| Yougoslavie | 63 | 60 | 65 | 78 | 52 | 71 | 84 | 76 [e] | 27 [e] | -64.5 |

All totals exclude Yugoslavia / Tous les totaux excluent la Yougoslavie

# FOREIGN TRADE
## PIG MEAT / VIANDE DE PORC

### IMPORTS / IMPORTATIONS

Thousand metric tons - Dressed carcass weight · Milliers de tonnes métriques - Poids en carcasse parée

| | 1980/82 average | 1983 | 1984 | 1985 | 1986 | 1987 | 1988 | 1989 | 1990 | 1989/90 % change |
|---|---|---|---|---|---|---|---|---|---|---|
| OECD - Total | 2673 | 2931 | 3067 | 3333 | 3456 | 3733 | 3794 | 3831 | 4023 | 5.0 |
| OECD - North America | 294 | 376 | 552 | 627 | 565 | 598 | 595 | 501 | 489 | -2.4 |
| Canada | 18 | 20 | 18 | 21 | 18 | 22 | 14 | 13 | 13 | 0.0 |
| United States | 277 | 356 | 534 | 606 | 547 | 576 | 581 | 488 | 476 | -2.5 |
| Japan | 195 | 271 | 262 | 272 | 292 | 415 | 484 | 523 | 488 | -6.7 |
| OECD - Oceania | 1 | 1 | 2 | - | - | - | - | - | - | .. |
| Australia | - | - | 1 | - | - | - | - | - | - | .. |
| New Zealand | 1 | 1 | 1 | - | - | - | - | - | - | .. |
| OECD - Europe | 2183 | 2283 | 2251 | 2434 | 2599 | 2720 | 2715 | 2807 | 3046 | 8.5 |
| EC-12 Total | 2161 | 2271 | 2235 | 2423 | 2588 | 2697 | 2691 | 2784 | 3021 | 8.5 |
| Belgium / Luxembourg | 120 | 161 | 168 | 155 | 172 | 170 | 131 | 126 | 162 | 28.6 |
| Denmark | - | 1 | 1 | 2 | 3 | 4 | 9 | 15 | 14 | -6.7 |
| France | 421 | 437 | 435 | 461 | 493 | 537 | 537 | 518 | 508 | -1.9 |
| Germany | 570 | 598 | 597 | 652 | 618 | 678 | 746 | 727 | 948 | 30.4 |
| Greece | 28 | 60 | 56 | 64 | 68 | 82 | 56 | 83 | 67 | -19.3 |
| Ireland | 24 | 28 | 25 | 24 | 24 | 25 | 28 | 28 | 20 | -28.6 |
| Italy | 402 | 423 | 409 | 516 | 597 | 596 | 594 | 606 | 645 | 6.4 |
| Netherlands | 46 | 43 | 40 | 37 | 38 | 44 | 52 | 46 | 53 | 15.2 |
| Portugal | 3 | 7 | 2 | 21 | 15 | 10 | 26 | 34 | 24 | -29.4 |
| Spain | 7 | 17 | 21 | 19 | 101 | 70 | 40 | 85 | 77 | -9.4 |
| United Kingdom | 540 | 496 | 481 | 472 | 459 | 481 | 472 | 516 | 503 | -2.5 |
| Other OECD - Europe | 22 | 12 | 16 | 11 | 11 | 23 | 24 | 23 | 25 | 8.7 |
| Austria | 12 | 4 | 7 | 1 | 1 | 1 | 1 | 2 | 2 | 0.0 |
| Finland | - | - | - | - | - | - | 1 | - | - | .. |
| Norway | 4 | 2 | 2 | 4 | 2 | 2 | 2 | 2 | 1 | -50.0 |
| Sweden | 5 | 6 | 6 | 6 | 7 | 13 | 15 | 15 | 16 | 6.7 |
| Switzerland | 1 | - | 1 | - | 1 | 7 | 5 | 4 | 6 | 50.0 |
| Turkey | - | - | - | - | - | - | - | - | - | .. |
| Yugoslavia | 4 | 17 | 4 | 14 | 61 | 31 | 42 | 89 | 90 | 1.1 |

### EXPORTS / EXPORTATIONS

| | 1980/82 average | 1983 | 1984 | 1985 | 1986 | 1987 | 1988 | 1989 | 1990 | 1989/90 % change |
|---|---|---|---|---|---|---|---|---|---|---|
| OECD - Total | 2682 | 2856 [b] | 3021 | 3123 | 3242 | 3466 | 3688 | 3686 | 4032 | 9.4 |
| OECD - North America | 341 | 295 [b] | 400 | 397 | 350 | 390 | 482 | 489 | 491 | 0.4 |
| Canada | 154 | 193 | 325 | 338 | 310 | 339 | 385 | 362 | 363 | 0.3 |
| United States | 187 | 102 [b] | 75 | 59 | 40 | 51 | 97 | 127 | 128 | 0.8 |
| Japan | - | - | - | - | - | - | - | - | - | .. |
| OECD - Oceania | 5 | 5 | 6 | 6 | 3 | 7 | 8 | 6 | 6 | 0.0 |
| Australia | 3 | 3 | 4 | 4 | 3 | 7 | 8 | 6 | 6 | 0.0 |
| New Zealand | 2 | 2 | 2 | 2 | - | - | - | - | - | .. |
| OECD - Europe | 2336 | 2556 | 2615 | 2720 | 2889 | 3069 | 3198 | 3191 | 3535 | 10.8 |
| EC-12 Total | 2248 | 2472 | 2511 | 2612 | 2826 | 2996 | 3125 | 3113 | 3453 | 10.9 |
| Belgium / Luxembourg | 349 | 373 | 383 | 339 | 408 | 455 | 456 | 482 | 441 | -8.5 |
| Denmark | 727 | 782 | 780 | 811 | 814 | 805 | 845 | 843 | 873 | 3.6 |
| France | 64 | 67 | 66 | 82 | 119 | 152 | 209 | 201 | 223 | 10.9 |
| Germany | 95 | 130 | 140 | 139 | 173 | 173 | 180 | 178 | 446 | 150.6 |
| Greece | - | - | - | - | - | - | - | 1 | 1 | 0.0 |
| Ireland | 55 | 56 | 47 | 42 | 41 | 46 | 45 | 49 | 56 | 14.3 |
| Italy | 42 | 48 | 44 | 53 | 46 | 49 | 36 | 37 | 42 | 13.5 |
| Netherlands | 854 | 934 | 989 | 1070 | 1148 | 1249 | 1274 | 1239 | 1280 | 3.3 |
| Portugal | - | 4 | 4 | 4 | 4 | 4 | 5 | 6 | 5 | -16.7 |
| Spain | 1 | 5 | 3 | 4 | 4 | 3 | 4 | 6 | 16 | 166.7 |
| United Kingdom | 61 | 73 | 55 | 68 | 69 | 60 | 71 | 71 | 70 | -1.4 |
| Other OECD - Europe | 88 | 84 | 104 | 108 | 63 | 73 | 73 | 78 | 82 | 5.1 |
| Austria | 3 | 1 | 2 | 8 | 1 | 3 | 8 | 4 | 2 | -50.0 |
| Finland | 35 | 25 | 20 | 18 | 10 | 17 | 9 | 14 | 23 | 64.3 |
| Norway | 5 | 3 | 6 | 6 | 1 | 4 | 10 | 6 | 8 | 33.3 |
| Sweden | 44 | 53 | 75 | 75 | 51 | 46 | 45 | 53 | 47 | -11.3 |
| Switzerland | 1 | 2 | 1 | 1 | - | 3 | 1 | 1 | 2 | 100.0 |
| Turkey | - | - | - | - | - | - | - | - | - | .. |
| Yugoslavia | 27 | 51 | 53 | 62 | 28 | 36 | 42 | 25 | 24 | -4.0 |

All totals exclude Yugoslavia / Tous les totaux excluent la Yougoslavie

# COMMERCE EXTÉRIEUR
## VIANDE DE VOLAILLE / POULTRY MEAT [1]

### IMPORTATIONS / IMPORTS
Milliers de tonnes métriques - Poids en carcasse parée      Thousand metric tons - Dressed carcass weight

| | 1980/82 moyenne | 1983 | 1984 | 1985 | 1986 | 1987 | 1988 | 1989 | 1990 | 1989/90 % var |
|---|---|---|---|---|---|---|---|---|---|---|
| OCDE - Total | 593 | 646 | 694 | 743 | 860 | 964 | 1119 | 1203 | 1369 [e] | 13.8 |
| OCDE - Amérique du Nord | 27 | 36 | 45 | 34 | 28 | 45 | 47 | 42 | 45 [e] | 7.1 |
| Canada | 27 | 36 | 45 | 34 | 28 | 45 | 47 | 42 | 45 [e] | 7.1 |
| États-Unis | - | - | - | - | - | - | - | - | - | .. |
| Japon | 94 | 100 | 112 | 115 | 187 | 217 | 272 | 296 | 297 | 0.3 |
| OCDE - Océanie | - | - | - | - | - | - | - | - | - | .. |
| Australie | - | - | - | - | - | - | - | - | - | .. |
| Nouvelle Zélande | - | - | - | - | - | - | - | - | - | .. |
| OCDE - Europe | 472 | 510 | 537 | 594 | 645 | 702 | 800 | 865 | 1027 | 18.7 |
| CE-12 Total | 433 | 470 | 492 | 550 | 592 | 644 | 733 | 800 | 966 | 20.8 |
| Belgique / Luxembourg | 45 | 53 | 55 | 69 | 82 | 85 | 91 | 94 | 105 | 11.7 |
| Danemark | - | - | - | 3 | 4 | 4 | 4 | 5 | 7 | 40.0 |
| France | 21 | 33 | 30 | 33 | 31 | 48 | 53 | 65 | 71 | 9.2 |
| Allemagne | 277 | 254 | 256 | 261 | 265 | 283 | 315 | 335 | 397 | 18.5 |
| Grèce | 1 | 2 | 3 | 4 | 4 | 7 | 7 | 9 | 10 | 11.1 |
| Irlande | 9 | 11 | 9 | 11 | 12 | 13 | 12 | 11 | 12 | 9.1 |
| Italie | 18 | 22 | 31 | 41 | 35 | 33 | 46 | 51 | 48 | -5.9 |
| Pays-Bas | 23 | 24 | 27 | 30 | 44 | 47 | 67 | 76 | 100 | 31.6 |
| Portugal | - | - | - | - | - | - | - | - | 5 | .. |
| Espagne | 13 | 14 | 20 | 27 | 16 | 30 | 43 | 51 | 53 | 3.9 |
| Royaume-Uni | 25 | 57 | 61 | 71 | 99 | 94 | 95 | 103 | 158 | 53.4 |
| Autre pays européens de l'OCDE | 39 | 40 | 45 | 44 | 53 | 58 | 67 | 65 | 61 | -6.2 |
| Autriche | 11 | 11 | 11 | 11 | 15 | 16 | 20 | 21 | 20 | -4.8 |
| Finlande | - | - | - | - | - | - | - | - | - | .. |
| Norvège | - | - | 1 | 1 | 2 | 2 | 1 | - | - | .. |
| Suède | - | - | - | - | - | - | 1 | 1 | 1 | 0.0 |
| Suisse | 28 | 29 | 33 | 32 | 36 | 40 | 45 | 43 | 40 | -7.0 |
| Turquie | - | - | - | - | - | - | - | - | - | .. |
| Yougoslavie | 2 | 3 | 1 | 1 | 3 | 3 | 2 | 3 | 2 | -33.3 |

### EXPORTATIONS / EXPORTS

| | 1980/82 moyenne | 1983 | 1984 | 1985 | 1986 | 1987 | 1988 | 1989 | 1990 | 1989/90 % var |
|---|---|---|---|---|---|---|---|---|---|---|
| OCDE - Total | 1175 | 1074 [b] | 985 | 994 | 1133 | 1329 | 1427 | 1543 | 1811 [e] | 17.4 |
| OCDE - Amérique du Nord | 394 | 227 [b] | 211 | 216 | 278 | 369 | 388 | 405 | 560 [e] | 38.3 |
| Canada | 4 | 2 | 2 | 5 | 2 | 6 | 6 | 7 | 6 [e] | -14.3 |
| États-Unis | 390 | 225 [b] | 209 | 211 | 276 | 363 | 382 | 398 | 554 | 39.2 |
| Japon | 3 | 2 | 2 | 3 | 3 | 4 | 5 | 6 | 8 | 33.3 |
| OCDE - Océanie | 5 | 1 | 1 | 1 | 3 | 3 | 1 | 1 | 1 | 0.0 |
| Australie | 5 | 1 | 1 | 1 | 3 | 3 | 1 | 1 | 1 | 0.0 |
| Nouvelle Zélande | - | - | - | - | - | - | - | - | - | .. |
| OCDE - Europe | 773 | 844 | 771 | 774 | 849 | 953 | 1033 | 1131 | 1242 | 9.8 |
| CE-12 Total | 769 | 840 | 766 | 767 | 843 | 944 | 1029 | 1129 | 1240 | 9.8 |
| Belgique / Luxembourg | 27 | 29 | 33 | 42 | 50 | 60 | 73 | 86 | 101 | 17.4 |
| Danemark | 58 | 63 | 59 | 63 | 57 | 60 | 62 | 71 | 79 | 11.3 |
| France | 321 | 404 | 342 | 322 | 362 | 393 | 422 | 473 | 509 | 7.6 |
| Allemagne | 49 | 30 | 27 | 27 | 28 | 32 | 40 | 52 | 65 | 25.0 |
| Grèce | 2 | 1 | - | 1 | 1 | 2 | 2 | 2 | 2 | 0.0 |
| Irlande | 7 | 8 | 6 | 5 | 6 | 9 | 13 | 13 | 16 | 23.1 |
| Italie | 6 | 7 | 11 | 11 | 12 | 18 | 21 | 20 | 30 | 50.0 |
| Pays-Bas | 276 | 268 | 252 | 257 | 276 | 299 | 314 | 323 | 353 | 9.3 |
| Portugal | - | - | - | - | - | - | - | - | 2 | .. |
| Espagne | 3 | 4 | 4 | 2 | 6 | 11 | 9 | 9 | 7 | -22.2 |
| Royaume-Uni | 20 | 26 | 32 | 37 | 45 | 60 | 73 | 80 | 76 | -5.0 |
| Autre pays européens de l'OCDE | 4 | 4 | 5 | 7 | 6 | 9 | 4 | 2 | 2 | 0.0 |
| Autriche | 1 | 1 | 1 | 1 | 1 | 1 | 1 | 1 | 1 | 0.0 |
| Finlande | - | - | - | - | - | - | - | - | - | .. |
| Norvège | - | - | - | - | - | 1 | - | - | - | .. |
| Suède | 1 | 1 | 4 | 1 | 1 | 2 | - | - | - | .. |
| Suisse | - | 1 | - | - | - | - | 1 | - | - | .. |
| Turquie | 1 | 1 | - | 5 | 4 | 5 | 2 | 1 | 1 | 0.0 |
| Yougoslavie | 8 | 23 | 30 | 24 | 11 | 17 | 17 | 16 | 10 | -37.5 |

1. Poids éviscéré ou «prêt à cuire» / Eviscerated or ready-to-cook weight      All totals exclude Yugoslavia / Tous les totaux excluent la Yougoslavie

# FOREIGN TRADE
## MUTTON, LAMB AND GOAT MEAT / VIANDE DE MOUTON ET DE CHÈVRE

### IMPORTS / IMPORTATIONS

Thousand metric tons - Dressed carcass weight          Milliers de tonnes métriques - Poids en carcasse parée

| | 1980/82 average | 1983 | 1984 | 1985 | 1986 | 1987 | 1988 | 1989 | 1990 | 1989/90 % change |
|---|---|---|---|---|---|---|---|---|---|---|
| OECD - Total | 551 | 542 | 506 | 567 | 560 | 592 | 579 | 652 [e] | 708 [e] | 8.6 |
| OECD - North America | 24 | 23 | 20 | 30 | 36 | 36 | 38 | 42 | 39 | -7.1 |
| Canada | 12 | 15 | 11 | 13 | 17 | 16 | 15 | 13 | 12 | -7.7 |
| United States | 12 | 8 | 9 | 17 | 19 | 20 | 23 | 29 | 27 | -6.9 |
| Japan | 168 | 165 | 149 | 159 | 159 | 153 | 128 | 147 [e] | 143 [e] | -2.7 |
| OECD - Oceania | - | - | - | - | - | - | - | - | - | .. |
| Australia | - | - | - | - | - | - | - | - | - | .. |
| New Zealand | - | - | - | - | - | - | - | - | - | .. |
| OECD - Europe | 359 | 354 | 337 | 378 | 365 | 403 | 413 | 463 | 526 | 13.6 |
| EC-12 Total | 350 | 347 | 328 | 369 | 356 | 394 | 403 | 451 | 514 | 14.0 |
| Belgium / Luxembourg | 20 | 20 | 19 | 22 | 21 | 20 | 23 | 25 | 29 | 16.0 |
| Denmark | 2 | 2 | 2 | 2 | 2 | 3 | 3 | 3 | 4 | 33.3 |
| France | 52 | 65 | 71 | 76 | 94 | 109 | 121 | 138 | 153 | 10.9 |
| Germany | 37 | 36 | 30 | 37 | 35 | 33 | 34 | 43 | 51 | 18.6 |
| Greece | 9 | 20 | 17 | 17 | 18 | 15 | 16 | 20 | 18 | -10.0 |
| Ireland | 4 | 1 | 1 | 1 | - | 1 | 1 | 1 | 2 | 100.0 |
| Italy | 30 | 30 | 32 | 40 | 37 | 44 | 45 | 49 | 51 | 4.1 |
| Netherlands | 2 | 1 | 1 | 3 | 2 | 3 | 3 | 5 | 7 | 40.0 |
| Portugal | - | - | - | - | - | 4 | 4 | 6 | 11 | 83.3 |
| Spain | 1 | 1 | 1 | 1 | 9 | 13 | 20 | 22 | 31 | 40.9 |
| United Kingdom | 193 | 171 | 154 | 170 | 138 | 149 | 133 | 139 | 157 | 12.9 |
| Other OECD - Europe | 9 | 7 | 9 | 9 | 9 | 9 | 10 | 12 | 12 | 0.0 |
| Austria | 1 | 1 | 1 | 1 | 1 | 2 | 2 | 3 | 3 | 0.0 |
| Finland | - | - | - | - | - | - | - | - | - | .. |
| Norway | 2 | - | 1 | - | 1 | - | - | - | - | .. |
| Sweden | 1 | 1 | 1 | 1 | 1 | 2 | 2 | 2 | 2 | 0.0 |
| Switzerland | 5 | 5 | 6 | 7 | 6 | 5 | 6 | 7 | 7 | 0.0 |
| Turkey | - | - | - | - | - | - | - | - | - | .. |
| Yugoslavia | - | - | - | - | - | - | - | - | 3 | .. |

### EXPORTS / EXPORTATIONS

| | 1980/82 average | 1983 | 1984 | 1985 | 1986 | 1987 | 1988 | 1989 | 1990 | 1989/90 % change |
|---|---|---|---|---|---|---|---|---|---|---|
| OECD - Total | 989 | 1089 | 977 | 979 | 1044 | 1061 | 1069 | 1075 | 1010 | -6.0 |
| OECD - North America | 7 | 1 | 1 | 1 | 1 | 1 | 2 | 2 | 2 | 0.0 |
| Canada | - | - | - | - | - | - | 1 | 1 | 1 | 0.0 |
| United States | 7 | 1 | 1 | 1 | 1 | 1 | 1 | 1 | 1 | 0.0 |
| Japan | - | - | - | - | - | - | - | - | - | .. |
| OECD - Oceania | 834 | 882 | 795 | 820 | 874 | 871 | 771 | 761 | 697 | -8.4 |
| Australia | 349 | 304 | 256 | 293 | 349 | 346 | 333 | 294 | 326 | 10.9 |
| New Zealand | 485 | 578 | 539 | 527 | 525 | 525 | 438 | 467 | 371 | -20.6 |
| OECD - Europe | 149 | 206 | 181 | 158 | 169 | 189 | 296 | 312 | 311 | -0.3 |
| EC-12 Total | 94 | 116 | 114 | 123 | 134 | 167 | 197 | 212 | 239 | 12.7 |
| Belgium / Luxembourg | 5 | 7 | 7 | 9 | 7 | 6 | 9 | 10 | 12 | 20.0 |
| Denmark | - | - | - | - | - | - | - | - | - | .. |
| France | 5 | 7 | 7 | 7 | 8 | 10 | 10 | 13 | 17 | 30.8 |
| Germany | 7 | 5 | 4 | 7 | 7 | 6 | 6 | 6 | 13 | 116.7 |
| Greece | - | - | 1 | - | - | - | 1 | 1 | 1 | 0.0 |
| Ireland | 17 | 16 | 18 | 26 | 23 | 26 | 28 | 40 | 60 | 50.0 |
| Italy | - | - | - | - | - | 2 | 3 | 3 | 3 | 0.0 |
| Netherlands | 16 | 16 | 13 | 14 | 12 | 15 | 13 | 15 | 21 | 40.0 |
| Portugal | - | - | - | - | - | - | - | 1 | 1 | 0.0 |
| Spain | 1 | 1 | 1 | 1 | 6 | 11 | 28 | 12 | 6 | -50.0 |
| United Kingdom | 42 | 64 | 63 | 59 | 71 | 91 | 99 | 111 | 105 | -5.4 |
| Other OECD - Europe | 55 | 90 | 67 | 35 | 35 | 22 | 99 | 100 | 72 | -28.0 |
| Austria | - | - | - | - | - | - | - | - | - | .. |
| Finland | - | - | - | - | - | - | - | - | - | .. |
| Norway | - | - | - | - | - | - | - | 2 | 2 | 0.0 |
| Sweden | - | - | - | - | - | - | - | - | - | .. |
| Switzerland | - | - | - | - | - | - | - | - | - | .. |
| Turkey | 55 | 90 | 67 | 35 | 35 | 22 | 99 | 98 | 70 | -28.6 |
| Yugoslavia | 5 | 7 | 26 | 6 | 4 | 7 | 5 | 5 | 3 | -40.0 |

All totals exclude Yugoslavia / Tous les totaux excluent la Yugoslavie

# COMMERCE EXTÉRIEUR
## VIANDE D'ÉQUIDÉS / HORSE MEAT [1]

## IMPORTATIONS / IMPORTS
*Milliers de tonnes métriques - Poids en carcasse parée*                                          *Thousand metric tons - Dressed carcass weight*

|  | 1980/82 moyenne | 1983 | 1984 | 1985 | 1986 | 1987 | 1988 | 1989 | 1990 | 1989/90 % var |
|---|---|---|---|---|---|---|---|---|---|---|
| OCDE - Total | 267 | 237 | 232 | 234 | 217 | 231 | 237 | 246 | 249 e | 1.2 |
| OCDE - Amérique du Nord | - | - | - | - | - | - | - | - | - | .. |
| Canada | - | - | - | - | - | - | - | - | - | .. |
| États-Unis | - | - | - | - | - | - | - | - | - | .. |
| Japon | 78 | 65 | 62 | 60 | 53 | 50 | 55 | 56 | 54 e | -3.6 |
| OCDE - Océanie | - | - | - | - | - | - | - | - | - | .. |
| Australie | - | - | - | - | - | - | - | - | - | .. |
| Nouvelle Zélande | - | - | - | - | - | - | - | - | - | .. |
| OCDE - Europe | 189 | 172 | 170 | 174 | 164 | 181 | 182 | 190 | 195 | 2.6 |
| CE-12 Total | 185 | 168 | 166 | 170 | 159 | 175 | 176 | 184 | 188 | 2.2 |
| Belgique / Luxembourg | 36 | 34 | 32 | 34 | 35 | 40 | 38 | 39 | 42 | 7.7 |
| Danemark | - | - | - | - | - | - | - | - | - | .. |
| France | 69 | 61 | 59 | 53 | 46 | 50 | 52 | 54 | 52 | -3.7 |
| Allemagne | 2 | 2 | 3 | 2 | 2 | 3 | 3 | 4 | 4 | 0.0 |
| Grèce | - | - | - | - | - | - | - | - | - | .. |
| Irlande | - | - | - | - | - | - | - | - | - | .. |
| Italie | 43 | 42 | 42 | 53 | 48 | 54 | 55 | 57 | 61 | 7.0 |
| Pays-Bas | 32 | 27 | 27 | 25 | 25 | 27 | 26 | 27 | 26 | -3.7 |
| Portugal | - | - | - | - | - | - | - | - | - | .. |
| Espagne | - | - | - | - | - | - | - | - | - | .. |
| Royaume-Uni | 2 | 2 | 3 | 3 | 3 | 1 | 2 | 3 | 3 | 0.0 |
| Autre pays européens de l'OCDE | 4 | 4 | 4 | 4 | 5 | 6 | 6 | 6 | 7 | 16.7 |
| Autriche | 1 | 1 | 1 | 1 | 1 | 1 | 1 | 1 | 1 | 0.0 |
| Finlande | - | - | - | - | - | - | - | - | - | .. |
| Norvège | - | - | - | - | - | - | - | - | - | .. |
| Suède | - | - | - | - | 1 | 2 | 1 | 1 | 1 | 0.0 |
| Suisse | 3 | 3 | 3 | 3 | 3 | 3 | 4 | 4 | 5 | 25.0 |
| Turquie | - | - | - | - | - | - | - | - | - | .. |
| Yougoslavie | - | - | - | - | - | - | - | - | - | .. |

## EXPORTATIONS / EXPORTS

|  | 1980/82 moyenne | 1983 | 1984 | 1985 | 1986 | 1987 | 1988 | 1989 | 1990 | 1989/90 % var |
|---|---|---|---|---|---|---|---|---|---|---|
| OCDE - Total | 46 | 44 | 43 | 39 | 36 | 38 | 37 | 40 | 33 | -17.5 |
| OCDE - Amérique du Nord | - | - | - | - | - | - | - | - | - | .. |
| Canada | - | - | - | - | - | - | - | - | - | .. |
| États-Unis | - | - | - | - | - | - | - | - | - | .. |
| Japon | - | - | - | - | - | - | - | - | - | .. |
| OCDE - Océanie | - | - | - | - | - | - | - | - | - | .. |
| Australie | - | - | - | - | - | - | - | - | - | .. |
| Nouvelle Zélande | - | - | - | - | - | - | - | - | - | .. |
| OCDE - Europe | 46 | 44 | 43 | 39 | 36 | 38 | 37 | 40 | 33 | -17.5 |
| CE-12 Total | 43 | 43 | 41 | 38 | 35 | 37 | 36 | 39 | 32 | -17.9 |
| Belgique / Luxembourg | 8 | 9 | 9 | 10 | 10 | 11 | 13 | 14 | 13 | -7.1 |
| Danemark | 1 | - | - | - | - | - | - | - | - | .. |
| France | 2 | 2 | 3 | 3 | 5 | 6 | 7 | 7 | 4 | -42.9 |
| Allemagne | 5 | 5 | 6 | 6 | 4 | 4 | 3 | 4 | 3 | -25.0 |
| Grèce | 2 | 1 | - | - | 1 | - | - | - | - | .. |
| Irlande | 3 | 2 | 2 | 2 | 1 | 1 | - | 1 | - | -100.0 |
| Italie | - | - | - | - | - | 1 | 1 | - | - | .. |
| Pays-Bas | 14 | 15 | 12 | 9 | 8 | 8 | 7 | 9 | 8 | -11.1 |
| Portugal | - | - | - | - | - | - | - | - | - | .. |
| Espagne | 1 | - | - | - | - | - | - | - | - | .. |
| Royaume-Uni | 8 | 9 | 9 | 8 | 6 | 6 | 5 | 4 | 4 | 0.0 |
| Autre pays européens de l'OCDE | 3 | 1 | 2 | 1 | 1 | 1 | 1 | 1 | 1 | 0.0 |
| Autriche | - | - | - | - | - | - | - | - | - | .. |
| Finlande | - | - | - | - | - | - | - | - | - | .. |
| Norvège | - | - | - | - | - | - | - | - | - | .. |
| Suède | - | - | - | - | - | - | - | - | - | .. |
| Suisse | - | - | - | - | - | - | - | - | - | .. |
| Turquie | 3 | 1 | 2 | 1 | 1 | 1 | 1 | 1 | 1 | 0.0 |
| Yougoslavie | 9 | 14 | 7 | 10 | 6 | 21 | 10 | 8 | 3 | -62.5 |

1. Y compris les mulets et les anes / Including mules and asses            All totals exclude Yugoslavia / Tous les totaux excluent la Yougoslavie

# FOREIGN TRADE
## OTHER MEAT / AUTRES VIANDES

### IMPORTS / IMPORTATIONS

*Thousand metric tons - Dressed carcass weight*          *Milliers de tonnes métriques - Poids en carcasse parée*

|  | 1980/82 average | 1983 | 1984 | 1985 | 1986 | 1987 | 1988 | 1989 | 1990 | 1989/90 % change |
|---|---|---|---|---|---|---|---|---|---|---|
| OECD - Total | 138 | 129 | 125 | 124 | 100 | 108 | 113 | 102 | 112 | 9.8 |
| OECD - North America | - | - | - | - | - | - | - | - | - | .. |
| Canada | - | - | - | - | - | - | - | - | - | .. |
| United States | - | - | - | - | - | - | - | - | - | .. |
| Japan | 21 | 19 | 17 | 17 | 4 | 1 | 1 | - | 1 | .. |
| OECD - Oceania | - | - | - | - | - | - | - | - | - | .. |
| Australia | - | - | - | - | - | - | - | - | - | .. |
| New Zealand | - | - | - | - | - | - | - | - | - | .. |
| OECD - Europe | 116 | 110 | 108 | 107 | 96 | 107 | 112 | 102 | 111 | 8.8 |
| EC-12 Total | 106 | 101 | 97 | 96 | 85 | 96 | 100 | 90 | 99 | 10.0 |
| Belgium / Luxembourg | 8 | 9 | 10 | 9 | 9 | 10 | 12 | 15 | 12 | -20.0 |
| Denmark | - | - | - | - | - | - | - | - | - | .. |
| France | 25 | 29 | 28 | 27 | 27 | 28 | 28 | 19 | 28 | 47.4 |
| Germany | 28 | 24 | 25 | 27 | 19 | 21 | 27 | 25 | 26 | 4.0 |
| Greece | - | - | - | - | - | 1 | - | - | - | .. |
| Ireland | - | - | - | - | - | - | 1 | 1 | 1 | 0.0 |
| Italy | 27 | 26 | 20 | 24 | 21 | 25 | 20 | 19 | 19 | 0.0 |
| Netherlands | 8 | 6 | 7 | 6 | 6 | 8 | 8 | 8 | 9 | 12.5 |
| Portugal | - | - | - | - | - | - | 1 | - | 1 | .. |
| Spain | 2 | - | 1 | - | - | - | 1 | 1 | 1 | 0.0 |
| United Kingdom | 7 | 7 | 6 | 3 | 3 | 3 | 2 | 2 | 2 | 0.0 |
| Other OECD - Europe | 10 | 9 | 11 | 11 | 11 | 11 | 12 | 12 | 12 | 0.0 |
| Austria | 2 | 2 | 3 | 3 | 3 | 2 | 3 | 3 | 2 | -33.3 |
| Finland | 1 | - | - | - | - | - | - | - | - | .. |
| Norway | - | - | - | - | - | - | - | - | - | .. |
| Sweden | 2 | 2 | 2 | 2 | 2 | 2 | 2 | 2 | 2 | 0.0 |
| Switzerland | 5 | 5 | 6 | 6 | 6 | 7 | 7 | 7 | 8 | 14.3 |
| Turkey | - | - | - | - | - | - | - | - | - | .. |
| Yugoslavia | - | - | - | - | - | - | - | - | - | .. |

### EXPORTS / EXPORTATIONS

|  | 1980/82 average | 1983 | 1984 | 1985 | 1986 | 1987 | 1988 | 1989 | 1990 | 1989/90 % change |
|---|---|---|---|---|---|---|---|---|---|---|
| OECD - Total | 46 | 43 | 43 | 54 | 54 | 42 | 48 | 51 | 51 | 0.0 |
| OECD - North America | - | - | - | - | - | - | - | - | - | .. |
| Canada | - | - | - | - | - | - | - | - | - | .. |
| United States | - | - | - | - | - | - | - | - | - | .. |
| Japan | - | - | - | - | - | - | - | - | - | .. |
| OECD - Oceania | 17 | 14 | 15 | 29 | 31 | 15 | 11 | 10 | 12 | 20.0 |
| Australia | 15 | 12 | 13 | 27 | 29 | 13 | 9 | 8 | 10 | 25.0 |
| New Zealand | 2 | 2 | 2 | 2 | 2 | 2 | 2 | 2 | 2 | 0.0 |
| OECD - Europe | 29 | 29 | 28 | 25 | 23 | 27 | 37 | 41 | 39 | -4.9 |
| EC-12 Total | 25 | 26 | 25 | 22 | 20 | 23 | 33 | 38 | 36 | -5.3 |
| Belgium / Luxembourg | 1 | 2 | 3 | 2 | 2 | 4 | 6 | 11 | 9 | -18.2 |
| Denmark | - | - | - | - | - | - | - | - | - | .. |
| France | 5 | 4 | 5 | 4 | 4 | 4 | 4 | 6 | 6 | 0.0 |
| Germany | 2 | 2 | 2 | 2 | 3 | 3 | 4 | 4 | 4 | 0.0 |
| Greece | - | - | 1 | - | - | - | - | - | - | .. |
| Ireland | - | - | - | - | - | - | 3 | 1 | 2 | 100.0 |
| Italy | 1 | - | 1 | 2 | 1 | 2 | 2 | 2 | 2 | 0.0 |
| Netherlands | 6 | 7 | 6 | 6 | 7 | 6 | 9 | 9 | 9 | 0.0 |
| Portugal | - | - | - | - | - | - | - | - | - | .. |
| Spain | 4 | 6 | 4 | 3 | 1 | 2 | 2 | 2 | 1 | -50.0 |
| United Kingdom | 6 | 5 | 3 | 3 | 2 | 2 | 3 | 3 | 3 | 0.0 |
| Other OECD - Europe | 4 | 3 | 3 | 3 | 3 | 4 | 4 | 3 | 3 | 0.0 |
| Austria | 4 | 3 | 3 | 3 | 3 | 4 | 4 | 3 | 3 | 0.0 |
| Finland | - | - | - | - | - | - | - | - | - | .. |
| Norway | - | - | - | - | - | - | - | - | - | .. |
| Sweden | - | - | - | - | - | - | - | - | - | .. |
| Switzerland | - | - | - | - | - | - | - | - | - | .. |
| Turkey | - | - | - | - | - | - | - | - | - | .. |
| Yugoslavia | - | 1 | 1 | - | - | 2 | - | - | - | .. |

All totals exclude Yugoslavia / Tous les totaux excluent la Yougoslavie

# COMMERCE EXTÉRIEUR
## ABATS COMESTIBLES / EDIBLE OFFALS [1]

## IMPORTATIONS / IMPORTS

*Milliers de tonnes métriques - Poids en carcasse parée*  *Thousand metric tons - Dressed carcass weight*

| | 1980/82 moyenne | 1983 | 1984 | 1985 | 1986 | 1987 | 1988 | 1989 | 1990 | 1989/90 % var |
|---|---|---|---|---|---|---|---|---|---|---|
| OCDE - Total | 641 | 657 | 642 | 690 | 665 | 661 [e] | 656 [e] | 608 [e] | 636 [e] | 4.6 |
| OCDE - Amérique du Nord | 17 | 25 | 29 | 34 | 36 | 38 | 40 | 44 | 43 [e] | -2.3 |
| Canada | 5 | 10 | 8 | 11 | 13 | 14 | 13 | 14 | 16 | 14.3 |
| États-Unis | 12 | 15 | 21 | 23 | 23 | 24 | 27 | 30 | 27 [e] | -10.0 |
| Japon | 60 | 65 | 71 | 82 | 97 | 100 [e] | 95 [e] | 97 [e] | 97 [e] | 0.0 |
| OCDE - Océanie | - | 1 | 2 | 2 | 1 | 2 | 2 | 2 | 2 | 0.0 |
| Australie | - | 1 | 2 | 2 | 1 | 2 | 2 | 2 | 2 | 0.0 |
| Nouvelle Zélande | - | - | - | - | - | - | - | - | - | .. |
| OCDE - Europe | 563 | 566 | 540 | 572 | 531 | 521 | 519 | 465 | 494 | 6.2 |
| CE-12 Total | 554 | 560 | 534 | 567 | 526 | 516 | 513 | 461 | 490 | 6.3 |
| Belgique / Luxembourg | 50 | 34 | 38 | 36 | 39 | 38 | 45 | 45 | 48 | 6.7 |
| Danemark | - | - | - | - | - | 1 | 1 | 2 | 2 | 0.0 |
| France | 191 | 190 | 177 | 180 | 177 | 182 | 181 | 140 | 150 | 7.1 |
| Allemagne | 80 | 91 | 81 | 80 | 65 | 61 | 63 | 63 | 99 | 57.1 |
| Grèce | 4 | 8 | 9 | 10 | 12 | 14 | 8 | 11 | 10 | -9.1 |
| Irlande | 7 | 6 | 6 | 6 | 9 | 12 | 8 | 9 | 5 | -44.4 |
| Italie | 42 | 40 | 36 | 43 | 49 | 46 | 45 | 48 | 44 | -8.3 |
| Pays-Bas | 42 | 41 | 43 | 44 | 28 | 15 | 34 | 34 | 36 | 5.9 |
| Portugal | 2 | 6 | 6 | 7 | 9 | 10 | 7 | 5 | 5 | 0.0 |
| Espagne | 4 | 17 | 19 | 25 | 25 | 31 | 15 | 15 | 13 | -13.3 |
| Royaume-Uni | 133 | 127 | 119 | 136 | 113 | 106 | 106 | 89 | 78 | -12.4 |
| Autre pays européens de l'OCDE | 9 | 6 | 6 | 5 | 5 | 5 | 6 | 4 | 4 | 0.0 |
| Autriche | 3 | 2 | 2 | 1 | 1 | 1 | - | 1 | 1 | 0.0 |
| Finlande | 1 | - | - | - | - | - | 1 | - | - | .. |
| Norvège | 2 | 2 | 2 | 2 | 2 | 1 | 2 | - | 1 | .. |
| Suède | - | - | - | - | - | 1 | 1 | 1 | - | -100.0 |
| Suisse | 3 | 2 | 2 | 2 | 2 | 2 | 2 | 2 | 2 | 0.0 |
| Turquie | - | - | - | - | - | - | - | - | - | .. |
| Yougoslavie | 4 | 8 | 3 | 2 | 2 | 1 | 3 | 1 | 7 | 600.0 |

## EXPORTATIONS / EXPORTS

| | 1980/82 moyenne | 1983 | 1984 | 1985 | 1986 | 1987 | 1988 | 1989 | 1990 | 1989/90 % var |
|---|---|---|---|---|---|---|---|---|---|---|
| OCDE - Total | 702 | 725 | 767 | 809 | 806 | 788 | 838 | 850 | 802 [e] | -5.6 |
| OCDE - Amérique du Nord | 260 | 280 | 282 | 295 | 297 | 277 | 306 | 309 | 301 [e] | -2.6 |
| Canada | 39 | 46 | 49 | 43 | 43 | 42 | 61 | 67 | 60 [e] | -10.4 |
| États-Unis | 221 | 234 | 233 | 252 | 254 | 235 | 245 | 242 | 241 [e] | -0.4 |
| Japon | - | - | - | - | - | - | - | - | - | .. |
| OCDE - Océanie | 99 | 100 | 98 | 118 | 103 | 114 | 114 | 109 | 100 | -8.3 |
| Australie | 53 | 51 | 49 | 67 | 60 | 59 | 62 | 60 | 60 | 0.0 |
| Nouvelle Zélande | 46 | 49 | 49 | 51 | 43 | 55 | 52 | 49 | 40 | -18.4 |
| OCDE - Europe | 343 | 345 | 387 | 396 | 406 | 397 | 418 | 432 | 401 | -7.2 |
| CE-12 Total | 337 | 339 | 381 | 389 | 400 | 387 | 415 | 427 | 395 | -7.5 |
| Belgique / Luxembourg | 60 | 50 | 43 | 42 | 51 | 53 | 48 | 47 | 45 | -4.3 |
| Danemark | 21 | 25 | 27 | 25 | 27 | 26 | 27 | 24 | 26 | 8.3 |
| France | 47 | 45 | 48 | 50 | 55 | 56 | 57 | 52 | 23 | -55.8 |
| Allemagne | 38 | 39 | 42 | 45 | 54 | 53 | 54 | 57 | 56 | -1.8 |
| Grèce | - | - | - | - | - | - | 1 | 1 | 1 | 0.0 |
| Irlande | 42 | 40 | 62 | 67 | 81 | 79 | 71 | 80 | 72 | -10.0 |
| Italie | 11 | 8 | 9 | 8 | 5 | 4 | 9 | 8 | 11 | 37.5 |
| Pays-Bas | 92 | 108 | 124 | 124 | 99 | 86 | 126 | 130 | 133 | 2.3 |
| Portugal | - | 3 | 3 | 4 | 3 | 4 | - | 1 | 1 | 0.0 |
| Espagne | 9 | 4 | 7 | 8 | 8 | 6 | 4 | 5 | 5 | 0.0 |
| Royaume-Uni | 16 | 17 | 16 | 16 | 17 | 20 | 18 | 22 | 22 | 0.0 |
| Autre pays européens de l'OCDE | 6 | 6 | 6 | 7 | 6 | 10 | 3 | 5 | 6 | 20.0 |
| Autriche | 1 | 1 | 1 | 1 | 1 | 1 | 1 | 1 | 1 | 0.0 |
| Finlande | - | - | - | - | - | - | - | - | 1 | .. |
| Norvège | 1 | - | - | - | - | - | - | - | 1 | .. |
| Suède | 4 | 4 | 4 | 5 | 4 | 3 | 2 | 4 | 3 | -25.0 |
| Suisse | - | 1 | 1 | 1 | 1 | 6 | - | - | - | .. |
| Turquie | - | - | - | - | - | - | - | - | - | .. |
| Yougoslavie | 13 | 20 | 1 | 5 | 14 | 8 | 2 | - | 2 | .. |

1. Poids de produit / Product weight

All totals exclude Yugoslavia / Tous les totaux excluent la Yougoslavie

# CONSUMPTION
## TOTAL MEAT / TOTAL VIANDE

*Thousand metric tons - Dressed carcass weight*      *Milliers de tonnes métriques - Poids en carcasse parée*

| | 1980/82 average | 1983 | 1984 | 1985 | 1986 | 1987 | 1988 | 1989 | 1990 | 1989/90 % change |
|---|---|---|---|---|---|---|---|---|---|---|
| **OECD - Total** | 65091 | 66867 | 67672 | 69248 [b] | 69940 | 71558 [e] | 73337 [e] | 73739 [e] | 74160 [e] | 0.6 |
| **OECD - North America** | 28352 | 29383 | 29689 | 30504 | 30750 | 31235 | 32255 | 32547 | 32649 [e] | 0.3 |
| Canada | 2523 | 2557 | 2493 | 2583 | 2615 | 2640 | 2706 | 2696 | 2619 [e] | -2.9 |
| United States | 25829 | 26826 | 27196 | 27921 | 28135 | 28595 | 29549 | 29851 | 30030 [e] | 0.6 |
| **Japan** | 4118 | 4344 | 4442 | 4650 | 4882 | 5114 [e] | 5264 [e] | 5335 [e] | 5410 [e] | 1.4 |
| **OECD - Oceania** | 1883 | 1805 | 1919 | 1930 | 1930 | 2021 [e] | 2045 [e] | 2156 [e] | 2129 [e] | -1.3 |
| Australia | 1562 | 1506 | 1611 | 1615 | 1610 | 1698 [e] | 1672 [e] | 1824 [e] | 1798 [e] | -1.4 |
| New Zealand | 321 | 299 | 308 | 315 | 320 | 323 | 373 | 332 | 331 | -0.3 |
| **OECD - Europe** | 30739 | 31335 | 31622 | 32164 [b] | 32378 | 33188 | 33773 | 33701 [e] | 33972 [e] | 0.8 |
| **EC-12 Total** | 27323 | 27907 | 28105 | 28505 [b] | 28829 | 29676 | 30069 | 30006 | 30429 | 1.4 |
| Belgium / Luxembourg | 991 | 998 | 1031 | 1046 | 1050 | 1037 | 1025 | 1010 | 997 | -1.3 |
| Denmark | 415 | 411 | 429 | 461 | 519 | 533 | 535 | 542 | 541 | -0.2 |
| France | 5789 | 5825 | 5855 | 5822 | 5932 | 6022 | 6110 | 6168 | 6266 | 1.6 |
| Germany | 6094 | 6017 | 6053 | 6129 | 6228 | 6331 | 6389 | 6205 | 6312 | 1.7 |
| Greece | 677 | 779 | 768 | 782 | 781 | 876 | 766 | 844 | 815 | -3.4 |
| Ireland | 333 | 344 | 323 | 320 [b] | 308 | 316 | 328 | 311 | 333 | 7.1 |
| Italy | 4435 | 4595 | 4613 | 4786 | 4804 | 4869 | 4949 | 5050 | 5018 | -0.6 |
| Netherlands | 1110 | 1081 | 1110 | 1142 | 1152 | 1255 | 1290 | 1277 | 1309 | 2.5 |
| Portugal | 534 | 574 | 551 | 558 | 600 | 659 | 673 | 729 | 762 | 4.5 |
| Spain | 2769 | 3142 | 3227 | 3227 | 3182 | 3340 | 3616 | 3648 | 3812 | 4.5 |
| United Kingdom | 4175 | 4141 | 4145 | 4232 | 4273 | 4438 | 4388 | 4222 | 4264 | 1.0 |
| **Other OECD - Europe** | 3416 | 3428 | 3517 | 3659 | 3549 | 3512 | 3704 | 3695 [e] | 3543 [e] | -4.1 |
| Austria | 661 | 674 | 679 | 674 | 672 | 676 | 704 | 719 | 726 | 1.0 |
| Finland | 317 | 321 | 330 | 331 | 337 | 341 | 342 | 317 | 332 | 4.7 |
| Norway | 212 | 206 | 209 | 222 | 229 | 229 | 230 | 222 | 224 | 0.9 |
| Sweden | 524 | 512 | 487 | 492 | 489 | 492 | 506 | 510 | 516 | 1.2 |
| Switzerland | 553 | 552 | 552 | 567 | 570 | 577 | 582 | 579 | 571 | -1.4 |
| Turkey | 1149 | 1163 | 1260 | 1373 | 1252 | 1197 | 1340 | 1348 [e] | 1174 [e] | -12.9 |
| Yugoslavia | 1439 | 1417 | 1482 | 1453 | 1580 | 1618 | 1645 | 1671 | 1714 | 2.6 |

## TOTAL BEEF AND VEAL / TOTAL VIANDE BOVINE

| | 1980/82 average | 1983 | 1984 | 1985 | 1986 | 1987 | 1988 | 1989 | 1990 | 1989/90 % change |
|---|---|---|---|---|---|---|---|---|---|---|
| **OECD - Total** | 21909 | 22295 | 22498 | 22972 [b] | 23250 | 22949 [e] | 22864 [e] | 22498 [e] | 22186 [e] | -1.4 |
| **OECD - North America** | 11959 | 12487 | 12544 | 12792 | 13028 | 12625 | 12623 | 12232 | 12062 [e] | -1.4 |
| Canada | 1016 | 1039 | 1002 | 1026 | 1047 | 1023 | 1034 | 1028 | 1007 | -2.0 |
| United States | 10943 | 11448 | 11542 | 11766 | 11981 | 11602 | 11589 | 11204 | 11055 [e] | -1.3 |
| **Japan** | 639 | 724 | 752 | 774 | 817 | 893 | 973 | 996 | 1094 | 9.8 |
| **OECD - Oceania** | 884 | 806 | 812 | 785 | 809 | 805 [e] | 805 [e] | 844 [e] | 770 [e] | -8.8 |
| Australia | 736 | 684 | 692 | 666 | 690 | 678 [e] | 673 [e] | 719 [e] | 652 [e] | -9.3 |
| New Zealand | 148 | 122 | 120 | 119 | 119 | 127 | 132 | 125 | 118 | -5.6 |
| **OECD - Europe** | 8427 | 8278 | 8390 | 8621 [b] | 8596 | 8626 | 8463 | 8426 | 8260 | -2.0 |
| **EC-12 Total** | 7345 | 7182 | 7256 | 7423 [b] | 7469 | 7573 | 7327 | 7255 | 7159 | -1.3 |
| Belgium / Luxembourg | 275 | 257 | 262 | 270 | 253 | 249 | 225 | 215 | 205 | -4.7 |
| Denmark | 63 | 58 | 68 | 72 | 86 | 81 | 87 | 98 | 97 | -1.0 |
| France | 1730 | 1718 | 1755 | 1722 | 1758 | 1756 | 1694 | 1706 | 1676 | -1.8 |
| Germany | 1447 | 1365 | 1378 | 1410 | 1432 | 1448 | 1442 | 1414 | 1398 | -1.1 |
| Greece | 190 | 215 | 215 | 212 | 223 | 260 | 190 | 239 | 230 | -3.8 |
| Ireland | 89 | 85 | 84 | 77 [b] | 79 | 74 | 68 | 67 | 60 | -10.4 |
| Italy | 1458 | 1484 | 1468 | 1591 | 1587 | 1542 | 1530 | 1529 | 1471 | -3.8 |
| Netherlands | 293 | 263 | 268 | 275 | 238 | 289 | 285 | 294 | 291 | -1.0 |
| Portugal | 118 | 113 | 111 | 116 | 118 | 124 | 137 | 145 | 158 | 9.0 |
| Spain | 439 | 441 | 444 | 444 | 430 | 441 | 443 | 453 | 488 | 7.7 |
| United Kingdom | 1243 | 1183 | 1203 | 1234 | 1265 | 1309 | 1226 | 1095 | 1085 | -0.9 |
| **Other OECD - Europe** | 1082 | 1096 | 1134 | 1198 | 1127 | 1053 | 1136 | 1171 | 1101 | -6.0 |
| Austria | 189 | 182 | 181 | 170 | 168 | 164 | 165 | 167 | 169 | 1.2 |
| Finland | 108 | 103 | 106 | 104 | 104 | 104 | 103 | 103 | 109 | 5.8 |
| Norway | 75 | 67 | 66 | 74 | 78 | 76 | 80 | 74 | 77 | 4.1 |
| Sweden | 146 | 142 | 132 | 130 | 135 | 145 | 141 | 144 | 149 | 3.5 |
| Switzerland | 176 | 166 | 171 | 179 | 175 | 184 | 176 | 170 | 174 | 2.4 |
| Turkey | 388 | 436 | 478 | 541 | 467 | 380 | 471 | 513 | 423 | -17.5 |
| Yugoslavia | 320 | 325 | 333 | 315 | 301 | 321 | 316 | 369 | 391 | 6.0 |

All totals exclude Yugoslavia / Tous les totaux excluent la Yougoslavie

# CONSOMMATION
## VIANDE DE PORC / PIG MEAT

*Milliers de tonnes métriques - Poids en carcasse parée*        *Thousand metric tons - Dressed carcass weight*

| | 1980/82 moyenne | 1983 | 1984 | 1985 | 1986 | 1987 | 1988 | 1989 | 1990 | 1989/90 % var. |
|---|---|---|---|---|---|---|---|---|---|---|
| OCDE - Total | 22173 | 22695 | 22839 | 23168 | 23144 | 23755 | 24823 | 24809 | 24618 | -0.8 |
| OCDE - Amérique du Nord | 7996 | 7924 | 7889 | 8025 | 7677 | 7770 | 8354 | 8428 | 8120 | -3.7 |
| Canada | 900 | 891 | 837 | 860 | 845 | 846 | 889 | 911 | 848 | -6.9 |
| États-Unis | 7096 | 7033 | 7052 | 7165 | 6832 | 6924 | 7465 | 7517 | 7272 | -3.3 |
| Japon | 1643 | 1678 | 1697 | 1804 | 1890 | 1994 | 2041 | 2066 | 2066 | 0.0 |
| OCDE - Océanie | 263 | 284 | 342 | 309 | 298 | 326 | 340 | 349 | 357 | 2.3 |
| Australie | 228 | 245 | 300 | 263 | 250 | 281 | 294 | 304 | 314 | 3.3 |
| Nouvelle Zélande | 35 | 39 | 42 | 46 | 48 | 45 | 46 | 45 | 43 | -4.4 |
| OCDE - Europe | 12272 | 12809 | 12911 | 13030 | 13279 | 13665 | 14088 | 13966 | 14075 | 0.8 |
| CE-12 Total | 11143 | 11658 | 11784 | 11877 | 12127 | 12512 | 12893 | 12779 | 12894 | 0.9 |
| Belgique / Luxembourg | 429 | 453 | 473 | 470 | 482 | 466 | 482 | 482 | 465 | -3.5 |
| Danemark | 263 | 262 | 271 | 290 | 325 | 340 | 338 | 332 | 330 | -0.6 |
| France | 1937 | 1934 | 1946 | 1950 | 1964 | 2032 | 2107 | 2098 | 2101 | 0.1 |
| Allemagne | 3569 | 3605 | 3624 | 3665 | 3730 | 3792 | 3817 | 3645 | 3644 | 0.0 |
| Grèce | 176 | 209 | 201 | 211 | 221 | 246 | 216 | 233 | 213 | -8.6 |
| Irlande | 112 | 120 | 119 | 118 | 122 | 119 | 125 | 125 | 124 | -0.8 |
| Italie | 1395 | 1490 | 1532 | 1575 | 1604 | 1668 | 1712 | 1776 | 1814 | 2.1 |
| Pays-Bas | 588 | 585 | 596 | 602 | 624 | 641 | 686 | 664 | 682 | 2.7 |
| Portugal | 173 | 203 | 206 | 214 | 230 | 260 | 250 | 285 | 296 | 3.9 |
| Espagne | 1048 | 1359 | 1443 | 1402 | 1443 | 1515 | 1738 | 1753 | 1833 | 4.6 |
| Royaume-Uni | 1454 | 1438 | 1373 | 1380 | 1382 | 1433 | 1422 | 1386 | 1392 | 0.4 |
| Autre pays européens de l'OCDE | 1129 | 1151 | 1127 | 1153 | 1152 | 1153 | 1195 | 1187 | 1181 | -0.5 |
| Autriche | 343 | 360 | 360 | 367 | 361 | 364 | 395 | 397 | 402 | 1.3 |
| Finlande | 142 | 150 | 152 | 156 | 161 | 161 | 162 | 157 | 164 | 4.5 |
| Norvège | 82 | 81 | 81 | 84 | 85 | 87 | 85 | 81 | 77 | -4.9 |
| Suède | 281 | 269 | 258 | 262 | 260 | 257 | 270 | 269 | 264 | -1.9 |
| Suisse | 281 | 291 | 276 | 284 | 285 | 284 | 283 | 283 | 274 | -3.2 |
| Turquie | - | - | - | - | - | - | - | - | - | .. |
| Yougoslavie | 721 | 693 | 735 | 734 | 848 | 858 | 839 | 861 | 881 | 2.3 |

## VIANDE DE VOLAILLE / POULTRY MEAT [1]

| | 1980/82 moyenne | 1983 | 1984 | 1985 | 1986 | 1987 | 1988 | 1989 | 1990 | 1989/90 % var. |
|---|---|---|---|---|---|---|---|---|---|---|
| OCDE - Total | 13879 | 14678 | 15091 | 15749 | 16377 | 17521 | 18314 | 19146 | 19970 [e] | 4.3 |
| OCDE - Amérique du Nord | 6990 | 7536 | 7800 | 8245 | 8609 | 9407 | 9816 | 10434 | 11040 [e] | 5.8 |
| Canada | 551 | 571 | 596 | 636 | 656 | 709 | 736 | 715 | 721 [e] | 0.8 |
| États-Unis | 6438 | 6965 | 7204 | 7609 | 7953 | 8698 | 9080 | 9719 | 10319 | 6.2 |
| Japon | 1245 | 1359 | 1425 | 1466 | 1574 | 1641 | 1695 | 1697 | 1685 | -0.7 |
| OCDE - Océanie | 334 | 334 | 360 | 412 | 413 | 439 | 453 | 489 | 504 | 3.1 |
| Australie | 300 | 301 | 314 | 364 | 367 | 391 | 401 | 431 | 444 | 3.0 |
| Nouvelle Zélande | 34 | 33 | 46 | 48 | 46 | 48 | 52 | 58 | 60 | 3.4 |
| OCDE - Europe | 5311 | 5449 | 5506 | 5626 | 5781 | 6034 | 6350 | 6526 | 6741 | 3.3 |
| CE-12 Total | 4832 | 4991 | 4996 | 5119 | 5229 | 5442 | 5706 | 5858 | 6040 | 3.1 |
| Belgique / Luxembourg | 140 | 153 | 149 | 157 | 166 | 167 | 169 | 163 | 171 | 4.9 |
| Danemark | 45 | 50 | 50 | 56 | 60 | 60 | 60 | 60 | 60 | 0.0 |
| France | 905 | 966 | 951 | 979 | 1041 | 1031 | 1086 | 1183 | 1219 | 3.0 |
| Allemagne | 606 | 569 | 581 | 591 | 614 | 641 | 686 | 708 | 781 | 10.3 |
| Grèce | 129 | 154 | 155 | 156 | 151 | 156 | 155 | 160 | 166 | 3.8 |
| Irlande | 50 | 56 | 55 | 61 | 65 | 70 | 73 | 69 | 76 | 10.1 |
| Italie | 1031 | 1058 | 1040 | 1028 | 1024 | 1061 | 1097 | 1125 | 1118 | -0.6 |
| Pays-Bas | 143 | 170 | 184 | 198 | 208 | 232 | 246 | 256 | 264 | 3.1 |
| Portugal | 159 | 164 | 140 | 137 | 157 | 171 | 175 | 183 | 188 | 2.7 |
| Espagne | 848 | 823 | 806 | 840 | 764 | 805 | 853 | 870 | 880 | 1.1 |
| Royaume-Uni | 777 | 828 | 885 | 916 | 979 | 1048 | 1106 | 1081 | 1117 | 3.3 |
| Autre pays européens de l'OCDE | 479 | 458 | 510 | 507 | 552 | 592 | 644 | 668 | 701 | 4.9 |
| Autriche | 82 | 86 | 90 | 89 | 97 | 101 | 101 | 109 | 109 | 0.0 |
| Finlande | 16 | 18 | 20 | 21 | 22 | 26 | 28 | 30 | 33 | 10.0 |
| Norvège | 11 | 11 | 11 | 13 | 15 | 16 | 18 | 18 | 20 | 11.1 |
| Suède | 44 | 45 | 44 | 45 | 44 | 38 | 44 | 46 | 52 | 13.0 |
| Suisse | 51 | 53 | 59 | 59 | 63 | 66 | 75 | 76 | 73 | -3.9 |
| Turquie | 275 | 245 | 286 | 280 | 311 | 345 | 378 | 389 | 414 | 6.4 |
| Yougoslavie | 273 | 280 | 284 | 272 | 308 | 310 | 345 | 297 | 290 | -2.4 |

1. Poids éviscéré ou «prêt à cuire» / Eviscerated or ready-to-cook weight        All totals exclude Yugoslavia / Tous les totaux excluent la Yougoslavie

# CONSUMPTION
## MUTTON, LAMB AND GOAT MEAT / VIANDE DE MOUTON ET DE CHÈVRE

Thousand metric tons - Dressed carcass weight                                              Milliers de tonnes métriques - Poids en carcasse parée

| | 1980/82 average | 1983 | 1984 | 1985 | 1986 | 1987 | 1988 | 1989 | 1990 | 1989/90 % change |
|---|---|---|---|---|---|---|---|---|---|---|
| OECD - Total | 2200 | 2264 | 2294 | 2422 | 2300 | 2366 | 2380 | 2463 [e] | 2474 [e] | 0.4 |
| OECD - North America | 182 | 196 | 206 | 195 | 194 | 188 | 197 | 204 | 211 | 3.4 |
| Canada | 18 | 20 | 22 | 19 | 23 | 24 | 22 | 20 | 20 | 0.0 |
| United States | 164 | 176 | 184 | 176 | 171 | 164 | 175 | 184 | 191 | 3.8 |
| Japan | 168 | 165 | 149 | 160 | 161 | 153 | 128 | 147 [e] | 143 [e] | -2.7 |
| OECD - Oceania | 287 | 278 | 308 | 351 | 324 | 345 | 352 | 373 | 394 | 5.6 |
| Australia | 196 | 189 | 218 | 263 | 233 | 251 | 222 | 284 | 299 | 5.3 |
| New Zealand | 91 | 89 | 90 | 88 | 91 | 94 | 130 | 89 | 95 | 6.7 |
| OECD - Europe | 1562 | 1625 | 1631 | 1716 | 1621 | 1680 | 1703 | 1739 | 1726 | -0.7 |
| EC-12 Total | 1127 | 1201 | 1191 | 1216 | 1183 | 1236 | 1242 | 1322 | 1415 | 7.0 |
| Belgium / Luxembourg | 19 | 17 | 16 | 16 | 18 | 18 | 18 | 19 | 20 | 5.3 |
| Denmark | 2 | 2 | 3 | 3 | 3 | 4 | 4 | 4 | 5 | 25.0 |
| France | 226 | 236 | 238 | 242 | 248 | 258 | 262 | 276 | 312 | 13.0 |
| Germany | 52 | 54 | 49 | 53 | 51 | 53 | 53 | 62 | 67 | 8.1 |
| Greece | 130 | 139 | 135 | 139 | 124 | 141 | 141 | 145 | 143 | -1.4 |
| Ireland | 27 | 25 | 24 | 24 | 24 | 24 | 23 | 25 | 27 | 8.0 |
| Italy | 83 | 81 | 86 | 89 | 86 | 89 | 93 | 102 | 103 | 1.0 |
| Netherlands | 8 | 6 | 6 | 7 | 8 | 9 | 10 | 13 | 18 | 38.5 |
| Portugal | 24 | 27 | 26 | 25 | 25 | 30 | 32 | 33 | 35 | 6.1 |
| Spain | 139 | 202 | 207 | 210 | 213 | 227 | 224 | 228 | 248 | 8.8 |
| United Kingdom | 417 | 412 | 401 | 408 | 383 | 383 | 382 | 415 | 437 | 5.3 |
| Other OECD - Europe | 436 | 424 | 440 | 500 | 438 | 444 | 461 | 417 | 311 | -25.4 |
| Austria | 4 | 5 | 5 | 5 | 5 | 7 | 7 | 8 | 9 | 12.5 |
| Finland | 1 | 1 | 1 | 1 | 1 | 1 | 1 | 1 | 1 | 0.0 |
| Norway | 22 | 23 | 27 | 25 | 26 | 25 | 23 | 25 | 25 | 0.0 |
| Sweden | 5 | 6 | 6 | 6 | 7 | 7 | 6 | 6 | 7 | 16.7 |
| Switzerland | 9 | 9 | 10 | 11 | 11 | 10 | 11 | 12 | 12 | 0.0 |
| Turkey | 394 | 380 | 391 | 452 | 388 | 394 | 413 | 365 | 257 | -29.6 |
| Yugoslavia | 54 | 55 | 37 | 53 | 57 | 59 | 63 | 66 | 68 | 3.0 |

## HORSE MEAT / VIANDE D'ÉQUIDÉS [1]

| | 1980/82 average | 1983 | 1984 | 1985 | 1986 | 1987 | 1988 | 1989 | 1990 | 1989/90 % change |
|---|---|---|---|---|---|---|---|---|---|---|
| OECD - Total | 313 | 274 | 269 | 269 | 250 | 261 | 265 | 267 | 270 [e] | 1.1 |
| OECD - North America | - | - | - | - | - | - | - | - | - | .. |
| Canada | - | - | - | - | - | - | - | - | - | .. |
| United States | - | - | - | - | - | - | - | - | - | .. |
| Japan | 82 | 70 | 68 | 66 | 58 | 55 | 59 | 61 | 59 [e] | -3.3 |
| OECD - Oceania | - | - | - | - | - | - | - | - | - | .. |
| Australia | - | - | - | - | - | - | - | - | - | .. |
| New Zealand | - | - | - | - | - | - | - | - | - | .. |
| OECD - Europe | 231 | 204 | 201 | 203 | 192 | 206 | 206 | 206 | 211 | 2.4 |
| EC-12 Total | 220 | 194 | 191 | 193 | 182 | 194 | 193 | 194 | 198 | 2.1 |
| Belgium / Luxembourg | 33 | 28 | 26 | 27 | 27 | 31 | 28 | 27 | 30 | 11.1 |
| Denmark | 2 | 1 | 1 | 1 | 1 | 1 | 1 | 1 | 1 | 0.0 |
| France | 85 | 74 | 71 | 64 | 54 | 58 | 60 | 60 | 58 | -3.3 |
| Germany | 6 | 6 | 5 | 5 | 5 | 6 | 5 | 5 | 5 | 0.0 |
| Greece | 1 | - | - | - | - | 1 | 1 | 1 | - | -100.0 |
| Ireland | - | - | - | - | - | - | - | - | - | .. |
| Italy | 58 | 57 | 58 | 65 | 65 | 66 | 68 | 72 | 76 | 5.6 |
| Netherlands | 25 | 18 | 20 | 21 | 21 | 23 | 23 | 21 | 20 | -4.8 |
| Portugal | 1 | 1 | 2 | 1 | 1 | 1 | 1 | 1 | 1 | 0.0 |
| Spain | 10 | 9 | 8 | 8 | 7 | 7 | 6 | 6 | 7 | 16.7 |
| United Kingdom | - | - | - | 1 | 1 | - | - | - | - | .. |
| Other OECD - Europe | 11 | 10 | 10 | 10 | 10 | 12 | 13 | 12 | 13 | 8.3 |
| Austria | 1 | 1 | 1 | 1 | 1 | 1 | 2 | 2 | 2 | 0.0 |
| Finland | 1 | 1 | 1 | 1 | 1 | 1 | 1 | 1 | 1 | 0.0 |
| Norway | 1 | 1 | 1 | 1 | 1 | 1 | 1 | 1 | 1 | 0.0 |
| Sweden | 3 | 3 | 2 | 3 | 3 | 4 | 3 | 3 | 3 | 0.0 |
| Switzerland | 4 | 4 | 5 | 4 | 4 | 5 | 6 | 5 | 6 | 20.0 |
| Turkey | - | - | - | - | - | - | - | - | - | .. |
| Yugoslavia | - | - | - | - | - | - | - | - | - | .. |

1. Including mules and asses / Y compris les mulets et les anes                All totals exclude Yugoslavia / Tous les totaux excluent la Yougoslavie

# CONSOMMATION
## AUTRES VIANDES / OTHER MEAT

*Milliers de tonnes métriques - Poids en carcasse parée* — *Thousand metric tons - Dressed carcass weight*

| | 1980/82 moyenne | 1983 | 1984 | 1985 | 1986 | 1987 | 1988 | 1989 | 1990 | 1989/90 % var. |
|---|---|---|---|---|---|---|---|---|---|---|
| OCDE - Total | 1129 | 1082 | 1091 | 1085 | 1046 | 1071 | 1097 | 1080 | 1078 | -0.2 |
| OCDE - Amérique du Nord | 230 | 235 | 240 | 243 | 244 | 250 | 250 | 250 | 250 | 0.0 |
| Canada | - | - | - | - | - | - | - | - | - | .. |
| États-Unis | 230 | 235 | 240 | 243 | 244 | 250 | 250 | 250 | 250 | 0.0 |
| Japon | 40 | 40 | 33 | 32 | 18 | 6 | 3 | 1 | 3 | 200.0 |
| OCDE - Océanie | 29 | 33 | 32 | 13 | 12 | 23 | 14 | 16 | 4 | -75.0 |
| Australie | 29 | 33 | 32 | 13 | 12 | 23 | 14 | 16 | 4 | -75.0 |
| Nouvelle Zélande | - | - | - | - | - | - | - | - | - | .. |
| OCDE - Europe | 829 | 774 | 786 | 797 | 772 | 792 | 830 | 813 | 821 | 1.0 |
| CE-12 Total | 772 | 713 | 723 | 732 | 716 | 735 | 772 | 751 | 760 | 1.2 |
| Belgique / Luxembourg | 20 | 22 | 22 | 24 | 25 | 25 | 26 | 26 | 28 | 7.7 |
| Danemark | 3 | 3 | 3 | 3 | 3 | 3 | 3 | 3 | 3 | 0.0 |
| France | 304 | 294 | 292 | 293 | 292 | 296 | 314 | 313 | 322 | 2.9 |
| Allemagne | 68 | 61 | 61 | 63 | 53 | 55 | 60 | 58 | 59 | 1.7 |
| Grèce | 6 | 5 | 4 | 5 | 4 | 6 | 5 | 5 | 5 | 0.0 |
| Irlande | - | - | - | - | - | - | 1 | 1 | 1 | 0.0 |
| Italie | 214 | 217 | 216 | 222 | 221 | 226 | 236 | 229 | 218 | -4.8 |
| Pays-Bas | 2 | - | 2 | 1 | 1 | 4 | 5 | 2 | 4 | 100.0 |
| Portugal | 8 | 14 | 16 | 16 | 16 | 16 | 18 | 22 | 24 | 9.1 |
| Espagne | 137 | 88 | 96 | 97 | 93 | 95 | 97 | 84 | 87 | 3.6 |
| Royaume-Uni | 9 | 9 | 11 | 8 | 8 | 9 | 7 | 8 | 9 | 12.5 |
| Autre pays européens de l'OCDE | 58 | 61 | 63 | 65 | 56 | 57 | 58 | 62 | 61 | -1.6 |
| Autriche | 7 | 6 | 7 | 7 | 5 | 4 | 5 | 7 | 6 | -14.3 |
| Finlande | 11 | 11 | 13 | 11 | 11 | 11 | 11 | 12 | 11 | -8.3 |
| Norvège | 7 | 8 | 8 | 10 | 9 | 9 | 9 | 9 | 10 | 11.1 |
| Suède | 23 | 27 | 25 | 27 | 21 | 22 | 23 | 24 | 23 | -4.2 |
| Suisse | 9 | 9 | 10 | 10 | 10 | 11 | 10 | 10 | 11 | 10.0 |
| Turquie | - | - | - | - | - | - | - | - | - | .. |
| Yougoslavie | 6 | 5 | 7 | 8 | 8 | 6 | 8 | 7 | 7 | 0.0 |

## ABATS COMESTIBLES / EDIBLE OFFALS [1]

| | 1980/82 moyenne | 1983 | 1984 | 1985 | 1986 | 1987 | 1988 | 1989 | 1990 | 1989/90 % var. |
|---|---|---|---|---|---|---|---|---|---|---|
| OCDE - Total | 3488 | 3579 | 3590 | 3583 | 3573 | 3635 [e] | 3594 [e] | 3476 [e] | 3564 [e] | 2.5 |
| OCDE - Amérique du Nord | 994 | 1005 | 1010 | 1004 | 998 | 995 | 1015 | 999 | 966 [e] | -3.3 |
| Canada | 37 | 36 | 36 | 42 | 44 | 38 | 25 | 22 | 23 [e] | 4.5 |
| États-Unis | 957 | 969 | 974 | 962 | 954 | 957 | 990 | 977 | 943 [e] | -3.5 |
| Japon | 301 | 308 | 318 | 348 | 364 | 372 [e] | 365 [e] | 367 [e] | 360 [e] | -1.9 |
| OCDE - Océanie | 86 | 70 | 65 | 60 | 74 | 83 | 81 | 85 | 100 | 17.6 |
| Australie | 73 | 54 | 55 | 46 | 58 | 74 | 68 | 70 | 85 | 21.4 |
| Nouvelle Zélande | 13 | 16 | 10 | 14 | 16 | 9 | 13 | 15 | 15 | 0.0 |
| OCDE - Europe | 2108 | 2196 | 2197 | 2171 | 2137 | 2185 | 2133 | 2025 | 2138 | 5.6 |
| CE-12 Total | 1885 | 1968 | 1964 | 1945 | 1923 | 1984 | 1936 | 1847 | 1963 | 6.3 |
| Belgique / Luxembourg | 75 | 68 | 83 | 82 | 79 | 81 | 77 | 78 | 78 | 0.0 |
| Danemark | 37 | 35 | 33 | 36 | 41 | 44 | 42 | 44 | 45 | 2.3 |
| France | 602 | 603 | 602 | 572 | 575 | 591 | 587 | 532 | 578 | 8.6 |
| Allemagne | 346 | 357 | 355 | 342 | 343 | 336 | 326 | 313 | 358 | 14.4 |
| Grèce | 47 | 57 | 58 | 59 | 58 | 66 | 58 | 61 | 58 | -4.9 |
| Irlande | 55 | 58 | 41 | 40 | 18 | 29 | 38 | 24 | 45 | 87.5 |
| Italie | 197 | 208 | 213 | 216 | 217 | 217 | 213 | 217 | 218 | 0.5 |
| Pays-Bas | 51 | 39 | 34 | 38 | 52 | 57 | 35 | 27 | 30 | 11.1 |
| Portugal | 50 | 52 | 50 | 49 | 53 | 57 | 60 | 60 | 60 | 0.0 |
| Espagne | 148 | 220 | 223 | 226 | 232 | 250 | 255 | 254 | 269 | 5.9 |
| Royaume-Uni | 276 | 271 | 272 | 285 | 255 | 256 | 245 | 237 | 224 | -5.5 |
| Autre pays européens de l'OCDE | 222 | 228 | 233 | 226 | 214 | 201 | 197 | 178 | 175 | -1.7 |
| Autriche | 35 | 34 | 35 | 35 | 35 | 35 | 29 | 29 | 29 | 0.0 |
| Finlande | 38 | 37 | 37 | 37 | 37 | 37 | 36 | 13 | 13 | 0.0 |
| Norvège | 14 | 15 | 15 | 15 | 19 | 15 | 14 | 14 | 14 | 0.0 |
| Suède | 21 | 20 | 20 | 19 | 19 | 19 | 19 | 18 | 18 | 0.0 |
| Suisse | 22 | 20 | 21 | 20 | 22 | 17 | 21 | 23 | 21 | -8.7 |
| Turquie | 93 | 102 | 105 | 100 | 86 | 78 | 78 | 81 | 80 | -1.2 |
| Yougoslavie | 65 | 59 | 86 | 71 | 58 | 64 | 74 | 71 | 77 | 8.5 |

1. Poids de produit / Product weight

All totals exclude Yugoslavia / Tous les totaux excluent la Yougoslavie

# CONSUMPTION PER HEAD
## TOTAL MEAT / TOTAL VIANDE

*Kilogrammes per year - Dressed carcass weight*                              *Kilogrammes par an - Poids en carcasse parée*

| | 1980/82 average | 1983 | 1984 | 1985 | 1986 | 1987 | 1988 | 1989 | 1990 | 1989/90 % change |
|---|---|---|---|---|---|---|---|---|---|---|
| OECD - Total | 82.8 | 83.8 | 84.3 | 85.7 [b] | 85.9 | 87.3 [e] | 88.9 [e] | 88.7 [e] | 88.3 [e] | -0.4 |
| OECD - North America | 111.4 | 113.2 | 113.3 | 115.3 | 115.2 | 115.9 | 118.5 | 118.3 | 117.4 [e] | -0.8 |
| Canada | 103.6 | 103.1 | 99.7 | 102.6 | 103.1 | 102.9 | 104.3 | 102.7 | 98.4 [e] | -4.2 |
| United States | 112.2 | 114.3 | 114.7 | 116.7 | 116.4 | 117.2 | 120.0 | 120.0 | 119.5 [e] | -0.5 |
| Japan | 35.0 | 36.4 | 37.0 | 38.5 | 40.2 | 41.9 [e] | 42.9 [e] | 43.3 [e] | 43.8 [e] | 1.1 |
| OECD - Oceania | 104.0 | 96.9 | 101.9 | 101.2 | 100.0 | 103.3 [e] | 103.0 [e] | 106.9 [e] | 104.0 [e] | -2.6 |
| Australia | 104.6 | 97.8 | 103.4 | 102.3 | 100.5 | 104.4 [e] | 101.1 [e] | 108.4 [e] | 105.2 [e] | -2.9 |
| New Zealand | 101.1 | 92.6 | 94.5 | 95.9 | 97.6 | 97.6 | 112.1 | 99.3 | 98.0 | -1.4 |
| OECD - Europe | 77.6 | 78.3 | 78.7 | 79.6 [b] | 79.7 | 81.3 | 82.3 | 81.5 [e] | 81.4 [e] | -0.2 |
| EC-12 Total | 85.7 | 87.1 | 87.5 | 88.6 [b] | 89.3 | 91.7 | 92.6 | 92.0 | 92.8 | 0.8 |
| Belgium / Luxembourg | 97.0 | 97.6 | 100.9 | 102.3 | 102.6 | 101.3 | 99.9 | 97.9 | 96.1 | -1.8 |
| Denmark | 81.0 | 80.4 | 83.9 | 90.1 | 101.3 | 104.0 | 104.3 | 105.6 | 105.3 | -0.3 |
| France | 106.9 | 106.4 | 106.6 | 105.5 | 107.1 | 108.3 | 109.3 | 109.8 | 111.0 | 1.1 |
| Germany | 98.9 | 98.0 | 98.9 | 100.4 | 102.0 | 103.7 | 104.0 | 100.1 | 100.1 | 0.0 |
| Greece | 69.7 | 79.1 | 77.6 | 78.7 | 78.4 | 87.7 | 76.5 | 84.1 | 80.4 | -4.5 |
| Ireland | 96.9 | 98.1 | 91.5 | 90.4 [b] | 87.0 | 89.2 | 92.7 | 88.5 | 95.1 | 7.4 |
| Italy | 78.5 | 80.9 | 81.0 | 83.8 | 84.0 | 84.9 | 86.2 | 87.8 | 87.0 | -0.8 |
| Netherlands | 78.0 | 75.2 | 77.0 | 78.8 | 79.1 | 85.6 | 87.4 | 86.0 | 87.6 | 1.9 |
| Portugal | 53.9 | 57.1 | 54.4 | 54.8 | 58.7 | 64.2 | 65.3 | 70.5 | 73.5 | 4.2 |
| Spain | 73.6 | 82.5 | 84.4 | 84.0 | 82.3 | 86.3 | 93.2 | 93.8 | 97.8 | 4.3 |
| United Kingdom | 74.1 | 73.5 | 73.4 | 74.7 | 75.3 | 78.0 | 76.9 | 73.8 | 74.3 | 0.7 |
| Other OECD - Europe | 44.4 | 43.1 | 43.5 | 44.5 | 42.6 | 41.6 | 43.2 | 42.3 [e] | 39.6 [e] | -6.4 |
| Austria | 87.4 | 89.2 | 89.9 | 89.2 | 88.8 | 89.2 | 92.7 | 94.3 | 94.1 | -0.2 |
| Finland | 66.1 | 66.1 | 67.6 | 67.5 | 68.5 | 69.1 | 69.1 | 63.9 | 66.6 | 4.4 |
| Norway | 51.7 | 49.9 | 50.5 | 53.5 | 54.9 | 54.7 | 54.6 | 52.5 | 52.8 | 0.5 |
| Sweden | 62.9 | 61.5 | 58.4 | 58.9 | 58.4 | 58.6 | 60.0 | 60.0 | 60.2 | 0.3 |
| Switzerland | 86.0 | 85.2 | 84.9 | 86.8 | 86.7 | 87.2 | 87.2 | 86.1 | 84.0 | -2.4 |
| Turkey | 25.1 | 24.1 | 25.5 | 27.1 | 24.2 | 22.7 | 24.8 | 24.4 [e] | 20.5 [e] | -15.8 |
| Yugoslavia | 64.0 | 62.1 | 64.5 | 62.8 | 67.9 | 69.1 | 69.8 | 70.5 | 72.0 | 2.1 |

## TOTAL BEEF AND VEAL / TOTAL VIANDE BOVINE

| | 1980/82 average | 1983 | 1984 | 1985 | 1986 | 1987 | 1988 | 1989 | 1990 | 1989/90 % change |
|---|---|---|---|---|---|---|---|---|---|---|
| OECD - Total | 27.9 | 28.0 | 28.0 | 28.4 [b] | 28.6 | 28.0 [e] | 27.7 [e] | 27.1 [e] | 26.4 [e] | -2.3 |
| OECD - North America | 47.0 | 48.1 | 47.9 | 48.4 | 48.8 | 46.8 | 46.4 | 44.5 | 43.4 [e] | -2.5 |
| Canada | 41.7 | 41.9 | 40.1 | 40.7 | 41.3 | 39.9 | 39.9 | 39.2 | 37.8 | -3.4 |
| United States | 47.5 | 48.8 | 48.7 | 49.2 | 49.6 | 47.6 | 47.1 | 45.0 | 44.0 [e] | -2.4 |
| Japan | 5.4 | 6.1 | 6.3 | 6.4 | 6.7 | 7.3 | 7.9 | 8.1 | 8.9 | 9.5 |
| OECD - Oceania | 48.8 | 43.3 | 43.1 | 41.2 | 41.9 | 41.1 [e] | 40.5 [e] | 41.8 [e] | 37.6 [e] | -10.1 |
| Australia | 49.3 | 44.4 | 44.4 | 42.2 | 43.1 | 41.7 [e] | 40.7 [e] | 42.7 [e] | 38.2 [e] | -10.7 |
| New Zealand | 46.6 | 37.8 | 36.8 | 36.2 | 36.3 | 38.4 | 39.7 | 37.4 | 34.9 | -6.6 |
| OECD - Europe | 21.3 | 20.7 | 20.9 | 21.3 [b] | 21.2 | 21.1 | 20.6 | 20.4 | 19.8 | -3.0 |
| EC-12 Total | 23.0 | 22.4 | 22.6 | 23.1 [b] | 23.1 | 23.4 | 22.6 | 22.3 | 21.8 | -1.9 |
| Belgium / Luxembourg | 26.9 | 25.1 | 25.6 | 26.4 | 24.7 | 24.3 | 21.9 | 20.8 | 19.8 | -5.2 |
| Denmark | 12.4 | 11.3 | 13.3 | 14.1 | 16.8 | 15.8 | 17.0 | 19.1 | 18.9 | -1.2 |
| France | 31.9 | 31.4 | 31.9 | 31.2 | 31.7 | 31.6 | 30.3 | 30.4 | 29.7 | -2.2 |
| Germany | 23.5 | 22.2 | 22.5 | 23.1 | 23.5 | 23.7 | 23.5 | 22.8 | 22.2 | -2.8 |
| Greece | 19.5 | 21.8 | 21.7 | 21.3 | 22.4 | 26.0 | 19.0 | 23.8 | 22.7 | -4.8 |
| Ireland | 26.0 | 24.3 | 23.8 | 21.8 [b] | 22.3 | 20.9 | 19.2 | 19.1 | 17.1 | -10.1 |
| Italy | 25.8 | 26.1 | 25.8 | 27.8 | 27.7 | 26.9 | 26.6 | 26.6 | 25.5 | -4.0 |
| Netherlands | 20.6 | 18.3 | 18.6 | 19.0 | 16.3 | 19.7 | 19.3 | 19.8 | 19.5 | -1.6 |
| Portugal | 11.9 | 11.2 | 11.0 | 11.4 | 11.5 | 12.1 | 13.3 | 14.0 | 15.2 | 8.6 |
| Spain | 11.7 | 11.6 | 11.6 | 11.6 | 11.1 | 11.4 | 11.4 | 11.6 | 12.5 | 7.5 |
| United Kingdom | 22.1 | 21.0 | 21.3 | 21.8 | 22.3 | 23.0 | 21.5 | 19.1 | 18.9 | -1.2 |
| Other OECD - Europe | 14.1 | 13.8 | 14.0 | 14.6 | 13.5 | 12.5 | 13.2 | 13.4 | 12.3 | -8.3 |
| Austria | 25.0 | 24.1 | 24.0 | 22.5 | 22.2 | 21.7 | 21.7 | 21.9 | 21.9 | 0.0 |
| Finland | 22.6 | 21.2 | 21.7 | 21.2 | 21.1 | 21.1 | 20.8 | 20.7 | 21.9 | 5.4 |
| Norway | 18.4 | 16.2 | 15.9 | 17.8 | 18.7 | 18.2 | 18.2 | 17.5 | 18.2 | 3.7 |
| Sweden | 17.5 | 17.0 | 15.8 | 15.6 | 16.1 | 17.3 | 16.7 | 17.0 | 17.4 | 2.6 |
| Switzerland | 27.3 | 25.6 | 26.3 | 27.4 | 26.6 | 27.8 | 26.4 | 25.3 | 25.6 | 1.3 |
| Turkey | 8.5 | 9.0 | 9.7 | 10.7 | 9.0 | 7.2 | 8.7 | 9.3 | 7.4 | -20.3 |
| Yugoslavia | 14.3 | 14.3 | 14.5 | 13.6 | 12.9 | 13.7 | 13.4 | 15.6 | 16.4 | 5.5 |

All totals exclude Yugoslavia / Tous les totaux excluent la Yougoslavie

44

# CONSOMMATION PAR TÊTE
## VIANDE DE PORC / PIG MEAT

*Kilogrammes par an - Poids en carcasse parée*          *Kilogrammes per year - Dressed carcass weight*

| | 1980/82 moyenne | 1983 | 1984 | 1985 | 1986 | 1987 | 1988 | 1989 | 1990 | 1989/90 % var. |
|---|---|---|---|---|---|---|---|---|---|---|
| OCDE - Total | 28.2 | 28.5 | 28.4 | 28.7 | 28.4 | 29.0 | 30.1 | 29.8 | 29.3 | -1.7 |
| OCDE - Amérique du Nord | 31.4 | 30.5 | 30.1 | 30.3 | 28.8 | 28.8 | 30.7 | 30.6 | 29.2 | -4.7 |
| Canada | 37.0 | 35.9 | 33.5 | 34.2 | 33.3 | 33.0 | 34.3 | 34.7 | 31.9 | -8.2 |
| États-Unis | 30.9 | 30.0 | 29.8 | 29.9 | 28.3 | 28.4 | 30.3 | 30.2 | 28.9 | -4.3 |
| Japon | 14.0 | 14.1 | 14.1 | 14.9 | 15.6 | 16.3 | 16.6 | 16.8 | 16.7 | -0.3 |
| OCDE - Océanie | 14.5 | 15.2 | 18.2 | 16.2 | 15.4 | 16.7 | 17.1 | 17.3 | 17.4 | 0.8 |
| Australie | 15.3 | 15.9 | 19.3 | 16.7 | 15.6 | 17.3 | 17.8 | 18.1 | 18.4 | 1.8 |
| Nouvelle Zélande | 10.9 | 12.1 | 12.9 | 14.0 | 14.6 | 13.6 | 13.8 | 13.5 | 12.7 | -5.5 |
| OCDE - Europe | 31.0 | 32.0 | 32.1 | 32.3 | 32.7 | 33.5 | 34.3 | 33.8 | 33.7 | -0.2 |
| CE-12 Total | 34.9 | 36.4 | 36.7 | 36.9 | 37.6 | 38.7 | 39.7 | 39.2 | 39.3 | 0.3 |
| Belgique / Luxembourg | 42.0 | 44.3 | 46.3 | 46.0 | 47.1 | 45.5 | 47.0 | 46.7 | 44.8 | -4.1 |
| Danemark | 51.3 | 51.2 | 53.0 | 56.7 | 63.5 | 66.3 | 65.9 | 64.7 | 64.2 | -0.8 |
| France | 35.7 | 35.3 | 35.4 | 35.3 | 35.5 | 36.5 | 37.7 | 37.4 | 37.2 | -0.3 |
| Allemagne | 57.9 | 58.7 | 59.2 | 60.1 | 61.1 | 62.1 | 62.1 | 58.8 | 57.8 | -1.7 |
| Grèce | 18.1 | 21.2 | 20.3 | 21.2 | 22.2 | 24.6 | 21.6 | 23.2 | 21.0 | -9.5 |
| Irlande | 32.4 | 34.2 | 33.7 | 33.3 | 34.5 | 33.6 | 35.3 | 35.6 | 35.4 | -0.5 |
| Italie | 24.7 | 26.2 | 26.9 | 27.6 | 28.0 | 29.1 | 29.8 | 30.9 | 31.5 | 1.9 |
| Pays-Bas | 41.3 | 40.7 | 41.3 | 41.5 | 42.8 | 43.7 | 46.5 | 44.7 | 45.6 | 2.1 |
| Portugal | 17.5 | 20.2 | 20.3 | 21.0 | 22.5 | 25.3 | 24.3 | 27.6 | 28.5 | 3.5 |
| Espagne | 27.9 | 35.7 | 37.7 | 36.5 | 37.3 | 39.1 | 44.8 | 45.1 | 47.0 | 4.4 |
| Royaume-Uni | 25.8 | 25.5 | 24.3 | 24.4 | 24.3 | 25.2 | 24.9 | 24.2 | 24.2 | 0.1 |
| Autre pays européens de l'OCDE | 14.7 | 14.5 | 13.9 | 14.0 | 13.8 | 13.7 | 13.9 | 13.6 | 13.2 | -2.9 |
| Autriche | 45.4 | 47.7 | 47.7 | 48.6 | 47.7 | 48.1 | 52.0 | 52.1 | 52.1 | 0.1 |
| Finlande | 29.5 | 30.9 | 31.1 | 31.8 | 32.7 | 32.6 | 32.8 | 31.6 | 32.9 | 4.1 |
| Norvège | 19.9 | 19.6 | 19.6 | 20.2 | 20.4 | 20.8 | 20.2 | 19.2 | 18.2 | -5.3 |
| Suède | 33.8 | 32.3 | 30.9 | 31.4 | 31.1 | 30.6 | 32.0 | 31.7 | 30.8 | -2.7 |
| Suisse | 43.7 | 44.9 | 42.4 | 43.5 | 43.4 | 42.9 | 42.4 | 42.1 | 40.3 | -4.2 |
| Turquie | - | - | - | - | - | - | - | - | - | .. |
| Yougoslavie | 32.1 | 30.4 | 32.0 | 31.7 | 36.4 | 36.7 | 35.6 | 36.3 | 37.0 | 1.9 |

## VIANDE DE VOLAILLE / POULTRY MEAT [1]

| | 1980/82 moyenne | 1983 | 1984 | 1985 | 1986 | 1987 | 1988 | 1989 | 1990 | 1989/90 % var. |
|---|---|---|---|---|---|---|---|---|---|---|
| OCDE - Total | 17.7 | 18.4 | 18.8 | 19.5 | 20.1 | 21.4 | 22.2 | 23.0 | 23.8 [e] | 3.3 |
| OCDE - Amérique du Nord | 27.5 | 29.0 | 29.8 | 31.2 | 32.2 | 34.9 | 36.1 | 37.9 | 39.7 [e] | 4.7 |
| Canada | 22.6 | 23.0 | 23.8 | 25.3 | 25.9 | 27.6 | 28.4 | 27.2 | 27.1 [e] | -0.5 |
| États-Unis | 28.0 | 29.7 | 30.4 | 31.8 | 32.9 | 35.7 | 36.9 | 39.1 | 41.0 | 5.1 |
| Japon | 10.6 | 11.4 | 11.9 | 12.1 | 13.0 | 13.4 | 13.8 | 13.8 | 13.6 | -1.0 |
| OCDE - Océanie | 18.4 | 17.9 | 19.1 | 21.6 | 21.4 | 22.4 | 22.8 | 24.2 | 24.6 | 1.6 |
| Australie | 20.1 | 19.6 | 20.2 | 23.1 | 22.9 | 24.0 | 24.2 | 25.6 | 26.0 | 1.5 |
| Nouvelle Zélande | 10.8 | 10.2 | 14.1 | 14.6 | 14.0 | 14.5 | 15.6 | 17.3 | 17.8 | 2.3 |
| OCDE - Europe | 13.4 | 13.6 | 13.7 | 13.9 | 14.2 | 14.8 | 15.5 | 15.8 | 16.1 | 2.3 |
| CE-12 Total | 15.2 | 15.6 | 15.6 | 15.9 | 16.2 | 16.8 | 17.6 | 18.0 | 18.4 | 2.5 |
| Belgique / Luxembourg | 13.7 | 15.0 | 14.6 | 15.4 | 16.2 | 16.3 | 16.5 | 15.8 | 16.5 | 4.3 |
| Danemark | 8.8 | 9.8 | 9.8 | 11.0 | 11.7 | 11.7 | 11.7 | 11.7 | 11.7 | -0.2 |
| France | 16.7 | 17.7 | 17.3 | 17.7 | 18.8 | 18.5 | 19.4 | 21.1 | 21.6 | 2.5 |
| Allemagne | 9.8 | 9.3 | 9.5 | 9.7 | 10.1 | 10.5 | 11.2 | 11.4 | 12.4 | 8.4 |
| Grèce | 13.2 | 15.6 | 15.7 | 15.7 | 15.2 | 15.6 | 15.5 | 15.9 | 16.4 | 2.7 |
| Irlande | 14.5 | 16.0 | 15.6 | 17.2 | 18.4 | 19.8 | 20.6 | 19.6 | 21.7 | 10.5 |
| Italie | 18.2 | 18.6 | 18.3 | 18.0 | 17.9 | 18.5 | 19.1 | 19.6 | 19.4 | -0.8 |
| Pays-Bas | 10.0 | 11.8 | 12.8 | 13.7 | 14.3 | 15.8 | 16.7 | 17.2 | 17.7 | 2.5 |
| Portugal | 16.1 | 16.3 | 13.8 | 13.5 | 15.3 | 16.7 | 17.0 | 17.7 | 18.1 | 2.4 |
| Espagne | 22.5 | 21.6 | 21.1 | 21.9 | 19.8 | 20.8 | 22.0 | 22.4 | 22.6 | 0.9 |
| Royaume-Uni | 13.8 | 14.7 | 15.7 | 16.2 | 17.2 | 18.4 | 19.4 | 18.9 | 19.5 | 3.0 |
| Autre pays européens de l'OCDE | 6.2 | 5.8 | 6.3 | 6.2 | 6.6 | 7.0 | 7.5 | 7.7 | 7.8 | 2.4 |
| Autriche | 10.8 | 11.4 | 11.9 | 11.8 | 12.8 | 13.3 | 13.3 | 14.3 | 14.1 | -1.1 |
| Finlande | 3.3 | 3.7 | 4.1 | 4.3 | 4.5 | 5.3 | 5.7 | 6.0 | 6.6 | 9.6 |
| Norvège | 2.6 | 2.7 | 2.7 | 3.1 | 3.6 | 3.8 | 4.3 | 4.3 | 4.7 | 10.7 |
| Suède | 5.3 | 5.4 | 5.3 | 5.4 | 5.3 | 4.5 | 5.2 | 5.4 | 6.1 | 12.1 |
| Suisse | 7.9 | 8.2 | 9.1 | 9.0 | 9.6 | 10.0 | 11.2 | 11.3 | 10.7 | -5.0 |
| Turquie | 6.0 | 5.1 | 5.8 | 5.5 | 6.0 | 6.5 | 7.0 | 7.0 | 7.2 | 2.9 |
| Yougoslavie | 12.2 | 12.3 | 12.4 | 11.8 | 13.2 | 13.2 | 14.6 | 12.5 | 12.2 | -2.8 |

1. Poids éviscéré ou «prêt à cuire» / Eviscerated or ready-to-cook weight       All totals exclude Yugoslavia / Tous les totaux excluent la Yougoslavie

# CONSUMPTION PER HEAD
## MUTTON, LAMB AND GOAT MEAT / VIANDE DE MOUTON ET DE CHÈVRE
*Kilogrammes per year - Dressed carcass weight*          *Kilogrammes par an - Poids en carcasse parée*

| | 1980/82 average | 1983 | 1984 | 1985 | 1986 | 1987 | 1988 | 1989 | 1990 | 1989/90 % change |
|---|---|---|---|---|---|---|---|---|---|---|
| OECD - Total | 2.8 | 2.8 | 2.9 | 3.0 | 2.8 | 2.9 | 2.9 | 3.0 e | 2.9 e | -0.5 |
| OECD - North America | 0.7 | 0.8 | 0.8 | 0.7 | 0.7 | 0.7 | 0.7 | 0.7 | 0.8 | 2.3 |
| Canada | 0.7 | 0.8 | 0.9 | 0.8 | 0.9 | 0.9 | 0.8 | 0.8 | 0.8 | -1.4 |
| United States | 0.7 | 0.7 | 0.8 | 0.7 | 0.7 | 0.7 | 0.7 | 0.7 | 0.8 | 2.7 |
| Japan | 1.4 | 1.4 | 1.2 | 1.3 | 1.3 | 1.3 | 1.0 | 1.2 e | 1.2 e | -3.1 |
| OECD - Oceania | 15.9 | 14.9 | 16.3 | 18.4 | 16.8 | 17.6 | 17.7 | 18.5 | 19.3 | 4.1 |
| Australia | 13.1 | 12.3 | 14.0 | 16.7 | 14.5 | 15.4 | 13.4 | 16.9 | 17.5 | 3.7 |
| New Zealand | 28.7 | 27.6 | 27.6 | 26.8 | 27.8 | 28.4 | 39.1 | 26.6 | 28.1 | 5.6 |
| OECD - Europe | 3.9 | 4.1 | 4.1 | 4.2 | 4.0 | 4.1 | 4.1 | 4.2 | 4.1 | -1.7 |
| EC-12 Total | 3.5 | 3.7 | 3.7 | 3.8 | 3.7 | 3.8 | 3.8 | 4.1 | 4.3 | 6.4 |
| Belgium / Luxembourg | 1.9 | 1.7 | 1.6 | 1.6 | 1.8 | 1.8 | 1.8 | 1.8 | 1.9 | 4.7 |
| Denmark | 0.5 | 0.4 | 0.6 | 0.6 | 0.6 | 0.8 | 0.8 | 0.8 | 1.0 | 24.8 |
| France | 4.2 | 4.3 | 4.3 | 4.4 | 4.5 | 4.6 | 4.7 | 4.9 | 5.5 | 12.5 |
| Germany | 0.8 | 0.9 | 0.8 | 0.9 | 0.8 | 0.9 | 0.9 | 1.0 | 1.1 | 6.2 |
| Greece | 13.3 | 14.1 | 13.6 | 14.0 | 12.4 | 14.1 | 14.1 | 14.5 | 14.1 | -2.4 |
| Ireland | 7.7 | 7.1 | 6.8 | 6.8 | 6.8 | 6.8 | 6.5 | 7.1 | 7.7 | 8.4 |
| Italy | 1.5 | 1.4 | 1.5 | 1.6 | 1.5 | 1.6 | 1.6 | 1.8 | 1.8 | 0.8 |
| Netherlands | 0.5 | 0.4 | 0.4 | 0.5 | 0.5 | 0.6 | 0.7 | 0.9 | 1.2 | 37.6 |
| Portugal | 2.4 | 2.7 | 2.6 | 2.5 | 2.4 | 2.9 | 3.1 | 3.2 | 3.4 | 5.7 |
| Spain | 3.7 | 5.3 | 5.4 | 5.5 | 5.5 | 5.9 | 5.8 | 5.9 | 6.4 | 8.6 |
| United Kingdom | 7.4 | 7.3 | 7.1 | 7.2 | 6.7 | 6.7 | 6.7 | 7.3 | 7.6 | 5.0 |
| Other OECD - Europe | 5.7 | 5.3 | 5.4 | 6.1 | 5.3 | 5.3 | 5.4 | 4.8 | 3.5 | -27.2 |
| Austria | 0.5 | 0.7 | 0.7 | 0.7 | 0.7 | 0.9 | 0.9 | 1.0 | 1.2 | 11.2 |
| Finland | 0.2 | 0.2 | 0.2 | 0.2 | 0.2 | 0.2 | 0.2 | 0.2 | 0.2 | -0.4 |
| Norway | 5.4 | 5.6 | 6.5 | 6.0 | 6.2 | 6.0 | 5.5 | 5.9 | 5.9 | -0.4 |
| Sweden | 0.6 | 0.7 | 0.7 | 0.7 | 0.8 | 0.8 | 0.7 | 0.7 | 0.8 | 15.7 |
| Switzerland | 1.5 | 1.4 | 1.5 | 1.7 | 1.7 | 1.5 | 1.6 | 1.8 | 1.8 | -1.1 |
| Turkey | 8.6 | 7.9 | 7.9 | 8.9 | 7.5 | 7.5 | 7.7 | 6.6 | 4.5 | -31.9 |
| Yugoslavia | 2.4 | 2.4 | 1.6 | 2.3 | 2.4 | 2.5 | 2.7 | 2.8 | 2.9 | 2.6 |

## HORSE MEAT / VIANDE D'ÉQUIDÉS [1]

| | 1980/82 average | 1983 | 1984 | 1985 | 1986 | 1987 | 1988 | 1989 | 1990 | 1989/90 % change |
|---|---|---|---|---|---|---|---|---|---|---|
| OECD - Total | 0.4 | 0.3 | 0.3 | 0.3 | 0.3 | 0.3 | 0.3 | 0.3 | 0.3 e | 0.2 |
| OECD - North America | - | - | - | - | - | - | - | - | - | .. |
| Canada | - | - | - | - | - | - | - | - | - | .. |
| United States | - | - | - | - | - | - | - | - | - | .. |
| Japan | 0.7 | 0.6 | 0.6 | 0.5 | 0.5 | 0.5 | 0.5 | 0.5 | 0.5 e | -3.6 |
| OECD - Oceania | - | - | - | - | - | - | - | - | - | .. |
| Australia | - | - | - | - | - | - | - | - | - | .. |
| New Zealand | - | - | - | - | - | - | - | - | - | .. |
| OECD - Europe | 0.6 | 0.5 | 0.5 | 0.5 | 0.5 | 0.5 | 0.5 | 0.5 | 0.5 | 1.4 |
| EC-12 Total | 0.7 | 0.6 | 0.6 | 0.6 | 0.6 | 0.6 | 0.6 | 0.6 | 0.6 | 1.4 |
| Belgium / Luxembourg | 3.2 | 2.7 | 2.5 | 2.6 | 2.6 | 3.0 | 2.7 | 2.6 | 2.9 | 10.5 |
| Denmark | 0.3 | 0.2 | 0.2 | 0.2 | 0.2 | 0.2 | 0.2 | 0.2 | 0.2 | -0.2 |
| France | 1.6 | 1.4 | 1.3 | 1.2 | 1.0 | 1.0 | 1.1 | 1.1 | 1.0 | -3.8 |
| Germany | 0.1 | 0.1 | 0.1 | 0.1 | 0.1 | 0.1 | 0.1 | 0.1 | 0.1 | -1.7 |
| Greece | 0.1 | - | - | - | - | 0.1 | 0.1 | 0.1 | - | -100.0 |
| Ireland | - | - | - | - | - | - | - | - | - | .. |
| Italy | 1.0 | 1.0 | 1.0 | 1.1 | 1.1 | 1.2 | 1.2 | 1.3 | 1.3 | 5.3 |
| Netherlands | 1.8 | 1.3 | 1.4 | 1.4 | 1.4 | 1.6 | 1.6 | 1.4 | 1.3 | -5.4 |
| Portugal | 0.1 | 0.1 | 0.2 | 0.1 | 0.1 | 0.1 | 0.1 | 0.1 | 0.1 | -0.3 |
| Spain | 0.3 | 0.2 | 0.2 | 0.2 | 0.2 | 0.2 | 0.2 | 0.2 | 0.2 | 16.4 |
| United Kingdom | - | - | - | - | - | - | - | - | - | .. |
| Other OECD - Europe | 0.1 | 0.1 | 0.1 | 0.1 | 0.1 | 0.1 | 0.2 | 0.1 | 0.1 | 5.7 |
| Austria | 0.1 | 0.1 | 0.1 | 0.1 | 0.1 | 0.1 | 0.3 | 0.3 | 0.3 | -1.1 |
| Finland | 0.2 | 0.2 | 0.2 | 0.2 | 0.2 | 0.2 | 0.2 | 0.2 | 0.2 | -0.4 |
| Norway | 0.2 | 0.2 | 0.2 | 0.2 | 0.2 | 0.2 | 0.2 | 0.2 | 0.2 | -0.4 |
| Sweden | 0.4 | 0.4 | 0.2 | 0.4 | 0.4 | 0.5 | 0.4 | 0.4 | 0.4 | -0.9 |
| Switzerland | 0.7 | 0.6 | 0.8 | 0.6 | 0.6 | 0.8 | 0.9 | 0.7 | 0.9 | 18.7 |
| Turkey | - | - | - | - | - | - | - | - | - | .. |
| Yugoslavia | - | - | - | - | - | - | - | - | - | .. |

1. Including mules and asses / Y compris les mulets et les anes        All totals exclude Yugoslavia / Tous les totaux excluent la Yougoslavie

# CONSOMMATION PAR TÊTE
## AUTRES VIANDES / OTHER MEAT

*Kilogrammes par an - Poids en carcasse parée*                                                                                          *Kilogrammes per year - Dressed carcass weight*

| | 1980/82 moyenne | 1983 | 1984 | 1985 | 1986 | 1987 | 1988 | 1989 | 1990 | 1989/90 % var. |
|---|---|---|---|---|---|---|---|---|---|---|
| OCDE - Total | 1.4 | 1.4 | 1.4 | 1.3 | 1.3 | 1.3 | 1.3 | 1.3 | 1.3 | -1.1 |
| OCDE - Amérique du Nord | 0.9 | 0.9 | 0.9 | 0.9 | 0.9 | 0.9 | 0.9 | 0.9 | 0.9 | -1.1 |
| Canada | - | - | - | - | - | - | - | - | - | .. |
| États-Unis | 1.0 | 1.0 | 1.0 | 1.0 | 1.0 | 1.0 | 1.0 | 1.0 | 1.0 | -1.0 |
| Japon | 0.3 | 0.3 | 0.3 | 0.3 | 0.1 | - | - | - | - | 199.0 |
| OCDE - Océanie | 1.6 | 1.8 | 1.7 | 0.7 | 0.6 | 1.2 | 0.7 | 0.8 | 0.2 | -75.4 |
| Australie | 1.9 | 2.1 | 2.1 | 0.8 | 0.7 | 1.4 | 0.8 | 1.0 | 0.2 | -75.4 |
| Nouvelle Zélande | - | - | - | - | - | - | - | - | - | .. |
| OCDE - Europe | 2.1 | 1.9 | 2.0 | 2.0 | 1.9 | 1.9 | 2.0 | 2.0 | 2.0 | 0.0 |
| CE-12 Total | 2.4 | 2.2 | 2.3 | 2.3 | 2.2 | 2.3 | 2.4 | 2.3 | 2.3 | 0.6 |
| Belgique / Luxembourg | 2.0 | 2.2 | 2.2 | 2.3 | 2.4 | 2.4 | 2.5 | 2.5 | 2.7 | 7.1 |
| Danemark | 0.6 | 0.6 | 0.6 | 0.6 | 0.6 | 0.6 | 0.6 | 0.6 | 0.6 | -0.2 |
| France | 5.6 | 5.4 | 5.3 | 5.3 | 5.3 | 5.3 | 5.6 | 5.6 | 5.7 | 2.4 |
| Allemagne | 1.1 | 1.0 | 1.0 | 1.0 | 0.9 | 0.9 | 1.0 | 0.9 | 0.9 | 0.0 |
| Grèce | 0.6 | 0.5 | 0.4 | 0.5 | 0.4 | 0.6 | 0.5 | 0.5 | 0.5 | -1.1 |
| Irlande | 0.1 | - | - | - | - | - | 0.3 | 0.3 | 0.3 | 0.3 |
| Italie | 3.8 | 3.8 | 3.8 | 3.9 | 3.9 | 3.9 | 4.1 | 4.0 | 3.8 | -5.0 |
| Pays-Bas | 0.1 | - | 0.1 | 0.1 | 0.1 | 0.3 | 0.3 | 0.1 | 0.3 | 98.7 |
| Portugal | 0.8 | 1.4 | 1.6 | 1.6 | 1.6 | 1.6 | 1.7 | 2.1 | 2.3 | 8.8 |
| Espagne | 3.6 | 2.3 | 2.5 | 2.5 | 2.4 | 2.5 | 2.5 | 2.2 | 2.2 | 3.4 |
| Royaume-Uni | 0.2 | 0.2 | 0.2 | 0.1 | 0.1 | 0.2 | 0.1 | 0.1 | 0.2 | 12.2 |
| Autre pays européens de l'OCDE | 0.7 | 0.8 | 0.8 | 0.8 | 0.7 | 0.7 | 0.7 | 0.7 | 0.7 | -4.0 |
| Autriche | 1.0 | 0.8 | 0.9 | 0.9 | 0.7 | 0.5 | 0.7 | 0.9 | 0.8 | -15.3 |
| Finlande | 2.3 | 2.3 | 2.7 | 2.2 | 2.2 | 2.2 | 2.2 | 2.4 | 2.2 | -8.7 |
| Norvège | 1.8 | 1.9 | 1.9 | 2.4 | 2.2 | 2.1 | 2.1 | 2.1 | 2.4 | 10.7 |
| Suède | 2.7 | 3.2 | 3.0 | 3.2 | 2.5 | 2.6 | 2.7 | 2.8 | 2.7 | -5.0 |
| Suisse | 1.5 | 1.4 | 1.5 | 1.5 | 1.5 | 1.7 | 1.5 | 1.5 | 1.6 | 8.8 |
| Turquie | - | - | - | - | - | - | - | - | - | .. |
| Yougoslavie | 0.3 | 0.2 | 0.3 | 0.3 | 0.3 | 0.3 | 0.3 | 0.3 | 0.3 | -0.5 |

## ABATS COMESTIBLES / EDIBLE OFFALS [1]

| | 1980/82 moyenne | 1983 | 1984 | 1985 | 1986 | 1987 | 1988 | 1989 | 1990 | 1989/90 % var. |
|---|---|---|---|---|---|---|---|---|---|---|
| OCDE - Total | 4.4 | 4.5 | 4.5 | 4.4 | 4.4 | 4.4 e | 4.4 e | 4.2 e | 4.2 e | 1.6 |
| OCDE - Amérique du Nord | 3.9 | 3.9 | 3.9 | 3.8 | 3.7 | 3.7 | 3.7 | 3.6 | 3.5 e | -4.3 |
| Canada | 1.5 | 1.5 | 1.4 | 1.7 | 1.7 | 1.5 | 1.0 | 0.8 | 0.9 e | 3.1 |
| États-Unis | 4.2 | 4.1 | 4.1 | 4.0 | 3.9 | 3.9 | 4.0 | 3.9 | 3.8 e | -4.5 |
| Japon | 2.6 | 2.6 | 2.6 | 2.9 | 3.0 | 3.0 e | 3.0 e | 3.0 e | 2.9 e | -2.2 |
| OCDE - Océanie | 4.7 | 3.8 | 3.5 | 3.1 | 3.8 | 4.2 | 4.1 | 4.2 | 4.9 | 16.0 |
| Australie | 4.9 | 3.5 | 3.5 | 2.9 | 3.6 | 4.5 | 4.1 | 4.2 | 5.0 | 19.6 |
| Nouvelle Zélande | 4.1 | 5.0 | 3.1 | 4.3 | 4.9 | 2.7 | 3.9 | 4.5 | 4.4 | -1.1 |
| OCDE - Europe | 5.3 | 5.5 | 5.5 | 5.4 | 5.3 | 5.4 | 5.2 | 4.9 e | 5.1 e | 4.5 |
| CE-12 Total | 5.9 | 6.1 | 6.1 | 6.0 | 6.0 | 6.1 | 6.0 | 5.7 | 6.0 | 5.6 |
| Belgique / Luxembourg | 7.4 | 6.7 | 8.1 | 8.0 | 7.7 | 7.9 | 7.5 | 7.6 | 7.5 | -0.6 |
| Danemark | 7.2 | 6.8 | 6.5 | 7.0 | 8.0 | 8.6 | 8.2 | 8.6 | 8.8 | 2.1 |
| France | 11.1 | 11.0 | 11.0 | 10.4 | 10.4 | 10.6 | 10.5 | 9.5 | 10.2 | 8.1 |
| Allemagne | 5.6 | 5.8 | 5.8 | 5.6 | 5.6 | 5.5 | 5.3 | 5.0 | 5.7 | 12.4 |
| Grèce | 4.8 | 5.8 | 5.9 | 5.9 | 5.8 | 6.6 | 5.8 | 6.1 | 5.7 | -5.9 |
| Irlande | 16.1 | 16.5 | 11.6 | 11.3 | 5.1 | 8.2 | 10.7 | 6.8 | 12.8 | 88.1 |
| Italie | 3.5 | 3.7 | 3.7 | 3.8 | 3.8 | 3.8 | 3.7 | 3.8 | 3.8 | 0.2 |
| Pays-Bas | 3.6 | 2.7 | 2.4 | 2.6 | 3.6 | 3.9 | 2.4 | 1.8 | 2.0 | 10.4 |
| Portugal | 5.1 | 5.2 | 4.9 | 4.8 | 5.2 | 5.6 | 5.8 | 5.8 | 5.8 | -0.3 |
| Espagne | 3.9 | 5.8 | 5.8 | 5.9 | 6.0 | 6.5 | 6.6 | 6.5 | 6.9 | 5.7 |
| Royaume-Uni | 4.9 | 4.8 | 4.8 | 5.0 | 4.5 | 4.5 | 4.3 | 4.1 | 3.9 | -5.8 |
| Autre pays européens de l'OCDE | 2.9 | 2.9 | 2.9 | 2.8 | 2.6 | 2.4 | 2.3 | 2.0 e | 2.0 e | -4.1 |
| Autriche | 4.6 | 4.5 | 4.6 | 4.6 | 4.6 | 4.6 | 3.8 | 3.8 | 3.8 | -1.1 |
| Finlande | 8.0 | 7.6 | 7.6 | 7.5 | 7.5 | 7.5 | 7.3 | 2.6 | 2.6 | -0.4 |
| Norvège | 3.4 | 3.6 | 3.6 | 3.6 | 3.6 | 3.6 | 3.3 | 3.3 | 3.3 | -0.4 |
| Suède | 2.5 | 2.4 | 2.4 | 2.3 | 2.3 | 2.3 | 2.3 | 2.1 | 2.1 | -0.9 |
| Suisse | 3.4 | 3.1 | 3.2 | 3.1 | 3.3 | 2.6 | 3.1 | 3.4 | 3.1 | -9.7 |
| Turquie | 2.0 | 2.1 | 2.1 | 2.0 | 1.7 | 1.5 | 1.4 | 1.5 e | 1.4 e | -4.5 |
| Yougoslavie | 2.9 | 2.6 | 3.7 | 3.1 | 2.5 | 2.7 | 3.1 | 3.0 | 3.2 | 8.0 |

1. Poids de produit / Product weight                                                                     All totals exclude Yugoslavia / Tous les totaux excluent la Yougoslavie

# COUNTRY TABLES - TABLEAUX PAR PAYS

# CANADA

## BEEF / VIANDE DE BŒUF

*Thousand metric tons - Dressed carcass weight*

| | 1984 | 1985 | 1986 | 1987 | 1988 | 1989 | 1990 | 1989/90 % change |
|---|---|---|---|---|---|---|---|---|
| Number of animals slaughtered *(thousands)* | 3566.0 | 3603.0 | 3530.0 | 3263.0 | 3158.0 | 3196.0 | 3021.0 | -5.5 |
| Average dressed carcass weight *(kilogrammes)* | 266.0 | 273.0 | 280.0 | 286.0 | 294.0 | 291.0 | 291.0 | 0.0 |
| **Gross indigenous production** | **1018.0** | **1063.0** | **1035.0** | **978.0** | **1054.0** | **1059.0** | **1109.0** | **4.7** |
| *Minus:* Meat equivalent of exported live animals | 78.0 | 92.0 | 62.0 | 67.0 | 137.0 | 133.0 | 246.0 | 85.0 |
| *Plus:* Meat from slaughterings of imported live animals | 8.0 | 14.0 | 17.0 | 21.0 | 11.0 | 4.0 | 13.0 | 225.0 |
| **Total meat production from slaughtered animals** | **948.0** | **985.0** | **990.0** | **932.0** | **928.0** | **930.0** | **876.0** | **-5.8** |
| *Minus:* Exports of meat | 105.0 | 116.0 | 102.0 | 89.0 | 82.0 | 104.0 | 105.0 | 1.0 |
| *Plus:* Imports of meat | 115.0 | 115.0 | 110.0 | 134.0 | 153.0 | 158.0 | 185.0 | 17.1 |
| *Minus:* Stock variations | -2.0 | 2.0 | -4.0 | -2.0 | 5.0 | - | -3.0 | |
| **Meat consumption** | **960.0** | **982.0** | **1002.0** | **979.0** | **994.0** | **984.0** | **959.0** | **-2.5** |
| Consumption per head *(kilogrammes per year)* | 38.4 | 39.0 | 39.5 | 38.2 | 38.3 | 37.5 | 36.0 | -3.9 |

## VEAL / VIANDE DE VEAU

| | 1984 | 1985 | 1986 | 1987 | 1988 | 1989 | 1990 | 1989/90 % change |
|---|---|---|---|---|---|---|---|---|
| Number of animals slaughtered *(thousands)* | 652.0 | 632.0 | 620.0 | 565.0 | 546.0 | 578.0 | 578.0 | 0.0 |
| Average dressed carcass weight *(kilogrammes)* | 64.0 | 69.0 | 73.0 | 83.0 | 82.0 | 83.0 | 83.0 | 0.0 |
| **Gross indigenous production** | **48.0** | **47.0** | **46.0** | **49.0** | **49.0** | **52.0** | **53.0** | **1.9** |
| *Minus:* Meat equivalent of exported live animals | 7.0 | 3.0 | 2.0 | 3.0 | 4.0 | 4.0 | 5.0 | 25.0 |
| *Plus:* Meat from slaughterings of imported live animals | 1.0 | - | 1.0 | 1.0 | - | - | - | .. |
| **Total meat production from slaughtered animals** | **42.0** | **44.0** | **45.0** | **47.0** | **45.0** | **48.0** | **48.0** | **0.0** |
| *Minus:* Exports of meat | 1.0 | 1.0 | 2.0 | 4.0 | 4.0 | 5.0 | 5.0 | 0.0 |
| *Plus:* Imports of meat | 1.0 | 1.0 | 2.0 | 1.0 | - | - | 5.0 | .. |
| *Minus:* Stock variations | - | - | - | - | 1.0 | -1.0 | - | |
| **Meat consumption** | **42.0** | **44.0** | **45.0** | **44.0** | **40.0** | **44.0** | **48.0** | **9.1** |
| Consumption per head *(kilogrammes per year)* | 1.7 | 1.7 | 1.8 | 1.7 | 1.5 | 1.7 | 1.8 | 7.6 |

## BEEF AND VEAL / TOTAL VIANDE BOVINE

| | 1984 | 1985 | 1986 | 1987 | 1988 | 1989 | 1990 | 1989/90 % change |
|---|---|---|---|---|---|---|---|---|
| Number of animals slaughtered *(thousands)* | 4218.0 | 4235.0 | 4150.0 | 3828.0 | 3704.0 | 3774.0 | 3599.0 | -4.6 |
| Average dressed carcass weight *(kilogrammes)* | 234.7 | 243.0 | 249.4 | 255.7 | 262.7 | 259.1 | 256.7 | -0.9 |
| **Gross indigenous production** | **1066.0** | **1110.0** | **1081.0** | **1027.0** | **1103.0** | **1111.0** | **1162.0** | **4.6** |
| *Minus:* Meat equivalent of exported live animals | 85.0 | 95.0 | 64.0 | 70.0 | 141.0 | 137.0 | 251.0 | 83.2 |
| *Plus:* Meat from slaughterings of imported live animals | 9.0 | 14.0 | 18.0 | 22.0 | 11.0 | 4.0 | 13.0 | 225.0 |
| **Total meat production from slaughtered animals** | **990.0** | **1029.0** | **1035.0** | **979.0** | **973.0** | **978.0** | **924.0** | **-5.5** |
| *Minus:* Exports of meat | 106.0 | 117.0 | 104.0 | 93.0 | 86.0 | 109.0 | 110.0 | 0.9 |
| *Plus:* Imports of meat | 116.0 | 116.0 | 112.0 | 135.0 | 153.0 | 158.0 | 190.0 | 20.3 |
| *Minus:* Stock variations | -2.0 | 2.0 | -4.0 | -2.0 | 6.0 | -1.0 | -3.0 | |
| **Meat consumption** | **1002.0** | **1026.0** | **1047.0** | **1023.0** | **1034.0** | **1028.0** | **1007.0** | **-2.0** |
| Consumption per head *(kilogrammes per year)* | 40.1 | 40.7 | 41.3 | 39.9 | 39.9 | 39.2 | 37.8 | -3.4 |

# CANADA

*Milliers de tonnes métriques - Poids en carcasse parée*

## *VIANDE DE PORC / PIG MEAT*

| | 1984 | 1985 | 1986 | 1987 | 1988 | 1989 | 1990 | 1989/90 % var. |
|---|---|---|---|---|---|---|---|---|
| Nombre d'animaux abattus *(milliers)* | 13886.0 | 14452.0 | 14444.0 | 14854.0 | 15553.0 | 15579.0 | 14908.0 | -4.3 |
| Poids moyen en carcasse parée *(kilogrammes)* | 75.0 | 75.0 | 76.0 | 76.0 | 77.0 | 76.0 | 76.0 | 0.0 |
| **Production indigène brute** | **1145.0** | **1175.0** | **1136.0** | **1163.0** | **1256.0** | **1260.0** | **1198.0** | -4.9 |
| *Moins:* Équivalent en viande des animaux exportés vivants | 101.0 | 87.0 | 38.0 | 33.0 | 66.0 | 77.0 | 66.0 | -14.3 |
| *Plus:* Viande provenant des abbattages d'animaux importés vivants | - | - | - | - | - | 1.0 | 1.0 | 0.0 |
| **Production totale de viande provenant des abattages** | **1044.0** | **1088.0** | **1098.0** | **1130.0** | **1190.0** | **1184.0** | **1133.0** | -4.3 |
| *Moins:* Exportations de viande | 224.0 | 251.0 | 272.0 | 301.0 | 319.0 | 285.0 | 297.0 | 4.2 |
| *Plus:* Importations de viande | 18.0 | 21.0 | 18.0 | 22.0 | 14.0 | 12.0 | 12.0 | 0.0 |
| *Moins:* Variations des stocks | 1.0 | -2.0 | -1.0 | - | -4.0 | - | - | |
| **Consommation de viande** | **837.0** | **860.0** | **845.0** | **851.0** | **889.0** | **911.0** | **848.0** | -6.9 |
| Consommation par tête *(kilogrammes par an)* | 33.5 | 34.2 | 33.3 | 33.2 | 34.3 | 34.7 | 31.9 | -8.2 |

## *VIANDE DE VOLAILLE / POULTRY MEAT*

| | 1984 | 1985 | 1986 | 1987 | 1988 | 1989 | 1990 | 1989/90 % var. |
|---|---|---|---|---|---|---|---|---|
| Nombre d'animaux abattus *(milliers)* | | | | | | | | |
| Poids moyen en carcasse parée *(kilogrammes)* | | | | | | | | |
| **Production indigène brute** | **558.0** | **608.0** | **628.0** | **683.0** | **685.0** | **686.0** | **685.0** ᵉ | -0.1 |
| *Moins:* Équivalent en viande des animaux exportés vivants | - | - | - | - | - | - | - | .. |
| *Plus:* Viande provenant des abbattages d'animaux importés vivants | - | - | - | - | - | - | - | .. |
| **Production totale de viande provenant des abattages** | **558.0** | **608.0** | **628.0** | **683.0** | **685.0** | **686.0** | **685.0** ᵉ | -0.1 |
| *Moins:* Exportations de viande | 2.0 | 5.0 | 2.0 | 6.0 | 6.0 | 7.0 | 6.0 ᵉ | -14.3 |
| *Plus:* Importations de viande | 45.0 | 34.0 | 28.0 | 45.0 | 47.0 | 42.0 | 45.0 ᵉ | 7.1 |
| *Moins:* Variations des stocks | 5.0 | 1.0 | -2.0 | 13.0 | -10.0 | 6.0 | 3.0 ᵉ | |
| **Consommation de viande** | **596.0** | **636.0** | **656.0** | **709.0** | **736.0** | **715.0** | **721.0** ᵉ | 0.8 |
| Consommation par tête *(kilogrammes par an)* | 23.8 | 25.3 | 25.9 | 27.6 | 28.4 | 27.2 | 27.1 ᵉ | -0.5 |

## *VIANDE DE MOUTON ET DE CHÈVRE / MUTTON, LAMB AND GOAT MEAT*

| | 1984 | 1985 | 1986 | 1987 | 1988 | 1989 | 1990 | 1989/90 % var. |
|---|---|---|---|---|---|---|---|---|
| Nombre d'animaux abattus *(milliers)* | 467.0 | 419.0 | 397.0 | 382.0 | 390.0 | 442.0 | 435.0 | -1.6 |
| Poids moyen en carcasse parée *(kilogrammes)* | 19.0 | 19.0 | 20.0 | 21.0 | 21.0 | 19.0 | 20.0 | 5.3 |
| **Production indigène brute** | **8.0** | **7.0** | **7.0** | **7.0** | **8.0** | **8.0** | **9.0** | 12.5 |
| *Moins:* Équivalent en viande des animaux exportés vivants | - | - | - | - | 1.0 | 1.0 | 1.0 | 0.0 |
| *Plus:* Viande provenant des abbattages d'animaux importés vivants | 1.0 | 1.0 | 1.0 | 1.0 | 1.0 | 1.0 | 1.0 | 0.0 |
| **Production totale de viande provenant des abattages** | **9.0** | **8.0** | **8.0** | **8.0** | **8.0** | **8.0** | **9.0** | 12.5 |
| *Moins:* Exportations de viande | - | - | - | - | - | - | - | .. |
| *Plus:* Importations de viande | 10.0 | 12.0 | 16.0 | 15.0 | 14.0 | 12.0 | 12.0 | 0.0 |
| *Moins:* Variations des stocks | -3.0 | 1.0 | 1.0 | -1.0 | - | - | - | |
| **Consommation de viande** | **22.0** | **19.0** | **23.0** | **24.0** | **22.0** | **20.0** | **21.0** | 5.0 |
| Consommation par tête *(kilogrammes par an)* | 0.9 | 0.8 | 0.9 | 0.9 | 0.8 | 0.8 | 0.8 | 3.6 |

# CANADA

*Thousand metric tons - Dressed carcass weight*

| | 1984 | 1985 | 1986 | 1987 | 1988 | 1989 | 1990 | 1989/90 % change |
|---|---|---|---|---|---|---|---|---|
| Number of animals slaughtered *(thousands)* | - | - | - | - | - | - | - | .. |
| Average dressed carcass weight *(kilogrammes)* | - | - | - | - | - | - | - | .. |
| Gross indigenous production | • | • | • | • | • | • | • | .. |
| *Minus:* Meat equivalent of exported live animals | - | - | - | - | - | - | - | .. |
| *Plus:* Meat from slaughterings of imported live animals | - | - | - | - | - | - | - | .. |
| Total meat production from slaughtered animals | • | • | • | • | • | • | • | .. |
| *Minus:* Exports of meat | - | - | - | - | - | - | - | .. |
| *Plus:* Imports of meat | - | - | - | - | - | - | - | .. |
| *Minus:* Stock variations | - | - | - | - | - | - | - | |
| Meat consumption | • | • | • | • | • | • | • | .. |
| Consumption per head *(kilogrammes per year)* | - | - | - | - | - | - | - | .. |

## OTHER MEAT / AUTRES VIANDES

| | 1984 | 1985 | 1986 | 1987 | 1988 | 1989 | 1990 | 1989/90 % change |
|---|---|---|---|---|---|---|---|---|
| Number of animals slaughtered *(thousands)* | | | | | | | | |
| Average dressed carcass weight *(kilogrammes)* | | | | | | | | |
| Gross indigenous production | • | • | • | • | • | • | • | .. |
| *Minus:* Meat equivalent of exported live animals | - | - | - | - | - | - | - | .. |
| *Plus:* Meat from slaughterings of imported live animals | - | - | - | - | - | - | - | .. |
| Total meat production from slaughtered animals | • | • | • | • | • | • | • | .. |
| *Minus:* Exports of meat | - | - | - | - | - | - | - | .. |
| *Plus:* Imports of meat | - | - | - | - | - | - | - | .. |
| *Minus:* Stock variations | - | - | - | - | - | - | - | |
| Meat consumption | • | • | • | • | • | • | • | .. |
| Consumption per head *(kilogrammes per year)* | - | - | - | - | - | - | - | .. |

## EDIBLE OFFALS / ABATS COMESTIBLES

| | 1984 | 1985 | 1986 | 1987 | 1988 | 1989 | 1990 | 1989/90 % change |
|---|---|---|---|---|---|---|---|---|
| Number of animals slaughtered *(thousands)* | | | | | | | | |
| Average dressed carcass weight *(kilogrammes)* | | | | | | | | |
| Gross indigenous production | 77.0 | 76.0 | 72.0 | 68.0 | 72.0 | 74.0 | 68.0 e | -8.1 |
| *Minus:* Meat equivalent of exported live animals | 11.0 | 9.0 | 5.0 | 3.0 | 6.0 | 7.0 | 5.0 e | -28.6 |
| *Plus:* Meat from slaughterings of imported live animals | 1.0 | 1.0 | 1.0 | 1.0 | - | - | - | .. |
| Total meat production from slaughtered animals | 67.0 | 68.0 | 68.0 | 66.0 | 66.0 | 67.0 | 63.0 | -6.0 |
| *Minus:* Exports of meat | 38.0 | 34.0 | 38.0 | 39.0 | 55.0 | 60.0 | 55.0 e | -8.3 |
| *Plus:* Imports of meat | 7.0 | 10.0 | 12.0 | 13.0 | 13.0 | 14.0 | 16.0 | 14.3 |
| *Minus:* Stock variations | - | 2.0 | -2.0 | 2.0 | -1.0 | -1.0 | 1.0 | |
| Meat consumption | 36.0 | 42.0 | 44.0 | 38.0 | 25.0 | 22.0 | 23.0 e | 4.5 |
| Consumption per head *(kilogrammes per year)* | 1.4 | 1.7 | 1.7 | 1.5 | 1.0 | 0.8 | 0.9 e | 3.1 |

# CANADA

*Milliers de tonnes métriques - Poids en carcasse parée*

## TOTAL VIANDE / TOTAL MEAT

| | 1984 | 1985 | 1986 | 1987 | 1988 | 1989 | 1990 | 1989/90 % var. |
|---|---|---|---|---|---|---|---|---|
| **Nombre d'animaux abattus** *(milliers)* | | | | | | | | |
| **Poids moyen en carcasse parée** *(kilogrammes)* | | | | | | | | |
| **Production indigène brute** | 2854.0 | 2976.0 | 2924.0 | 2948.0 | 3124.0 | 3139.0 | 3122.0 ᵉ | -0.5 |
| *Moins:* Équivalent en viande des animaux exportés vivants | 197.0 | 191.0 | 107.0 | 106.0 | 214.0 | 222.0 | 323.0 ᵉ | 45.5 |
| *Plus:* Viande provenant des abbattages d'animaux importés vivants | 11.0 | 16.0 | 20.0 | 24.0 | 12.0 | 6.0 | 15.0 | 150.0 |
| **Production totale de viande provenant des abattages** | 2668.0 | 2801.0 | 2837.0 | 2866.0 | 2922.0 | 2923.0 | 2814.0 ᵉ | -3.7 |
| *Moins:* Exportations de viande | 370.0 | 407.0 | 416.0 | 439.0 | 466.0 | 461.0 | 468.0 ᵉ | 1.5 |
| *Plus:* Importations de viande | 196.0 | 193.0 | 186.0 | 230.0 | 241.0 | 238.0 | 270.0 ᵉ | 13.4 |
| *Moins:* Variations des stocks | 1.0 | 4.0 | -8.0 | 12.0 | -9.0 | 4.0 | 1.0 ᵉ | |
| **Consommation de viande** | 2493.0 | 2583.0 | 2615.0 | 2645.0 | 2706.0 | 2696.0 | 2615.0 ᵉ | -3.0 |
| **Consommation par tête** *(kilogrammes par an)* | 99.7 | 102.6 | 103.1 | 103.1 | 104.3 | 102.7 | 98.2 ᵉ | -4.3 |

## PRODUCTION INDIGENE BRUTE DE VIANDE
## MEAT GROSS INDIGENOUS PRODUCTION

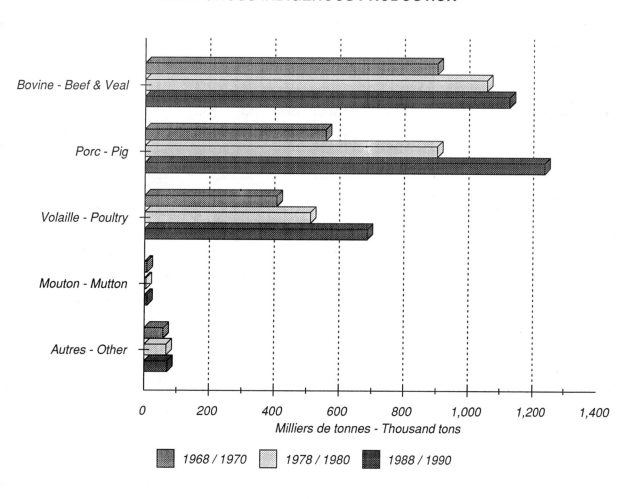

Milliers de tonnes - Thousand tons

■ 1968 / 1970   □ 1978 / 1980   ■ 1988 / 1990

# UNITED STATES

## BEEF / VIANDE DE BŒUF

*Thousand metric tons - Dressed carcass weight*

| | 1984 | 1985 | 1986 | 1987 | 1988 | 1989 | 1990 | 1989/90 % change |
|---|---|---|---|---|---|---|---|---|
| Number of animals slaughtered *(thousands)* | 37582.0 | 36293.0 | 37288.0 | 35647.0 | 35079.0 | 33916.0 | 33439.0 | -1.4 |
| Average dressed carcass weight *(kilogrammes)* | 285.0 | 297.0 | 297.0 | 300.0 | 305.0 | 316.0 | 309.0 | -2.2 |
| Gross indigenous production | 10592.0 | 10657.0 | 10860.0 | 10532.0 | 10568.0 | 10273.0 | 9986.0 | -2.8 |
| *Minus:* Meat equivalent of exported live animals | 27.0 | 42.0 | 36.0 | 43.0 | 102.0 | 51.0 | 36.0 | -29.4 |
| *Plus:* Meat from slaughterings of imported live animals | 139.0 | 148.0 | 231.0 | 200.0 | 234.0 | 250.0 | 366.0 | 46.4 |
| Total meat production from slaughtered animals | 10704.0 | 10763.0 | 11055.0 | 10689.0 | 10700.0 | 10472.0 | 10316.0 | -1.5 |
| *Minus:* Exports of meat | 147.0 | 147.0 | 234.0 | 273.0 | 308.0 | 464.0 | 456.0 | -1.7 |
| *Plus:* Imports of meat | 827.0 | 939.0 | 966.0 | 1029.0 | 1079.0 | 988.0 | 1069.0 | 8.2 |
| *Minus:* Stock variations | 20.0 | -24.0 | -4.0 | -12.0 | 16.0 | -40.0 | 28.0 | |
| Meat consumption | 11364.0 | 11579.0 | 11791.0 | 11457.0 | 11455.0 | 11036.0 | 10901.0 | -1.2 |
| Consumption per head *(kilogrammes per year)* | 47.9 | 48.4 | 48.8 | 47.0 | 46.5 | 44.4 | 43.4 | -2.3 |

## VEAL / VIANDE DE VEAU

| | 1984 | 1985 | 1986 | 1987 | 1988 | 1989 | 1990 | 1989/90 % change |
|---|---|---|---|---|---|---|---|---|
| Number of animals slaughtered *(thousands)* | 3293.0 | 3385.0 | 3408.0 | 2815.0 | 2506.0 | 2172.0 | 1838.0 | -15.4 |
| Average dressed carcass weight *(kilogrammes)* | 65.0 | 67.0 | 68.0 | 67.0 | 72.0 | 74.0 | 81.0 | 9.5 |
| Gross indigenous production | 225.0 | 234.0 | 231.0 | 189.0 | 180.0 | 161.0 | 148.0 | -8.1 |
| *Minus:* Meat equivalent of exported live animals | - | - | - | - | - | - | - | .. |
| *Plus:* Meat from slaughterings of imported live animals | - | - | - | - | - | - | - | .. |
| Total meat production from slaughtered animals | 225.0 | 234.0 | 231.0 | 189.0 | 180.0 | 161.0 | 148.0 | -8.1 |
| *Minus:* Exports of meat | 3.0 | 2.0 | 2.0 | 3.0 | 5.0 | 4.0 [e] | 4.0 [e] | 0.0 |
| *Plus:* Imports of meat | 11.0 | 9.0 | 12.0 | 11.0 | 12.0 | 11.0 [e] | 11.0 [e] | 0.0 |
| *Minus:* Stock variations | 2.0 | -1.0 | -2.0 | -1.0 | - | - | 1.0 | |
| Meat consumption | 231.0 | 242.0 | 243.0 | 198.0 | 187.0 | 168.0 [e] | 154.0 [e] | -8.3 |
| Consumption per head *(kilogrammes per year)* | 1.0 | 1.0 | 1.0 | 0.8 | 0.8 | 0.7 [e] | 0.6 [e] | -9.3 |

## BEEF AND VEAL / TOTAL VIANDE BOVINE

| | 1984 | 1985 | 1986 | 1987 | 1988 | 1989 | 1990 | 1989/90 % change |
|---|---|---|---|---|---|---|---|---|
| Number of animals slaughtered *(thousands)* | 40875.0 | 39678.0 | 40696.0 | 38462.0 | 37585.0 | 36088.0 | 35277.0 | -2.2 |
| Average dressed carcass weight *(kilogrammes)* | 267.4 | 277.2 | 277.3 | 282.8 | 289.5 | 294.6 | 296.6 | 0.7 |
| Gross indigenous production | 10817.0 | 10891.0 | 11091.0 | 10721.0 | 10748.0 | 10434.0 | 10134.0 | -2.9 |
| *Minus:* Meat equivalent of exported live animals | 27.0 | 42.0 | 36.0 | 43.0 | 102.0 | 51.0 | 36.0 | -29.4 |
| *Plus:* Meat from slaughterings of imported live animals | 139.0 | 148.0 | 231.0 | 200.0 | 234.0 | 250.0 | 366.0 | 46.4 |
| Total meat production from slaughtered animals | 10929.0 | 10997.0 | 11286.0 | 10878.0 | 10880.0 | 10633.0 | 10464.0 | -1.6 |
| *Minus:* Exports of meat | 150.0 | 149.0 | 236.0 | 276.0 | 313.0 | 468.0 [e] | 460.0 [e] | -1.7 |
| *Plus:* Imports of meat | 838.0 | 948.0 | 978.0 | 1040.0 | 1091.0 | 999.0 [e] | 1080.0 [e] | 8.1 |
| *Minus:* Stock variations | 22.0 | -25.0 | -6.0 | -13.0 | 16.0 | -40.0 | 29.0 | |
| Meat consumption | 11595.0 | 11821.0 | 12034.0 | 11655.0 | 11642.0 | 11204.0 [e] | 11055.0 [e] | -1.3 |
| Consumption per head *(kilogrammes per year)* | 48.9 | 49.4 | 49.8 | 47.8 | 47.3 | 45.0 [e] | 44.0 [e] | -2.4 |

# ÉTATS UNIS

*Milliers de tonnes métriques - Poids en carcasse parée*

## VIANDE DE PORC / PIG MEAT

| | 1984 | 1985 | 1986 | 1987 | 1988 | 1989 | 1990 | 1989/90 % var. |
|---|---|---|---|---|---|---|---|---|
| Nombre d'animaux abattus *(milliers)* | 85168.0 | 84292.0 | 79598.0 | 81081.0 | 87795.0 | 88693.0 | 85431.0 | -3.7 |
| Poids moyen en carcasse parée *(kilogrammes)* | 78.0 | 79.0 | 80.0 | 80.0 | 81.0 | 81.0 | 82.0 | 1.2 |
| Production indigène brute | 6619.0 | 6623.0 | 6342.0 | 6487.0 | 7056.0 | 7099.0 | 6916.0 | -2.6 |
| *Moins:* Équivalent en viande des animaux exportés vivants | 1.0 | 1.0 | 1.0 | 1.0 | 8.0 | 8.0 | 20.0 | 150.0 |
| *Plus:* Viande provenant des abbattages d'animaux importés vivants | 101.0 | 94.0 | 38.0 | 34.0 | 65.0 | 82.0 | 69.0 | -15.9 |
| Production totale de viande provenant des abattages | 6719.0 | 6716.0 | 6379.0 | 6520.0 | 7113.0 | 7173.0 | 6965.0 | -2.9 |
| *Moins:* Exportations de viande | 74.0 | 58.0 | 39.0 | 50.0 | 89.0 | 119.0 | 108.0 | -9.2 |
| *Plus:* Importations de viande | 433.0 | 512.0 | 509.0 | 542.0 | 516.0 | 406.0 | 407.0 | 0.2 |
| *Moins:* Variations des stocks | -13.0 | -27.0 | -16.0 | 48.0 | 35.0 | -57.0 | -8.0 | |
| Consommation de viande | 7091.0 | 7197.0 | 6865.0 | 6964.0 | 7505.0 | 7517.0 | 7272.0 | -3.3 |
| Consommation par tête *(kilogrammes par an)* | 29.9 | 30.1 | 28.4 | 28.5 | 30.5 | 30.2 | 28.9 | -4.3 |

## VIANDE DE VOLAILLE / POULTRY MEAT

| | 1984 | 1985 | 1986 | 1987 | 1988 | 1989 | 1990 | 1989/90 % var. |
|---|---|---|---|---|---|---|---|---|
| Nombre d'animaux abattus *(milliers)* | | | | | | | | |
| Poids moyen en carcasse parée *(kilogrammes)* | | | | | | | | |
| Production indigène brute | 7427.0 | 7865.0 | 8263.0 | 9100.0 | 9426.0 | 10105.0 | 10878.0 | 7.6 |
| *Moins:* Équivalent en viande des animaux exportés vivants | - | - | - | - | - | - | - | .. |
| *Plus:* Viande provenant des abbattages d'animaux importés vivants | - | - | - | - | - | - | - | .. |
| Production totale de viande provenant des abattages | 7427.0 | 7865.0 | 8263.0 | 9100.0 | 9426.0 | 10105.0 | 10878.0 | 7.6 |
| *Moins:* Exportations de viande | 209.0 | 211.0 | 276.0 | 363.0 | 382.0 | 398.0 | 554.0 | 39.2 |
| *Plus:* Importations de viande | - | - | - | - | - | - | - | .. |
| *Moins:* Variations des stocks | -8.0 | 23.0 | 13.0 | 16.0 | -59.0 | -12.0 | 5.0 | |
| Consommation de viande | 7226.0 | 7631.0 | 7974.0 | 8721.0 | 9103.0 | 9719.0 | 10319.0 | 6.2 |
| Consommation par tête *(kilogrammes par an)* | 30.5 | 31.9 | 33.0 | 35.8 | 37.0 | 39.1 | 41.0 | 5.1 |

## VIANDE DE MOUTON ET DE CHÈVRE / MUTTON, LAMB AND GOAT MEAT

| | 1984 | 1985 | 1986 | 1987 | 1988 | 1989 | 1990 | 1989/90 % var. |
|---|---|---|---|---|---|---|---|---|
| Nombre d'animaux abattus *(milliers)* | 6758.0 | 6078.0 | 5635.0 | 5200.0 | 5293.0 | 5464.0 | 5750.0 | 5.2 |
| Poids moyen en carcasse parée *(kilogrammes)* | 24.0 | 26.0 | 27.0 | 26.0 | 28.0 | 28.0 | 29.0 | 3.6 |
| Production indigène brute | 172.0 | 163.0 | 153.0 | 143.0 | 152.0 | 157.0 | 165.0 | 5.1 |
| *Moins:* Équivalent en viande des animaux exportés vivants | - | - | - | - | - | - | - | .. |
| *Plus:* Viande provenant des abbattages d'animaux importés vivants | - | - | - | - | - | - | - | .. |
| Production totale de viande provenant des abattages | 172.0 | 163.0 | 153.0 | 143.0 | 152.0 | 157.0 | 165.0 | 5.1 |
| *Moins:* Exportations de viande | 1.0 | 1.0 | 1.0 | 1.0 | 1.0 | 1.0 | 1.0 | 0.0 |
| *Plus:* Importations de viande | 9.0 | 17.0 | 19.0 | 20.0 | 23.0 | 29.0 | 27.0 | -6.9 |
| *Moins:* Variations des stocks | -4.0 | 3.0 | - | -2.0 | -1.0 | 1.0 | - | |
| Consommation de viande | 184.0 | 176.0 | 171.0 | 164.0 | 175.0 | 184.0 | 191.0 | 3.8 |
| Consommation par tête *(kilogrammes par an)* | 0.8 | 0.7 | 0.7 | 0.7 | 0.7 | 0.7 | 0.8 | 2.7 |

# UNITED STATES

## HORSE MEAT / VIANDE D'ÉQUIDÉS

| | 1984 | 1985 | 1986 | 1987 | 1988 | 1989 | 1990 | 1989/90 % change |
|---|---|---|---|---|---|---|---|---|
| Number of animals slaughtered *(thousands)* | - | - | - | - | - | - | - | .. |
| Average dressed carcass weight *(kilogrammes)* | - | - | - | - | - | - | - | .. |
| Gross indigenous production | . | . | . | . | . | . | . | .. |
| *Minus:* Meat equivalent of exported live animals | - | - | - | - | - | - | - | .. |
| *Plus:* Meat from slaughterings of imported live animals | - | - | - | - | - | - | - | .. |
| Total meat production from slaughtered animals | . | . | . | . | . | . | . | .. |
| *Minus:* Exports of meat | - | - | - | - | - | - | - | .. |
| *Plus:* Imports of meat | - | - | - | - | - | - | - | .. |
| *Minus:* Stock variations | - | - | - | - | - | - | - | |
| Meat consumption | . | . | . | . | . | . | . | .. |
| Consumption per head *(kilogrammes per year)* | - | - | - | - | - | - | - | .. |

## OTHER MEAT / AUTRES VIANDES

| | 1984 | 1985 | 1986 | 1987 | 1988 | 1989 | 1990 | 1989/90 % change |
|---|---|---|---|---|---|---|---|---|
| Number of animals slaughtered *(thousands)* | | | | | | | | |
| Average dressed carcass weight *(kilogrammes)* | | | | | | | | |
| Gross indigenous production | 240.0 ᵉ | 243.0 ᵉ | 244.0 ᵉ | 250.0 ᵉ | 250.0 ᵉ | 250.0 ᵉ | 250.0 ᵉ | 0.0 |
| *Minus:* Meat equivalent of exported live animals | - | - | - | - | - | - | - | .. |
| *Plus:* Meat from slaughterings of imported live animals | - | - | - | - | - | - | - | .. |
| Total meat production from slaughtered animals | 240.0 ᵉ | 243.0 ᵉ | 244.0 ᵉ | 250.0 ᵉ | 250.0 ᵉ | 250.0 ᵉ | 250.0 ᵉ | 0.0 |
| *Minus:* Exports of meat | - | - | - | - | - | - | - | .. |
| *Plus:* Imports of meat | - | - | - | - | - | - | - | .. |
| *Minus:* Stock variations | - | - | - | - | - | - | - | |
| Meat consumption | 240.0 ᵉ | 243.0 ᵉ | 244.0 ᵉ | 250.0 ᵉ | 250.0 ᵉ | 250.0 ᵉ | 250.0 ᵉ | 0.0 |
| Consumption per head *(kilogrammes per year)* | 1.0 ᵉ | 1.0 ᵉ | 1.0 ᵉ | 1.0 ᵉ | 1.0 ᵉ | 1.0 ᵉ | 1.0 ᵉ | -1.0 |

## EDIBLE OFFALS / ABATS COMESTIBLES

| | 1984 | 1985 | 1986 | 1987 | 1988 | 1989 | 1990 | 1989/90 % change |
|---|---|---|---|---|---|---|---|---|
| Number of animals slaughtered *(thousands)* | | | | | | | | |
| Average dressed carcass weight *(kilogrammes)* | | | | | | | | |
| Gross indigenous production | 1186.0 | 1191.0 | 1185.0 | 1168.0 | 1208.0 | 1189.0 | 1157.0 | -2.7 |
| *Minus:* Meat equivalent of exported live animals | 1.0 | 2.0 | 2.0 | 2.0 | 5.0 | 2.0 | 2.0 ᵉ | 0.0 |
| *Plus:* Meat from slaughterings of imported live animals | 15.0 | 17.0 | 17.0 | 14.0 | 21.0 | 23.0 | 21.0 ᵉ | -8.7 |
| Total meat production from slaughtered animals | 1200.0 | 1206.0 | 1200.0 | 1180.0 | 1224.0 | 1210.0 | 1176.0 ᵉ | -2.8 |
| *Minus:* Exports of meat | 232.0 | 250.0 | 252.0 | 232.0 | 240.0 | 240.0 | 239.0 ᵉ | -0.4 |
| *Plus:* Imports of meat | 6.0 | 6.0 | 6.0 | 10.0 | 6.0 | 7.0 | 6.0 ᵉ | -14.3 |
| *Minus:* Stock variations | - | - | - | - | - | - | - | |
| Meat consumption | 974.0 | 962.0 | 954.0 | 958.0 | 990.0 | 977.0 | 943.0 ᵉ | -3.5 |
| Consumption per head *(kilogrammes per year)* | 4.1 | 4.0 | 3.9 | 3.9 | 4.0 | 3.9 | 3.8 ᵉ | -4.5 |

# ÉTATS UNIS

*Milliers de tonnes métriques - Poids en carcasse parée*

| | 1984 | 1985 | 1986 | 1987 | 1988 | 1989 | 1990 | 1989/90 % var. |
|---|---|---|---|---|---|---|---|---|
| **Nombre d'animaux abattus** *(milliers)* | | | | | | | | |
| **Poids moyen en carcasse parée** *(kilogrammes)* | | | | | | | | |
| **Production indigène brute** | 26461.0 | 26976.0 | 27278.0 | 27869.0 | 28840.0 | 29234.0 | 29500.0 | 0.9 |
| *Moins:* Équivalent en viande des animaux exportés vivants | 29.0 | 45.0 | 39.0 | 46.0 | 115.0 | 61.0 | 58.0 ᵉ | -4.9 |
| *Plus:* Viande provenant des abbattages d'animaux importés vivants | 255.0 | 259.0 | 286.0 | 248.0 | 320.0 | 355.0 | 456.0 ᵉ | 28.5 |
| **Production totale de viande provenant des abattages** | 26687.0 | 27190.0 | 27525.0 | 28071.0 | 29045.0 | 29528.0 | 29898.0 ᵉ | 1.3 |
| *Moins:* Exportations de viande | 666.0 | 669.0 | 804.0 | 922.0 | 1025.0 | 1226.0 ᵉ | 1362.0 ᵉ | 11.1 |
| *Plus:* Importations de viande | 1286.0 | 1483.0 | 1512.0 | 1612.0 | 1636.0 | 1441.0 ᵉ | 1520.0 ᵉ | 5.5 |
| *Moins:* Variations des stocks | -3.0 | -26.0 | -9.0 | 49.0 | -9.0 | -108.0 | 26.0 | |
| **Consommation de viande** | 27310.0 | 28030.0 | 28242.0 | 28712.0 | 29665.0 | 29851.0 ᵉ | 30030.0 ᵉ | 0.6 |
| **Consommation par tête** *(kilogrammes par an)* | 115.2 | 117.1 | 116.9 | 117.7 | 120.4 | 120.0 ᵉ | 119.5 ᵉ | -0.5 |

## PRODUCTION INDIGENE BRUTE DE VIANDE
## MEAT GROSS INDIGENOUS PRODUCTION

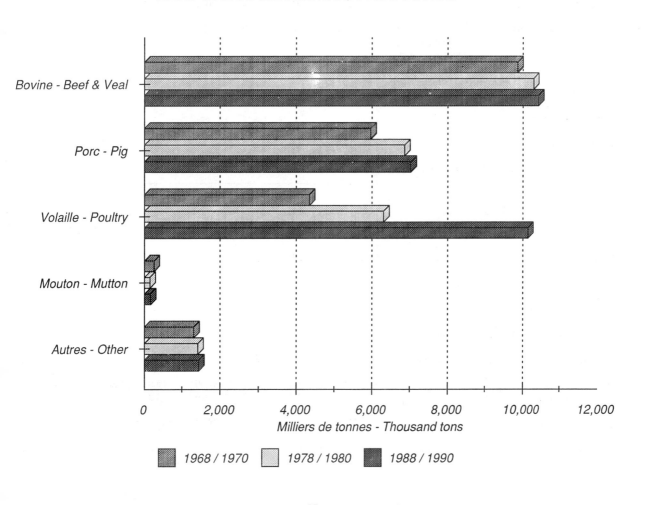

# JAPAN

## BEEF / VIANDE DE BŒUF

| | 1984 | 1985 | 1986 | 1987 | 1988 | 1989 | 1990 | 1989/90 % change |
|---|---|---|---|---|---|---|---|---|
| Number of animals slaughtered *(thousands)* | 1493.0 | 1536.0 | 1524.0 | 1485.0 | 1442.0 | 1376.0 | 1434.0 [e] | 4.2 |
| Average dressed carcass weight *(kilogrammes)* | 360.0 | 361.0 | 368.0 | 382.0 | 394.0 | 391.0 | 386.0 [e] | -1.3 |
| Gross indigenous production | 537.0 | 554.0 | 561.0 | 567.0 | 568.0 | 538.0 | 553.0 | 2.8 |
| *Minus:* Meat equivalent of exported live animals | - | - | - | - | - | - | - | .. |
| *Plus:* Meat from slaughterings of imported live animals | - | - | - | - | - | - | - | .. |
| Total meat production from slaughtered animals | 537.0 | 554.0 | 561.0 | 567.0 | 568.0 | 538.0 | 553.0 | 2.8 |
| *Minus:* Exports of meat | - | - | - | - | - | - | - | .. |
| *Plus:* Imports of meat | 213.0 | 225.0 | 268.0 | 319.0 | 408.0 | 520.0 | 549.0 | 5.6 |
| *Minus:* Stock variations | - | 7.0 | 14.0 | -6.0 | 4.0 | 63.0 | 9.0 | |
| Meat consumption | 750.0 | 772.0 | 815.0 | 892.0 | 972.0 | 995.0 | 1093.0 | 9.8 |
| Consumption per head *(kilogrammes per year)* | 6.2 | 6.4 | 6.7 | 7.3 | 7.9 | 8.1 | 8.8 | 9.5 |

## VEAL / VIANDE DE VEAU

| | 1984 | 1985 | 1986 | 1987 | 1988 | 1989 | 1990 | 1989/90 % change |
|---|---|---|---|---|---|---|---|---|
| Number of animals slaughtered *(thousands)* | 44.0 | 39.0 | 30.0 | 22.0 | 18.0 | 16.0 | 19.0 [e] | 18.8 |
| Average dressed carcass weight *(kilogrammes)* | 40.0 [e] | 40.0 [e] | 40.0 [e] | 40.0 [e] | 40.0 [e] | 40.0 [e] | 40.0 [e] | 0.0 |
| Gross indigenous production | 2.0 | 2.0 | 2.0 | 1.0 | 1.0 | 1.0 | 1.0 | 0.0 |
| *Minus:* Meat equivalent of exported live animals | - | - | - | - | - | - | - | .. |
| *Plus:* Meat from slaughterings of imported live animals | - | - | - | - | - | - | - | .. |
| Total meat production from slaughtered animals | 2.0 | 2.0 | 2.0 | 1.0 | 1.0 | 1.0 | 1.0 | 0.0 |
| *Minus:* Exports of meat | - | - | - | - | - | - | - | .. |
| *Plus:* Imports of meat | - | - | - | - | - | - | - | .. |
| *Minus:* Stock variations | - | - | - | - | - | - | - | |
| Meat consumption | 2.0 | 2.0 | 2.0 | 1.0 | 1.0 | 1.0 | 1.0 | 0.0 |
| Consumption per head *(kilogrammes per year)* | - | - | - | - | - | - | - | -0.3 |

## BEEF AND VEAL / TOTAL VIANDE BOVINE

| | 1984 | 1985 | 1986 | 1987 | 1988 | 1989 | 1990 | 1989/90 % change |
|---|---|---|---|---|---|---|---|---|
| Number of animals slaughtered *(thousands)* | 1537.0 | 1575.0 | 1554.0 | 1507.0 | 1460.0 | 1392.0 | 1453.0 [e] | 4.4 |
| Average dressed carcass weight *(kilogrammes)* | 350.7 | 353.0 | 362.3 | 376.9 | 389.7 | 387.2 | 381.3 [e] | -1.5 |
| Gross indigenous production | 539.0 | 556.0 | 563.0 | 568.0 | 569.0 | 539.0 | 554.0 | 2.8 |
| *Minus:* Meat equivalent of exported live animals | - | - | - | - | - | - | - | .. |
| *Plus:* Meat from slaughterings of imported live animals | - | - | - | - | - | - | - | .. |
| Total meat production from slaughtered animals | 539.0 | 556.0 | 563.0 | 568.0 | 569.0 | 539.0 | 554.0 | 2.8 |
| *Minus:* Exports of meat | - | - | - | - | - | - | - | .. |
| *Plus:* Imports of meat | 213.0 | 225.0 | 268.0 | 319.0 | 408.0 | 520.0 | 549.0 | 5.6 |
| *Minus:* Stock variations | - | 7.0 | 14.0 | -6.0 | 4.0 | 63.0 | 9.0 | |
| Meat consumption | 752.0 | 774.0 | 817.0 | 893.0 | 973.0 | 996.0 | 1094.0 | 9.8 |
| Consumption per head *(kilogrammes per year)* | 6.3 | 6.4 | 6.7 | 7.3 | 7.9 | 8.1 | 8.9 | 9.5 |

# JAPON

*Milliers de tonnes métriques - Poids en carcasse parée*

## VIANDE DE PORC / PIG MEAT

|  | 1984 | 1985 | 1986 | 1987 | 1988 | 1989 | 1990 | 1989/90 % var. |
|---|---|---|---|---|---|---|---|---|
| Nombre d'animaux abattus *(milliers)* | 19258.0 | 20638.0 | 20996.0 | 21428.0 | 21234.0 | 21417.0 | 21360.0 <sup>e</sup> | -0.3 |
| Poids moyen en carcasse parée *(kilogrammes)* | 74.0 | 74.0 | 74.0 | 74.0 | 74.0 | 75.0 | 72.0 <sup>e</sup> | -4.0 |
| Production indigène brute | 1433.0 | 1550.0 | 1558.0 | 1592.0 | 1577.0 | 1597.0 | 1536.0 | -3.8 |
| *Moins:* Équivalent en viande des animaux exportés vivants | - | - | - | - | - | - | - | .. |
| *Plus:* Viande provenant des abbattages d'animaux importés vivants | - | - | - | - | - | - | - | .. |
| Production totale de viande provenant des abattages | 1433.0 | 1550.0 | 1558.0 | 1592.0 | 1577.0 | 1597.0 | 1536.0 | -3.8 |
| *Moins:* Exportations de viande | - | - | - | - | - | - | - | .. |
| *Plus:* Importations de viande | 262.0 | 272.0 | 292.0 | 415.0 | 484.0 | 523.0 | 488.0 | -6.7 |
| *Moins:* Variations des stocks | -2.0 | 18.0 | -40.0 | 13.0 | 20.0 | 54.0 | -42.0 | |
| Consommation de viande | 1697.0 | 1804.0 | 1890.0 | 1994.0 | 2041.0 | 2066.0 | 2066.0 | 0.0 |
| Consommation par tête *(kilogrammes par an)* | 14.1 | 14.9 | 15.6 | 16.3 | 16.6 | 16.8 | 16.7 | -0.3 |

## VIANDE DE VOLAILLE / POULTRY MEAT

|  | 1984 | 1985 | 1986 | 1987 | 1988 | 1989 | 1990 | 1989/90 % var. |
|---|---|---|---|---|---|---|---|---|
| Nombre d'animaux abattus *(milliers)* | | | | | | | | |
| Poids moyen en carcasse parée *(kilogrammes)* | | | | | | | | |
| Production indigène brute | 1325.0 | 1354.0 | 1398.0 | 1437.0 | 1436.0 | 1417.0 | 1387.0 | -2.1 |
| *Moins:* Équivalent en viande des animaux exportés vivants | - | - | - | - | - | - | - | .. |
| *Plus:* Viande provenant des abbattages d'animaux importés vivants | - | - | - | - | - | - | - | .. |
| Production totale de viande provenant des abattages | 1325.0 | 1354.0 | 1398.0 | 1437.0 | 1436.0 | 1417.0 | 1387.0 | -2.1 |
| *Moins:* Exportations de viande | 2.0 | 3.0 | 3.0 | 4.0 | 5.0 | 6.0 | 8.0 | 33.3 |
| *Plus:* Importations de viande | 112.0 | 115.0 | 187.0 | 217.0 | 272.0 | 296.0 | 297.0 | 0.3 |
| *Moins:* Variations des stocks | 10.0 | - | 8.0 | 9.0 | 8.0 | 10.0 | -9.0 | |
| Consommation de viande | 1425.0 | 1466.0 | 1574.0 | 1641.0 | 1695.0 | 1697.0 | 1685.0 | -0.7 |
| Consommation par tête *(kilogrammes par an)* | 11.9 | 12.1 | 13.0 | 13.4 | 13.8 | 13.8 | 13.6 | -1.0 |

## VIANDE DE MOUTON ET DE CHÈVRE / MUTTON, LAMB AND GOAT MEAT

|  | 1984 | 1985 | 1986 | 1987 | 1988 | 1989 | 1990 | 1989/90 % var. |
|---|---|---|---|---|---|---|---|---|
| Nombre d'animaux abattus *(milliers)* | 9.0 | 12.0 | 13.0 | 14.0 | 14.0 | 14.0 <sup>e</sup> | 14.0 <sup>e</sup> | 0.0 |
| Poids moyen en carcasse parée *(kilogrammes)* | 23.0 <sup>e</sup> | 23.0 <sup>e</sup> | 23.0 <sup>e</sup> | 23.0 <sup>e</sup> | 23.0 <sup>e</sup> | 23.0 <sup>e</sup> | 23.0 <sup>e</sup> | 0.0 |
| Production indigène brute | . | . | . | . | . | . | . | .. |
| *Moins:* Équivalent en viande des animaux exportés vivants | - | - | - | - | - | - | - | .. |
| *Plus:* Viande provenant des abbattages d'animaux importés vivants | - | - | - | - | - | - | - | .. |
| Production totale de viande provenant des abattages | . | . | . | . | . | . | . | .. |
| *Moins:* Exportations de viande | - | - | - | - | - | - | - | .. |
| *Plus:* Importations de viande | 149.0 | 159.0 | 159.0 | 153.0 | 128.0 | 147.0 <sup>e</sup> | 143.0 <sup>e</sup> | -2.7 |
| *Moins:* Variations des stocks | - | -1.0 | -2.0 | - | - | - | - | |
| Consommation de viande | 149.0 | 160.0 | 161.0 | 153.0 | 128.0 | 147.0 <sup>e</sup> | 143.0 <sup>e</sup> | -2.7 |
| Consommation par tête *(kilogrammes par an)* | 1.2 | 1.3 | 1.3 | 1.3 | 1.0 | 1.2 <sup>e</sup> | 1.2 <sup>e</sup> | -3.1 |

# JAPAN

## HORSE MEAT / VIANDE D'ÉQUIDÉS

*Thousand metric tons - Dressed carcass weight*

| | 1984 | 1985 | 1986 | 1987 | 1988 | 1989 | 1990 | 1989/90 % change |
|---|---|---|---|---|---|---|---|---|
| Number of animals slaughtered *(thousands)* | 16.0 | 17.0 | 17.0 | 15.0 | 12.0 | 13.0 | 13.0 [e] | 0.0 |
| Average dressed carcass weight *(kilogrammes)* | 340.0 | 324.0 | 335.0 | 335.0 | 341.0 | 337.0 | 336.0 [e] | -0.3 |
| **Gross indigenous production** | **6.0** | **6.0** | **5.0** | **5.0** | **4.0** | **5.0** | **5.0** | 0.0 |
| *Minus:* Meat equivalent of exported live animals | - | - | - | - | - | - | - | .. |
| *Plus:* Meat from slaughterings of imported live animals | - | - | - | - | - | - | - | .. |
| **Total meat production from slaughtered animals** | **6.0** | **6.0** | **5.0** | **5.0** | **4.0** | **5.0** | **5.0** | 0.0 |
| *Minus:* Exports of meat | - | - | - | - | - | - | - | .. |
| *Plus:* Imports of meat | 62.0 | 60.0 | 53.0 | 50.0 | 55.0 | 56.0 | 54.0 [e] | -3.6 |
| *Minus:* Stock variations | - | - | - | - | - | - | - | |
| **Meat consumption** | **68.0** | **66.0** | **58.0** | **55.0** | **59.0** | **61.0** | **59.0** [e] | -3.3 |
| Consumption per head *(kilogrammes per year)* | 0.6 | 0.5 | 0.5 | 0.5 | 0.5 | 0.5 | 0.5 [e] | -3.6 |

## OTHER MEAT / AUTRES VIANDES[1]

| | 1984 | 1985 | 1986 | 1987 | 1988 | 1989 | 1990 | 1989/90 % change |
|---|---|---|---|---|---|---|---|---|
| Number of animals slaughtered *(thousands)* | | | | | | | | |
| Average dressed carcass weight *(kilogrammes)* | | | | | | | | |
| **Gross indigenous production** | **16.0** | **15.0** | **14.0** | **5.0** | **2.0** | **1.0** | **2.0** | 100.0 |
| *Minus:* Meat equivalent of exported live animals | - | - | - | - | - | - | - | .. |
| *Plus:* Meat from slaughterings of imported live animals | - | - | - | - | - | - | - | .. |
| **Total meat production from slaughtered animals** | **16.0** | **15.0** | **14.0** | **5.0** | **2.0** | **1.0** | **2.0** | 100.0 |
| *Minus:* Exports of meat | - | - | - | - | - | - | - | .. |
| *Plus:* Imports of meat | 17.0 | 17.0 | 4.0 | 1.0 | 1.0 | - | 1.0 | .. |
| *Minus:* Stock variations | - | - | - | - | - | - | - | |
| **Meat consumption** | **33.0** | **32.0** | **18.0** | **6.0** | **3.0** | **1.0** | **3.0** | 200.0 |
| Consumption per head *(kilogrammes per year)* | 0.3 | 0.3 | 0.1 | - | - | - | - | 199.0 |

## EDIBLE OFFALS / ABATS COMESTIBLES

| | 1984 | 1985 | 1986 | 1987 | 1988 | 1989 | 1990 | 1989/90 % change |
|---|---|---|---|---|---|---|---|---|
| Number of animals slaughtered *(thousands)* | | | | | | | | |
| Average dressed carcass weight *(kilogrammes)* | | | | | | | | |
| **Gross indigenous production** | **247.0** | **266.0** | **267.0** | **272.0** | **270.0** | **270.0** | **263.0** | -2.6 |
| *Minus:* Meat equivalent of exported live animals | - | - | - | - | - | - | - | .. |
| *Plus:* Meat from slaughterings of imported live animals | - | - | - | - | - | - | - | .. |
| **Total meat production from slaughtered animals** | **247.0** | **266.0** | **267.0** | **272.0** | **270.0** | **270.0** | **263.0** | -2.6 |
| *Minus:* Exports of meat | - | - | - | - | - | - | - | .. |
| *Plus:* Imports of meat | 71.0 | 82.0 | 97.0 | 100.0 [e] | 95.0 [e] | 97.0 [e] | 97.0 [e] | 0.0 |
| *Minus:* Stock variations | - | - | - | - | - | - | - | |
| **Meat consumption** | **318.0** | **348.0** | **364.0** | **372.0** [e] | **365.0** [e] | **367.0** [e] | **360.0** [e] | -1.9 |
| Consumption per head *(kilogrammes per year)* | 2.6 | 2.9 | 3.0 | 3.0 [e] | 3.0 [e] | 3.0 [e] | 2.9 [e] | -2.2 |

(1) Whale meat / Viande de baleine

# JAPON

*Milliers de tonnes métriques - Poids en carcasse parée*

*TOTAL VIANDE / TOTAL MEAT*

| | 1984 | 1985 | 1986 | 1987 | 1988 | 1989 | 1990 | 1989/90 % var. |
|---|---|---|---|---|---|---|---|---|
| **Nombre d'animaux abattus** *(milliers)* | | | | | | | | |
| **Poids moyen en carcasse parée** *(kilogrammes)* | | | | | | | | |
| **Production indigène brute** | **3566.0** | **3747.0** | **3805.0** | **3879.0** | **3858.0** | **3829.0** | **3747.0** | -2.1 |
| *Moins:* Équivalent en viande des animaux exportés vivants | - | - | - | - | - | - | - | .. |
| *Plus:* Viande provenant des abbattages d'animaux importés vivants | - | - | - | - | - | - | - | .. |
| **Production totale de viande provenant des abattages** | **3566.0** | **3747.0** | **3805.0** | **3879.0** | **3858.0** | **3829.0** | **3747.0** | -2.1 |
| *Moins:* Exportations de viande | 2.0 | 3.0 | 3.0 | 4.0 | 5.0 | 6.0 | 8.0 | 33.3 |
| *Plus:* Importations de viande | 886.0 | 930.0 | 1060.0 | 1255.0 [e] | 1443.0 [e] | 1639.0 [e] | 1629.0 [e] | -0.6 |
| *Moins:* Variations des stocks | 8.0 | 24.0 | -20.0 | 16.0 | 32.0 | 127.0 | -42.0 | |
| **Consommation de viande** | **4442.0** | **4650.0** | **4882.0** | **5114.0** [e] | **5264.0** [e] | **5335.0** [e] | **5410.0** [e] | 1.4 |
| **Consommation par tête** *(kilogrammes par an)* | 37.0 | 38.5 | 40.2 | 41.9 [e] | 42.9 [e] | 43.3 [e] | 43.8 [e] | 1.1 |

## PRODUCTION INDIGENE BRUTE DE VIANDE
## MEAT GROSS INDIGENOUS PRODUCTION

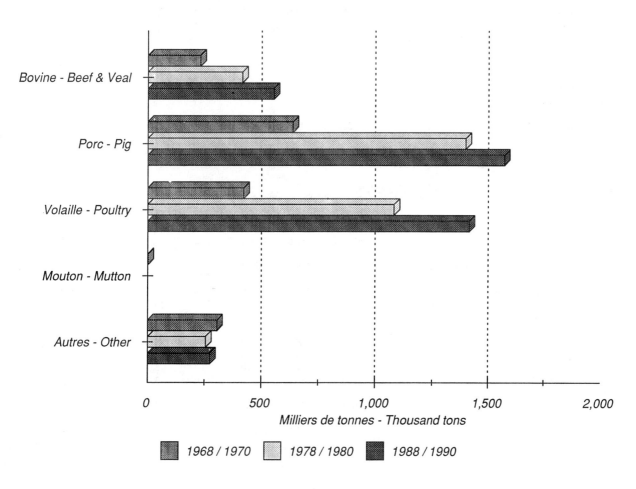

*Milliers de tonnes - Thousand tons*

■ 1968 / 1970    ☐ 1978 / 1980    ■ 1988 / 1990

# AUSTRALIA

## BEEF / VIANDE DE BŒUF

*Thousand metric tons - Dressed carcass weight*

| | 1984 | 1985 | 1986 | 1987 | 1988 | 1989 | 1990 | 1989/90 % change |
|---|---|---|---|---|---|---|---|---|
| Number of animals slaughtered *(thousands)* | 5608.0 | 5958.0 | 6598.0 | 6860.0 | 6696.0 | 6512.0 | 7099.0 | 9.0 |
| Average dressed carcass weight *(kilogrammes)* | 216.0 | 216.0 | 215.0 | 220.0 | 224.0 | 234.0 | 235.0 | 0.4 |
| Gross indigenous production | 1233.0 | 1299.0 | 1435.0 | 1526.0 | 1516.0 | 1541.0 | 1680.0 | 9.0 |
| *Minus:* Meat equivalent of exported live animals | 19.0 | 13.0 | 14.0 | 14.0 | 16.0 | 14.0 | 15.0 [e] | 7.1 |
| *Plus:* Meat from slaughterings of imported live animals | - | - | - | - | - | - | - | .. |
| Total meat production from slaughtered animals | 1214.0 | 1286.0 | 1421.0 | 1512.0 | 1500.0 | 1527.0 | 1665.0 [e] | 9.0 |
| *Minus:* Exports of meat | 565.0 | 647.0 | 764.0 | 866.0 | 860.0 | 842.0 | 1042.0 | 23.8 |
| *Plus:* Imports of meat | 4.0 | 2.0 | 3.0 | 3.0 [e] | 3.0 [e] | 3.0 [e] | 3.0 [e] | 0.0 |
| *Minus:* Stock variations | -6.0 | 8.0 | 5.0 | 2.0 | -3.0 | -6.0 | 2.0 | |
| Meat consumption | 659.0 | 633.0 | 655.0 | 647.0 [e] | 646.0 [e] | 694.0 [e] | 624.0 [e] | -10.1 |
| Consumption per head *(kilogrammes per year)* | 42.3 | 40.1 | 40.9 | 39.8 [e] | 39.1 [e] | 41.2 [e] | 36.5 [e] | -11.4 |

## VEAL / VIANDE DE VEAU

| | 1984 | 1985 | 1986 | 1987 | 1988 | 1989 | 1990 | 1989/90 % change |
|---|---|---|---|---|---|---|---|---|
| Number of animals slaughtered *(thousands)* | 1217.0 | 1193.0 | 1261.0 | 1188.0 | 1026.0 | 973.0 | 1047.0 | 7.6 |
| Average dressed carcass weight *(kilogrammes)* | 32.0 | 33.0 | 33.0 | 32.0 | 34.0 | 34.0 | 35.0 | 2.9 |
| Gross indigenous production | 39.0 | 39.0 | 42.0 | 38.0 | 35.0 | 33.0 | 37.0 | 12.1 |
| *Minus:* Meat equivalent of exported live animals | - | - | - | - | - | - | - | .. |
| *Plus:* Meat from slaughterings of imported live animals | - | - | - | - | - | - | - | .. |
| Total meat production from slaughtered animals | 39.0 | 39.0 | 42.0 | 38.0 | 35.0 | 33.0 | 37.0 | 12.1 |
| *Minus:* Exports of meat | 6.0 | 6.0 | 7.0 | 7.0 | 8.0 | 8.0 | 9.0 | 12.5 |
| *Plus:* Imports of meat | - | - | - | - | - | - | - | .. |
| *Minus:* Stock variations | - | - | - | - | - | - | - | |
| Meat consumption | 33.0 | 33.0 | 35.0 | 31.0 | 27.0 | 25.0 | 28.0 | 12.0 |
| Consumption per head *(kilogrammes per year)* | 2.1 | 2.1 | 2.2 | 1.9 | 1.6 | 1.5 | 1.6 | 10.3 |

## BEEF AND VEAL / TOTAL VIANDE BOVINE

| | 1984 | 1985 | 1986 | 1987 | 1988 | 1989 | 1990 | 1989/90 % change |
|---|---|---|---|---|---|---|---|---|
| Number of animals slaughtered *(thousands)* | 6825.0 | 7151.0 | 7859.0 | 8048.0 | 7722.0 | 7485.0 | 8146.0 | 8.8 |
| Average dressed carcass weight *(kilogrammes)* | 183.6 | 185.3 | 186.2 | 192.6 | 198.8 | 208.4 | 208.9 | 0.2 |
| Gross indigenous production | 1272.0 | 1338.0 | 1477.0 | 1564.0 | 1551.0 | 1574.0 | 1717.0 | 9.1 |
| *Minus:* Meat equivalent of exported live animals | 19.0 | 13.0 | 14.0 | 14.0 | 16.0 | 14.0 | 15.0 [e] | 7.1 |
| *Plus:* Meat from slaughterings of imported live animals | - | - | - | - | - | - | - | .. |
| Total meat production from slaughtered animals | 1253.0 | 1325.0 | 1463.0 | 1550.0 | 1535.0 | 1560.0 | 1702.0 [e] | 9.1 |
| *Minus:* Exports of meat | 571.0 | 653.0 | 771.0 | 873.0 | 868.0 | 850.0 | 1051.0 | 23.6 |
| *Plus:* Imports of meat | 4.0 | 2.0 | 3.0 | 3.0 [e] | 3.0 [e] | 3.0 [e] | 3.0 [e] | 0.0 |
| *Minus:* Stock variations | -6.0 | 8.0 | 5.0 | 2.0 | -3.0 | -6.0 | 2.0 | |
| Meat consumption | 692.0 | 666.0 | 690.0 | 678.0 [e] | 673.0 [e] | 719.0 [e] | 652.0 [e] | -9.3 |
| Consumption per head *(kilogrammes per year)* | 44.4 | 42.2 | 43.1 | 41.7 [e] | 40.7 [e] | 42.7 [e] | 38.2 [e] | -10.7 |

# AUSTRALIE

*Milliers de tonnes métriques - Poids en carcasse parée*

## VIANDE DE PORC / PIG MEAT

|  | 1984 | 1985 | 1986 | 1987 | 1988 | 1989 | 1990 | 1989/90 % var. |
|---|---|---|---|---|---|---|---|---|
| Nombre d'animaux abattus *(milliers)* | 4473.0 | 4539.0 | 4627.0 | 4793.0 | 4962.0 | 4941.0 | 4944.0 | 0.1 |
| Poids moyen en carcasse parée *(kilogrammes)* | 57.0 | 59.0 | 54.0 | 60.0 | 61.0 | 63.0 | 65.0 | 3.2 |
| Production indigène brute | 303.0 | 268.0 | 251.0 | 288.0 | 303.0 | 310.0 | 319.0 | 2.9 |
| *Moins:* Équivalent en viande des animaux exportés vivants | - | - | - | - | - | - | - | .. |
| *Plus:* Viande provenant des abbattages d'animaux importés vivants | - | - | - | - | - | - | - | .. |
| Production totale de viande provenant des abattages | 303.0 | 268.0 | 251.0 | 288.0 | 303.0 | 310.0 | 319.0 | 2.9 |
| *Moins:* Exportations de viande | 4.0 | 4.0 | 3.0 | 7.0 | 8.0 | 6.0 | 6.0 | 0.0 |
| *Plus:* Importations de viande | 1.0 | - | - | - | - | - | - | .. |
| *Moins:* Variations des stocks | - | 1.0 | -2.0 | - | 1.0 | - | -1.0 |  |
| Consommation de viande | 300.0 | 263.0 | 250.0 | 281.0 | 294.0 | 304.0 | 314.0 | 3.3 |
| Consommation par tête *(kilogrammes par an)* | 19.3 | 16.7 | 15.6 | 17.3 | 17.8 | 18.1 | 18.4 | 1.8 |

## VIANDE DE VOLAILLE / POULTRY MEAT

|  | 1984 | 1985 | 1986 | 1987 | 1988 | 1989 | 1990 | 1989/90 % var. |
|---|---|---|---|---|---|---|---|---|
| Nombre d'animaux abattus *(milliers)* |  |  |  |  |  |  |  |  |
| Poids moyen en carcasse parée *(kilogrammes)* |  |  |  |  |  |  |  |  |
| Production indigène brute | 315.0 | 365.0 | 370.0 | 394.0 | 402.0 | 432.0 | 445.0 | 3.0 |
| *Moins:* Équivalent en viande des animaux exportés vivants | - | - | - | - | - | - | - | .. |
| *Plus:* Viande provenant des abbattages d'animaux importés vivants | - | - | - | - | - | - | - | .. |
| Production totale de viande provenant des abattages | 315.0 | 365.0 | 370.0 | 394.0 | 402.0 | 432.0 | 445.0 | 3.0 |
| *Moins:* Exportations de viande | 1.0 | 1.0 | 3.0 | 3.0 | 1.0 | 1.0 | 1.0 | 0.0 |
| *Plus:* Importations de viande | - | - | - | - | - | - | - | .. |
| *Moins:* Variations des stocks | - | - | - | - | - | - | - |  |
| Consommation de viande | 314.0 | 364.0 | 367.0 | 391.0 | 401.0 | 431.0 | 444.0 | 3.0 |
| Consommation par tête *(kilogrammes par an)* | 20.2 | 23.1 | 22.9 | 24.0 | 24.2 | 25.6 | 26.0 | 1.5 |

## VIANDE DE MOUTON ET DE CHÈVRE / MUTTON, LAMB AND GOAT MEAT

|  | 1984 | 1985 | 1986 | 1987 | 1988 | 1989 | 1990 | 1989/90 % var. |
|---|---|---|---|---|---|---|---|---|
| Nombre d'animaux abattus *(milliers)* | 25800.0 | 30400.0 | 32500.0 | 32800.0 | 29800.0 | 30600.0 | 33900.0 | 10.8 |
| Poids moyen en carcasse parée *(kilogrammes)* | 19.0 | 18.0 | 18.0 | 18.0 | 18.0 | 19.0 | 19.0 | 0.0 |
| Production indigène brute | 475.0 | 556.0 | 585.0 | 599.0 | 551.0 | 583.0 | 649.0 | 11.3 |
| *Moins:* Équivalent en viande des animaux exportés vivants | 126.0 | 125.0 | 128.0 | 129.0 | 131.0 | 102.0 | 68.0 | -33.3 |
| *Plus:* Viande provenant des abbattages d'animaux importés vivants | - | - | - | - | - | - | - | .. |
| Production totale de viande provenant des abattages | 349.0 | 431.0 | 457.0 | 470.0 | 420.0 | 481.0 | 581.0 | 20.8 |
| *Moins:* Exportations de viande | 130.0 | 168.0 | 221.0 | 217.0 | 202.0 | 192.0 | 258.0 | 34.4 |
| *Plus:* Importations de viande | - | - | - | - | - | - | - | .. |
| *Moins:* Variations des stocks | 1.0 | - | 3.0 | 2.0 | -4.0 | 5.0 | 24.0 |  |
| Consommation de viande | 218.0 | 263.0 | 233.0 | 251.0 | 222.0 | 284.0 | 299.0 | 5.3 |
| Consommation par tête *(kilogrammes par an)* | 14.0 | 16.7 | 14.5 | 15.4 | 13.4 | 16.9 | 17.5 | 3.7 |

# AUSTRALIA

## HORSE MEAT / VIANDE D'ÉQUIDÉS

| | 1984 | 1985 | 1986 | 1987 | 1988 | 1989 | 1990 | 1989/90 % change |
|---|---|---|---|---|---|---|---|---|
| Number of animals slaughtered *(thousands)* | - | - | - | - | - | - | - | .. |
| Average dressed carcass weight *(kilogrammes)* | - | - | - | - | - | - | - | .. |
| Gross indigenous production | - | - | - | - | - | - | - | .. |
| *Minus:* Meat equivalent of exported live animals | - | - | - | - | - | - | - | .. |
| *Plus:* Meat from slaughterings of imported live animals | - | - | - | - | - | - | - | .. |
| Total meat production from slaughtered animals | - | - | - | - | - | - | - | .. |
| *Minus:* Exports of meat | - | - | - | - | - | - | - | .. |
| *Plus:* Imports of meat | - | - | - | - | - | - | - | .. |
| *Minus:* Stock variations | - | - | - | - | - | - | - | |
| Meat consumption | - | - | - | - | - | - | - | .. |
| Consumption per head *(kilogrammes per year)* | - | - | - | - | - | - | - | .. |

## OTHER MEAT / AUTRES VIANDES

| | 1984 | 1985 | 1986 | 1987 | 1988 | 1989 | 1990 | 1989/90 % change |
|---|---|---|---|---|---|---|---|---|
| Number of animals slaughtered *(thousands)* | | | | | | | | |
| Average dressed carcass weight *(kilogrammes)* | | | | | | | | |
| Gross indigenous production | 45.0 | 40.0 | 41.0 | 36.0 | 23.0 | 24.0 | 14.0 | -41.7 |
| *Minus:* Meat equivalent of exported live animals | - | - | - | - | - | - | - | .. |
| *Plus:* Meat from slaughterings of imported live animals | - | - | - | - | - | - | - | .. |
| Total meat production from slaughtered animals | 45.0 | 40.0 | 41.0 | 36.0 | 23.0 | 24.0 | 14.0 | -41.7 |
| *Minus:* Exports of meat | 13.0 | 27.0 | 29.0 | 13.0 | 9.0 | 8.0 | 10.0 | 25.0 |
| *Plus:* Imports of meat | - | - | - | - | - | - | - | .. |
| *Minus:* Stock variations | - | - | - | - | - | - | - | |
| Meat consumption | 32.0 | 13.0 | 12.0 | 23.0 | 14.0 | 16.0 | 4.0 | -75.0 |
| Consumption per head *(kilogrammes per year)* | 2.1 | 0.8 | 0.7 | 1.4 | 0.8 | 1.0 | 0.2 | -75.4 |

## EDIBLE OFFALS / ABATS COMESTIBLES

| | 1984 | 1985 | 1986 | 1987 | 1988 | 1989 | 1990 | 1989/90 % change |
|---|---|---|---|---|---|---|---|---|
| Number of animals slaughtered *(thousands)* | | | | | | | | |
| Average dressed carcass weight *(kilogrammes)* | | | | | | | | |
| Gross indigenous production | 103.0 | 111.0 | 117.0 | 131.0 | 128.0 | 128.0 | 143.0 | 11.7 |
| *Minus:* Meat equivalent of exported live animals | - | - | - | - | - | - | - | .. |
| *Plus:* Meat from slaughterings of imported live animals | - | - | - | - | - | - | - | .. |
| Total meat production from slaughtered animals | 103.0 | 111.0 | 117.0 | 131.0 | 128.0 | 128.0 | 143.0 | 11.7 |
| *Minus:* Exports of meat | 49.0 | 67.0 | 60.0 | 59.0 | 62.0 | 60.0 | 60.0 | 0.0 |
| *Plus:* Imports of meat | 2.0 | 2.0 | 1.0 | 2.0 | 2.0 | 2.0 | 2.0 | 0.0 |
| *Minus:* Stock variations | 1.0 | - | - | - | - | - | - | |
| Meat consumption | 55.0 | 46.0 | 58.0 | 74.0 | 68.0 | 70.0 | 85.0 | 21.4 |
| Consumption per head *(kilogrammes per year)* | 3.5 | 2.9 | 3.6 | 4.5 | 4.1 | 4.2 | 5.0 | 19.6 |

# AUSTRALIE

*Milliers de tonnes métriques - Poids en carcasse parée*

| | 1984 | 1985 | 1986 | 1987 | 1988 | 1989 | 1990 | 1989/90 % var. |
|---|---|---|---|---|---|---|---|---|
| Nombre d'animaux abattus *(milliers)* | | | | | | | | |
| Poids moyen en carcasse parée *(kilogrammes)* | | | | | | | | |
| Production indigène brute | 2513.0 | 2678.0 | 2841.0 | 3012.0 | 2958.0 | 3051.0 | 3287.0 | 7.7 |
| *Moins:* Équivalent en viande des animaux exportés vivants | 145.0 | 138.0 | 142.0 | 143.0 | 147.0 | 116.0 | 83.0 ᵉ | -28.4 |
| *Plus:* Viande provenant des abbattages d'animaux importés vivants | - | - | - | - | - | - | - | .. |
| Production totale de viande provenant des abattages | 2368.0 | 2540.0 | 2699.0 | 2869.0 | 2811.0 | 2935.0 | 3204.0 ᵉ | 9.2 |
| *Moins:* Exportations de viande | 768.0 | 920.0 | 1087.0 | 1172.0 | 1150.0 | 1117.0 | 1386.0 | 24.1 |
| *Plus:* Importations de viande | 7.0 | 4.0 | 4.0 | 5.0 ᵉ | 5.0 ᵉ | 5.0 ᵉ | 5.0 ᵉ | 0.0 |
| *Moins:* Variations des stocks | -4.0 | 9.0 | 6.0 | 4.0 | -6.0 | -1.0 | 25.0 | |
| Consommation de viande | 1611.0 | 1615.0 | 1610.0 | 1698.0 ᵉ | 1672.0 ᵉ | 1824.0 ᵉ | 1798.0 ᵉ | -1.4 |
| Consommation par tête *(kilogrammes par an)* | 103.4 | 102.3 | 100.5 | 104.4 ᵉ | 101.1 ᵉ | 108.4 ᵉ | 105.2 ᵉ | -2.9 |

## PRODUCTION INDIGENE BRUTE DE VIANDE
## *MEAT GROSS INDIGENOUS PRODUCTION*

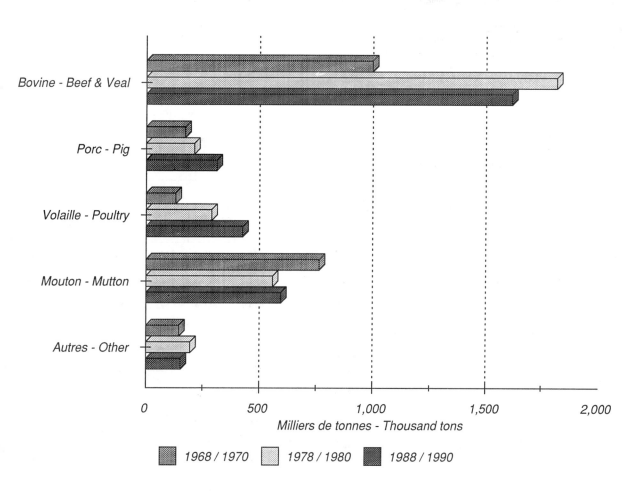

# NEW ZEALAND

## BEEF / VIANDE DE BŒUF

| | 1984 | 1985 | 1986 | 1987 | 1988 | 1989 | 1990 | 1989/90 % change |
|---|---|---|---|---|---|---|---|---|
| Number of animals slaughtered *(thousands)* | 2597.0 | 2817.0 | 2834.0 | 3149.0 | 3140.0 | 3165.0 | 2671.0 | -15.6 |
| Average dressed carcass weight *(kilogrammes)* | 166.7 | 172.9 | 164.4 | 176.2 | 182.2 | 170.9 | 179.3 | 4.9 |
| **Gross indigenous production** | **433.0** | **487.0** | **466.0** | **555.0** | **572.0** | **541.0** | **479.0** | -11.5 |
| *Minus:* Meat equivalent of exported live animals | - | - | - | - | - | - | - | .. |
| *Plus:* Meat from slaughterings of imported live animals | - | - | - | - | - | - | - | .. |
| **Total meat production from slaughtered animals** | **433.0** | **487.0** | **466.0** | **555.0** | **572.0** | **541.0** | **479.0** | -11.5 |
| *Minus:* Exports of meat | 282.0 | 360.0 | 329.0 | 434.0 | 435.0 | 441.0 | 377.0 | -14.5 |
| *Plus:* Imports of meat | - | - | - | - | - | - | - | .. |
| *Minus:* Stock variations | 31.0 | 8.0 | 18.0 | -6.0 | 5.0 | -25.0 | -16.0 | |
| **Meat consumption** | **120.0** | **119.0** | **119.0** | **127.0** | **132.0** | **125.0** | **118.0** | -5.6 |
| Consumption per head *(kilogrammes per year)* | 36.8 | 36.2 | 36.3 | 38.4 | 39.7 | 37.4 | 34.9 | -6.6 |

## VEAL / VIANDE DE VEAU

| | 1984 | 1985 | 1986 | 1987 | 1988 | 1989 | 1990 | 1989/90 % change |
|---|---|---|---|---|---|---|---|---|
| **Number of animals slaughtered** *(thousands)* | - | - | - | - | - | - | - | .. |
| Average dressed carcass weight *(kilogrammes)* | - | - | - | - | - | - | - | .. |
| **Gross indigenous production** | • | • | • | • | • | • | • | .. |
| *Minus:* Meat equivalent of exported live animals | - | - | - | - | - | - | - | .. |
| *Plus:* Meat from slaughterings of imported live animals | - | - | - | - | - | - | - | .. |
| **Total meat production from slaughtered animals** | • | • | • | • | • | • | • | .. |
| *Minus:* Exports of meat | - | - | - | - | - | - | - | .. |
| *Plus:* Imports of meat | - | - | - | - | - | - | - | .. |
| *Minus:* Stock variations | - | - | - | - | - | - | - | .. |
| **Meat consumption** | • | • | • | • | • | • | • | .. |
| Consumption per head *(kilogrammes per year)* | - | - | - | - | - | - | - | .. |

## BEEF AND VEAL / TOTAL VIANDE BOVINE

| | 1984 | 1985 | 1986 | 1987 | 1988 | 1989 | 1990 | 1989/90 % change |
|---|---|---|---|---|---|---|---|---|
| Number of animals slaughtered *(thousands)* | 2597.0 | 2817.0 | 2834.0 | 3149.0 | 3140.0 | 3165.0 | 2671.0 | -15.6 |
| Average dressed carcass weight *(kilogrammes)* | 166.7 | 172.9 | 164.4 | 176.2 | 182.2 | 170.9 | 179.3 | 4.9 |
| **Gross indigenous production** | **433.0** | **487.0** | **466.0** | **555.0** | **572.0** | **541.0** | **479.0** | -11.5 |
| *Minus:* Meat equivalent of exported live animals | - | - | - | - | - | - | - | .. |
| *Plus:* Meat from slaughterings of imported live animals | - | - | - | - | - | - | - | .. |
| **Total meat production from slaughtered animals** | **433.0** | **487.0** | **466.0** | **555.0** | **572.0** | **541.0** | **479.0** | -11.5 |
| *Minus:* Exports of meat | 282.0 | 360.0 | 329.0 | 434.0 | 435.0 | 441.0 | 377.0 | -14.5 |
| *Plus:* Imports of meat | - | - | - | - | - | - | - | .. |
| *Minus:* Stock variations | 31.0 | 8.0 | 18.0 | -6.0 | 5.0 | -25.0 | -16.0 | |
| **Meat consumption** | **120.0** | **119.0** | **119.0** | **127.0** | **132.0** | **125.0** | **118.0** | -5.6 |
| Consumption per head *(kilogrammes per year)* | 36.8 | 36.2 | 36.3 | 38.4 | 39.7 | 37.4 | 34.9 | -6.6 |

# NOUVELLE ZÉLANDE

*Milliers de tonnes métriques - Poids en carcasse parée*

## VIANDE DE PORC / PIG MEAT

| | 1984 | 1985 | 1986 | 1987 | 1988 | 1989 | 1990 | 1989/90 % var. |
|---|---|---|---|---|---|---|---|---|
| Nombre d'animaux abattus *(milliers)* | 768.0 | 849.0 | 843.0 | 774.0 | 782.0 | 781.0 | 749.0 | -4.1 |
| Poids moyen en carcasse parée *(kilogrammes)* | 56.0 | 57.0 | 57.0 | 58.0 | 59.0 | 58.0 | 57.0 | -1.7 |
| **Production indigène brute** | **43.0** | **48.0** | **48.0** | **45.0** | **46.0** | **45.0** | **43.0** | -4.4 |
| *Moins:* Équivalent en viande des animaux exportés vivants | - | - | - | - | - | - | - | .. |
| *Plus:* Viande provenant des abbattages d'animaux importés vivants | - | - | - | - | - | - | - | .. |
| **Production totale de viande provenant des abattages** | **43.0** | **48.0** | **48.0** | **45.0** | **46.0** | **45.0** | **43.0** | -4.4 |
| *Moins:* Exportations de viande | 2.0 | 2.0 | - | - | - | - | - | .. |
| *Plus:* Importations de viande | 1.0 | - | - | - | - | - | - | .. |
| *Moins:* Variations des stocks | - | - | - | - | - | - | - | |
| **Consommation de viande** | **42.0** | **46.0** | **48.0** | **45.0** | **46.0** | **45.0** | **43.0** | -4.4 |
| Consommation par tête *(kilogrammes par an)* | 12.9 | 14.0 | 14.6 | 13.6 | 13.8 | 13.5 | 12.7 | -5.5 |

## VIANDE DE VOLAILLE / POULTRY MEAT

| | 1984 | 1985 | 1986 | 1987 | 1988 | 1989 | 1990 | 1989/90 % var. |
|---|---|---|---|---|---|---|---|---|
| Nombre d'animaux abattus *(milliers)* | | | | | | | | |
| Poids moyen en carcasse parée *(kilogrammes)* | | | | | | | | |
| **Production indigène brute** | **46.0** | **48.0** | **46.0** | **48.0** | **52.0** | **58.0** | **60.0** | 3.4 |
| *Moins:* Équivalent en viande des animaux exportés vivants | - | - | - | - | - | - | - | .. |
| *Plus:* Viande provenant des abbattages d'animaux importés vivants | - | - | - | - | - | - | - | .. |
| **Production totale de viande provenant des abattages** | **46.0** | **48.0** | **46.0** | **48.0** | **52.0** | **58.0** | **60.0** | 3.4 |
| *Moins:* Exportations de viande | - | - | - | - | - | - | - | .. |
| *Plus:* Importations de viande | - | - | - | - | - | - | - | .. |
| *Moins:* Variations des stocks | - | - | - | - | - | - | - | |
| **Consommation de viande** | **46.0** | **48.0** | **46.0** | **48.0** | **52.0** | **58.0** | **60.0** | 3.4 |
| Consommation par tête *(kilogrammes par an)* | 14.1 | 14.6 | 14.0 | 14.5 | 15.6 | 17.3 | 17.8 | 2.3 |

## VIANDE DE MOUTON ET DE CHÈVRE / MUTTON, LAMB AND GOAT MEAT

| | 1984 | 1985 | 1986 | 1987 | 1988 | 1989 | 1990 | 1989/90 % var. |
|---|---|---|---|---|---|---|---|---|
| Nombre d'animaux abattus *(milliers)* | 43606.0 | 50701.0 | 41378.0 | 40929.0 | 38341.0 | 40059.0 | 32824.0 | -18.1 |
| Poids moyen en carcasse parée *(kilogrammes)* | 15.0 | 14.0 | 15.0 | 15.0 | 16.0 | 15.0 | 16.0 | 6.7 |
| **Production indigène brute** | **668.0** | **728.0** | **611.0** | **610.0** | **604.0** | **612.0** | **535.0** | -12.6 |
| *Moins:* Équivalent en viande des animaux exportés vivants | - | - | - | - | - | - | - | .. |
| *Plus:* Viande provenant des abbattages d'animaux importés vivants | - | - | - | - | - | - | - | .. |
| **Production totale de viande provenant des abattages** | **668.0** | **728.0** | **611.0** | **610.0** | **604.0** | **612.0** | **535.0** | -12.6 |
| *Moins:* Exportations de viande | 539.0 | 527.0 | 525.0 | 525.0 | 438.0 | 467.0 | 371.0 | -20.6 |
| *Plus:* Importations de viande | - | - | - | - | - | - | - | .. |
| *Moins:* Variations des stocks | 39.0 | 113.0 | -5.0 | -9.0 | 36.0 | 56.0 | 69.0 | |
| **Consommation de viande** | **90.0** | **88.0** | **91.0** | **94.0** | **130.0** | **89.0** | **95.0** | 6.7 |
| Consommation par tête *(kilogrammes par an)* | 27.6 | 26.8 | 27.8 | 28.4 | 39.1 | 26.6 | 28.1 | 5.6 |

# NEW ZEALAND

## HORSE MEAT / VIANDE D'ÉQUIDÉS

| | 1984 | 1985 | 1986 | 1987 | 1988 | 1989 | 1990 | 1989/90 % change |
|---|---|---|---|---|---|---|---|---|
| **Number of animals slaughtered** *(thousands)* | - | - | - | - | - | - | - | .. |
| **Average dressed carcass weight** *(kilogrammes)* | - | - | - | - | - | - | - | .. |
| **Gross indigenous production** | · | · | · | · | · | · | · | .. |
| *Minus:* Meat equivalent of exported live animals | - | - | - | - | - | - | - | .. |
| *Plus:* Meat from slaughterings of imported live animals | - | - | - | - | - | - | - | .. |
| **Total meat production from slaughtered animals** | · | · | · | · | · | · | · | .. |
| *Minus:* Exports of meat | - | - | - | - | - | - | - | .. |
| *Plus:* Imports of meat | - | - | - | - | - | - | - | .. |
| *Minus:* Stock variations | - | - | - | - | - | - | - | |
| **Meat consumption** | · | · | · | · | · | · | · | .. |
| **Consumption per head** *(kilogrammes per year)* | - | - | - | - | - | - | - | .. |

## OTHER MEAT / AUTRES VIANDES

| | 1984 | 1985 | 1986 | 1987 | 1988 | 1989 | 1990 | 1989/90 % change |
|---|---|---|---|---|---|---|---|---|
| **Number of animals slaughtered** *(thousands)* | | | | | | | | |
| **Average dressed carcass weight** *(kilogrammes)* | | | | | | | | |
| **Gross indigenous production** | 2.0 | 2.0 | 2.0 | 2.0 | 2.0 | 2.0 | 2.0 | 0.0 |
| *Minus:* Meat equivalent of exported live animals | - | - | - | - | - | - | - | .. |
| *Plus:* Meat from slaughterings of imported live animals | - | - | - | - | - | - | - | .. |
| **Total meat production from slaughtered animals** | 2.0 | 2.0 | 2.0 | 2.0 | 2.0 | 2.0 | 2.0 | 0.0 |
| *Minus:* Exports of meat | 2.0 | 2.0 | 2.0 | 2.0 | 2.0 | 2.0 | 2.0 | 0.0 |
| *Plus:* Imports of meat | - | - | - | - | - | - | - | .. |
| *Minus:* Stock variations | - | - | - | - | - | - | - | |
| **Meat consumption** | · | · | · | · | · | · | · | .. |
| **Consumption per head** *(kilogrammes per year)* | - | - | - | - | - | - | - | .. |

## EDIBLE OFFALS / ABATS COMESTIBLES

| | 1984 | 1985 | 1986 | 1987 | 1988 | 1989 | 1990 | 1989/90 % change |
|---|---|---|---|---|---|---|---|---|
| **Number of animals slaughtered** *(thousands)* | | | | | | | | |
| **Average dressed carcass weight** *(kilogrammes)* | | | | | | | | |
| **Gross indigenous production** | 59.0 | 65.0 | 59.0 | 64.0 | 65.0 | 64.0 | 55.0 | -14.1 |
| *Minus:* Meat equivalent of exported live animals | - | - | - | - | - | - | - | .. |
| *Plus:* Meat from slaughterings of imported live animals | - | - | - | - | - | - | - | .. |
| **Total meat production from slaughtered animals** | 59.0 | 65.0 | 59.0 | 64.0 | 65.0 | 64.0 | 55.0 | -14.1 |
| *Minus:* Exports of meat | 49.0 | 51.0 | 43.0 | 55.0 | 52.0 | 49.0 | 40.0 | -18.4 |
| *Plus:* Imports of meat | - | - | - | - | - | - | - | .. |
| *Minus:* Stock variations | - | - | - | - | - | - | - | |
| **Meat consumption** | 10.0 | 14.0 | 16.0 | 9.0 | 13.0 | 15.0 | 15.0 | 0.0 |
| **Consumption per head** *(kilogrammes per year)* | 3.1 | 4.3 | 4.9 | 2.7 | 3.9 | 4.5 | 4.4 | -1.1 |

# NOUVELLE ZÉLANDE

*Milliers de tonnes métriques - Poids en carcasse parée*

*TOTAL VIANDE / TOTAL MEAT*

| | 1984 | 1985 | 1986 | 1987 | 1988 | 1989 | 1990 | 1989/90 % var. |
|---|---|---|---|---|---|---|---|---|
| **Nombre d'animaux abattus** *(milliers)* | | | | | | | | |
| **Poids moyen en carcasse parée** *(kilogrammes)* | | | | | | | | |
| **Production indigène brute** | 1251.0 | 1378.0 | 1232.0 | 1324.0 | 1341.0 | 1322.0 | 1174.0 | -11.2 |
| *Moins:* Équivalent en viande des animaux exportés vivants | - | - | - | - | - | - | - | .. |
| *Plus:* Viande provenant des abbattages d'animaux importés vivants | - | - | - | - | - | - | - | .. |
| **Production totale de viande provenant des abattages** | 1251.0 | 1378.0 | 1232.0 | 1324.0 | 1341.0 | 1322.0 | 1174.0 | -11.2 |
| *Moins:* Exportations de viande | 874.0 | 942.0 | 899.0 | 1016.0 | 927.0 | 959.0 | 790.0 | -17.6 |
| *Plus:* Importations de viande | 1.0 | - | - | - | - | - | - | .. |
| *Moins:* Variations des stocks | 70.0 | 121.0 | 13.0 | -15.0 | 41.0 | 31.0 | 53.0 | |
| **Consommation de viande** | 308.0 | 315.0 | 320.0 | 323.0 | 373.0 | 332.0 | 331.0 | -0.3 |
| **Consommation par tête** *(kilogrammes par an)* | 94.5 | 95.9 | 97.6 | 97.6 | 112.1 | 99.3 | 98.0 | -1.4 |

## PRODUCTION INDIGENE BRUTE DE VIANDE
## *MEAT GROSS INDIGENOUS PRODUCTION*

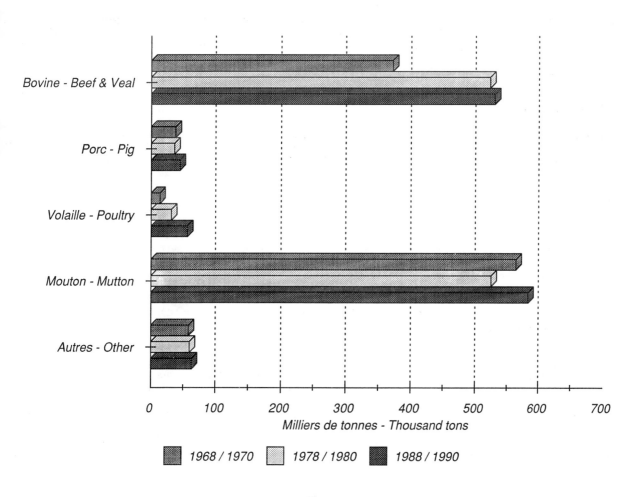

*Milliers de tonnes - Thousand tons*

■ *1968 / 1970*   ☐ *1978 / 1980*   ■ *1988 / 1990*

# EUROPEAN COMMUNITY (EC-12)

## BEEF / VIANDE DE BŒUF

*Thousand metric tons - Dressed carcass weight*

| | 1984 | 1985 | 1986 | 1987 | 1988 | 1989 | 1990 | 1989/90 % change |
|---|---|---|---|---|---|---|---|---|
| Number of animals slaughtered *(thousands)* | 24097.0 | 23693.0 [b] | 24524.0 [b] | 24475.0 | 22714.0 | 21963.0 | 23417.0 | 6.6 |
| Average dressed carcass weight *(kilogrammes)* | 291.2 | 293.0 [b] | 292.3 [b] | 295.1 | 300.7 | 304.2 | 306.6 | 0.8 |
| **Gross indigenous production** | **7005.0** | **6868.0** [b] | **7083.0** [b] | **7128.0** | **6743.0** | **6541.0** | **6948.0** | 6.2 |
| *Minus:* Meat equivalent of exported live animals | 316.0 | 312.0 [b] | 358.0 [b] | 320.0 | 325.0 | 325.0 | 330.0 | 1.5 |
| *Plus:* Meat from slaughterings of imported live animals | 327.0 | 387.0 | 443.0 [b] | 415.0 | 412.0 | 466.0 | 562.0 | 20.6 |
| **Total meat production from slaughtered animals** | **7016.0** | **6943.0** [b] | **7168.0** [b] | **7223.0** | **6830.0** | **6682.0** | **7180.0** | 7.5 |
| *Minus:* Exports of meat | 1819.0 | 1905.0 [b] | 2338.0 [b] | 2126.0 | 1952.0 | 2290.0 | 2156.0 | -5.9 |
| *Plus:* Imports of meat | 1457.0 | 1659.0 | 1677.0 [b] | 1743.0 | 1661.0 | 1735.0 | 1771.0 | 2.1 |
| *Minus:* Stock variations | 332.0 | 193.0 [b] | -154.0 [b] | 90.0 | -41.0 | -431.0 | 338.0 | |
| **Meat consumption** | **6322.0** | **6504.0** [b] | **6661.0** [b] | **6750.0** | **6580.0** | **6558.0** | **6457.0** | -1.5 |
| Consumption per head *(kilogrammes per year)* | 19.7 | 20.2 [b] | 20.6 [b] | 20.9 | 20.3 | 20.1 | 19.7 | -2.1 |

## VEAL / VIANDE DE VEAU

| | 1984 | 1985 | 1986 | 1987 | 1988 | 1989 | 1990 | 1989/90 % change |
|---|---|---|---|---|---|---|---|---|
| Number of animals slaughtered *(thousands)* | 7991.0 | 7784.0 [b] | 7236.0 [b] | 7271.0 | 6658.0 | 6071.0 | 6073.0 | 0.0 |
| Average dressed carcass weight *(kilogrammes)* | 123.5 | 126.2 [b] | 124.1 [b] | 126.1 | 129.0 | 129.8 | 131.9 | 1.6 |
| **Gross indigenous production** | **1021.0** | **1008.0** | **931.0** | **938.0** | **874.0** | **799.0** | **793.0** | -0.8 |
| *Minus:* Meat equivalent of exported live animals | 82.0 | 73.0 | 84.0 | 80.0 | 66.0 | 65.0 | 58.0 | -10.8 |
| *Plus:* Meat from slaughterings of imported live animals | 48.0 | 47.0 | 51.0 | 59.0 | 51.0 | 54.0 | 66.0 | 22.2 |
| **Total meat production from slaughtered animals** | **987.0** | **982.0** | **898.0** | **917.0** | **859.0** | **788.0** | **801.0** | 1.6 |
| *Minus:* Exports of meat | 187.0 | 195.0 | 200.0 | 192.0 | 220.0 | 154.0 | 161.0 | 4.5 |
| *Plus:* Imports of meat | 134.0 | 132.0 | 110.0 | 97.0 | 107.0 | 63.0 | 63.0 | 0.0 |
| *Minus:* Stock variations | - | - | - | - | -1.0 | - | 1.0 | |
| **Meat consumption** | **934.0** | **919.0** | **808.0** | **822.0** | **747.0** | **697.0** | **702.0** | 0.7 |
| Consumption per head *(kilogrammes per year)* | 2.9 | 2.9 | 2.5 | 2.5 | 2.3 | 2.1 | 2.1 | 0.1 |

## BEEF AND VEAL / TOTAL VIANDE BOVINE

| | 1984 | 1985 | 1986 | 1987 | 1988 | 1989 | 1990 | 1989/90 % change |
|---|---|---|---|---|---|---|---|---|
| Number of animals slaughtered *(thousands)* | 32088.0 | 31477.0 [b] | 31760.0 [b] | 31746.0 | 29372.0 | 28034.0 | 29490.0 | 5.2 |
| Average dressed carcass weight *(kilogrammes)* | 249.4 | 251.8 [b] | 254.0 [b] | 256.4 | 261.8 | 266.5 | 270.6 | 1.6 |
| **Gross indigenous production** | **8026.0** | **7876.0** [b] | **8014.0** | **8066.0** | **7617.0** | **7340.0** | **7741.0** | 5.5 |
| *Minus:* Meat equivalent of exported live animals | 398.0 | 385.0 [b] | 442.0 | 400.0 | 391.0 | 390.0 | 388.0 | -0.5 |
| *Plus:* Meat from slaughterings of imported live animals | 375.0 | 434.0 | 494.0 | 474.0 | 463.0 | 520.0 | 628.0 | 20.8 |
| **Total meat production from slaughtered animals** | **8003.0** | **7925.0** [b] | **8066.0** | **8140.0** | **7689.0** | **7470.0** | **7981.0** | 6.8 |
| *Minus:* Exports of meat | 2006.0 | 2100.0 [b] | 2538.0 | 2318.0 | 2172.0 | 2444.0 | 2317.0 | -5.2 |
| *Plus:* Imports of meat | 1591.0 | 1791.0 | 1787.0 | 1840.0 | 1768.0 | 1798.0 | 1834.0 | 2.0 |
| *Minus:* Stock variations | 332.0 | 193.0 [b] | -154.0 | 90.0 | -42.0 | -431.0 | 339.0 | |
| **Meat consumption** | **7256.0** | **7423.0** [b] | **7469.0** | **7572.0** | **7327.0** | **7255.0** | **7159.0** | -1.3 |
| Consumption per head *(kilogrammes per year)* | 22.6 | 23.1 [b] | 23.1 | 23.4 | 22.6 | 22.3 | 21.8 | -1.9 |

# COMMUNAUTÉ EUROPÉENNE (CE-12)

*Milliers de tonnes métriques - Poids en carcasse parée*

## VIANDE DE PORC / PIG MEAT

| | 1984 | 1985 | 1986 | 1987 | 1988 | 1989 | 1990 | 1989/90 % var. |
|---|---|---|---|---|---|---|---|---|
| Nombre d'animaux abattus *(milliers)* | 149822.0 | 150514.0 | 154366.0 | 158766.0 | 163550.0 | 159128.0 | 162061.0 | 1.8 |
| Poids moyen en carcasse parée *(kilogrammes)* | 80.6 | 80.4 | 80.4 | 80.9 | 81.6 | 82.4 | 83.6 | 1.4 |
| **Production indigène brute** | **12042.0** | **12075.0** | **12365.0** | **12828.0** | **13319.0** | **13103.0** | **13350.0** | 1.9 |
| *Moins:* Équivalent en viande des animaux exportés vivants | 349.0 | 367.0 | 434.0 | 467.0 | 426.0 | 390.0 | 394.0 | 1.0 |
| *Plus:* Viande provenant des abbattages d'animaux importés vivants | 381.0 | 397.0 | 487.0 | 487.0 | 449.0 | 406.0 | 586.0 | 44.3 |
| **Production totale de viande provenant des abattages** | **12074.0** | **12105.0** | **12418.0** | **12848.0** | **13342.0** | **13119.0** | **13542.0** | 3.2 |
| *Moins:* Exportations de viande | 2162.0 | 2245.0 | 2392.0 | 2529.0 | 2699.0 | 2723.0 | 3059.0 | 12.3 |
| *Plus:* Importations de viande | 1854.0 | 2026.0 | 2101.0 | 2210.0 | 2242.0 | 2378.0 | 2435.0 | 2.4 |
| *Moins:* Variations des stocks | -18.0 | 9.0 | - | 17.0 | -8.0 | -5.0 | 24.0 | |
| **Consommation de viande** | **11784.0** | **11877.0** | **12127.0** | **12512.0** | **12893.0** | **12779.0** | **12894.0** | 0.9 |
| Consommation par tête *(kilogrammes par an)* | 36.7 | 36.9 | 37.6 | 38.7 | 39.7 | 39.2 | 39.3 | 0.3 |

## VIANDE DE VOLAILLE / POULTRY MEAT

| | 1984 | 1985 | 1986 | 1987 | 1988 | 1989 | 1990 | 1989/90 % var. |
|---|---|---|---|---|---|---|---|---|
| Nombre d'animaux abattus *(milliers)* | | | | | | | | |
| Poids moyen en carcasse parée *(kilogrammes)* | | | | | | | | |
| **Production indigène brute** | **5261.0** | **5331.0** | **5443.0** | **5783.0** | **5996.0** | **6122.0** | **6336.0** | 3.5 |
| *Moins:* Équivalent en viande des animaux exportés vivants | 57.0 | 73.0 | 79.0 | 93.0 | 86.0 | 97.0 | 123.0 | 26.8 |
| *Plus:* Viande provenant des abbattages d'animaux importés vivants | 57.0 | 70.0 | 78.0 | 90.0 | 90.0 | 98.0 | 127.0 | 29.6 |
| **Production totale de viande provenant des abattages** | **5261.0** | **5328.0** | **5442.0** | **5780.0** | **6000.0** | **6123.0** | **6340.0** | 3.5 |
| *Moins:* Exportations de viande | 710.0 | 694.0 | 764.0 | 851.0 | 943.0 | 1032.0 | 1117.0 | 8.2 |
| *Plus:* Importations de viande | 435.0 | 480.0 | 514.0 | 554.0 | 643.0 | 705.0 | 839.0 | 19.0 |
| *Moins:* Variations des stocks | -9.0 | -5.0 | -37.0 | 41.0 | -6.0 | -65.0 | 22.0 | |
| **Consommation de viande** | **4995.0** | **5119.0** | **5229.0** | **5442.0** | **5706.0** | **5861.0** | **6040.0** | 3.1 |
| Consommation par tête *(kilogrammes par an)* | 15.6 | 15.9 | 16.2 | 16.8 | 17.6 | 18.0 | 18.4 | 2.4 |

## VIANDE DE MOUTON ET DE CHÈVRE / MUTTON, LAMB AND GOAT MEAT

| | 1984 | 1985 | 1986 | 1987 | 1988 | 1989 | 1990 | 1989/90 % var. |
|---|---|---|---|---|---|---|---|---|
| Nombre d'animaux abattus *(milliers)* | 69574.0 | 70845.0 | 66815.0 | 71084.0 | 74071.0 | 77340.0 | 82461.0 | 6.6 |
| Poids moyen en carcasse parée *(kilogrammes)* | 14.1 | 14.1 | 14.4 | 14.3 | 14.1 | 14.3 | 14.4 | 0.7 |
| **Production indigène brute** | **963.0** | **980.0** | **946.0** | **1003.0** | **1031.0** | **1083.0** | **1153.0** | 6.5 |
| *Moins:* Équivalent en viande des animaux exportés vivants | 28.0 | 33.0 | 33.0 | 44.0 | 53.0 | 51.0 | 73.0 | 43.1 |
| *Plus:* Viande provenant des abbattages d'animaux importés vivants | 44.0 | 53.0 | 48.0 | 58.0 | 64.0 | 71.0 | 104.0 | 46.5 |
| **Production totale de viande provenant des abattages** | **979.0** | **1000.0** | **961.0** | **1017.0** | **1042.0** | **1103.0** | **1184.0** | 7.3 |
| *Moins:* Exportations de viande | 87.0 | 90.0 | 101.0 | 123.0 | 144.0 | 162.0 | 166.0 | 2.5 |
| *Plus:* Importations de viande | 285.0 | 316.0 | 308.0 | 336.0 | 339.0 | 381.0 | 410.0 | 7.6 |
| *Moins:* Variations des stocks | -14.0 | 10.0 | -15.0 | -6.0 | -5.0 | - | 13.0 | |
| **Consommation de viande** | **1191.0** | **1216.0** | **1183.0** | **1236.0** | **1242.0** | **1322.0** | **1415.0** | 7.0 |
| Consommation par tête *(kilogrammes par an)* | 3.7 | 3.8 | 3.7 | 3.8 | 3.8 | 4.1 | 4.3 | 6.4 |

# EUROPEAN COMMUNITY (EC-12)

## HORSE MEAT / VIANDE D'ÉQUIDÉS

*Thousand metric tons - Dressed carcass weight*

| | 1984 | 1985 | 1986 | 1987 | 1988 | 1989 | 1990 | 1989/90 % change |
|---|---|---|---|---|---|---|---|---|
| Number of animals slaughtered *(thousands)* | 513.0 | 524.0 | 456.0 | 438.0 | 409.0 | 403.0 | 396.0 | -1.7 |
| Average dressed carcass weight *(kilogrammes)* | 220.3 | 223.3 | 217.1 | 226.0 | 222.5 | 215.9 | 219.7 | 1.8 |
| **Gross indigenous production** | **66.0** | **61.0** | **58.0** | **55.0** | **52.0** | **49.0** | **42.0** | -14.3 |
| *Minus:* Meat equivalent of exported live animals | 14.0 | 12.0 | 15.0 | 15.0 | 15.0 | 18.0 | 13.0 | -27.8 |
| *Plus:* Meat from slaughterings of imported live animals | 61.0 | 68.0 | 56.0 | 59.0 | 54.0 | 56.0 | 58.0 | 3.6 |
| **Total meat production from slaughtered animals** | **113.0** | **117.0** | **99.0** | **99.0** | **91.0** | **87.0** | **87.0** | 0.0 |
| *Minus:* Exports of meat | 28.0 | 26.0 | 20.0 | 22.0 | 21.0 | 22.0 | 19.0 | -13.6 |
| *Plus:* Imports of meat | 105.0 | 102.0 | 103.0 | 116.0 | 122.0 | 128.0 | 130.0 | 1.6 |
| *Minus:* Stock variations | - | - | - | -1.0 | -1.0 | - | - | |
| **Meat consumption** | **190.0** | **193.0** | **182.0** | **194.0** | **193.0** | **193.0** | **198.0** | 2.6 |
| Consumption per head *(kilogrammes per year)* | 0.6 | 0.6 | 0.6 | 0.6 | 0.6 | 0.6 | 0.6 | 2.0 |

## OTHER MEAT / AUTRES VIANDES

| | 1984 | 1985 | 1986 | 1987 | 1988 | 1989 | 1990 | 1989/90 % change |
|---|---|---|---|---|---|---|---|---|
| Number of animals slaughtered *(thousands)* | | | | | | | | |
| Average dressed carcass weight *(kilogrammes)* | | | | | | | | |
| **Gross indigenous production** | **651.0** | **658.0** | **651.0** | **662.0** | **705.0** | **699.0** | **697.0** | -0.3 |
| *Minus:* Meat equivalent of exported live animals | 1.0 | 1.0 | 2.0 | 2.0 | 3.0 | 4.0 | 4.0 | 0.0 |
| *Plus:* Meat from slaughterings of imported live animals | 4.0 | 5.0 | 5.0 | 9.0 | 8.0 | 8.0 | 10.0 | 25.0 |
| **Total meat production from slaughtered animals** | **654.0** | **662.0** | **654.0** | **669.0** | **710.0** | **703.0** | **703.0** | 0.0 |
| *Minus:* Exports of meat | 24.0 | 21.0 | 18.0 | 21.0 | 30.0 | 34.0 | 32.0 | -5.9 |
| *Plus:* Imports of meat | 93.0 | 91.0 | 80.0 | 87.0 | 92.0 | 82.0 | 89.0 | 8.5 |
| *Minus:* Stock variations | - | - | - | - | - | - | - | |
| **Meat consumption** | **723.0** | **732.0** | **716.0** | **735.0** | **772.0** | **751.0** | **760.0** | 1.2 |
| Consumption per head *(kilogrammes per year)* | 2.3 | 2.3 | 2.2 | 2.3 | 2.4 | 2.3 | 2.3 | 0.6 |

## EDIBLE OFFALS / ABATS COMESTIBLES

| | 1984 | 1985 | 1986 | 1987 | 1988 | 1989 | 1990 | 1989/90 % change |
|---|---|---|---|---|---|---|---|---|
| Number of animals slaughtered *(thousands)* | | | | | | | | |
| Average dressed carcass weight *(kilogrammes)* | | | | | | | | |
| **Gross indigenous production** | **1808.0** | **1770.0** | **1800.0** | **1857.0** | **1839.0** | **1807.0** | **1869.0** | 3.4 |
| *Minus:* Meat equivalent of exported live animals | 70.0 | 66.0 | 78.0 | 76.0 | 71.0 | 70.0 | 70.0 | 0.0 |
| *Plus:* Meat from slaughterings of imported live animals | 77.0 | 81.0 | 90.0 | 92.0 | 87.0 | 86.0 | 106.0 | 23.3 |
| **Total meat production from slaughtered animals** | **1815.0** | **1785.0** | **1812.0** | **1873.0** | **1855.0** | **1823.0** | **1905.0** | 4.5 |
| *Minus:* Exports of meat | 311.0 | 323.0 | 322.0 | 311.0 | 343.0 | 357.0 | 351.0 | -1.7 |
| *Plus:* Imports of meat | 458.0 | 486.0 | 436.0 | 424.0 | 426.0 | 375.0 | 402.0 | 7.2 |
| *Minus:* Stock variations | -3.0 | 3.0 | 3.0 | 2.0 | 1.0 | -6.0 | 1.0 | |
| **Meat consumption** | **1965.0** | **1945.0** | **1923.0** | **1984.0** | **1937.0** | **1847.0** | **1955.0** | 5.8 |
| Consumption per head *(kilogrammes per year)* | 6.1 | 6.0 | 6.0 | 6.1 | 6.0 | 5.7 | 6.0 | 5.2 |

# COMMUNAUTÉ EUROPÉENNE (CE-12)

*Milliers de tonnes métriques - Poids en carcasse parée*

**TOTAL VIANDE / TOTAL MEAT**

| | 1984 | 1985 | 1986 | 1987 | 1988 | 1989 | 1990 | 1989/90 % var. |
|---|---|---|---|---|---|---|---|---|
| **Nombre d'animaux abattus** *(milliers)* | | | | | | | | |
| **Poids moyen en carcasse parée** *(kilogrammes)* | | | | | | | | |
| **Production indigène brute** | 28817.0 | 28751.0 [b] | 29277.0 | 30254.0 | 30559.0 | 30203.0 | 31188.0 | 3.3 |
| *Moins:* Équivalent en viande des animaux exportés vivants | 917.0 | 937.0 [b] | 1083.0 | 1097.0 | 1045.0 | 1020.0 | 1065.0 | 4.4 |
| *Plus:* Viande provenant des abbattages d'animaux importés vivants | 999.0 | 1108.0 | 1258.0 | 1269.0 | 1215.0 | 1245.0 | 1619.0 | 30.0 |
| **Production totale de viande provenant des abattages** | 28899.0 | 28922.0 [b] | 29452.0 | 30426.0 | 30729.0 | 30428.0 | 31742.0 | 4.3 |
| *Moins:* Exportations de viande | 5328.0 | 5499.0 [b] | 6155.0 | 6175.0 | 6352.0 | 6774.0 | 7061.0 | 4.2 |
| *Plus:* Importations de viande | 4821.0 | 5292.0 | 5329.0 | 5567.0 | 5632.0 | 5847.0 | 6139.0 | 5.0 |
| *Moins:* Variations des stocks | 288.0 | 210.0 [b] | -203.0 | 143.0 | -61.0 | -507.0 | 399.0 | |
| **Consommation de viande** | 28104.0 | 28505.0 [b] | 28829.0 | 29675.0 | 30070.0 | 30008.0 | 30421.0 | 1.4 |
| **Consommation par tête** *(kilogrammes par an)* | 87.5 | 88.6 [b] | 89.3 | 91.7 | 92.6 | 92.1 | 92.7 | 0.8 |

## PRODUCTION INDIGENE BRUTE DE VIANDE
## MEAT GROSS INDIGENOUS PRODUCTION

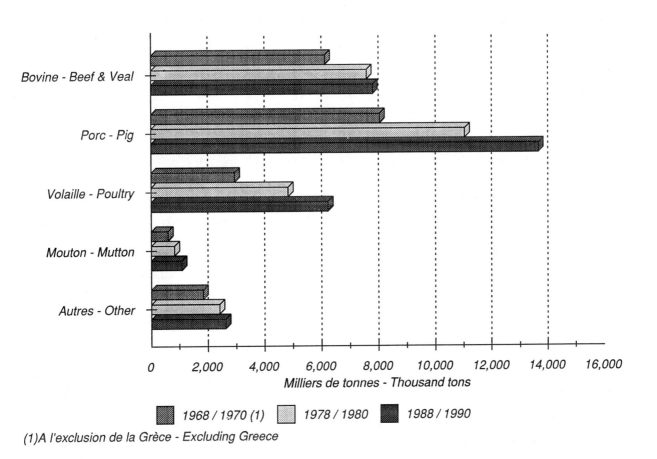

Milliers de tonnes - Thousand tons

■ 1968 / 1970 (1)    ☐ 1978 / 1980    ■ 1988 / 1990

*(1)A l'exclusion de la Grèce - Excluding Greece*

# BELGIUM - LUXEMBOURG ECONOMIC UNION

## BEEF / VIANDE DE BŒUF

*Thousand metric tons - Dressed carcass weight*

|  | 1984 | 1985 | 1986 | 1987 | 1988 | 1989 | 1990 | 1989/90 % change |
|---|---|---|---|---|---|---|---|---|
| Number of animals slaughtered *(thousands)* | 771.0 | 764.0 | 737.0 | 720.0 | 694.0 | 661.0 | 697.0 | 5.4 |
| Average dressed carcass weight *(kilogrammes)* | 365.0 | 375.0 | 389.0 | 391.0 | 397.0 | 408.0 | 410.0 | 0.5 |
| Gross indigenous production | 290.0 | 299.0 | 303.0 | 290.0 | 292.0 | 285.0 | 289.0 | 1.4 |
| *Minus:* Meat equivalent of exported live animals | 18.0 | 21.0 | 26.0 | 18.0 | 25.0 | 29.0 | 19.0 | -34.5 |
| *Plus:* Meat from slaughterings of imported live animals | 9.0 | 8.0 | 9.0 | 10.0 | 9.0 | 14.0 | 16.0 | 14.3 |
| Total meat production from slaughtered animals | 281.0 | 286.0 | 286.0 | 282.0 | 276.0 | 270.0 | 286.0 | 5.9 |
| *Minus:* Exports of meat | 80.0 | 75.0 | 87.0 | 98.0 | 110.0 | 113.0 | 141.0 | 24.8 |
| *Plus:* Imports of meat | 31.0 | 29.0 | 27.0 | 29.0 | 26.0 | 28.0 | 28.0 | 0.0 |
| *Minus:* Stock variations | 3.0 | 2.0 | 4.0 | -1.0 | -5.0 | -5.0 | -2.0 | |
| Meat consumption | 229.0 | 238.0 | 222.0 | 214.0 | 197.0 | 190.0 | 175.0 | -7.9 |
| Consumption per head *(kilogrammes per year)* | 22.4 | 23.3 | 21.7 | 20.9 | 19.2 | 18.4 | 16.9 | -8.4 |

## VEAL / VIANDE DE VEAU

|  | 1984 | 1985 | 1986 | 1987 | 1988 | 1989 | 1990 | 1989/90 % change |
|---|---|---|---|---|---|---|---|---|
| Number of animals slaughtered *(thousands)* | 290.0 | 304.0 | 301.0 | 335.0 | 291.0 | 233.0 | 239.0 | 2.6 |
| Average dressed carcass weight *(kilogrammes)* | 131.0 | 132.0 | 132.0 | 133.0 | 141.0 | 151.0 | 153.0 | 1.3 |
| Gross indigenous production | 40.0 | 43.0 | 42.0 | 46.0 | 44.0 | 38.0 | 37.0 | -2.6 |
| *Minus:* Meat equivalent of exported live animals | 5.0 | 6.0 | 6.0 | 6.0 | 6.0 | 6.0 | 5.0 | -16.7 |
| *Plus:* Meat from slaughterings of imported live animals | 3.0 | 3.0 | 4.0 | 4.0 | 3.0 | 3.0 | 4.0 | 33.3 |
| Total meat production from slaughtered animals | 38.0 | 40.0 | 40.0 | 44.0 | 41.0 | 35.0 | 36.0 | 2.9 |
| *Minus:* Exports of meat | 9.0 | 11.0 | 12.0 | 12.0 | 15.0 | 12.0 | 8.0 | -33.3 |
| *Plus:* Imports of meat | 4.0 | 3.0 | 3.0 | 3.0 | 2.0 | 2.0 | 2.0 | 0.0 |
| *Minus:* Stock variations | - | - | - | - | - | - | - | |
| Meat consumption | 33.0 | 32.0 | 31.0 | 35.0 | 28.0 | 25.0 | 30.0 | 20.0 |
| Consumption per head *(kilogrammes per year)* | 3.2 | 3.1 | 3.0 | 3.4 | 2.7 | 2.4 | 2.9 | 19.3 |

## BEEF AND VEAL / TOTAL VIANDE BOVINE

|  | 1984 | 1985 | 1986 | 1987 | 1988 | 1989 | 1990 | 1989/90 % change |
|---|---|---|---|---|---|---|---|---|
| Number of animals slaughtered *(thousands)* | 1061.0 | 1068.0 | 1038.0 | 1055.0 | 985.0 | 894.0 | 936.0 | 4.7 |
| Average dressed carcass weight *(kilogrammes)* | 300.7 | 305.2 | 314.1 | 309.0 | 321.8 | 341.2 | 344.0 | 0.8 |
| Gross indigenous production | 330.0 | 342.0 | 345.0 | 336.0 | 336.0 | 323.0 | 326.0 | 0.9 |
| *Minus:* Meat equivalent of exported live animals | 23.0 | 27.0 | 32.0 | 24.0 | 31.0 | 35.0 | 24.0 | -31.4 |
| *Plus:* Meat from slaughterings of imported live animals | 12.0 | 11.0 | 13.0 | 14.0 | 12.0 | 17.0 | 20.0 | 17.6 |
| Total meat production from slaughtered animals | 319.0 | 326.0 | 326.0 | 326.0 | 317.0 | 305.0 | 322.0 | 5.6 |
| *Minus:* Exports of meat | 89.0 | 86.0 | 99.0 | 110.0 | 125.0 | 125.0 | 149.0 | 19.2 |
| *Plus:* Imports of meat | 35.0 | 32.0 | 30.0 | 32.0 | 28.0 | 30.0 | 30.0 | 0.0 |
| *Minus:* Stock variations | 3.0 | 2.0 | 4.0 | -1.0 | -5.0 | -5.0 | -2.0 | |
| Meat consumption | 262.0 | 270.0 | 253.0 | 249.0 | 225.0 | 215.0 | 205.0 | -4.7 |
| Consumption per head *(kilogrammes per year)* | 25.6 | 26.4 | 24.7 | 24.3 | 21.9 | 20.8 | 19.8 | -5.2 |

# UNION ÉCONOMIQUE BELGO - LUXEMBOURGEOISE

Milliers de tonnes métriques - Poids en carcasse parée

*VIANDE DE PORC / PIG MEAT*

| | 1984 | 1985 | 1986 | 1987 | 1988 | 1989 | 1990 | 1989/90 % var. |
|---|---|---|---|---|---|---|---|---|
| Nombre d'animaux abattus *(milliers)* | 8452.0 | 8390.0 | 8617.0 | 9093.0 | 9279.0 | 9492.0 | 8480.0 | -10.7 |
| Poids moyen en carcasse parée *(kilogrammes)* | 86.0 | 86.0 | 87.0 | 87.0 | 88.0 | 88.0 | 94.0 | 6.8 |
| **Production indigène brute** | **684.0** | **676.0** | **701.0** | **753.0** | **806.0** | **830.0** | **747.0** | -10.0 |
| *Moins:* Équivalent en viande des animaux exportés vivants | 59.0 | 40.0 | 60.0 | 73.0 | 79.0 | 79.0 | 47.0 | -40.5 |
| *Plus:* Viande provenant des abbattages d'animaux importés vivants | 109.0 | 89.0 | 106.0 | 107.0 | 87.0 | 79.0 | 87.0 | 10.1 |
| **Production totale de viande provenant des abattages** | **734.0** | **725.0** | **747.0** | **787.0** | **814.0** | **830.0** | **787.0** | -5.2 |
| *Moins:* Exportations de viande | 324.0 | 299.0 | 348.0 | 382.0 | 377.0 | 403.0 | 394.0 | -2.2 |
| *Plus:* Importations de viande | 59.0 | 66.0 | 66.0 | 63.0 | 44.0 | 47.0 | 75.0 | 59.6 |
| *Moins:* Variations des stocks | -4.0 | 22.0 | -17.0 | 2.0 | -1.0 | -8.0 | 3.0 | |
| **Consommation de viande** | **473.0** | **470.0** | **482.0** | **466.0** | **482.0** | **482.0** | **465.0** | -3.5 |
| Consommation par tête *(kilogrammes par an)* | 46.3 | 46.0 | 47.1 | 45.5 | 47.0 | 46.7 | 44.8 | -4.1 |

*VIANDE DE VOLAILLE / POULTRY MEAT*

| | 1984 | 1985 | 1986 | 1987 | 1988 | 1989 | 1990 | 1989/90 % var. |
|---|---|---|---|---|---|---|---|---|
| Nombre d'animaux abattus *(milliers)* | | | | | | | | |
| Poids moyen en carcasse parée *(kilogrammes)* | | | | | | | | |
| **Production indigène brute** | **126.0** | **131.0** | **134.0** | **141.0** | **152.0** | **154.0** | **167.0** | 8.4 |
| *Moins:* Équivalent en viande des animaux exportés vivants | 5.0 | 7.0 | 9.0 | 12.0 | 12.0 | 18.0 | 20.0 | 11.1 |
| *Plus:* Viande provenant des abbattages d'animaux importés vivants | 23.0 | 35.0 | 43.0 | 43.0 | 41.0 | 42.0 | 44.0 | 4.8 |
| **Production totale de viande provenant des abattages** | **144.0** | **159.0** | **168.0** | **172.0** | **181.0** | **178.0** | **191.0** | 7.3 |
| *Moins:* Exportations de viande | 28.0 | 35.0 | 41.0 | 48.0 | 61.0 | 68.0 | 81.0 | 19.1 |
| *Plus:* Importations de viande | 32.0 | 34.0 | 39.0 | 42.0 | 50.0 | 52.0 | 61.0 | 17.3 |
| *Moins:* Variations des stocks | -1.0 | 1.0 | - | -1.0 | 1.0 | -1.0 | - | |
| **Consommation de viande** | **149.0** | **157.0** | **166.0** | **167.0** | **169.0** | **163.0** | **171.0** | 4.9 |
| Consommation par tête *(kilogrammes par an)* | 14.6 | 15.4 | 16.2 | 16.3 | 16.5 | 15.8 | 16.5 | 4.3 |

*VIANDE DE MOUTON ET DE CHÈVRE / MUTTON, LAMB AND GOAT MEAT*

| | 1984 | 1985 | 1986 | 1987 | 1988 | 1989 | 1990 | 1989/90 % var. |
|---|---|---|---|---|---|---|---|---|
| Nombre d'animaux abattus *(milliers)* | 343.0 | 369.0 | 315.0 | 355.0 | 324.0 | 347.0 | 373.0 | 7.5 |
| Poids moyen en carcasse parée *(kilogrammes)* | 15.0 | 22.0 | 29.0 | 31.0 | 27.0 | 28.0 | 27.0 | -3.6 |
| **Production indigène brute** | **4.0** | **3.0** | **4.0** | **4.0** | **4.0** | **4.0** | **3.0** | -25.0 |
| *Moins:* Équivalent en viande des animaux exportés vivants | 3.0 | 4.0 | 3.0 | 2.0 | 5.0 | 5.0 | 7.0 | 40.0 |
| *Plus:* Viande provenant des abbattages d'animaux importés vivants | 7.0 | 9.0 | 7.0 | 5.0 | 8.0 | 8.0 | 11.0 | 37.5 |
| **Production totale de viande provenant des abattages** | **8.0** | **8.0** | **8.0** | **7.0** | **7.0** | **7.0** | **7.0** | 0.0 |
| *Moins:* Exportations de viande | 4.0 | 5.0 | 4.0 | 4.0 | 4.0 | 5.0 | 5.0 | 0.0 |
| *Plus:* Importations de viande | 12.0 | 13.0 | 14.0 | 15.0 | 15.0 | 17.0 | 18.0 | 5.9 |
| *Moins:* Variations des stocks | - | - | - | - | - | - | - | |
| **Consommation de viande** | **16.0** | **16.0** | **18.0** | **18.0** | **18.0** | **19.0** | **20.0** | 5.3 |
| Consommation par tête *(kilogrammes par an)* | 1.6 | 1.6 | 1.8 | 1.8 | 1.8 | 1.8 | 1.9 | 4.7 |

# BELGIUM - LUXEMBOURG ECONOMIC UNION

## HORSE MEAT / VIANDE D'ÉQUIDÉS

*Thousand metric tons - Dressed carcass weight*

|  | 1984 | 1985 | 1986 | 1987 | 1988 | 1989 | 1990 | 1989/90 % change |
|---|---|---|---|---|---|---|---|---|
| Number of animals slaughtered *(thousands)* | 26.0 | 24.0 | 17.0 | 15.0 | 14.0 | 11.0 | 10.0 | -9.1 |
| Average dressed carcass weight *(kilogrammes)* | 241.0 | 238.0 | 243.0 | 247.0 | 245.0 | 239.0 | 262.0 | 9.6 |
| Gross indigenous production | 3.0 | 3.0 | 2.0 | 2.0 | 3.0 | 2.0 | 1.0 | -50.0 |
| *Minus:* Meat equivalent of exported live animals | 1.0 | 1.0 | 1.0 | 1.0 | 1.0 | 2.0 | 1.0 | -50.0 |
| *Plus:* Meat from slaughterings of imported live animals | 4.0 | 4.0 | 3.0 | 3.0 | 2.0 | 3.0 | 3.0 | 0.0 |
| Total meat production from slaughtered animals | 6.0 | 6.0 | 4.0 | 4.0 | 4.0 | 3.0 | 3.0 | 0.0 |
| *Minus:* Exports of meat | 8.0 | 9.0 | 9.0 | 10.0 | 12.0 | 12.0 | 12.0 | 0.0 |
| *Plus:* Imports of meat | 28.0 | 30.0 | 32.0 | 37.0 | 36.0 | 36.0 | 39.0 | 8.3 |
| *Minus:* Stock variations | - | - | - | - | - | - | - | |
| Meat consumption | 26.0 | 27.0 | 27.0 | 31.0 | 28.0 | 27.0 | 30.0 | 11.1 |
| Consumption per head *(kilogrammes per year)* | 2.5 | 2.6 | 2.6 | 3.0 | 2.7 | 2.6 | 2.9 | 10.5 |

## OTHER MEAT / AUTRES VIANDES

|  | 1984 | 1985 | 1986 | 1987 | 1988 | 1989 | 1990 | 1989/90 % change |
|---|---|---|---|---|---|---|---|---|
| Number of animals slaughtered *(thousands)* | | | | | | | | |
| Average dressed carcass weight *(kilogrammes)* | | | | | | | | |
| Gross indigenous production | 15.0 | 17.0 | 18.0 | 19.0 | 20.0 | 22.0 | 25.0 | 13.6 |
| *Minus:* Meat equivalent of exported live animals | - | - | - | - | - | 1.0 | 1.0 | 0.0 |
| *Plus:* Meat from slaughterings of imported live animals | 1.0 | 1.0 | 1.0 | 2.0 | 2.0 | 3.0 | 3.0 | 0.0 |
| Total meat production from slaughtered animals | 16.0 | 18.0 | 19.0 | 21.0 | 22.0 | 24.0 | 27.0 | 12.5 |
| *Minus:* Exports of meat | 3.0 | 2.0 | 2.0 | 4.0 | 6.0 | 10.0 | 8.0 | -20.0 |
| *Plus:* Imports of meat | 9.0 | 8.0 | 8.0 | 8.0 | 10.0 | 12.0 | 9.0 | -25.0 |
| *Minus:* Stock variations | - | - | - | - | - | - | - | |
| Meat consumption | 22.0 | 24.0 | 25.0 | 25.0 | 26.0 | 26.0 | 28.0 | 7.7 |
| Consumption per head *(kilogrammes per year)* | 2.2 | 2.3 | 2.4 | 2.4 | 2.5 | 2.5 | 2.7 | 7.1 |

## EDIBLE OFFALS / ABATS COMESTIBLES

|  | 1984 | 1985 | 1986 | 1987 | 1988 | 1989 | 1990 | 1989/90 % change |
|---|---|---|---|---|---|---|---|---|
| Number of animals slaughtered *(thousands)* | | | | | | | | |
| Average dressed carcass weight *(kilogrammes)* | | | | | | | | |
| Gross indigenous production | 88.0 | 88.0 | 91.0 | 96.0 | 80.0 | 80.0 | 75.0 | -6.3 |
| *Minus:* Meat equivalent of exported live animals | 7.0 | 5.0 | 8.0 | 9.0 | 8.0 | 8.0 | 5.0 | -37.5 |
| *Plus:* Meat from slaughterings of imported live animals | 12.0 | 10.0 | 11.0 | 11.0 | 7.0 | 7.0 | 8.0 | 14.3 |
| Total meat production from slaughtered animals | 93.0 | 93.0 | 94.0 | 98.0 | 79.0 | 79.0 | 78.0 | -1.3 |
| *Minus:* Exports of meat | 36.0 | 37.0 | 43.0 | 44.0 | 40.0 | 39.0 | 40.0 | 2.6 |
| *Plus:* Imports of meat | 26.0 | 26.0 | 28.0 | 27.0 | 38.0 | 38.0 | 40.0 | 5.3 |
| *Minus:* Stock variations | - | - | - | - | - | - | - | |
| Meat consumption | 83.0 | 82.0 | 79.0 | 81.0 | 77.0 | 78.0 | 78.0 | 0.0 |
| Consumption per head *(kilogrammes per year)* | 8.1 | 8.0 | 7.7 | 7.9 | 7.5 | 7.6 | 7.5 | -0.6 |

# UNION ÉCONOMIQUE BELGO - LUXEMBOURGEOISE

*Milliers de tonnes métriques - Poids en carcasse parée*

*TOTAL VIANDE / TOTAL MEAT*

| | 1984 | 1985 | 1986 | 1987 | 1988 | 1989 | 1990 | 1989/90 % var. |
|---|---|---|---|---|---|---|---|---|
| **Nombre d'animaux abattus** *(milliers)* | | | | | | | | |
| **Poids moyen en carcasse parée** *(kilogrammes)* | | | | | | | | |
| **Production indigène brute** | **1250.0** | **1260.0** | **1295.0** | **1351.0** | **1401.0** | **1415.0** | **1344.0** | **-5.0** |
| *Moins:* Équivalent en viande des animaux exportés vivants | 98.0 | 84.0 | 113.0 | 121.0 | 136.0 | 148.0 | 105.0 | -29.1 |
| *Plus:* Viande provenant des abbattages d'animaux importés vivants | 168.0 | 159.0 | 184.0 | 185.0 | 159.0 | 159.0 | 176.0 | 10.7 |
| **Production totale de viande provenant des abattages** | **1320.0** | **1335.0** | **1366.0** | **1415.0** | **1424.0** | **1426.0** | **1415.0** | **-0.8** |
| *Moins:* Exportations de viande | 492.0 | 473.0 | 546.0 | 602.0 | 625.0 | 662.0 | 689.0 | 4.1 |
| *Plus:* Importations de viande | 201.0 | 209.0 | 217.0 | 224.0 | 221.0 | 232.0 | 272.0 | 17.2 |
| *Moins:* Variations des stocks | -2.0 | 25.0 | -13.0 | - | -5.0 | -14.0 | 1.0 | |
| **Consommation de viande** | **1031.0** | **1046.0** | **1050.0** | **1037.0** | **1025.0** | **1010.0** | **997.0** | **-1.3** |
| **Consommation par tête** *(kilogrammes par an)* | 100.9 | 102.3 | 102.6 | 101.3 | 99.9 | 97.9 | 96.1 | -1.8 |

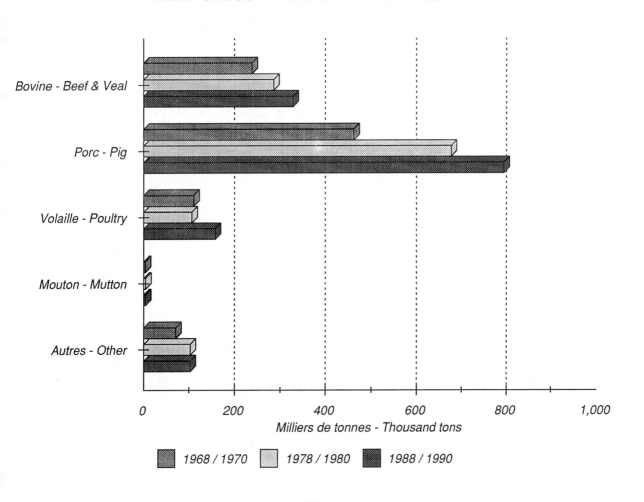

## PRODUCTION INDIGENE BRUTE DE VIANDE
## MEAT GROSS INDIGENOUS PRODUCTION

Bovine - Beef & Veal
Porc - Pig
Volaille - Poultry
Mouton - Mutton
Autres - Other

Milliers de tonnes - Thousand tons

1968 / 1970      1978 / 1980      1988 / 1990

# DENMARK

_Thousand metric tons - Dressed carcass weight_

| | 1984 | 1985 | 1986 | 1987 | 1988 | 1989 | 1990 | 1989/90 % change |
|---|---|---|---|---|---|---|---|---|
| Number of animals slaughtered _(thousands)_ | 1034.0 | 974.0 | 970.0 | 922.0 | 851.0 | 787.0 | 761.0 | -3.3 |
| Average dressed carcass weight _(kilogrammes)_ | 235.0 | 239.0 | 248.0 | 252.0 | 253.0 | 258.0 | 263.0 | 1.9 |
| Gross indigenous production | **243.0** | **234.0** | **241.0** | **233.0** | **215.0** | **203.0** | **201.0** | -1.0 |
| _Minus:_ Meat equivalent of exported live animals | - | - | - | - | - | - | - | .. |
| _Plus:_ Meat from slaughterings of imported live animals | - | - | - | - | - | - | - | .. |
| Total meat production from slaughtered animals | **243.0** | **234.0** | **241.0** | **233.0** | **215.0** | **203.0** | **201.0** | -1.0 |
| _Minus:_ Exports of meat | 176.0 | 165.0 | 189.0 | 175.0 | 168.0 | 156.0 | 133.0 | -14.7 |
| _Plus:_ Imports of meat | 6.0 | 12.0 | 18.0 | 24.0 | 26.0 | 30.0 | 41.0 | 36.7 |
| _Minus:_ Stock variations | 9.0 | 11.0 | -14.0 | 3.0 | -12.0 | -20.0 | 13.0 | |
| Meat consumption | **64.0** | **70.0** | **84.0** | **79.0** | **85.0** | **97.0** | **96.0** | -1.0 |
| Consumption per head _(kilogrammes per year)_ | 12.5 | 13.7 | 16.4 | 15.4 | 16.6 | 18.9 | 18.7 | -1.2 |

## VEAL / VIANDE DE VEAU

| | 1984 | 1985 | 1986 | 1987 | 1988 | 1989 | 1990 | 1989/90 % change |
|---|---|---|---|---|---|---|---|---|
| Number of animals slaughtered _(thousands)_ | 56.0 | 57.0 | 43.0 | 40.0 | 36.0 | 29.0 | 27.0 | -6.9 |
| Average dressed carcass weight _(kilogrammes)_ | 62.0 | 70.0 | 49.0 | 45.0 | 47.0 | 48.0 | 45.0 | -6.3 |
| Gross indigenous production | **4.0** | **2.0** | **2.0** | **2.0** | **2.0** | **1.0** | **1.0** | 0.0 |
| _Minus:_ Meat equivalent of exported live animals | - | - | - | - | - | - | - | .. |
| _Plus:_ Meat from slaughterings of imported live animals | - | - | - | - | - | - | - | .. |
| Total meat production from slaughtered animals | **4.0** | **2.0** | **2.0** | **2.0** | **2.0** | **1.0** | **1.0** | 0.0 |
| _Minus:_ Exports of meat | - | - | - | - | - | - | - | .. |
| _Plus:_ Imports of meat | - | - | - | - | - | - | - | .. |
| _Minus:_ Stock variations | - | - | - | - | - | - | - | |
| Meat consumption | **4.0** | **2.0** | **2.0** | **2.0** | **2.0** | **1.0** | **1.0** | 0.0 |
| Consumption per head _(kilogrammes per year)_ | 0.8 | 0.4 | 0.4 | 0.4 | 0.4 | 0.2 | 0.2 | -0.2 |

## BEEF AND VEAL / TOTAL VIANDE BOVINE

| | 1984 | 1985 | 1986 | 1987 | 1988 | 1989 | 1990 | 1989/90 % change |
|---|---|---|---|---|---|---|---|---|
| Number of animals slaughtered _(thousands)_ | 1090.0 | 1031.0 | 1013.0 | 962.0 | 887.0 | 816.0 | 788.0 | -3.4 |
| Average dressed carcass weight _(kilogrammes)_ | 226.6 | 228.9 | 239.9 | 244.3 | 244.6 | 250.0 | 256.3 | 2.5 |
| Gross indigenous production | **247.0** | **236.0** | **243.0** | **235.0** | **217.0** | **204.0** | **202.0** | -1.0 |
| _Minus:_ Meat equivalent of exported live animals | - | - | - | - | - | - | - | .. |
| _Plus:_ Meat from slaughterings of imported live animals | - | - | - | - | - | - | - | .. |
| Total meat production from slaughtered animals | **247.0** | **236.0** | **243.0** | **235.0** | **217.0** | **204.0** | **202.0** | -1.0 |
| _Minus:_ Exports of meat | 176.0 | 165.0 | 189.0 | 175.0 | 168.0 | 156.0 | 133.0 | -14.7 |
| _Plus:_ Imports of meat | 6.0 | 12.0 | 18.0 | 24.0 | 26.0 | 30.0 | 41.0 | 36.7 |
| _Minus:_ Stock variations | 9.0 | 11.0 | -14.0 | 3.0 | -12.0 | -20.0 | 13.0 | |
| Meat consumption | **68.0** | **72.0** | **86.0** | **81.0** | **87.0** | **98.0** | **97.0** | -1.0 |
| Consumption per head _(kilogrammes per year)_ | 13.3 | 14.1 | 16.8 | 15.8 | 17.0 | 19.1 | 18.9 | -1.2 |

# DANEMARK

*Milliers de tonnes métriques - Poids en carcasse parée*

## VIANDE DE PORC / PIG MEAT

|  | 1984 | 1985 | 1986 | 1987 | 1988 | 1989 | 1990 | 1989/90 % var. |
|---|---|---|---|---|---|---|---|---|
| Nombre d'animaux abattus *(milliers)* | 14785.0 | 15203.0 | 16101.0 | 16074.0 | 16196.0 | 15962.0 | 16416.0 | 2.8 |
| Poids moyen en carcasse parée *(kilogrammes)* | 70.0 | 71.0 | 71.0 | 71.0 | 72.0 | 73.0 | 74.0 | 1.4 |
| **Production indigène brute** | **1039.0** | **1086.0** | **1146.0** | **1150.0** | **1169.0** | **1164.0** | **1208.0** | 3.8 |
| *Moins:* Équivalent en viande des animaux exportés vivants | 4.0 | 3.0 | 2.0 | 1.0 | 1.0 | 1.0 | 1.0 | 0.0 |
| *Plus:* Viande provenant des abbattages d'animaux importés vivants | - | - | - | - | - | - | - | .. |
| Production totale de viande provenant des abattages | 1035.0 | 1083.0 | 1144.0 | 1149.0 | 1168.0 | 1163.0 | 1207.0 | 3.8 |
| *Moins:* Exportations de viande | 776.0 | 808.0 | 812.0 | 804.0 | 844.0 | 842.0 | 872.0 | 3.6 |
| *Plus:* Importations de viande | 1.0 | 2.0 | 3.0 | 4.0 | 9.0 | 15.0 | 14.0 | -6.7 |
| *Moins:* Variations des stocks | -11.0 | -13.0 | 10.0 | 9.0 | -5.0 | 4.0 | 19.0 |  |
| **Consommation de viande** | **271.0** | **290.0** | **325.0** | **340.0** | **338.0** | **332.0** | **330.0** | -0.6 |
| Consommation par tête *(kilogrammes par an)* | 53.0 | 56.7 | 63.5 | 66.3 | 65.9 | 64.7 | 64.2 | -0.8 |

## VIANDE DE VOLAILLE / POULTRY MEAT

|  | 1984 | 1985 | 1986 | 1987 | 1988 | 1989 | 1990 | 1989/90 % var. |
|---|---|---|---|---|---|---|---|---|
| Nombre d'animaux abattus *(milliers)* |  |  |  |  |  |  |  |  |
| Poids moyen en carcasse parée *(kilogrammes)* |  |  |  |  |  |  |  |  |
| **Production indigène brute** | **110.0** | **115.0** | **116.0** | **113.0** | **117.0** | **128.0** | **132.0** | 3.1 |
| *Moins:* Équivalent en viande des animaux exportés vivants | - | - | - | - | - | - | - | .. |
| *Plus:* Viande provenant des abbattages d'animaux importés vivants | - | - | - | - | - | - | - | .. |
| Production totale de viande provenant des abattages | 110.0 | 115.0 | 116.0 | 113.0 | 117.0 | 128.0 | 132.0 | 3.1 |
| *Moins:* Exportations de viande | 59.0 | 63.0 | 57.0 | 60.0 | 62.0 | 71.0 | 79.0 | 11.3 |
| *Plus:* Importations de viande | - | 3.0 | 4.0 | 4.0 | 4.0 | 5.0 | 7.0 | 40.0 |
| *Moins:* Variations des stocks | 1.0 | -1.0 | 3.0 | -3.0 | -1.0 | 2.0 | - |  |
| **Consommation de viande** | **50.0** | **56.0** | **60.0** | **60.0** | **60.0** | **60.0** | **60.0** | 0.0 |
| Consommation par tête *(kilogrammes par an)* | 9.8 | 11.0 | 11.7 | 11.7 | 11.7 | 11.7 | 11.7 | -0.2 |

## VIANDE DE MOUTON ET DE CHÈVRE / MUTTON, LAMB AND GOAT MEAT

|  | 1984 | 1985 | 1986 | 1987 | 1988 | 1989 | 1990 | 1989/90 % var. |
|---|---|---|---|---|---|---|---|---|
| Nombre d'animaux abattus *(milliers)* | 25.0 | 29.0 | 35.0 | 41.0 | 48.0 | 54.0 | 71.0 | 31.5 |
| Poids moyen en carcasse parée *(kilogrammes)* | 24.0 | 28.0 | 23.0 | 25.0 | 23.0 | 24.0 | 21.0 | -12.5 |
| **Production indigène brute** | **1.0** | **1.0** | **1.0** | **1.0** | **1.0** | **1.0** | **1.0** | 0.0 |
| *Moins:* Équivalent en viande des animaux exportés vivants | - | - | - | - | - | - | - | .. |
| *Plus:* Viande provenant des abbattages d'animaux importés vivants | - | - | - | - | - | - | - | .. |
| Production totale de viande provenant des abattages | 1.0 | 1.0 | 1.0 | 1.0 | 1.0 | 1.0 | 1.0 | 0.0 |
| *Moins:* Exportations de viande | - | - | - | - | - | - | - | .. |
| *Plus:* Importations de viande | 2.0 | 2.0 | 2.0 | 3.0 | 3.0 | 3.0 | 4.0 | 33.3 |
| *Moins:* Variations des stocks | - | - | - | - | - | - | - |  |
| **Consommation de viande** | **3.0** | **3.0** | **3.0** | **4.0** | **4.0** | **4.0** | **5.0** | 25.0 |
| Consommation par tête *(kilogrammes par an)* | 0.6 | 0.6 | 0.6 | 0.8 | 0.8 | 0.8 | 1.0 | 24.8 |

# DENMARK

|  | 1984 | 1985 | 1986 | 1987 | 1988 | 1989 | 1990 | 1989/90 % change |
|---|---|---|---|---|---|---|---|---|
| Number of animals slaughtered *(thousands)* | 4.0 | 3.0 | 3.0 | 3.0 | 3.0 | 3.0 | 3.0 | 0.0 |
| Average dressed carcass weight *(kilogrammes)* | 300.0 | 300.0 | 300.0 | 300.0 | 300.0 | 300.0 | 300.0 | 0.0 |
| Gross indigenous production | 1.0 | 1.0 | 1.0 | 1.0 | 1.0 | 1.0 | 1.0 | 0.0 |
| *Minus:* Meat equivalent of exported live animals | - | - | - | - | - | - | - | .. |
| *Plus:* Meat from slaughterings of imported live animals | - | - | - | - | - | - | - | .. |
| Total meat production from slaughtered animals | 1.0 | 1.0 | 1.0 | 1.0 | 1.0 | 1.0 | 1.0 | 0.0 |
| *Minus:* Exports of meat | - | - | - | - | - | - | - | .. |
| *Plus:* Imports of meat | - | - | - | - | - | - | - | .. |
| *Minus:* Stock variations | - | - | - | - | - | - | - | |
| Meat consumption | 1.0 | 1.0 | 1.0 | 1.0 | 1.0 | 1.0 | 1.0 | 0.0 |
| Consumption per head *(kilogrammes per year)* | 0.2 | 0.2 | 0.2 | 0.2 | 0.2 | 0.2 | 0.2 | -0.2 |

## OTHER MEAT / AUTRES VIANDES

|  | 1984 | 1985 | 1986 | 1987 | 1988 | 1989 | 1990 | 1989/90 % change |
|---|---|---|---|---|---|---|---|---|
| Number of animals slaughtered *(thousands)* | | | | | | | | |
| Average dressed carcass weight *(kilogrammes)* | | | | | | | | |
| Gross indigenous production | 3.0 | 3.0 | 3.0 | 3.0 | 3.0 | 3.0 | 3.0 | 0.0 |
| *Minus:* Meat equivalent of exported live animals | - | - | - | - | - | - | - | .. |
| *Plus:* Meat from slaughterings of imported live animals | - | - | - | - | - | - | - | .. |
| Total meat production from slaughtered animals | 3.0 | 3.0 | 3.0 | 3.0 | 3.0 | 3.0 | 3.0 | 0.0 |
| *Minus:* Exports of meat | - | - | - | - | - | - | - | .. |
| *Plus:* Imports of meat | - | - | - | - | - | - | - | .. |
| *Minus:* Stock variations | - | - | - | - | - | - | - | |
| Meat consumption | 3.0 | 3.0 | 3.0 | 3.0 | 3.0 | 3.0 | 3.0 | 0.0 |
| Consumption per head *(kilogrammes per year)* | 0.6 | 0.6 | 0.6 | 0.6 | 0.6 | 0.6 | 0.6 | -0.2 |

## EDIBLE OFFALS / ABATS COMESTIBLES

|  | 1984 | 1985 | 1986 | 1987 | 1988 | 1989 | 1990 | 1989/90 % change |
|---|---|---|---|---|---|---|---|---|
| Number of animals slaughtered *(thousands)* | | | | | | | | |
| Average dressed carcass weight *(kilogrammes)* | | | | | | | | |
| Gross indigenous production | 60.0 | 61.0 | 68.0 | 69.0 | 68.0 | 66.0 | 69.0 | 4.5 |
| *Minus:* Meat equivalent of exported live animals | - | - | - | - | - | - | - | .. |
| *Plus:* Meat from slaughterings of imported live animals | - | - | - | - | - | - | - | .. |
| Total meat production from slaughtered animals | 60.0 | 61.0 | 68.0 | 69.0 | 68.0 | 66.0 | 69.0 | 4.5 |
| *Minus:* Exports of meat | 27.0 | 25.0 | 27.0 | 26.0 | 27.0 | 24.0 | 26.0 | 8.3 |
| *Plus:* Imports of meat | - | - | - | 1.0 | 1.0 | 2.0 | 2.0 | 0.0 |
| *Minus:* Stock variations | - | - | - | - | - | - | - | |
| Meat consumption | 33.0 | 36.0 | 41.0 | 44.0 | 42.0 | 44.0 | 45.0 | 2.3 |
| Consumption per head *(kilogrammes per year)* | 6.5 | 7.0 | 8.0 | 8.6 | 8.2 | 8.6 | 8.8 | 2.1 |

# DANEMARK

*Milliers de tonnes métriques - Poids en carcasse parée*

TOTAL VIANDE / TOTAL MEAT

| | 1984 | 1985 | 1986 | 1987 | 1988 | 1989 | 1990 | 1989/90 % var. |
|---|---|---|---|---|---|---|---|---|
| **Nombre d'animaux abattus** *(milliers)* | | | | | | | | |
| **Poids moyen en carcasse parée** *(kilogrammes)* | | | | | | | | |
| **Production indigène brute** | 1461.0 | 1503.0 | 1578.0 | 1572.0 | 1576.0 | 1567.0 | 1616.0 | 3.1 |
| *Moins:* Équivalent en viande des animaux exportés vivants | 4.0 | 3.0 | 2.0 | 1.0 | 1.0 | 1.0 | 1.0 | 0.0 |
| *Plus:* Viande provenant des abattages d'animaux importés vivants | - | - | - | - | - | - | - | .. |
| **Production totale de viande provenant des abattages** | 1457.0 | 1500.0 | 1576.0 | 1571.0 | 1575.0 | 1566.0 | 1615.0 | 3.1 |
| *Moins:* Exportations de viande | 1038.0 | 1061.0 | 1085.0 | 1065.0 | 1101.0 | 1093.0 | 1110.0 | 1.6 |
| *Plus:* Importations de viande | 9.0 | 19.0 | 27.0 | 36.0 | 43.0 | 55.0 | 68.0 | 23.6 |
| *Moins:* Variations des stocks | -1.0 | -3.0 | -1.0 | 9.0 | -18.0 | -14.0 | 32.0 | |
| **Consommation de viande** | 429.0 | 461.0 | 519.0 | 533.0 | 535.0 | 542.0 | 541.0 | -0.2 |
| **Consommation par tête** *(kilogrammes par an)* | 83.9 | 90.1 | 101.3 | 104.0 | 104.3 | 105.6 | 105.3 | -0.3 |

## PRODUCTION INDIGENE BRUTE DE VIANDE
## MEAT GROSS INDIGENOUS PRODUCTION

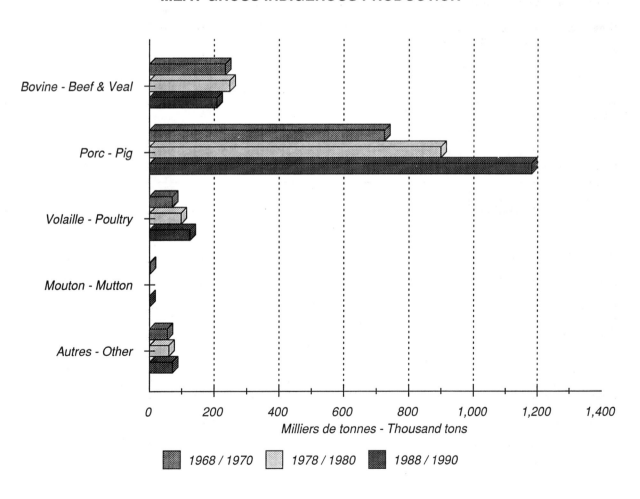

1968 / 1970    1978 / 1980    1988 / 1990

# FRANCE

*BEEF / VIANDE DE BŒUF*               *Thousand metric tons - Dressed carcass weight*

| | 1984 | 1985 | 1986 | 1987 | 1988 | 1989 | 1990 | 1989/90 % change |
|---|---|---|---|---|---|---|---|---|
| Number of animals slaughtered *(thousands)* | 4914.0 | 4682.0 | 4699.0 | 4814.0 | 4484.0 | 4125.0 | 4262.0 | 3.3 |
| Average dressed carcass weight *(kilogrammes)* | 327.0 | 328.0 | 331.0 | 332.0 | 335.0 | 336.0 | 342.0 | 1.8 |
| **Gross indigenous production** | **1703.0** | **1652.0** | **1675.0** | **1740.0** | **1652.0** | **1531.0** | **1599.0** | 4.4 |
| *Minus:* Meat equivalent of exported live animals | 110.0 | 129.0 | 143.0 | 154.0 | 166.0 | 165.0 | 161.0 | -2.4 |
| *Plus:* Meat from slaughterings of imported live animals | 13.0 | 14.0 | 22.0 | 14.0 | 18.0 | 21.0 | 23.0 | 9.5 |
| **Total meat production from slaughtered animals** | **1606.0** | **1537.0** | **1554.0** | **1600.0** | **1504.0** | **1387.0** | **1461.0** | 5.3 |
| *Minus:* Exports of meat | 377.0 | 440.0 | 528.0 | 453.0 | 417.0 | 523.0 | 420.0 | -19.7 |
| *Plus:* Imports of meat | 266.0 | 301.0 | 301.0 | 287.0 | 283.0 | 330.0 | 372.0 | 12.7 |
| *Minus:* Stock variations | 112.0 | 33.0 | -70.0 | 39.0 | 1.0 | -208.0 | 51.0 | |
| **Meat consumption** | **1383.0** | **1365.0** | **1397.0** | **1395.0** | **1369.0** | **1402.0** | **1362.0** | -2.9 |
| Consumption per head *(kilogrammes per year)* | 25.2 | 24.7 | 25.2 | 25.1 | 24.5 | 25.0 | 24.1 | -3.3 |

## *VEAL / VIANDE DE VEAU*

| | 1984 | 1985 | 1986 | 1987 | 1988 | 1989 | 1990 | 1989/90 % change |
|---|---|---|---|---|---|---|---|---|
| Number of animals slaughtered *(thousands)* | 3338.0 | 3094.0 | 3078.0 | 3069.0 | 2745.0 | 2419.0 | 2411.0 | -0.3 |
| Average dressed carcass weight *(kilogrammes)* | 115.0 | 115.0 | 116.0 | 117.0 | 117.0 | 118.0 | 121.0 | 2.5 |
| **Gross indigenous production** | **418.0** | **387.0** | **393.0** | **389.0** | **351.0** | **312.0** | **313.0** | 0.3 |
| *Minus:* Meat equivalent of exported live animals | 41.0 | 38.0 | 45.0 | 39.0 | 35.0 | 33.0 | 30.0 | -9.1 |
| *Plus:* Meat from slaughterings of imported live animals | 8.0 | 7.0 | 8.0 | 10.0 | 6.0 | 7.0 | 9.0 | 28.6 |
| **Total meat production from slaughtered animals** | **385.0** | **356.0** | **356.0** | **360.0** | **322.0** | **286.0** | **292.0** | 2.1 |
| *Minus:* Exports of meat | 28.0 | 20.0 | 18.0 | 18.0 | 32.0 | 9.0 | 7.0 | -22.2 |
| *Plus:* Imports of meat | 15.0 | 21.0 | 23.0 | 19.0 | 35.0 | 27.0 | 29.0 | 7.4 |
| *Minus:* Stock variations | - | - | - | - | - | - | - | |
| **Meat consumption** | **372.0** | **357.0** | **361.0** | **361.0** | **325.0** | **304.0** | **314.0** | 3.3 |
| Consumption per head *(kilogrammes per year)* | 6.8 | 6.5 | 6.5 | 6.5 | 5.8 | 5.4 | 5.6 | 2.8 |

## *BEEF AND VEAL / TOTAL VIANDE BOVINE*

| | 1984 | 1985 | 1986 | 1987 | 1988 | 1989 | 1990 | 1989/90 % change |
|---|---|---|---|---|---|---|---|---|
| Number of animals slaughtered *(thousands)* | 8252.0 | 7776.0 | 7777.0 | 7883.0 | 7229.0 | 6544.0 | 6673.0 | 2.0 |
| Average dressed carcass weight *(kilogrammes)* | 241.3 | 243.4 | 245.6 | 248.6 | 252.6 | 255.7 | 262.7 | 2.8 |
| **Gross indigenous production** | **2121.0** | **2039.0** | **2068.0** | **2129.0** | **2003.0** | **1843.0** | **1912.0** | 3.7 |
| *Minus:* Meat equivalent of exported live animals | 151.0 | 167.0 | 188.0 | 193.0 | 201.0 | 198.0 | 191.0 | -3.5 |
| *Plus:* Meat from slaughterings of imported live animals | 21.0 | 21.0 | 30.0 | 24.0 | 24.0 | 28.0 | 32.0 | 14.3 |
| **Total meat production from slaughtered animals** | **1991.0** | **1893.0** | **1910.0** | **1960.0** | **1826.0** | **1673.0** | **1753.0** | 4.8 |
| *Minus:* Exports of meat | 405.0 | 460.0 | 546.0 | 471.0 | 449.0 | 532.0 | 427.0 | -19.7 |
| *Plus:* Imports of meat | 281.0 | 322.0 | 324.0 | 306.0 | 318.0 | 357.0 | 401.0 | 12.3 |
| *Minus:* Stock variations | 112.0 | 33.0 | -70.0 | 39.0 | 1.0 | -208.0 | 51.0 | |
| **Meat consumption** | **1755.0** | **1722.0** | **1758.0** | **1756.0** | **1694.0** | **1706.0** | **1676.0** | -1.8 |
| Consumption per head *(kilogrammes per year)* | 31.9 | 31.2 | 31.7 | 31.6 | 30.3 | 30.4 | 29.7 | -2.2 |

# FRANCE

*Milliers de tonnes métriques - Poids en carcasse parée*

## VIANDE DE PORC / PIG MEAT

| | 1984 | 1985 | 1986 | 1987 | 1988 | 1989 | 1990 | 1989/90 % var. |
|---|---|---|---|---|---|---|---|---|
| Nombre d'animaux abattus *(milliers)* | 19698.0 | 19531.0 | 19743.0 | 20398.0 | 21437.0 | 21126.0 | 21303.0 | 0.8 |
| Poids moyen en carcasse parée *(kilogrammes)* | 85.0 | 85.0 | 85.0 | 85.0 | 86.0 | 87.0 | 88.0 | 1.1 |
| **Production indigène brute** | **1575.0** | **1571.0** | **1591.0** | **1646.0** | **1779.0** | **1779.0** | **1816.0** | **2.1** |
| *Moins:* Équivalent en viande des animaux exportés vivants | 12.0 | 13.0 | 24.0 | 23.0 | 17.0 | 12.0 | 13.0 | 8.3 |
| *Plus:* Viande provenant des abbattages d'animaux importés vivants | 121.0 | 104.0 | 110.0 | 106.0 | 90.0 | 77.0 | 68.0 | -11.7 |
| **Production totale de viande provenant des abattages** | **1684.0** | **1662.0** | **1677.0** | **1729.0** | **1852.0** | **1844.0** | **1871.0** | **1.5** |
| *Moins:* Exportations de viande | 54.0 | 69.0 | 95.0 | 129.0 | 192.0 | 189.0 | 210.0 | 11.1 |
| *Plus:* Importations de viande | 314.0 | 357.0 | 383.0 | 431.0 | 447.0 | 441.0 | 440.0 | -0.2 |
| *Moins:* Variations des stocks | -2.0 | - | 1.0 | -1.0 | - | -2.0 | - | |
| **Consommation de viande** | **1946.0** | **1950.0** | **1964.0** | **2032.0** | **2107.0** | **2098.0** | **2101.0** | **0.1** |
| Consommation par tête *(kilogrammes par an)* | 35.4 | 35.3 | 35.5 | 36.5 | 37.7 | 37.4 | 37.2 | -0.3 |

## VIANDE DE VOLAILLE / POULTRY MEAT

| | 1984 | 1985 | 1986 | 1987 | 1988 | 1989 | 1990 | 1989/90 % var. |
|---|---|---|---|---|---|---|---|---|
| Nombre d'animaux abattus *(milliers)* | | | | | | | | |
| Poids moyen en carcasse parée *(kilogrammes)* | | | | | | | | |
| **Production indigène brute** | **1251.0** | **1267.0** | **1328.0** | **1408.0** | **1449.0** | **1557.0** | **1665.0** | **6.9** |
| *Moins:* Équivalent en viande des animaux exportés vivants | 5.0 | 8.0 | 8.0 | 10.0 | 9.0 | 10.0 | 12.0 | 20.0 |
| *Plus:* Viande provenant des abbattages d'animaux importés vivants | 6.0 | 6.0 | 5.0 | 4.0 | 4.0 | 5.0 | 4.0 | -20.0 |
| **Production totale de viande provenant des abattages** | **1252.0** | **1265.0** | **1325.0** | **1402.0** | **1444.0** | **1552.0** | **1657.0** | **6.8** |
| *Moins:* Exportations de viande | 337.0 | 314.0 | 354.0 | 383.0 | 413.0 | 463.0 | 497.0 | 7.3 |
| *Plus:* Importations de viande | 24.0 | 27.0 | 26.0 | 44.0 | 49.0 | 60.0 | 67.0 | 11.7 |
| *Moins:* Variations des stocks | -12.0 | -1.0 | -44.0 | 32.0 | -6.0 | -34.0 | 8.0 | |
| **Consommation de viande** | **951.0** | **979.0** | **1041.0** | **1031.0** | **1086.0** | **1183.0** | **1219.0** | **3.0** |
| Consommation par tête *(kilogrammes par an)* | 17.3 | 17.7 | 18.8 | 18.5 | 19.4 | 21.1 | 21.6 | 2.5 |

## VIANDE DE MOUTON ET DE CHÈVRE / MUTTON, LAMB AND GOAT MEAT

| | 1984 | 1985 | 1986 | 1987 | 1988 | 1989 | 1990 | 1989/90 % var. |
|---|---|---|---|---|---|---|---|---|
| Nombre d'animaux abattus *(milliers)* | 10360.0 | 10189.0 | 9788.0 | 9745.0 | 9714.0 | 9492.0 | 11265.0 | 18.7 |
| Poids moyen en carcasse parée *(kilogrammes)* | 17.0 | 17.0 | 17.0 | 17.0 | 17.0 | 17.0 | 17.0 | 0.0 |
| **Production indigène brute** | **174.0** | **173.0** | **162.0** | **159.0** | **151.0** | **151.0** | **177.0** | **17.2** |
| *Moins:* Équivalent en viande des animaux exportés vivants | 2.0 | 3.0 | 4.0 | 5.0 | 4.0 | 7.0 | 10.0 | 42.9 |
| *Plus:* Viande provenant des abbattages d'animaux importés vivants | 7.0 | 8.0 | 11.0 | 16.0 | 17.0 | 18.0 | 27.0 | 50.0 |
| **Production totale de viande provenant des abattages** | **179.0** | **178.0** | **169.0** | **170.0** | **164.0** | **162.0** | **194.0** | **19.8** |
| *Moins:* Exportations de viande | 5.0 | 4.0 | 4.0 | 5.0 | 6.0 | 6.0 | 7.0 | 16.7 |
| *Plus:* Importations de viande | 64.0 | 68.0 | 83.0 | 93.0 | 104.0 | 120.0 | 126.0 | 5.0 |
| *Moins:* Variations des stocks | - | - | - | - | - | - | 1.0 | |
| **Consommation de viande** | **238.0** | **242.0** | **248.0** | **258.0** | **262.0** | **276.0** | **312.0** | **13.0** |
| Consommation par tête *(kilogrammes par an)* | 4.3 | 4.4 | 4.5 | 4.6 | 4.7 | 4.9 | 5.5 | 12.5 |

# FRANCE

## HORSE MEAT / VIANDE D'ÉQUIDÉS

*Thousand metric tons - Dressed carcass weight*

|  | 1984 | 1985 | 1986 | 1987 | 1988 | 1989 | 1990 | 1989/90 % change |
|---|---|---|---|---|---|---|---|---|
| Number of animals slaughtered *(thousands)* | 100.0 | 97.0 | 70.0 | 68.0 | 57.0 | 50.0 | 46.0 | -8.0 |
| Average dressed carcass weight *(kilogrammes)* | 285.0 | 290.0 | 289.0 | 290.0 | 289.0 | 285.0 | 283.0 | -0.7 |
| **Gross indigenous production** | **15.0** | **14.0** | **13.0** | **14.0** | **15.0** | **13.0** | **10.0** | -23.1 |
| *Minus:* Meat equivalent of exported live animals | 2.0 | 2.0 | 4.0 | 5.0 | 6.0 | 6.0 | 4.0 | -33.3 |
| *Plus:* Meat from slaughterings of imported live animals | 16.0 | 16.0 | 11.0 | 11.0 | 8.0 | 7.0 | 7.0 | 0.0 |
| **Total meat production from slaughtered animals** | **29.0** | **28.0** | **20.0** | **20.0** | **17.0** | **14.0** | **13.0** | -7.1 |
| *Minus:* Exports of meat | 1.0 | 1.0 | 1.0 | 1.0 | 1.0 | 1.0 | - | -100.0 |
| *Plus:* Imports of meat | 43.0 | 37.0 | 35.0 | 39.0 | 44.0 | 47.0 | 45.0 | -4.3 |
| *Minus:* Stock variations | - | - | - | - | - | - | - | |
| **Meat consumption** | **71.0** | **64.0** | **54.0** | **58.0** | **60.0** | **60.0** | **58.0** | -3.3 |
| Consumption per head *(kilogrammes per year)* | 1.3 | 1.2 | 1.0 | 1.0 | 1.1 | 1.1 | 1.0 | -3.8 |

## OTHER MEAT / AUTRES VIANDES

|  | 1984 | 1985 | 1986 | 1987 | 1988 | 1989 | 1990 | 1989/90 % change |
|---|---|---|---|---|---|---|---|---|
| Number of animals slaughtered *(thousands)* | | | | | | | | |
| Average dressed carcass weight *(kilogrammes)* | | | | | | | | |
| **Gross indigenous production** | **269.0** | **270.0** | **269.0** | **272.0** | **290.0** | **300.0** | **300.0** | 0.0 |
| *Minus:* Meat equivalent of exported live animals | - | - | - | - | - | - | - | .. |
| *Plus:* Meat from slaughterings of imported live animals | 1.0 | 2.0 | 2.0 | 3.0 | 3.0 | 3.0 | 3.0 | 0.0 |
| **Total meat production from slaughtered animals** | **270.0** | **272.0** | **271.0** | **275.0** | **293.0** | **303.0** | **303.0** | 0.0 |
| *Minus:* Exports of meat | 5.0 | 4.0 | 4.0 | 4.0 | 4.0 | 6.0 | 6.0 | 0.0 |
| *Plus:* Imports of meat | 27.0 | 25.0 | 25.0 | 25.0 | 25.0 | 16.0 | 25.0 | 56.3 |
| *Minus:* Stock variations | - | - | - | - | - | - | - | |
| **Meat consumption** | **292.0** | **293.0** | **292.0** | **296.0** | **314.0** | **313.0** | **322.0** | 2.9 |
| Consumption per head *(kilogrammes per year)* | 5.3 | 5.3 | 5.3 | 5.3 | 5.6 | 5.6 | 5.7 | 2.4 |

## EDIBLE OFFALS / ABATS COMESTIBLES

|  | 1984 | 1985 | 1986 | 1987 | 1988 | 1989 | 1990 | 1989/90 % change |
|---|---|---|---|---|---|---|---|---|
| Number of animals slaughtered *(thousands)* | | | | | | | | |
| Average dressed carcass weight *(kilogrammes)* | | | | | | | | |
| **Gross indigenous production** | **473.0** | **442.0** | **453.0** | **465.0** | **463.0** | **444.0** | **451.0** | 1.6 |
| *Minus:* Meat equivalent of exported live animals | 20.0 | 22.0 | 26.0 | 26.0 | 26.0 | 26.0 | 26.0 | 0.0 |
| *Plus:* Meat from slaughterings of imported live animals | 18.0 | 16.0 | 18.0 | 18.0 | 18.0 | 18.0 | 18.0 | 0.0 |
| **Total meat production from slaughtered animals** | **471.0** | **436.0** | **445.0** | **457.0** | **455.0** | **436.0** | **443.0** | 1.6 |
| *Minus:* Exports of meat | 28.0 | 28.0 | 29.0 | 30.0 | 31.0 | 26.0 | 23.0 | -11.5 |
| *Plus:* Imports of meat | 159.0 | 164.0 | 159.0 | 164.0 | 163.0 | 122.0 | 150.0 | 23.0 |
| *Minus:* Stock variations | - | - | - | - | - | - | - | |
| **Meat consumption** | **602.0** | **572.0** | **575.0** | **591.0** | **587.0** | **532.0** | **570.0** | 7.1 |
| Consumption per head *(kilogrammes per year)* | 11.0 | 10.4 | 10.4 | 10.6 | 10.5 | 9.5 | 10.1 | 6.6 |

# FRANCE

*Milliers de tonnes métriques - Poids en carcasse parée*

*TOTAL VIANDE / TOTAL MEAT*

| | 1984 | 1985 | 1986 | 1987 | 1988 | 1989 | 1990 | 1989/90 % var. |
|---|---|---|---|---|---|---|---|---|
| **Nombre d'animaux abattus** *(milliers)* | | | | | | | | |
| **Poids moyen en carcasse parée** *(kilogrammes)* | | | | | | | | |
| **Production indigène brute** | 5878.0 | 5776.0 | 5884.0 | 6093.0 | 6150.0 | 6087.0 | 6331.0 | 4.0 |
| *Moins:* Équivalent en viande des animaux exportés vivants | 192.0 | 215.0 | 254.0 | 262.0 | 263.0 | 259.0 | 256.0 | -1.2 |
| *Plus:* Viande provenant des abbattages d'animaux importés vivants | 190.0 | 173.0 | 187.0 | 182.0 | 164.0 | 156.0 | 159.0 | 1.9 |
| **Production totale de viande provenant des abattages** | 5876.0 | 5734.0 | 5817.0 | 6013.0 | 6051.0 | 5984.0 | 6234.0 | 4.2 |
| *Moins:* Exportations de viande | 835.0 | 880.0 | 1033.0 | 1023.0 | 1096.0 | 1223.0 | 1170.0 | -4.3 |
| *Plus:* Importations de viande | 912.0 | 1000.0 | 1035.0 | 1102.0 | 1150.0 | 1163.0 | 1254.0 | 7.8 |
| *Moins:* Variations des stocks | 98.0 | 32.0 | -113.0 | 70.0 | -5.0 | -244.0 | 60.0 | |
| **Consommation de viande** | 5855.0 | 5822.0 | 5932.0 | 6022.0 | 6110.0 | 6168.0 | 6258.0 | 1.5 |
| **Consommation par tête** *(kilogrammes par an)* | 106.6 | 105.5 | 107.1 | 108.3 | 109.3 | 109.8 | 110.9 | 1.0 |

## PRODUCTION INDIGENE BRUTE DE VIANDE
## MEAT GROSS INDIGENOUS PRODUCTION

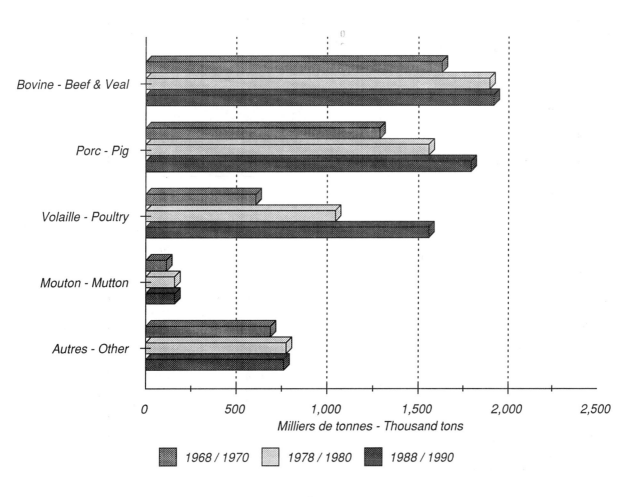

Milliers de tonnes - Thousand tons

■ 1968 / 1970   ☐ 1978 / 1980   ■ 1988 / 1990

# GERMANY[1]

## BEEF / VIANDE DE BŒUF

| | 1984 | 1985 | 1986 | 1987 | 1988 | 1989 | 1990 | 1989/90 % change |
|---|---|---|---|---|---|---|---|---|
| Number of animals slaughtered *(thousands)* | 5139.0 | 4976.0 | 5229.0 | 5174.0 | 4861.0 | 4706.0 | 5431.0 | 15.4 |
| Average dressed carcass weight *(kilogrammes)* | 298.0 | 300.0 | 308.0 | 308.0 | 314.0 | 322.0 | 318.0 | -1.2 |
| Gross indigenous production | 1552.0 | 1513.0 | 1654.0 | 1619.0 | 1539.0 | 1542.0 | 1625.0 | 5.4 |
| *Minus:* Meat equivalent of exported live animals | 59.0 | 57.0 | 68.0 | 55.0 | 47.0 | 67.0 | 75.0 | 11.9 |
| *Plus:* Meat from slaughterings of imported live animals | 38.0 | 37.0 | 25.0 | 28.0 | 36.0 | 38.0 | 179.0 | 371.1 |
| Total meat production from slaughtered animals | 1531.0 | 1493.0 | 1611.0 | 1592.0 | 1528.0 | 1513.0 | 1729.0 | 14.3 |
| *Minus:* Exports of meat | 444.0 | 433.0 | 576.0 | 463.0 | 467.0 | 601.0 | 680.0 | 13.1 |
| *Plus:* Imports of meat | 258.0 | 274.0 | 277.0 | 289.0 | 292.0 | 300.0 | 335.0 | 11.7 |
| *Minus:* Stock variations | 72.0 | 30.0 | -16.0 | 79.0 | 2.0 | -130.0 | 57.0 | |
| Meat consumption | 1273.0 | 1304.0 | 1328.0 | 1339.0 | 1351.0 | 1342.0 | 1327.0 | -1.1 |
| Consumption per head *(kilogrammes per year)* | 20.8 | 21.4 | 21.7 | 21.9 | 22.0 | 21.6 | 21.0 | -2.8 |

## VEAL / VIANDE DE VEAU

| | 1984 | 1985 | 1986 | 1987 | 1988 | 1989 | 1990 | 1989/90 % change |
|---|---|---|---|---|---|---|---|---|
| Number of animals slaughtered *(thousands)* | 708.0 | 708.0 | 707.0 | 729.0 | 639.0 | 500.0 | 514.0 | 2.8 |
| Average dressed carcass weight *(kilogrammes)* | 117.0 | 117.0 | 119.0 | 122.0 | 126.0 | 127.0 | 125.0 | -1.6 |
| Gross indigenous production | 85.0 | 83.0 | 85.0 | 85.0 | 74.0 | 59.0 | 51.0 | -13.6 |
| *Minus:* Meat equivalent of exported live animals | 14.0 | 11.0 | 12.0 | 9.0 | 8.0 | 9.0 | 7.0 | -22.2 |
| *Plus:* Meat from slaughterings of imported live animals | 12.0 | 11.0 | 11.0 | 13.0 | 14.0 | 13.0 | 20.0 | 53.8 |
| Total meat production from slaughtered animals | 83.0 | 83.0 | 84.0 | 89.0 | 80.0 | 63.0 | 64.0 | 1.6 |
| *Minus:* Exports of meat | 5.0 | 4.0 | 3.0 | 3.0 | 6.0 | 3.0 | 4.0 | 33.3 |
| *Plus:* Imports of meat | 27.0 | 27.0 | 23.0 | 23.0 | 17.0 | 12.0 | 11.0 | -8.3 |
| *Minus:* Stock variations | - | - | - | - | - | - | - | |
| Meat consumption | 105.0 | 106.0 | 104.0 | 109.0 | 91.0 | 72.0 | 71.0 | -1.4 |
| Consumption per head *(kilogrammes per year)* | 1.7 | 1.7 | 1.7 | 1.8 | 1.5 | 1.2 | 1.1 | -3.1 |

## BEEF AND VEAL / TOTAL VIANDE BOVINE

| | 1984 | 1985 | 1986 | 1987 | 1988 | 1989 | 1990 | 1989/90 % change |
|---|---|---|---|---|---|---|---|---|
| Number of animals slaughtered *(thousands)* | 5847.0 | 5684.0 | 5936.0 | 5903.0 | 5500.0 | 5206.0 | 5945.0 | 14.2 |
| Average dressed carcass weight *(kilogrammes)* | 276.0 | 277.3 | 285.5 | 284.8 | 292.4 | 302.7 | 301.6 | -0.4 |
| Gross indigenous production | 1637.0 | 1596.0 | 1739.0 | 1704.0 | 1613.0 | 1601.0 | 1676.0 | 4.7 |
| *Minus:* Meat equivalent of exported live animals | 73.0 | 68.0 | 80.0 | 64.0 | 55.0 | 76.0 | 82.0 | 7.9 |
| *Plus:* Meat from slaughterings of imported live animals | 50.0 | 48.0 | 36.0 | 41.0 | 50.0 | 51.0 | 199.0 | 290.2 |
| Total meat production from slaughtered animals | 1614.0 | 1576.0 | 1695.0 | 1681.0 | 1608.0 | 1576.0 | 1793.0 | 13.8 |
| *Minus:* Exports of meat | 449.0 | 437.0 | 579.0 | 466.0 | 473.0 | 604.0 | 684.0 | 13.2 |
| *Plus:* Imports of meat | 285.0 | 301.0 | 300.0 | 312.0 | 309.0 | 312.0 | 346.0 | 10.9 |
| *Minus:* Stock variations | 72.0 | 30.0 | -16.0 | 79.0 | 2.0 | -130.0 | 57.0 | |
| Meat consumption | 1378.0 | 1410.0 | 1432.0 | 1448.0 | 1442.0 | 1414.0 | 1398.0 | -1.1 |
| Consumption per head *(kilogrammes per year)* | 22.5 | 23.1 | 23.5 | 23.7 | 23.5 | 22.8 | 22.2 | -2.8 |

(1) Territory prior to unification / Territoire avant l'unification

# ALLEMAGNE[1]

*Milliers de tonnes métriques - Poids en carcasse parée*

## VIANDE DE PORC / PIG MEAT

| | 1984 | 1985 | 1986 | 1987 | 1988 | 1989 | 1990 | 1989/90 % var. |
|---|---|---|---|---|---|---|---|---|
| Nombre d'animaux abattus *(milliers)* | 38652.0 | 38732.0 | 39443.0 | 39507.0 | 38931.0 | 36369.0 | 37906.0 | 4.2 |
| Poids moyen en carcasse parée *(kilogrammes)* | 83.0 | 84.0 | 85.0 | 85.0 | 86.0 | 87.0 | 89.0 | 2.3 |
| Production indigène brute | 3161.0 | 3151.0 | 3288.0 | 3286.0 | 3250.0 | 3094.0 | 3142.0 | 1.6 |
| *Moins:* Équivalent en viande des animaux exportés vivants | 26.0 | 25.0 | 41.0 | 38.0 | 32.0 | 35.0 | 59.0 | 68.6 |
| *Plus:* Viande provenant des abbattages d'animaux importés vivants | 87.0 | 117.0 | 89.0 | 117.0 | 124.0 | 102.0 | 274.0 | 168.6 |
| Production totale de viande provenant des abattages | 3222.0 | 3243.0 | 3336.0 | 3365.0 | 3342.0 | 3161.0 | 3357.0 | 6.2 |
| *Moins:* Exportations de viande | 114.0 | 114.0 | 132.0 | 135.0 | 148.0 | 143.0 | 387.0 | 170.6 |
| *Plus:* Importations de viande | 510.0 | 535.0 | 529.0 | 561.0 | 622.0 | 625.0 | 674.0 | 7.8 |
| *Moins:* Variations des stocks | -6.0 | -1.0 | 3.0 | -1.0 | -1.0 | -2.0 | - | |
| Consommation de viande | 3624.0 | 3665.0 | 3730.0 | 3792.0 | 3817.0 | 3645.0 | 3644.0 | 0.0 |
| Consommation par tête *(kilogrammes par an)* | 59.2 | 60.1 | 61.1 | 62.1 | 62.1 | 58.8 | 57.8 | -1.7 |

## VIANDE DE VOLAILLE / POULTRY MEAT

| | 1984 | 1985 | 1986 | 1987 | 1988 | 1989 | 1990 | 1989/90 % var. |
|---|---|---|---|---|---|---|---|---|
| Nombre d'animaux abattus *(milliers)* | | | | | | | | |
| Poids moyen en carcasse parée *(kilogrammes)* | | | | | | | | |
| Production indigène brute | 352.0 | 357.0 | 377.0 | 390.0 | 411.0 | 425.0 | 449.0 | 5.6 |
| *Moins:* Équivalent en viande des animaux exportés vivants | 3.0 | 3.0 | 4.0 | 6.0 | 8.0 | 11.0 | 20.0 | 81.8 |
| *Plus:* Viande provenant des abbattages d'animaux importés vivants | 12.0 | 12.0 | 11.0 | 18.0 | 18.0 | 17.0 | 27.0 | 58.8 |
| Production totale de viande provenant des abattages | 361.0 | 366.0 | 384.0 | 402.0 | 421.0 | 431.0 | 456.0 | 5.8 |
| *Moins:* Exportations de viande | 25.0 | 24.0 | 24.0 | 26.0 | 32.0 | 41.0 | 45.0 | 9.8 |
| *Plus:* Importations de viande | 244.0 | 249.0 | 254.0 | 265.0 | 297.0 | 318.0 | 370.0 | 16.4 |
| *Moins:* Variations des stocks | - | - | - | - | - | - | - | |
| Consommation de viande | 580.0 | 591.0 | 614.0 | 641.0 | 686.0 | 708.0 | 781.0 | 10.3 |
| Consommation par tête *(kilogrammes par an)* | 9.5 | 9.7 | 10.1 | 10.5 | 11.2 | 11.4 | 12.4 | 8.4 |

## VIANDE DE MOUTON ET DE CHÈVRE / MUTTON, LAMB AND GOAT MEAT

| | 1984 | 1985 | 1986 | 1987 | 1988 | 1989 | 1990 | 1989/90 % var. |
|---|---|---|---|---|---|---|---|---|
| Nombre d'animaux abattus *(milliers)* | 1339.0 | 1322.0 | 1249.0 | 1428.0 | 1466.0 | 1549.0 | 1878.0 | 21.2 |
| Poids moyen en carcasse parée *(kilogrammes)* | 21.0 | 21.0 | 20.0 | 21.0 | 20.0 | 20.0 | 20.0 | 0.0 |
| Production indigène brute | 23.0 | 23.0 | 23.0 | 26.0 | 25.0 | 25.0 | 29.0 | 16.0 |
| *Moins:* Équivalent en viande des animaux exportés vivants | 4.0 | 6.0 | 6.0 | 5.0 | 4.0 | 4.0 | 10.0 | 150.0 |
| *Plus:* Viande provenant des abbattages d'animaux importés vivants | 9.0 | 10.0 | 9.0 | 8.0 | 8.0 | 10.0 | 18.0 | 80.0 |
| Production totale de viande provenant des abattages | 28.0 | 27.0 | 26.0 | 29.0 | 29.0 | 31.0 | 37.0 | 19.4 |
| *Moins:* Exportations de viande | 1.0 | 1.0 | 1.0 | 1.0 | 2.0 | 2.0 | 3.0 | 50.0 |
| *Plus:* Importations de viande | 22.0 | 27.0 | 26.0 | 25.0 | 26.0 | 33.0 | 33.0 | 0.0 |
| *Moins:* Variations des stocks | - | - | - | - | - | - | - | |
| Consommation de viande | 49.0 | 53.0 | 51.0 | 53.0 | 53.0 | 62.0 | 67.0 | 8.1 |
| Consommation par tête *(kilogrammes par an)* | 0.8 | 0.9 | 0.8 | 0.9 | 0.9 | 1.0 | 1.1 | 6.2 |

(1) Territoire avant l'unification / Territory prior to unification

# GERMANY[1]

## HORSE MEAT / VIANDE D'ÉQUIDÉS

*Thousand metric tons - Dressed carcass weight*

|  | 1984 | 1985 | 1986 | 1987 | 1988 | 1989 | 1990 | 1989/90 % change |
|---|---|---|---|---|---|---|---|---|
| Number of animals slaughtered *(thousands)* | 26.0 | 24.0 | 18.0 | 17.0 | 16.0 | 16.0 | 15.0 | -6.3 |
| Average dressed carcass weight *(kilogrammes)* | 273.0 | 278.0 | 268.0 | 270.0 | 266.0 | 261.0 | 267.0 | 2.3 |
| **Gross indigenous production** | **8.0** | **9.0** | **7.0** | **7.0** | **5.0** | **5.0** | **4.0** | -20.0 |
| *Minus:* Meat equivalent of exported live animals | 4.0 | 4.0 | 4.0 | 4.0 | 3.0 | 4.0 | 3.0 | -25.0 |
| *Plus:* Meat from slaughterings of imported live animals | 3.0 | 2.0 | 2.0 | 2.0 | 2.0 | 3.0 | 3.0 | 0.0 |
| **Total meat production from slaughtered animals** | **7.0** | **7.0** | **5.0** | **5.0** | **4.0** | **4.0** | **4.0** | 0.0 |
| *Minus:* Exports of meat | 2.0 | 2.0 | - | - | - | - | - | .. |
| *Plus:* Imports of meat | - | - | - | 1.0 | 1.0 | 1.0 | 1.0 | 0.0 |
| *Minus:* Stock variations | - | - | - | - | - | - | - | |
| **Meat consumption** | **5.0** | **5.0** | **5.0** | **6.0** | **5.0** | **5.0** | **5.0** | 0.0 |
| Consumption per head *(kilogrammes per year)* | 0.1 | 0.1 | 0.1 | 0.1 | 0.1 | 0.1 | 0.1 | -1.7 |

## OTHER MEAT / AUTRES VIANDES

|  | 1984 | 1985 | 1986 | 1987 | 1988 | 1989 | 1990 | 1989/90 % change |
|---|---|---|---|---|---|---|---|---|
| Number of animals slaughtered *(thousands)* | | | | | | | | |
| Average dressed carcass weight *(kilogrammes)* | | | | | | | | |
| **Gross indigenous production** | **38.0** | **38.0** | **37.0** | **37.0** | **37.0** | **37.0** | **37.0** | 0.0 |
| *Minus:* Meat equivalent of exported live animals | - | - | - | - | - | - | - | .. |
| *Plus:* Meat from slaughterings of imported live animals | - | - | - | 1.0 | 1.0 | 1.0 | 1.0 | 0.0 |
| **Total meat production from slaughtered animals** | **38.0** | **38.0** | **37.0** | **38.0** | **38.0** | **38.0** | **38.0** | 0.0 |
| *Minus:* Exports of meat | 2.0 | 2.0 | 3.0 | 3.0 | 4.0 | 4.0 | 4.0 | 0.0 |
| *Plus:* Imports of meat | 25.0 | 27.0 | 19.0 | 20.0 | 26.0 | 24.0 | 25.0 | 4.2 |
| *Minus:* Stock variations | - | - | - | - | - | - | - | |
| **Meat consumption** | **61.0** | **63.0** | **53.0** | **55.0** | **60.0** | **58.0** | **59.0** | 1.7 |
| Consumption per head *(kilogrammes per year)* | 1.0 | 1.0 | 0.9 | 0.9 | 1.0 | 0.9 | 0.9 | 0.0 |

## EDIBLE OFFALS / ABATS COMESTIBLES

|  | 1984 | 1985 | 1986 | 1987 | 1988 | 1989 | 1990 | 1989/90 % change |
|---|---|---|---|---|---|---|---|---|
| Number of animals slaughtered *(thousands)* | | | | | | | | |
| Average dressed carcass weight *(kilogrammes)* | | | | | | | | |
| **Gross indigenous production** | **316.0** | **307.0** | **332.0** | **328.0** | **317.0** | **307.0** | **315.0** | 2.6 |
| *Minus:* Meat equivalent of exported live animals | 9.0 | 8.0 | 10.0 | 9.0 | 7.0 | 9.0 | 11.0 | 22.2 |
| *Plus:* Meat from slaughterings of imported live animals | 10.0 | 12.0 | 9.0 | 11.0 | 12.0 | 11.0 | 34.0 | 209.1 |
| **Total meat production from slaughtered animals** | **317.0** | **311.0** | **331.0** | **330.0** | **322.0** | **309.0** | **338.0** | 9.4 |
| *Minus:* Exports of meat | 33.0 | 37.0 | 44.0 | 44.0 | 47.0 | 48.0 | 45.0 | -6.3 |
| *Plus:* Imports of meat | 72.0 | 68.0 | 56.0 | 50.0 | 51.0 | 52.0 | 65.0 | 25.0 |
| *Minus:* Stock variations | - | - | - | - | - | - | - | |
| **Meat consumption** | **356.0** | **342.0** | **343.0** | **336.0** | **326.0** | **313.0** | **358.0** | 14.4 |
| Consumption per head *(kilogrammes per year)* | 5.8 | 5.6 | 5.6 | 5.5 | 5.3 | 5.0 | 5.7 | 12.4 |

(1) Territory prior to unification / Territoire avant l'unification

# ALLEMAGNE[1]

*Milliers de tonnes métriques - Poids en carcasse parée*

*TOTAL VIANDE / TOTAL MEAT*

| | 1984 | 1985 | 1986 | 1987 | 1988 | 1989 | 1990 | 1989/90 % var. |
|---|---|---|---|---|---|---|---|---|
| **Nombre d'animaux abattus** *(milliers)* | | | | | | | | |
| **Poids moyen en carcasse parée** *(kilogrammes)* | | | | | | | | |
| **Production indigène brute** | **5535.0** | **5481.0** | **5803.0** | **5778.0** | **5658.0** | **5494.0** | **5652.0** | 2.9 |
| *Moins:* Équivalent en viande des animaux exportés vivants | 119.0 | 114.0 | 145.0 | 126.0 | 109.0 | 139.0 | 185.0 | 33.1 |
| *Plus:* Viande provenant des abbattages d'animaux importés vivants | 171.0 | 201.0 | 156.0 | 198.0 | 215.0 | 195.0 | 556.0 | 185.1 |
| **Production totale de viande provenant des abattages** | **5587.0** | **5568.0** | **5814.0** | **5850.0** | **5764.0** | **5550.0** | **6023.0** | 8.5 |
| *Moins:* Exportations de viande | 626.0 | 617.0 | 783.0 | 675.0 | 706.0 | 842.0 | 1168.0 | 38.7 |
| *Plus:* Importations de viande | 1158.0 | 1207.0 | 1184.0 | 1234.0 | 1332.0 | 1365.0 | 1514.0 | 10.9 |
| *Moins:* Variations des stocks | 66.0 | 29.0 | -13.0 | 78.0 | 1.0 | -132.0 | 57.0 | |
| **Consommation de viande** | **6053.0** | **6129.0** | **6228.0** | **6331.0** | **6389.0** | **6205.0** | **6312.0** | 1.7 |
| **Consommation par tête** *(kilogrammes par an)* | 98.9 | 100.4 | 102.0 | 103.7 | 104.0 | 100.1 | 100.1 | 0.0 |

(1) Territoire avant l'unification / Territory prior to unification

## PRODUCTION INDIGENE BRUTE DE VIANDE
## MEAT GROSS INDIGENOUS PRODUCTION

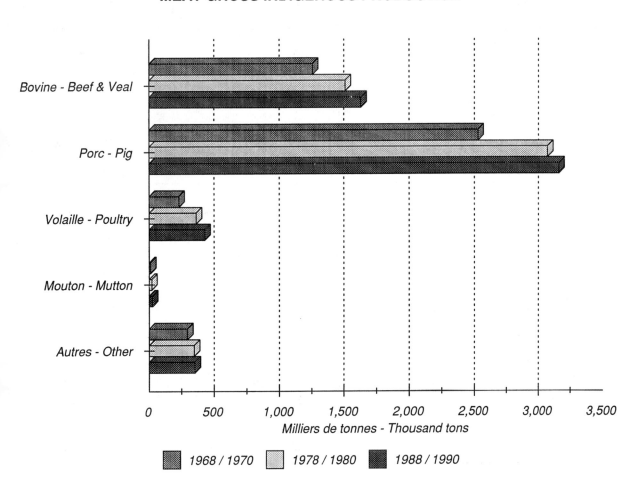

Milliers de tonnes - Thousand tons

■ 1968 / 1970    □ 1978 / 1980    ■ 1988 / 1990

# GREECE

## BEEF / VIANDE DE BŒUF

*Thousand metric tons - Dressed carcass weight*

| | 1984 | 1985 | 1986 | 1987 | 1988 | 1989 | 1990 | 1989/90 % change |
|---|---|---|---|---|---|---|---|---|
| Number of animals slaughtered *(thousands)* | 351.0 | 334.0 | 328.0 | 337.0 | 324.0 | 304.0 | 314.0 | 3.3 |
| Average dressed carcass weight *(kilogrammes)* | 223.0 | 227.0 | 231.0 | 235.0 | 235.0 | 247.0 | 240.0 | -2.8 |
| **Gross indigenous production** | **74.0** | **69.0** | **68.0** | **64.0** | **67.0** | **58.0** | **60.0** | 3.4 |
| *Minus:* Meat equivalent of exported live animals | - | - | - | - | - | - | - | .. |
| *Plus:* Meat from slaughterings of imported live animals | 4.0 | 8.0 | 8.0 | 16.0 | 9.0 | 17.0 | 16.0 | -5.9 |
| **Total meat production from slaughtered animals** | **78.0** | **77.0** | **76.0** | **80.0** | **76.0** | **75.0** | **76.0** | 1.3 |
| *Minus:* Exports of meat | - | - | - | - | 2.0 | 1.0 | 1.0 | 0.0 |
| *Plus:* Imports of meat | 86.0 | 99.0 | 121.0 | 158.0 | 92.0 | 152.0 | 147.0 | -3.3 |
| *Minus:* Stock variations | -2.0 | 3.0 | -2.0 | -1.0 | 3.0 | - | -1.0 | |
| **Meat consumption** | **166.0** | **173.0** | **199.0** | **239.0** | **163.0** | **226.0** | **223.0** | -1.3 |
| Consumption per head *(kilogrammes per year)* | 16.8 | 17.4 | 20.0 | 23.9 | 16.3 | 22.5 | 22.0 | -2.4 |

## VEAL / VIANDE DE VEAU

| | 1984 | 1985 | 1986 | 1987 | 1988 | 1989 | 1990 | 1989/90 % change |
|---|---|---|---|---|---|---|---|---|
| Number of animals slaughtered *(thousands)* | 57.0 | 56.0 | 52.0 | 55.0 | 55.0 | 62.0 | 55.0 | -11.3 |
| Average dressed carcass weight *(kilogrammes)* | 114.0 | 113.0 | 113.0 | 114.0 | 114.0 | 125.0 | 116.0 | -7.2 |
| **Gross indigenous production** | **6.0** | **6.0** | **6.0** | **6.0** | **6.0** | **8.0** | **6.0** | -25.0 |
| *Minus:* Meat equivalent of exported live animals | - | - | - | - | - | - | - | .. |
| *Plus:* Meat from slaughterings of imported live animals | 1.0 | - | - | - | - | - | - | .. |
| **Total meat production from slaughtered animals** | **7.0** | **6.0** | **6.0** | **6.0** | **6.0** | **8.0** | **6.0** | -25.0 |
| *Minus:* Exports of meat | - | - | - | - | - | - | - | .. |
| *Plus:* Imports of meat | 42.0 | 33.0 | 18.0 | 15.0 | 21.0 | 5.0 | 1.0 | -80.0 |
| *Minus:* Stock variations | - | - | - | - | - | - | - | |
| **Meat consumption** | **49.0** | **39.0** | **24.0** | **21.0** | **27.0** | **13.0** | **7.0** | -46.2 |
| Consumption per head *(kilogrammes per year)* | 4.9 | 3.9 | 2.4 | 2.1 | 2.7 | 1.3 | 0.7 | -46.7 |

## BEEF AND VEAL / TOTAL VIANDE BOVINE

| | 1984 | 1985 | 1986 | 1987 | 1988 | 1989 | 1990 | 1989/90 % change |
|---|---|---|---|---|---|---|---|---|
| Number of animals slaughtered *(thousands)* | 408.0 | 390.0 | 380.0 | 392.0 | 379.0 | 366.0 | 369.0 | 0.8 |
| Average dressed carcass weight *(kilogrammes)* | 208.3 | 212.8 | 215.8 | 219.4 | 216.4 | 226.8 | 222.2 | -2.0 |
| **Gross indigenous production** | **80.0** | **75.0** | **74.0** | **70.0** | **73.0** | **66.0** | **66.0** | 0.0 |
| *Minus:* Meat equivalent of exported live animals | - | - | - | - | - | - | - | .. |
| *Plus:* Meat from slaughterings of imported live animals | 5.0 | 8.0 | 8.0 | 16.0 | 9.0 | 17.0 | 16.0 | -5.9 |
| **Total meat production from slaughtered animals** | **85.0** | **83.0** | **82.0** | **86.0** | **82.0** | **83.0** | **82.0** | -1.2 |
| *Minus:* Exports of meat | - | - | - | - | 2.0 | 1.0 | 1.0 | 0.0 |
| *Plus:* Imports of meat | 128.0 | 132.0 | 139.0 | 173.0 | 113.0 | 157.0 | 148.0 | -5.7 |
| *Minus:* Stock variations | -2.0 | 3.0 | -2.0 | -1.0 | 3.0 | - | -1.0 | |
| **Meat consumption** | **215.0** | **212.0** | **223.0** | **260.0** | **190.0** | **239.0** | **230.0** | -3.8 |
| Consumption per head *(kilogrammes per year)* | 21.7 | 21.3 | 22.4 | 26.0 | 19.0 | 23.8 | 22.7 | -4.8 |

# GRÈCE

*Milliers de tonnes métriques - Poids en carcasse parée*

## VIANDE DE PORC / PIG MEAT

| | 1984 | 1985 | 1986 | 1987 | 1988 | 1989 | 1990 | 1989/90 % var. |
|---|---|---|---|---|---|---|---|---|
| Nombre d'animaux abattus *(milliers)* | 2262.0 | 2227.0 | 2347.0 | 2401.0 | 2365.0 | 2348.0 | 2264.0 | -3.6 |
| Poids moyen en carcasse parée *(kilogrammes)* | 66.0 | 64.0 | 65.0 | 68.0 | 68.0 | 64.0 | 65.0 | 1.6 |
| **Production indigène brute** | **146.0** | **147.0** | **153.0** | **164.0** | **160.0** | **151.0** | **147.0** | **-2.6** |
| *Moins:* Équivalent en viande des animaux exportés vivants | - | - | - | - | - | - | - | .. |
| *Plus:* Viande provenant des abbattages d'animaux importés vivants | - | - | - | - | - | - | - | .. |
| **Production totale de viande provenant des abattages** | **146.0** | **147.0** | **153.0** | **164.0** | **160.0** | **151.0** | **147.0** | **-2.6** |
| *Moins:* Exportations de viande | - | - | - | - | - | 1.0 | 1.0 | 0.0 |
| *Plus:* Importations de viande | 56.0 | 64.0 | 68.0 | 82.0 | 56.0 | 83.0 | 67.0 | -19.3 |
| *Moins:* Variations des stocks | 1.0 | - | - | - | - | - | - | |
| **Consommation de viande** | **201.0** | **211.0** | **221.0** | **246.0** | **216.0** | **233.0** | **213.0** | **-8.6** |
| **Consommation par tête** *(kilogrammes par an)* | 20.3 | 21.2 | 22.2 | 24.6 | 21.6 | 23.2 | 21.0 | -9.5 |

## VIANDE DE VOLAILLE / POULTRY MEAT

| | 1984 | 1985 | 1986 | 1987 | 1988 | 1989 | 1990 | 1989/90 % var. |
|---|---|---|---|---|---|---|---|---|
| Nombre d'animaux abattus *(milliers)* | | | | | | | | |
| Poids moyen en carcasse parée *(kilogrammes)* | | | | | | | | |
| **Production indigène brute** | **152.0** | **155.0** | **145.0** | **149.0** | **149.0** | **153.0** | **160.0** | **4.6** |
| *Moins:* Équivalent en viande des animaux exportés vivants | - | - | - | - | - | - | - | .. |
| *Plus:* Viande provenant des abbattages d'animaux importés vivants | - | - | - | - | - | - | - | .. |
| **Production totale de viande provenant des abattages** | **152.0** | **155.0** | **145.0** | **149.0** | **149.0** | **153.0** | **160.0** | **4.6** |
| *Moins:* Exportations de viande | - | 1.0 | 1.0 | 2.0 | 2.0 | 2.0 | 2.0 | 0.0 |
| *Plus:* Importations de viande | 3.0 | 4.0 | 4.0 | 7.0 | 7.0 | 9.0 | 10.0 | 11.1 |
| *Moins:* Variations des stocks | - | 2.0 | -3.0 | -2.0 | -1.0 | - | 2.0 | |
| **Consommation de viande** | **155.0** | **156.0** | **151.0** | **156.0** | **155.0** | **160.0** | **166.0** | **3.8** |
| **Consommation par tête** *(kilogrammes par an)* | 15.7 | 15.7 | 15.2 | 15.6 | 15.5 | 15.9 | 16.4 | 2.7 |

## VIANDE DE MOUTON ET DE CHÈVRE / MUTTON, LAMB AND GOAT MEAT

| | 1984 | 1985 | 1986 | 1987 | 1988 | 1989 | 1990 | 1989/90 % var. |
|---|---|---|---|---|---|---|---|---|
| Nombre d'animaux abattus *(milliers)* | 11499.0 | 11509.0 | 9960.0 | 12136.0 | 11794.0 | 12049.0 | 12213.0 | 1.4 |
| Poids moyen en carcasse parée *(kilogrammes)* | 11.0 | 11.0 | 11.0 | 10.0 | 11.0 | 11.0 | 11.0 | 0.0 |
| **Production indigène brute** | **120.0** | **121.0** | **106.0** | **124.0** | **127.0** | **128.0** | **128.0** | **0.0** |
| *Moins:* Équivalent en viande des animaux exportés vivants | - | - | - | - | - | 1.0 | - | -100.0 |
| *Plus:* Viande provenant des abbattages d'animaux importés vivants | 2.0 | 1.0 | - | 1.0 | 1.0 | 2.0 | 1.0 | -50.0 |
| **Production totale de viande provenant des abattages** | **122.0** | **122.0** | **106.0** | **125.0** | **128.0** | **129.0** | **129.0** | **0.0** |
| *Moins:* Exportations de viande | 1.0 | - | - | - | 1.0 | 1.0 | 1.0 | 0.0 |
| *Plus:* Importations de viande | 15.0 | 16.0 | 18.0 | 14.0 | 15.0 | 20.0 | 17.0 | -15.0 |
| *Moins:* Variations des stocks | 1.0 | -1.0 | - | -2.0 | 1.0 | 2.0 | 2.0 | |
| **Consommation de viande** | **135.0** | **139.0** | **124.0** | **141.0** | **141.0** | **146.0** | **143.0** | **-2.1** |
| **Consommation par tête** *(kilogrammes par an)* | 13.6 | 14.0 | 12.4 | 14.1 | 14.1 | 14.6 | 14.1 | -3.1 |

# GREECE

## HORSE MEAT / VIANDE D'ÉQUIDÉS

*Thousand metric tons - Dressed carcass weight*

| | 1984 | 1985 | 1986 | 1987 | 1988 | 1989 | 1990 | 1989/90 % change |
|---|---|---|---|---|---|---|---|---|
| Number of animals slaughtered *(thousands)* | - | - | - | - | - | - | - | .. |
| Average dressed carcass weight *(kilogrammes)* | - | - | - | - | - | - | - | .. |
| Gross indigenous production | - | - | 1.0 | 1.0 | 1.0 | 1.0 | - | -100.0 |
| *Minus:* Meat equivalent of exported live animals | - | - | 1.0 | - | - | 1.0 | - | -100.0 |
| *Plus:* Meat from slaughterings of imported live animals | - | - | - | - | - | - | - | .. |
| Total meat production from slaughtered animals | - | - | - | 1.0 | 1.0 | - | - | .. |
| *Minus:* Exports of meat | - | - | - | - | - | - | - | .. |
| *Plus:* Imports of meat | - | - | - | - | - | - | - | .. |
| *Minus:* Stock variations | - | - | - | - | - | - | - | |
| Meat consumption | - | - | - | 1.0 | 1.0 | - | - | .. |
| Consumption per head *(kilogrammes per year)* | - | - | - | 0.1 | 0.1 | - | - | .. |

## OTHER MEAT / AUTRES VIANDES

| | 1984 | 1985 | 1986 | 1987 | 1988 | 1989 | 1990 | 1989/90 % change |
|---|---|---|---|---|---|---|---|---|
| Number of animals slaughtered *(thousands)* | | | | | | | | |
| Average dressed carcass weight *(kilogrammes)* | | | | | | | | |
| Gross indigenous production | 5.0 | 5.0 | 4.0 | 5.0 | 5.0 | 5.0 | 5.0 | 0.0 |
| *Minus:* Meat equivalent of exported live animals | - | - | - | - | - | - | - | .. |
| *Plus:* Meat from slaughterings of imported live animals | - | - | - | - | - | - | - | .. |
| Total meat production from slaughtered animals | 5.0 | 5.0 | 4.0 | 5.0 | 5.0 | 5.0 | 5.0 | 0.0 |
| *Minus:* Exports of meat | 1.0 | - | - | - | - | - | - | .. |
| *Plus:* Imports of meat | - | - | - | 1.0 | - | - | - | .. |
| *Minus:* Stock variations | - | - | - | - | - | - | - | |
| Meat consumption | 4.0 | 5.0 | 4.0 | 6.0 | 5.0 | 5.0 | 5.0 | 0.0 |
| Consumption per head *(kilogrammes per year)* | 0.4 | 0.5 | 0.4 | 0.6 | 0.5 | 0.5 | 0.5 | -1.1 |

## EDIBLE OFFALS / ABATS COMESTIBLES

| | 1984 | 1985 | 1986 | 1987 | 1988 | 1989 | 1990 | 1989/90 % change |
|---|---|---|---|---|---|---|---|---|
| Number of animals slaughtered *(thousands)* | | | | | | | | |
| Average dressed carcass weight *(kilogrammes)* | | | | | | | | |
| Gross indigenous production | 49.0 | 49.0 | 46.0 | 52.0 | 51.0 | 51.0 | 50.0 | -2.0 |
| *Minus:* Meat equivalent of exported live animals | - | - | - | - | - | - | - | .. |
| *Plus:* Meat from slaughterings of imported live animals | - | - | - | - | - | - | - | .. |
| Total meat production from slaughtered animals | 49.0 | 49.0 | 46.0 | 52.0 | 51.0 | 51.0 | 50.0 | -2.0 |
| *Minus:* Exports of meat | - | - | - | - | - | 1.0 | 1.0 | 0.0 |
| *Plus:* Imports of meat | 9.0 | 10.0 | 12.0 | 14.0 | 8.0 | 11.0 | 10.0 | -9.1 |
| *Minus:* Stock variations | - | - | - | - | - | - | 1.0 | |
| Meat consumption | 58.0 | 59.0 | 58.0 | 66.0 | 59.0 | 61.0 | 58.0 | -4.9 |
| Consumption per head *(kilogrammes per year)* | 5.9 | 5.9 | 5.8 | 6.6 | 5.9 | 6.1 | 5.7 | -5.9 |

# GRÈCE

*Milliers de tonnes métriques - Poids en carcasse parée*

*TOTAL VIANDE / TOTAL MEAT*

| | 1984 | 1985 | 1986 | 1987 | 1988 | 1989 | 1990 | 1989/90 % var. |
|---|---|---|---|---|---|---|---|---|
| **Nombre d'animaux abattus** *(milliers)* | | | | | | | | |
| **Poids moyen en carcasse parée** *(kilogrammes)* | | | | | | | | |
| **Production indigène brute** | 552.0 | 552.0 | 529.0 | 565.0 | 566.0 | 555.0 | 556.0 | 0.2 |
| *Moins:* Équivalent en viande des animaux exportés vivants | - | - | 1.0 | - | - | 2.0 | - | -100.0 |
| *Plus:* Viande provenant des abbattages d'animaux importés vivants | 7.0 | 9.0 | 8.0 | 17.0 | 10.0 | 19.0 | 17.0 | -10.5 |
| **Production totale de viande provenant des abattages** | 559.0 | 561.0 | 536.0 | 582.0 | 576.0 | 572.0 | 573.0 | 0.2 |
| *Moins:* Exportations de viande | 2.0 | 1.0 | 1.0 | 2.0 | 5.0 | 6.0 | 6.0 | 0.0 |
| *Plus:* Importations de viande | 211.0 | 226.0 | 241.0 | 291.0 | 199.0 | 280.0 | 252.0 | -10.0 |
| *Moins:* Variations des stocks | - | 4.0 | -5.0 | -5.0 | 3.0 | 2.0 | 4.0 | |
| **Consommation de viande** | 768.0 | 782.0 | 781.0 | 876.0 | 767.0 | 844.0 | 815.0 | -3.4 |
| **Consommation par tête** *(kilogrammes par an)* | 77.6 | 78.7 | 78.4 | 87.7 | 76.6 | 84.1 | 80.4 | -4.5 |

## PRODUCTION INDIGENE BRUTE DE VIANDE
## MEAT GROSS INDIGENOUS PRODUCTION

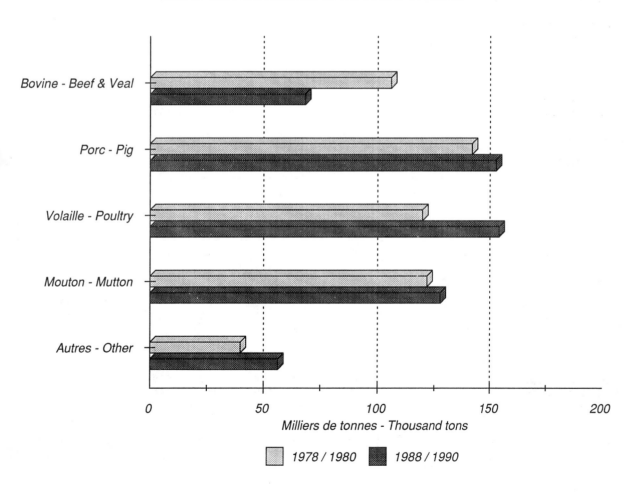

93

# IRELAND

## BEEF / VIANDE DE BŒUF

*Thousand metric tons - Dressed carcass weight*

|  | 1984 | 1985 | 1986 | 1987 | 1988 | 1989 | 1990 | 1989/90 % change |
|---|---|---|---|---|---|---|---|---|
| Number of animals slaughtered *(thousands)* | 1389.0 | 1515.0 [b] | 1692.0 | 1585.0 | 1452.0 | 1367.0 | 1576.0 | 15.3 |
| Average dressed carcass weight *(kilogrammes)* | 289.0 | 296.0 [b] | 299.0 | 302.0 | 316.0 | 316.0 | 327.0 | 3.5 |
| **Gross indigenous production** | **504.0** | **533.0** [b] | **558.0** | **512.0** | **520.0** | **480.0** | **569.0** | 18.5 |
| *Minus:* Meat equivalent of exported live animals | 109.0 | 88.0 [b] | 86.0 | 59.0 | 65.0 | 50.0 | 55.0 | 10.0 |
| *Plus:* Meat from slaughterings of imported live animals | 5.0 | 3.0 | 32.0 | 24.0 | 3.0 | 2.0 | - | -100.0 |
| **Total meat production from slaughtered animals** | **400.0** | **448.0** [b] | **504.0** | **477.0** | **458.0** | **432.0** | **514.0** | 19.0 |
| *Minus:* Exports of meat | 258.0 | 316.0 [b] | 414.0 | 431.0 | 365.0 | 438.0 | 370.0 | -15.5 |
| *Plus:* Imports of meat | 12.0 | 9.0 | 8.0 | 13.0 | 18.0 | 24.0 | 15.0 | -37.5 |
| *Minus:* Stock variations | 71.0 | 64.0 [b] | 19.0 | -15.0 | 43.0 | -49.0 | 99.0 | |
| **Meat consumption** | **83.0** | **77.0** [b] | **79.0** | **74.0** | **68.0** | **67.0** | **60.0** | -10.4 |
| Consumption per head *(kilogrammes per year)* | 23.5 | 21.8 [b] | 22.3 | 20.9 | 19.2 | 19.1 | 17.1 | -10.1 |

## VEAL / VIANDE DE VEAU

|  | 1984 | 1985 | 1986 | 1987 | 1988 | 1989 | 1990 | 1989/90 % change |
|---|---|---|---|---|---|---|---|---|
| Number of animals slaughtered *(thousands)* | 7.0 | 3.0 [b] | 4.0 | 3.0 | 2.0 | 3.0 | 3.0 | 0.0 |
| Average dressed carcass weight *(kilogrammes)* | 147.0 | 38.0 [b] | 38.0 [e] | 38.0 [e] | 38.0 [e] | 38.0 [e] | 38.0 [e] | 0.0 |
| **Gross indigenous production** | **1.0** | - | - | - | - | - | - | .. |
| *Minus:* Meat equivalent of exported live animals | - | - | - | - | - | - | - | .. |
| *Plus:* Meat from slaughterings of imported live animals | - | - | - | - | - | - | - | .. |
| **Total meat production from slaughtered animals** | **1.0** | - | - | - | - | - | - | .. |
| *Minus:* Exports of meat | - | - | - | - | 1.0 | - | - | .. |
| *Plus:* Imports of meat | - | - | - | - | - | - | - | .. |
| *Minus:* Stock variations | - | - | - | - | -1.0 | - | - | |
| **Meat consumption** | **1.0** | - | - | - | - | - | - | .. |
| Consumption per head *(kilogrammes per year)* | 0.3 | - | - | - | - | - | - | .. |

## BEEF AND VEAL / TOTAL VIANDE BOVINE

|  | 1984 | 1985 | 1986 | 1987 | 1988 | 1989 | 1990 | 1989/90 % change |
|---|---|---|---|---|---|---|---|---|
| Number of animals slaughtered *(thousands)* | 1396.0 | 1518.0 [b] | 1696.0 | 1588.0 | 1454.0 | 1370.0 | 1579.0 | 15.3 |
| Average dressed carcass weight *(kilogrammes)* | 287.2 | 295.1 [b] | 297.2 | 300.4 | 315.0 | 315.3 | 325.5 | 3.2 |
| **Gross indigenous production** | **505.0** | **533.0** [b] | **558.0** | **512.0** | **520.0** | **480.0** | **569.0** | 18.5 |
| *Minus:* Meat equivalent of exported live animals | 109.0 | 88.0 [b] | 86.0 | 59.0 | 65.0 | 50.0 | 55.0 | 10.0 |
| *Plus:* Meat from slaughterings of imported live animals | 5.0 | 3.0 | 32.0 | 24.0 | 3.0 | 2.0 | - | -100.0 |
| **Total meat production from slaughtered animals** | **401.0** | **448.0** [b] | **504.0** | **477.0** | **458.0** | **432.0** | **514.0** | 19.0 |
| *Minus:* Exports of meat | 258.0 | 316.0 [b] | 414.0 | 431.0 | 366.0 | 438.0 | 370.0 | -15.5 |
| *Plus:* Imports of meat | 12.0 | 9.0 | 8.0 | 13.0 | 18.0 | 24.0 | 15.0 | -37.5 |
| *Minus:* Stock variations | 71.0 | 64.0 [b] | 19.0 | -15.0 | 42.0 | -49.0 | 99.0 | |
| **Meat consumption** | **84.0** | **77.0** [b] | **79.0** | **74.0** | **68.0** | **67.0** | **60.0** | -10.4 |
| Consumption per head *(kilogrammes per year)* | 23.8 | 21.8 [b] | 22.3 | 20.9 | 19.2 | 19.1 | 17.1 | -10.1 |

# IRLANDE

*Milliers de tonnes métriques - Poids en carcasse parée*

*VIANDE DE PORC / PIG MEAT*

| | 1984 | 1985 | 1986 | 1987 | 1988 | 1989 | 1990 | 1989/90<br>% var. |
|---|---|---|---|---|---|---|---|---|
| Nombre d'animaux abattus *(milliers)* | 2224.0 | 2119.0 | 2158.0 | 2246.0 | 2295.0 | 2228.0 | 2375.0 | 6.6 |
| Poids moyen en carcasse parée *(kilogrammes)* | 65.0 | 64.0 | 64.0 | 64.0 | 64.0 | 65.0 | 66.0 | 1.5 |
| Production indigène brute | 141.0 | 136.0 | 139.0 | 140.0 | 142.0 | 146.0 | 160.0 | 9.6 |
| *Moins:* Équivalent en viande des animaux exportés vivants | 3.0 | 4.0 | 4.0 | 4.0 | 3.0 | 4.0 | 3.0 | -25.0 |
| *Plus:* Viande provenant des abbattages d'animaux importés vivants | 9.0 | 7.0 | 4.0 | 8.0 | 10.0 | 4.0 | 2.0 | -50.0 |
| Production totale de viande provenant des abattages | 147.0 | 139.0 | 139.0 | 144.0 | 149.0 | 146.0 | 159.0 | 8.9 |
| *Moins:* Exportations de viande | 44.0 | 38.0 | 37.0 | 42.0 | 42.0 | 45.0 | 53.0 | 17.8 |
| *Plus:* Importations de viande | 16.0 | 17.0 | 20.0 | 17.0 | 18.0 | 24.0 | 18.0 | -25.0 |
| *Moins:* Variations des stocks | - | - | - | - | - | - | - | |
| Consommation de viande | 119.0 | 118.0 | 122.0 | 119.0 | 125.0 | 125.0 | 124.0 | -0.8 |
| Consommation par tête *(kilogrammes par an)* | 33.7 | 33.3 | 34.5 | 33.6 | 35.3 | 35.6 | 35.4 | -0.5 |

*VIANDE DE VOLAILLE / POULTRY MEAT*

| | 1984 | 1985 | 1986 | 1987 | 1988 | 1989 | 1990 | 1989/90<br>% var. |
|---|---|---|---|---|---|---|---|---|
| Nombre d'animaux abattus *(milliers)* | | | | | | | | |
| Poids moyen en carcasse parée *(kilogrammes)* | | | | | | | | |
| Production indigène brute | 52.0 | 55.0 | 59.0 | 66.0 | 75.0 | 69.0 | 81.0 | 17.4 |
| *Moins:* Équivalent en viande des animaux exportés vivants | 1.0 | 1.0 | 1.0 | 1.0 | 1.0 | 1.0 | 1.0 | 0.0 |
| *Plus:* Viande provenant des abbattages d'animaux importés vivants | 2.0 | 2.0 | 2.0 | 3.0 | 3.0 | 3.0 | 4.0 | 33.3 |
| Production totale de viande provenant des abattages | 53.0 | 56.0 | 60.0 | 68.0 | 77.0 | 71.0 | 84.0 | 18.3 |
| *Moins:* Exportations de viande | 5.0 | 4.0 | 5.0 | 8.0 | 12.0 | 12.0 | 15.0 | 25.0 |
| *Plus:* Importations de viande | 7.0 | 9.0 | 10.0 | 10.0 | 9.0 | 8.0 | 8.0 | 0.0 |
| *Moins:* Variations des stocks | - | - | - | - | 1.0 | -2.0 | 1.0 | |
| Consommation de viande | 55.0 | 61.0 | 65.0 | 70.0 | 73.0 | 69.0 | 76.0 | 10.1 |
| Consommation par tête *(kilogrammes par an)* | 15.6 | 17.2 | 18.4 | 19.8 | 20.6 | 19.6 | 21.7 | 10.5 |

*VIANDE DE MOUTON ET DE CHÈVRE / MUTTON, LAMB AND GOAT MEAT*

| | 1984 | 1985 | 1986 | 1987 | 1988 | 1989 | 1990 | 1989/90<br>% var. |
|---|---|---|---|---|---|---|---|---|
| Nombre d'animaux abattus *(milliers)* | 1683.0 | 2081.0 | 2000.0 | 2070.0 | 2139.0 | 2848.0 | 3887.0 | 36.5 |
| Poids moyen en carcasse parée *(kilogrammes)* | 24.0 | 23.0 | 23.0 | 23.0 | 23.0 | 21.0 | 22.0 | 4.8 |
| Production indigène brute | 41.0 | 49.0 | 47.0 | 49.0 | 50.0 | 64.0 | 85.0 | 32.8 |
| *Moins:* Équivalent en viande des animaux exportés vivants | 1.0 | 2.0 | 1.0 | 2.0 | 2.0 | 2.0 | 5.0 | 150.0 |
| *Plus:* Viande provenant des abbattages d'animaux importés vivants | 1.0 | 1.0 | - | 1.0 | 1.0 | 1.0 | 2.0 | 100.0 |
| Production totale de viande provenant des abattages | 41.0 | 48.0 | 46.0 | 48.0 | 49.0 | 63.0 | 82.0 | 30.2 |
| *Moins:* Exportations de viande | 17.0 | 24.0 | 22.0 | 24.0 | 26.0 | 38.0 | 55.0 | 44.7 |
| *Plus:* Importations de viande | - | - | - | - | - | - | - | .. |
| *Moins:* Variations des stocks | - | - | - | - | - | - | - | |
| Consommation de viande | 24.0 | 24.0 | 24.0 | 24.0 | 23.0 | 25.0 | 27.0 | 8.0 |
| Consommation par tête *(kilogrammes par an)* | 6.8 | 6.8 | 6.8 | 6.8 | 6.5 | 7.1 | 7.7 | 8.4 |

# IRELAND

## HORSE MEAT / VIANDE D'ÉQUIDÉS

*Thousand metric tons - Dressed carcass weight*

| | 1984 | 1985 | 1986 | 1987 | 1988 | 1989 | 1990 | 1989/90 % change |
|---|---|---|---|---|---|---|---|---|
| Number of animals slaughtered *(thousands)* | 7.0 | 6.0 | 3.0 | 2.0 | 2.0 | 1.0 | 1.0 | 0.0 |
| Average dressed carcass weight *(kilogrammes)* | 271.0 | 262.0 | 231.0 | 252.0 [e] | 252.0 [e] | 252.0 [e] | 252.0 [e] | 0.0 |
| Gross indigenous production | 2.0 | 2.0 | 1.0 | 1.0 | - | 1.0 | - | -100.0 |
| *Minus:* Meat equivalent of exported live animals | - | - | - | - | - | - | - | .. |
| *Plus:* Meat from slaughterings of imported live animals | - | - | - | - | - | - | - | .. |
| Total meat production from slaughtered animals | 2.0 | 2.0 | 1.0 | 1.0 | - | 1.0 | - | -100.0 |
| *Minus:* Exports of meat | 2.0 | 2.0 | 1.0 | 1.0 | - | 1.0 | - | -100.0 |
| *Plus:* Imports of meat | - | - | - | - | - | - | - | .. |
| *Minus:* Stock variations | - | - | - | - | - | - | - | |
| Meat consumption | . | . | . | . | . | . | . | .. |
| Consumption per head *(kilogrammes per year)* | - | - | - | - | - | - | - | .. |

## OTHER MEAT / AUTRES VIANDES

| | 1984 | 1985 | 1986 | 1987 | 1988 | 1989 | 1990 | 1989/90 % change |
|---|---|---|---|---|---|---|---|---|
| Number of animals slaughtered *(thousands)* | | | | | | | | |
| Average dressed carcass weight *(kilogrammes)* | | | | | | | | |
| Gross indigenous production | . | . | . | . | 3.0 | 1.0 | 2.0 | 100.0 |
| *Minus:* Meat equivalent of exported live animals | - | - | - | - | - | - | - | .. |
| *Plus:* Meat from slaughterings of imported live animals | - | - | - | - | - | - | - | .. |
| Total meat production from slaughtered animals | . | . | . | . | 3.0 | 1.0 | 2.0 | 100.0 |
| *Minus:* Exports of meat | - | - | - | - | 3.0 | 1.0 | 2.0 | 100.0 |
| *Plus:* Imports of meat | - | - | - | - | 1.0 | 1.0 | 1.0 | 0.0 |
| *Minus:* Stock variations | - | - | - | - | - | - | - | |
| Meat consumption | . | . | . | . | 1.0 | 1.0 | 1.0 | 0.0 |
| Consumption per head *(kilogrammes per year)* | - | - | - | - | 0.3 | 0.3 | 0.3 | 0.3 |

## EDIBLE OFFALS / ABATS COMESTIBLES

| | 1984 | 1985 | 1986 | 1987 | 1988 | 1989 | 1990 | 1989/90 % change |
|---|---|---|---|---|---|---|---|---|
| Number of animals slaughtered *(thousands)* | | | | | | | | |
| Average dressed carcass weight *(kilogrammes)* | | | | | | | | |
| Gross indigenous production | 97.0 | 101.0 | 90.0 | 96.0 | 101.0 | 95.0 | 112.0 | 17.9 |
| *Minus:* Meat equivalent of exported live animals | 17.0 | 14.0 | 14.0 | 9.0 | 10.0 | 8.0 | 9.0 | 12.5 |
| *Plus:* Meat from slaughterings of imported live animals | 2.0 | 2.0 | 5.0 | 7.0 | 2.0 | 1.0 | - | -100.0 |
| Total meat production from slaughtered animals | 82.0 | 89.0 | 81.0 | 94.0 | 93.0 | 88.0 | 103.0 | 17.0 |
| *Minus:* Exports of meat | 45.0 | 53.0 | 67.0 | 70.0 | 61.0 | 72.0 | 63.0 | -12.5 |
| *Plus:* Imports of meat | 4.0 | 4.0 | 4.0 | 5.0 | 6.0 | 8.0 | 5.0 | -37.5 |
| *Minus:* Stock variations | - | - | - | - | - | - | - | |
| Meat consumption | 41.0 | 40.0 | 18.0 | 29.0 | 38.0 | 24.0 | 45.0 | 87.5 |
| Consumption per head *(kilogrammes per year)* | 11.6 | 11.3 | 5.1 | 8.2 | 10.7 | 6.8 | 12.8 | 88.1 |

# IRLANDE

*TOTAL VIANDE / TOTAL MEAT*

| | 1984 | 1985 | 1986 | 1987 | 1988 | 1989 | 1990 | 1989/90 % var. |
|---|---|---|---|---|---|---|---|---|
| **Nombre d'animaux abattus** *(milliers)* | | | | | | | | |
| **Poids moyen en carcasse parée** *(kilogrammes)* | | | | | | | | |
| **Production indigène brute** | **838.0** | **876.0** [b] | **894.0** | **864.0** | **891.0** | **856.0** | **1009.0** | 17.9 |
| *Moins:* Équivalent en viande des animaux exportés vivants | 131.0 | 109.0 [b] | 106.0 | 75.0 | 81.0 | 65.0 | 73.0 | 12.3 |
| *Plus:* Viande provenant des abbattages d'animaux importés vivants | 19.0 | 15.0 | 43.0 | 43.0 | 19.0 | 11.0 | 8.0 | -27.3 |
| **Production totale de viande provenant des abattages** | **726.0** | **782.0** [b] | **831.0** | **832.0** | **829.0** | **802.0** | **944.0** | 17.7 |
| *Moins:* Exportations de viande | 371.0 | 437.0 [b] | 546.0 | 576.0 | 510.0 | 607.0 | 558.0 | -8.1 |
| *Plus:* Importations de viande | 39.0 | 39.0 | 42.0 | 45.0 | 52.0 | 65.0 | 47.0 | -27.7 |
| *Moins:* Variations des stocks | 71.0 | 64.0 [b] | 19.0 | -15.0 | 43.0 | -51.0 | 100.0 | |
| **Consommation de viande** | **323.0** | **320.0** [b] | **308.0** | **316.0** | **328.0** | **311.0** | **333.0** | 7.1 |
| **Consommation par tête** *(kilogrammes par an)* | 91.5 | 90.4 [b] | 87.0 | 89.2 | 92.7 | 88.5 | 95.1 | 7.4 |

## PRODUCTION INDIGENE BRUTE DE VIANDE
## MEAT GROSS INDIGENOUS PRODUCTION

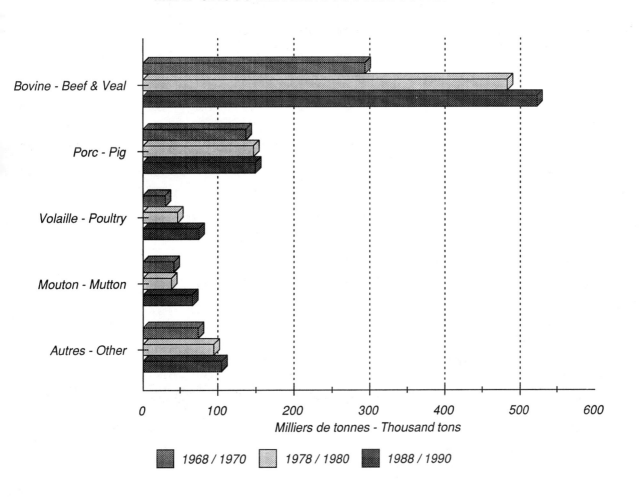

Milliers de tonnes - Thousand tons

■ 1968 / 1970    □ 1978 / 1980    ■ 1988 / 1990

# ITALY

*Thousand metric tons - Dressed carcass weight*

| | 1984 | 1985 | 1986 | 1987 | 1988 | 1989 | 1990 | 1989/90 % change |
|---|---|---|---|---|---|---|---|---|
| Number of animals slaughtered *(thousands)* | 3675.0 | 3700.0 | 3586.0 | 3430.0 | 3377.0 | 3293.0 | 3330.0 | 1.1 |
| Average dressed carcass weight *(kilogrammes)* | 272.0 | 272.0 | 274.0 | 282.0 | 281.0 | 283.0 | 285.0 | 0.7 |
| **Gross indigenous production** | **827.0** | **792.0** | **740.0** | **721.0** | **707.0** | **659.0** | **715.0** | 8.5 |
| *Minus:* Meat equivalent of exported live animals | 7.0 | 3.0 | 1.0 | - | - | - | 1.0 | .. |
| *Plus:* Meat from slaughterings of imported live animals | 182.0 | 221.0 | 243.0 | 245.0 | 242.0 | 277.0 | 233.0 | -15.9 |
| **Total meat production from slaughtered animals** | **1002.0** | **1010.0** | **982.0** | **966.0** | **949.0** | **936.0** | **947.0** | 1.2 |
| *Minus:* Exports of meat | 104.0 | 137.0 | 146.0 | 123.0 | 113.0 | 96.0 | 84.0 | -12.5 |
| *Plus:* Imports of meat | 392.0 | 495.0 | 453.0 | 450.0 | 426.0 | 426.0 | 412.0 | -3.3 |
| *Minus:* Stock variations | 41.0 | 8.0 | -71.0 | -13.0 | -41.0 | -39.0 | 33.0 | |
| **Meat consumption** | **1249.0** | **1360.0** | **1360.0** | **1306.0** | **1303.0** | **1305.0** | **1242.0** | -4.8 |
| Consumption per head *(kilogrammes per year)* | 21.9 | 23.8 | 23.8 | 22.8 | 22.7 | 22.7 | 21.5 | -5.0 |

## VEAL / VIANDE DE VEAU

| | 1984 | 1985 | 1986 | 1987 | 1988 | 1989 | 1990 | 1989/90 % change |
|---|---|---|---|---|---|---|---|---|
| Number of animals slaughtered *(thousands)* | 1459.0 | 1491.0 | 1515.0 | 1554.0 | 1572.0 | 1581.0 | 1555.0 | -1.6 |
| Average dressed carcass weight *(kilogrammes)* | 124.0 | 130.0 | 127.0 | 134.0 | 137.0 | 136.0 | 140.0 | 2.9 |
| **Gross indigenous production** | **160.0** | **175.0** | **179.0** | **191.0** | **201.0** | **200.0** | **204.0** | 2.0 |
| *Minus:* Meat equivalent of exported live animals | - | - | - | - | - | - | - | .. |
| *Plus:* Meat from slaughterings of imported live animals | 20.0 | 20.0 | 18.0 | 18.0 | 14.0 | 14.0 | 13.0 | -7.1 |
| **Total meat production from slaughtered animals** | **180.0** | **195.0** | **197.0** | **209.0** | **215.0** | **214.0** | **217.0** | 1.4 |
| *Minus:* Exports of meat | 1.0 | 4.0 | 2.0 | - | 3.0 | - | - | .. |
| *Plus:* Imports of meat | 40.0 | 40.0 | 32.0 | 27.0 | 15.0 | 10.0 | 12.0 | 20.0 |
| *Minus:* Stock variations | - | - | - | - | - | - | - | |
| **Meat consumption** | **219.0** | **231.0** | **227.0** | **236.0** | **227.0** | **224.0** | **229.0** | 2.2 |
| Consumption per head *(kilogrammes per year)* | 3.8 | 4.0 | 4.0 | 4.1 | 4.0 | 3.9 | 4.0 | 2.0 |

## BEEF AND VEAL / TOTAL VIANDE BOVINE

| | 1984 | 1985 | 1986 | 1987 | 1988 | 1989 | 1990 | 1989/90 % change |
|---|---|---|---|---|---|---|---|---|
| Number of animals slaughtered *(thousands)* | 5134.0 | 5191.0 | 5101.0 | 4984.0 | 4949.0 | 4874.0 | 4885.0 | 0.2 |
| Average dressed carcass weight *(kilogrammes)* | 230.2 | 232.1 | 231.1 | 235.8 | 235.2 | 235.9 | 238.3 | 1.0 |
| **Gross indigenous production** | **987.0** | **967.0** | **919.0** | **912.0** | **908.0** | **859.0** | **919.0** | 7.0 |
| *Minus:* Meat equivalent of exported live animals | 7.0 | 3.0 | 1.0 | - | - | - | 1.0 | .. |
| *Plus:* Meat from slaughterings of imported live animals | 202.0 | 241.0 | 261.0 | 263.0 | 256.0 | 291.0 | 246.0 | -15.5 |
| **Total meat production from slaughtered animals** | **1182.0** | **1205.0** | **1179.0** | **1175.0** | **1164.0** | **1150.0** | **1164.0** | 1.2 |
| *Minus:* Exports of meat | 105.0 | 141.0 | 148.0 | 123.0 | 116.0 | 96.0 | 84.0 | -12.5 |
| *Plus:* Imports of meat | 432.0 | 535.0 | 485.0 | 477.0 | 441.0 | 436.0 | 424.0 | -2.8 |
| *Minus:* Stock variations | 41.0 | 8.0 | -71.0 | -13.0 | -41.0 | -39.0 | 33.0 | |
| **Meat consumption** | **1468.0** | **1591.0** | **1587.0** | **1542.0** | **1530.0** | **1529.0** | **1471.0** | -3.8 |
| Consumption per head *(kilogrammes per year)* | 25.8 | 27.8 | 27.7 | 26.9 | 26.6 | 26.6 | 25.5 | -4.0 |

# ITALIE

*Milliers de tonnes métriques - Poids en carcasse parée*

*VIANDE DE PORC / PIG MEAT*

| | 1984 | 1985 | 1986 | 1987 | 1988 | 1989 | 1990 | 1989/90 % var. |
|---|---|---|---|---|---|---|---|---|
| Nombre d'animaux abattus *(milliers)* | 11447.0 | 11239.0 | 11073.0 | 11313.0 | 11737.0 | 11972.0 | 12134.0 | 1.4 |
| Poids moyen en carcasse parée *(kilogrammes)* | 106.0 | 106.0 | 106.0 | 109.0 | 108.0 | 108.0 | 110.0 | 1.9 |
| Production indigène brute | 1167.0 | 1112.0 | 1053.0 | 1121.0 | 1154.0 | 1207.0 | 1211.0 | 0.3 |
| *Moins:* Équivalent en viande des animaux exportés vivants | - | - | - | - | 1.0 | 1.0 | 1.0 | 0.0 |
| *Plus:* Viande provenant des abbattages d'animaux importés vivants | 51.0 | 75.0 | 119.0 | 110.0 | 115.0 | 103.0 | 122.0 | 18.4 |
| Production totale de viande provenant des abattages | 1218.0 | 1187.0 | 1172.0 | 1231.0 | 1268.0 | 1309.0 | 1332.0 | 1.8 |
| *Moins:* Exportations de viande | 44.0 | 53.0 | 46.0 | 49.0 | 35.0 | 36.0 | 41.0 | 13.9 |
| *Plus:* Importations de viande | 358.0 | 441.0 | 478.0 | 486.0 | 479.0 | 503.0 | 523.0 | 4.0 |
| *Moins:* Variations des stocks | - | - | - | - | - | - | - | |
| Consommation de viande | 1532.0 | 1575.0 | 1604.0 | 1668.0 | 1712.0 | 1776.0 | 1814.0 | 2.1 |
| Consommation par tête *(kilogrammes par an)* | 26.9 | 27.6 | 28.0 | 29.1 | 29.8 | 30.9 | 31.5 | 1.9 |

*VIANDE DE VOLAILLE / POULTRY MEAT*

| | 1984 | 1985 | 1986 | 1987 | 1988 | 1989 | 1990 | 1989/90 % var. |
|---|---|---|---|---|---|---|---|---|
| Nombre d'animaux abattus *(milliers)* | | | | | | | | |
| Poids moyen en carcasse parée *(kilogrammes)* | | | | | | | | |
| Production indigène brute | 1020.0 | 998.0 | 1001.0 | 1046.0 | 1072.0 | 1094.0 | 1100.0 | 0.5 |
| *Moins:* Équivalent en viande des animaux exportés vivants | 1.0 | 2.0 | 2.0 | 2.0 | 1.0 | 1.0 | 2.0 | 100.0 |
| *Plus:* Viande provenant des abbattages d'animaux importés vivants | 8.0 | 9.0 | 7.0 | 6.0 | 5.0 | 4.0 | 4.0 | 0.0 |
| Production totale de viande provenant des abattages | 1027.0 | 1005.0 | 1006.0 | 1050.0 | 1076.0 | 1097.0 | 1102.0 | 0.5 |
| *Moins:* Exportations de viande | 10.0 | 9.0 | 10.0 | 16.0 | 20.0 | 19.0 | 28.0 | 47.4 |
| *Plus:* Importations de viande | 23.0 | 32.0 | 28.0 | 27.0 | 41.0 | 47.0 | 44.0 | -6.4 |
| *Moins:* Variations des stocks | - | - | - | - | - | - | - | |
| Consommation de viande | 1040.0 | 1028.0 | 1024.0 | 1061.0 | 1097.0 | 1125.0 | 1118.0 | -0.6 |
| Consommation par tête *(kilogrammes par an)* | 18.3 | 18.0 | 17.9 | 18.5 | 19.1 | 19.6 | 19.4 | -0.8 |

*VIANDE DE MOUTON ET DE CHÈVRE / MUTTON, LAMB AND GOAT MEAT*

| | 1984 | 1985 | 1986 | 1987 | 1988 | 1989 | 1990 | 1989/90 % var. |
|---|---|---|---|---|---|---|---|---|
| Nombre d'animaux abattus *(milliers)* | 8047.0 | 8107.0 | 7959.0 | 8096.0 | 8433.0 | 9126.0 | 9602.0 | 5.2 |
| Poids moyen en carcasse parée *(kilogrammes)* | 9.0 | 9.0 | 8.0 | 9.0 | 9.0 | 9.0 | 10.0 | 11.1 |
| Production indigène brute | 54.0 | 49.0 | 49.0 | 47.0 | 51.0 | 56.0 | 56.0 | 0.0 |
| *Moins:* Équivalent en viande des animaux exportés vivants | - | - | - | - | - | - | - | .. |
| *Plus:* Viande provenant des abbattages d'animaux importés vivants | 17.0 | 21.0 | 18.0 | 23.0 | 22.0 | 24.0 | 29.0 | 20.8 |
| Production totale de viande provenant des abattages | 71.0 | 70.0 | 67.0 | 70.0 | 73.0 | 80.0 | 85.0 | 6.3 |
| *Moins:* Exportations de viande | - | - | - | 2.0 | 3.0 | 3.0 | 3.0 | 0.0 |
| *Plus:* Importations de viande | 15.0 | 19.0 | 19.0 | 21.0 | 23.0 | 25.0 | 22.0 | -12.0 |
| *Moins:* Variations des stocks | - | - | - | - | - | - | 1.0 | |
| Consommation de viande | 86.0 | 89.0 | 86.0 | 89.0 | 93.0 | 102.0 | 103.0 | 1.0 |
| Consommation par tête *(kilogrammes par an)* | 1.5 | 1.6 | 1.5 | 1.6 | 1.6 | 1.8 | 1.8 | 0.8 |

# ITALY

*Thousand metric tons - Dressed carcass weight*

|  | 1984 | 1985 | 1986 | 1987 | 1988 | 1989 | 1990 | 1989/90 % change |
|---|---|---|---|---|---|---|---|---|
| Number of animals slaughtered *(thousands)* | 256.0 | 271.0 | 263.0 | 257.0 | 252.0 | 258.0 | 259.0 | 0.4 |
| Average dressed carcass weight *(kilogrammes)* | 202.0 | 203.0 | 207.0 | 211.0 | 211.0 | 210.0 | 220.0 | 4.8 |
| **Gross indigenous production** | **16.0** | **12.0** | **17.0** | **13.0** | **14.0** | **15.0** | **15.0** | 0.0 |
| *Minus:* Meat equivalent of exported live animals | - | - | - | - | - | - | - | .. |
| *Plus:* Meat from slaughterings of imported live animals | 35.0 | 43.0 | 37.0 | 41.0 | 39.0 | 39.0 | 42.0 | 7.7 |
| **Total meat production from slaughtered animals** | **51.0** | **55.0** | **54.0** | **54.0** | **53.0** | **54.0** | **57.0** | 5.6 |
| *Minus:* Exports of meat | - | - | - | 1.0 | 1.0 | - | - | .. |
| *Plus:* Imports of meat | 7.0 | 10.0 | 11.0 | 13.0 | 16.0 | 18.0 | 19.0 | 5.6 |
| *Minus:* Stock variations | - | - | - | - | - | - | - | |
| **Meat consumption** | **58.0** | **65.0** | **65.0** | **66.0** | **68.0** | **72.0** | **76.0** | 5.6 |
| Consumption per head *(kilogrammes per year)* | 1.0 | 1.1 | 1.1 | 1.2 | 1.2 | 1.3 | 1.3 | 5.3 |

## OTHER MEAT / AUTRES VIANDES

|  | 1984 | 1985 | 1986 | 1987 | 1988 | 1989 | 1990 | 1989/90 % change |
|---|---|---|---|---|---|---|---|---|
| Number of animals slaughtered *(thousands)* | | | | | | | | |
| Average dressed carcass weight *(kilogrammes)* | | | | | | | | |
| **Gross indigenous production** | **197.0** | **200.0** | **201.0** | **203.0** | **218.0** | **212.0** | **201.0** | -5.2 |
| *Minus:* Meat equivalent of exported live animals | - | - | - | - | - | - | - | .. |
| *Plus:* Meat from slaughterings of imported live animals | 2.0 | 2.0 | 2.0 | 3.0 | 2.0 | 1.0 | 2.0 | 100.0 |
| **Total meat production from slaughtered animals** | **199.0** | **202.0** | **203.0** | **206.0** | **220.0** | **213.0** | **203.0** | -4.7 |
| *Minus:* Exports of meat | 1.0 | 2.0 | 1.0 | 2.0 | 2.0 | 2.0 | 2.0 | 0.0 |
| *Plus:* Imports of meat | 18.0 | 22.0 | 19.0 | 22.0 | 18.0 | 18.0 | 17.0 | -5.6 |
| *Minus:* Stock variations | - | - | - | - | - | - | - | |
| **Meat consumption** | **216.0** | **222.0** | **221.0** | **226.0** | **236.0** | **229.0** | **218.0** | -4.8 |
| Consumption per head *(kilogrammes per year)* | 3.8 | 3.9 | 3.9 | 3.9 | 4.1 | 4.0 | 3.8 | -5.0 |

## EDIBLE OFFALS / ABATS COMESTIBLES

|  | 1984 | 1985 | 1986 | 1987 | 1988 | 1989 | 1990 | 1989/90 % change |
|---|---|---|---|---|---|---|---|---|
| Number of animals slaughtered *(thousands)* | | | | | | | | |
| Average dressed carcass weight *(kilogrammes)* | | | | | | | | |
| **Gross indigenous production** | **186.0** | **181.0** | **173.0** | **175.0** | **177.0** | **177.0** | **185.0** | 4.5 |
| *Minus:* Meat equivalent of exported live animals | - | - | - | - | - | - | - | .. |
| *Plus:* Meat from slaughterings of imported live animals | 28.0 | 33.0 | 38.0 | 37.0 | 39.0 | 40.0 | 36.0 | -10.0 |
| **Total meat production from slaughtered animals** | **214.0** | **214.0** | **211.0** | **212.0** | **216.0** | **217.0** | **221.0** | 1.8 |
| *Minus:* Exports of meat | 9.0 | 8.0 | 5.0 | 4.0 | 9.0 | 8.0 | 11.0 | 37.5 |
| *Plus:* Imports of meat | 8.0 | 10.0 | 11.0 | 9.0 | 6.0 | 8.0 | 8.0 | 0.0 |
| *Minus:* Stock variations | - | - | - | - | - | - | - | |
| **Meat consumption** | **213.0** | **216.0** | **217.0** | **217.0** | **213.0** | **217.0** | **218.0** | 0.5 |
| Consumption per head *(kilogrammes per year)* | 3.7 | 3.8 | 3.8 | 3.8 | 3.7 | 3.8 | 3.8 | 0.2 |

# ITALIE

*Milliers de tonnes métriques - Poids en carcasse parée*

## TOTAL VIANDE / TOTAL MEAT

| | 1984 | 1985 | 1986 | 1987 | 1988 | 1989 | 1990 | 1989/90 % var. |
|---|---|---|---|---|---|---|---|---|
| **Nombre d'animaux abattus** *(milliers)* | | | | | | | | |
| **Poids moyen en carcasse parée** *(kilogrammes)* | | | | | | | | |
| **Production indigène brute** | 3627.0 | 3519.0 | 3413.0 | 3517.0 | 3594.0 | 3620.0 | 3687.0 | 1.9 |
| *Moins:* Équivalent en viande des animaux exportés vivants | 8.0 | 5.0 | 3.0 | 2.0 | 2.0 | 2.0 | 4.0 | 100.0 |
| *Plus:* Viande provenant des abbattages d'animaux importés vivants | 343.0 | 424.0 | 482.0 | 483.0 | 478.0 | 502.0 | 481.0 | -4.2 |
| **Production totale de viande provenant des abattages** | 3962.0 | 3938.0 | 3892.0 | 3998.0 | 4070.0 | 4120.0 | 4164.0 | 1.1 |
| *Moins:* Exportations de viande | 169.0 | 213.0 | 210.0 | 197.0 | 186.0 | 164.0 | 169.0 | 3.0 |
| *Plus:* Importations de viande | 861.0 | 1069.0 | 1051.0 | 1055.0 | 1024.0 | 1055.0 | 1057.0 | 0.2 |
| *Moins:* Variations des stocks | 41.0 | 8.0 | -71.0 | -13.0 | -41.0 | -39.0 | 34.0 | |
| **Consommation de viande** | 4613.0 | 4786.0 | 4804.0 | 4869.0 | 4949.0 | 5050.0 | 5018.0 | -0.6 |
| **Consommation par tête** *(kilogrammes par an)* | 81.0 | 83.8 | 84.0 | 84.9 | 86.2 | 87.8 | 87.0 | -0.8 |

## PRODUCTION INDIGENE BRUTE DE VIANDE
## *MEAT GROSS INDIGENOUS PRODUCTION*

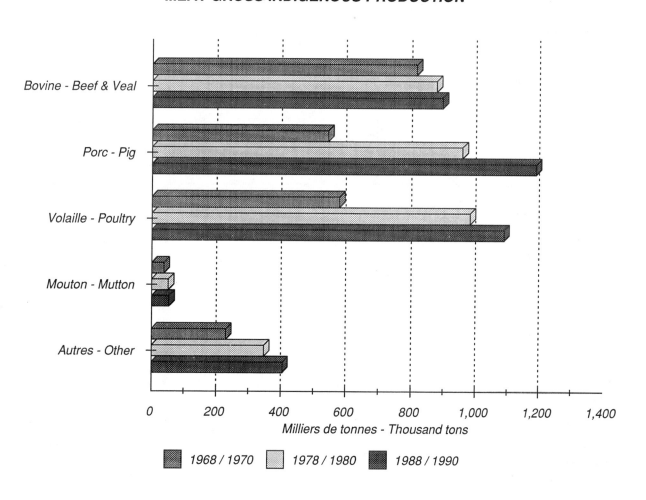

Milliers de tonnes - Thousand tons

1968 / 1970    1978 / 1980    1988 / 1990

# NETHERLANDS

## BEEF / VIANDE DE BŒUF

*Thousand metric tons - Dressed carcass weight*

| | 1984 | 1985 | 1986 | 1987 | 1988 | 1989 | 1990 | 1989/90 % change |
|---|---|---|---|---|---|---|---|---|
| Number of animals slaughtered *(thousands)* | 1246.0 | 1161.0 | 1230.0 | 1226.0 | 1119.0 | 1082.0 | 1178.0 | 8.9 |
| Average dressed carcass weight *(kilogrammes)* | 281.0 | 282.0 | 284.0 | 294.0 | 301.0 | 301.0 | 301.0 | 0.0 |
| Gross indigenous production | 349.0 | 326.0 | 329.0 | 342.0 | 317.0 | 300.0 | 320.0 | 6.7 |
| *Minus:* Meat equivalent of exported live animals | 7.0 | 9.0 | 7.0 | 8.0 | 6.0 | 8.0 | 11.0 | 37.5 |
| *Plus:* Meat from slaughterings of imported live animals | 9.0 | 17.0 | 27.0 | 27.0 | 26.0 | 35.0 | 45.0 | 28.6 |
| Total meat production from slaughtered animals | 351.0 | 334.0 | 349.0 | 361.0 | 337.0 | 327.0 | 354.0 | 8.3 |
| *Minus:* Exports of meat | 150.0 | 146.0 | 203.0 | 176.0 | 156.0 | 180.0 | 169.0 | -6.1 |
| *Plus:* Imports of meat | 60.0 | 66.0 | 74.0 | 77.0 | 81.0 | 73.0 | 79.0 | 8.2 |
| *Minus:* Stock variations | 15.0 | 3.0 | 12.0 | 4.0 | -6.0 | -37.0 | 1.0 | |
| Meat consumption | 246.0 | 251.0 | 208.0 | 258.0 | 268.0 | 257.0 | 263.0 | 2.3 |
| Consumption per head *(kilogrammes per year)* | 17.1 | 17.3 | 14.3 | 17.6 | 18.2 | 17.3 | 17.6 | 1.7 |

## VEAL / VIANDE DE VEAU

| | 1984 | 1985 | 1986 | 1987 | 1988 | 1989 | 1990 | 1989/90 % change |
|---|---|---|---|---|---|---|---|---|
| Number of animals slaughtered *(thousands)* | 1258.0 | 1274.0 | 1283.0 | 1242.0 | 1096.0 | 1034.0 | 1071.0 | 3.6 |
| Average dressed carcass weight *(kilogrammes)* | 131.0 | 144.0 | 148.0 | 150.0 | 154.0 | 154.0 | 154.0 | 0.0 |
| Gross indigenous production | 175.0 | 183.0 | 194.0 | 184.0 | 164.0 | 151.0 | 154.0 | 2.0 |
| *Minus:* Meat equivalent of exported live animals | 15.0 | 13.0 | 14.0 | 12.0 | 8.0 | 6.0 | 5.0 | -16.7 |
| *Plus:* Meat from slaughterings of imported live animals | 4.0 | 6.0 | 10.0 | 13.0 | 13.0 | 15.0 | 16.0 | 6.7 |
| Total meat production from slaughtered animals | 164.0 | 176.0 | 190.0 | 185.0 | 169.0 | 160.0 | 165.0 | 3.1 |
| *Minus:* Exports of meat | 143.0 | 155.0 | 163.0 | 155.0 | 158.0 | 126.0 | 138.0 | 9.5 |
| *Plus:* Imports of meat | 1.0 | 3.0 | 3.0 | 1.0 | 6.0 | 3.0 | 1.0 | -66.7 |
| *Minus:* Stock variations | - | - | - | - | - | - | - | |
| Meat consumption | 22.0 | 24.0 | 30.0 | 31.0 | 17.0 | 37.0 | 28.0 | -24.3 |
| Consumption per head *(kilogrammes per year)* | 1.5 | 1.7 | 2.1 | 2.1 | 1.2 | 2.5 | 1.9 | -24.8 |

## BEEF AND VEAL / TOTAL VIANDE BOVINE

| | 1984 | 1985 | 1986 | 1987 | 1988 | 1989 | 1990 | 1989/90 % change |
|---|---|---|---|---|---|---|---|---|
| Number of animals slaughtered *(thousands)* | 2504.0 | 2435.0 | 2513.0 | 2468.0 | 2215.0 | 2116.0 | 2249.0 | 6.3 |
| Average dressed carcass weight *(kilogrammes)* | 205.7 | 209.4 | 214.5 | 221.2 | 228.4 | 230.2 | 230.8 | 0.3 |
| Gross indigenous production | 524.0 | 509.0 | 523.0 | 526.0 | 481.0 | 451.0 | 474.0 | 5.1 |
| *Minus:* Meat equivalent of exported live animals | 22.0 | 22.0 | 21.0 | 20.0 | 14.0 | 14.0 | 16.0 | 14.3 |
| *Plus:* Meat from slaughterings of imported live animals | 13.0 | 23.0 | 37.0 | 40.0 | 39.0 | 50.0 | 61.0 | 22.0 |
| Total meat production from slaughtered animals | 515.0 | 510.0 | 539.0 | 546.0 | 506.0 | 487.0 | 519.0 | 6.6 |
| *Minus:* Exports of meat | 293.0 | 301.0 | 366.0 | 331.0 | 314.0 | 306.0 | 307.0 | 0.3 |
| *Plus:* Imports of meat | 61.0 | 69.0 | 77.0 | 78.0 | 87.0 | 76.0 | 80.0 | 5.3 |
| *Minus:* Stock variations | 15.0 | 3.0 | 12.0 | 4.0 | -6.0 | -37.0 | 1.0 | |
| Meat consumption | 268.0 | 275.0 | 238.0 | 289.0 | 285.0 | 294.0 | 291.0 | -1.0 |
| Consumption per head *(kilogrammes per year)* | 18.6 | 19.0 | 16.3 | 19.7 | 19.3 | 19.8 | 19.5 | -1.6 |

# PAYS - BAS

*Milliers de tonnes métriques - Poids en carcasse parée*

## VIANDE DE PORC / PIG MEAT

| | 1984 | 1985 | 1986 | 1987 | 1988 | 1989 | 1990 | 1989/90 % var. |
|---|---|---|---|---|---|---|---|---|
| Nombre d'animaux abattus *(milliers)* | 15511.0 | 16718.0 | 17905.0 | 19038.0 | 20125.0 | 19640.0 | 19941.0 | 1.5 |
| Poids moyen en carcasse parée *(kilogrammes)* | 84.0 | 84.0 | 81.0 | 80.0 | 81.0 | 82.0 | 83.0 | 1.2 |
| **Production indigène brute** | **1544.0** | **1635.0** | **1736.0** | **1846.0** | **1910.0** | **1852.0** | **1909.0** | 3.1 |
| *Moins:* Équivalent en viande des animaux exportés vivants | 239.0 | 268.0 | 295.0 | 320.0 | 285.0 | 249.0 | 253.0 | 1.6 |
| *Plus:* Viande provenant des abbattages d'animaux importés vivants | 1.0 | 1.0 | 3.0 | 2.0 | 6.0 | 4.0 | 5.0 | 25.0 |
| **Production totale de viande provenant des abattages** | **1306.0** | **1368.0** | **1444.0** | **1528.0** | **1631.0** | **1607.0** | **1661.0** | 3.4 |
| *Moins:* Exportations de viande | 750.0 | 802.0 | 853.0 | 929.0 | 989.0 | 990.0 | 1027.0 | 3.7 |
| *Plus:* Importations de viande | 39.0 | 36.0 | 35.0 | 42.0 | 46.0 | 42.0 | 48.0 | 14.3 |
| *Moins:* Variations des stocks | -1.0 | - | 2.0 | - | 2.0 | -5.0 | - | |
| **Consommation de viande** | **596.0** | **602.0** | **624.0** | **641.0** | **686.0** | **664.0** | **682.0** | 2.7 |
| Consommation par tête *(kilogrammes par an)* | 41.3 | 41.5 | 42.8 | 43.7 | 46.5 | 44.7 | 45.6 | 2.1 |

## VIANDE DE VOLAILLE / POULTRY MEAT

| | 1984 | 1985 | 1986 | 1987 | 1988 | 1989 | 1990 | 1989/90 % var. |
|---|---|---|---|---|---|---|---|---|
| Nombre d'animaux abattus *(milliers)* | | | | | | | | |
| Poids moyen en carcasse parée *(kilogrammes)* | | | | | | | | |
| **Production indigène brute** | **410.0** | **425.0** | **442.0** | **484.0** | **492.0** | **498.0** | **520.0** | 4.4 |
| *Moins:* Équivalent en viande des animaux exportés vivants | 39.0 | 49.0 | 51.0 | 56.0 | 50.0 | 50.0 | 61.0 | 22.0 |
| *Plus:* Viande provenant des abbattages d'animaux importés vivants | 5.0 | 5.0 | 7.0 | 11.0 | 15.0 | 22.0 | 39.0 | 77.3 |
| **Production totale de viande provenant des abattages** | **376.0** | **381.0** | **398.0** | **439.0** | **457.0** | **470.0** | **498.0** | 6.0 |
| *Moins:* Exportations de viande | 213.0 | 208.0 | 225.0 | 243.0 | 264.0 | 273.0 | 292.0 | 7.0 |
| *Plus:* Importations de viande | 22.0 | 25.0 | 37.0 | 36.0 | 52.0 | 54.0 | 61.0 | 13.0 |
| *Moins:* Variations des stocks | 1.0 | - | 2.0 | - | -1.0 | -5.0 | 3.0 | |
| **Consommation de viande** | **184.0** | **198.0** | **208.0** | **232.0** | **246.0** | **256.0** | **264.0** | 3.1 |
| Consommation par tête *(kilogrammes par an)* | 12.8 | 13.7 | 14.3 | 15.8 | 16.7 | 17.2 | 17.7 | 2.5 |

## VIANDE DE MOUTON ET DE CHÈVRE / MUTTON, LAMB AND GOAT MEAT

| | 1984 | 1985 | 1986 | 1987 | 1988 | 1989 | 1990 | 1989/90 % var. |
|---|---|---|---|---|---|---|---|---|
| Nombre d'animaux abattus *(milliers)* | 391.0 | 464.0 | 473.0 | 530.0 | 517.0 | 592.0 | 700.0 | 18.2 |
| Poids moyen en carcasse parée *(kilogrammes)* | 24.0 | 23.0 | 23.0 | 24.0 | 24.0 | 24.0 | 24.0 | 0.0 |
| **Production indigène brute** | **18.0** | **18.0** | **18.0** | **21.0** | **20.0** | **23.0** | **32.0** | 39.1 |
| *Moins:* Équivalent en viande des animaux exportés vivants | 8.0 | 8.0 | 7.0 | 8.0 | 8.0 | 9.0 | 15.0 | 66.7 |
| *Plus:* Viande provenant des abbattages d'animaux importés vivants | - | 1.0 | - | - | - | - | 1.0 | .. |
| **Production totale de viande provenant des abattages** | **10.0** | **11.0** | **11.0** | **13.0** | **12.0** | **14.0** | **18.0** | 28.6 |
| *Moins:* Exportations de viande | 5.0 | 6.0 | 5.0 | 7.0 | 5.0 | 6.0 | 6.0 | 0.0 |
| *Plus:* Importations de viande | 1.0 | 2.0 | 2.0 | 3.0 | 3.0 | 4.0 | 6.0 | 50.0 |
| *Moins:* Variations des stocks | - | - | - | - | - | - | - | |
| **Consommation de viande** | **6.0** | **7.0** | **8.0** | **9.0** | **10.0** | **12.0** | **18.0** | 50.0 |
| Consommation par tête *(kilogrammes par an)* | 0.4 | 0.5 | 0.5 | 0.6 | 0.7 | 0.8 | 1.2 | 49.0 |

# NETHERLANDS

## HORSE MEAT / VIANDE D'ÉQUIDÉS

*Thousand metric tons - Dressed carcass weight*

| | 1984 | 1985 | 1986 | 1987 | 1988 | 1989 | 1990 | 1989/90 % change |
|---|---|---|---|---|---|---|---|---|
| Number of animals slaughtered *(thousands)* | 9.0 | 12.0 | 9.0 | 7.0 | 6.0 | 5.0 | 4.0 | -20.0 |
| Average dressed carcass weight *(kilogrammes)* | 222.0 | 213.0 | 215.0 | 215.0 | 217.0 | 218.0 | 211.0 | -3.2 |
| **Gross indigenous production** | **5.0** | **5.0** | **4.0** | **4.0** | **4.0** | **3.0** | **2.0** | -33.3 |
| *Minus:* Meat equivalent of exported live animals | 4.0 | 3.0 | 3.0 | 3.0 | 3.0 | 3.0 | 3.0 | 0.0 |
| *Plus:* Meat from slaughterings of imported live animals | 1.0 | 1.0 | 1.0 | 1.0 | 1.0 | 1.0 | 1.0 | 0.0 |
| **Total meat production from slaughtered animals** | **2.0** | **3.0** | **2.0** | **2.0** | **2.0** | **1.0** | **-** | -100.0 |
| *Minus:* Exports of meat | 8.0 | 6.0 | 5.0 | 5.0 | 4.0 | 6.0 | 5.0 | -16.7 |
| *Plus:* Imports of meat | 26.0 | 24.0 | 24.0 | 26.0 | 25.0 | 26.0 | 25.0 | -3.8 |
| *Minus:* Stock variations | - | - | - | - | - | - | - | |
| **Meat consumption** | **20.0** | **21.0** | **21.0** | **23.0** | **23.0** | **21.0** | **20.0** | -4.8 |
| Consumption per head *(kilogrammes per year)* | 1.4 | 1.4 | 1.4 | 1.6 | 1.6 | 1.4 | 1.3 | -5.4 |

## OTHER MEAT / AUTRES VIANDES

| | 1984 | 1985 | 1986 | 1987 | 1988 | 1989 | 1990 | 1989/90 % change |
|---|---|---|---|---|---|---|---|---|
| Number of animals slaughtered *(thousands)* | | | | | | | | |
| Average dressed carcass weight *(kilogrammes)* | | | | | | | | |
| **Gross indigenous production** | **1.0** | **1.0** | **2.0** | **2.0** | **6.0** | **3.0** | **4.0** | 33.3 |
| *Minus:* Meat equivalent of exported live animals | 1.0 | 1.0 | 2.0 | 2.0 | 3.0 | 3.0 | 3.0 | 0.0 |
| *Plus:* Meat from slaughterings of imported live animals | - | - | - | - | - | - | 1.0 | .. |
| **Total meat production from slaughtered animals** | **-** | **-** | **-** | **-** | **3.0** | **-** | **2.0** | .. |
| *Minus:* Exports of meat | 5.0 | 5.0 | 5.0 | 4.0 | 6.0 | 6.0 | 6.0 | 0.0 |
| *Plus:* Imports of meat | 7.0 | 6.0 | 6.0 | 8.0 | 8.0 | 8.0 | 8.0 | 0.0 |
| *Minus:* Stock variations | - | - | - | - | - | - | - | |
| **Meat consumption** | **2.0** | **1.0** | **1.0** | **4.0** | **5.0** | **2.0** | **4.0** | 100.0 |
| Consumption per head *(kilogrammes per year)* | 0.1 | 0.1 | 0.1 | 0.3 | 0.3 | 0.1 | 0.3 | 98.7 |

## EDIBLE OFFALS / ABATS COMESTIBLES

| | 1984 | 1985 | 1986 | 1987 | 1988 | 1989 | 1990 | 1989/90 % change |
|---|---|---|---|---|---|---|---|---|
| Number of animals slaughtered *(thousands)* | | | | | | | | |
| Average dressed carcass weight *(kilogrammes)* | | | | | | | | |
| **Gross indigenous production** | **115.0** | **118.0** | **123.0** | **128.0** | **127.0** | **123.0** | **127.0** | 3.3 |
| *Minus:* Meat equivalent of exported live animals | 14.0 | 14.0 | 15.0 | 16.0 | 14.0 | 13.0 | 13.0 | 0.0 |
| *Plus:* Meat from slaughterings of imported live animals | 2.0 | 2.0 | 3.0 | 4.0 | 4.0 | 5.0 | 6.0 | 20.0 |
| **Total meat production from slaughtered animals** | **103.0** | **106.0** | **111.0** | **116.0** | **117.0** | **115.0** | **120.0** | 4.3 |
| *Minus:* Exports of meat | 110.0 | 110.0 | 84.0 | 70.0 | 112.0 | 117.0 | 120.0 | 2.6 |
| *Plus:* Imports of meat | 41.0 | 42.0 | 25.0 | 11.0 | 30.0 | 29.0 | 30.0 | 3.4 |
| *Minus:* Stock variations | - | - | - | - | - | - | - | |
| **Meat consumption** | **34.0** | **38.0** | **52.0** | **57.0** | **35.0** | **27.0** | **30.0** | 11.1 |
| Consumption per head *(kilogrammes per year)* | 2.4 | 2.6 | 3.6 | 3.9 | 2.4 | 1.8 | 2.0 | 10.4 |

# PAYS - BAS

*Milliers de tonnes métriques - Poids en carcasse parée*

## TOTAL VIANDE / TOTAL MEAT

| | 1984 | 1985 | 1986 | 1987 | 1988 | 1989 | 1990 | 1989/90 % var. |
|---|---|---|---|---|---|---|---|---|
| **Nombre d'animaux abattus** *(milliers)* | | | | | | | | |
| **Poids moyen en carcasse parée** *(kilogrammes)* | | | | | | | | |
| **Production indigène brute** | 2617.0 | 2711.0 | 2848.0 | 3011.0 | 3040.0 | 2953.0 | 3068.0 | 3.9 |
| *Moins:* Équivalent en viande des animaux exportés vivants | 327.0 | 365.0 | 394.0 | 425.0 | 377.0 | 341.0 | 364.0 | 6.7 |
| *Plus:* Viande provenant des abbattages d'animaux importés vivants | 22.0 | 33.0 | 51.0 | 58.0 | 65.0 | 82.0 | 114.0 | 39.0 |
| **Production totale de viande provenant des abattages** | 2312.0 | 2379.0 | 2505.0 | 2644.0 | 2728.0 | 2694.0 | 2818.0 | 4.6 |
| *Moins:* Exportations de viande | 1384.0 | 1438.0 | 1543.0 | 1589.0 | 1694.0 | 1704.0 | 1763.0 | 3.5 |
| *Plus:* Importations de viande | 197.0 | 204.0 | 206.0 | 204.0 | 251.0 | 239.0 | 258.0 | 7.9 |
| *Moins:* Variations des stocks | 15.0 | 3.0 | 16.0 | 4.0 | -5.0 | -47.0 | 4.0 | |
| **Consommation de viande** | 1110.0 | 1142.0 | 1152.0 | 1255.0 | 1290.0 | 1276.0 | 1309.0 | 2.6 |
| **Consommation par tête** *(kilogrammes par an)* | 77.0 | 78.8 | 79.1 | 85.6 | 87.4 | 85.9 | 87.6 | 1.9 |

## PRODUCTION INDIGENE BRUTE DE VIANDE
## MEAT GROSS INDIGENOUS PRODUCTION

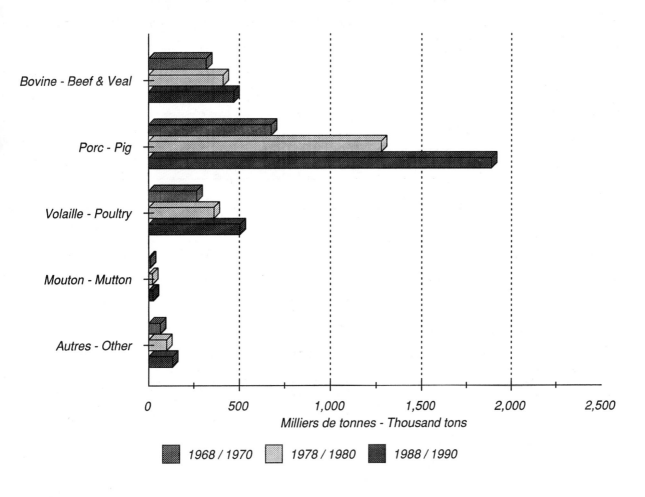

Milliers de tonnes - Thousand tons

■ 1968 / 1970    □ 1978 / 1980    ■ 1988 / 1990

105

# PORTUGAL

## BEEF / VIANDE DE BŒUF

*Thousand metric tons - Dressed carcass weight*

|  | 1984 | 1985 | 1986 | 1987 | 1988 | 1989 | 1990 | 1989/90 % change |
|---|---|---|---|---|---|---|---|---|
| Number of animals slaughtered *(thousands)* | 272.0 | 272.0 | 414.0 [b] | 416.0 | 421.0 | 502.0 | 435.0 | -13.3 |
| Average dressed carcass weight *(kilogrammes)* | 243.0 | 245.0 | 236.0 | 242.0 | 250.0 | 243.0 | 249.0 | 2.5 |
| **Gross indigenous production** | **93.0** | **89.0** | **95.0** | **95.0** | **106.0** | **114.0** | **105.0** | **-7.9** |
| *Minus:* Meat equivalent of exported live animals | - | - | - | - | - | - | - | .. |
| *Plus:* Meat from slaughterings of imported live animals | 2.0 | 5.0 | 4.0 | 5.0 | 3.0 | 4.0 | 5.0 | 25.0 |
| **Total meat production from slaughtered animals** | **95.0** | **94.0** | **99.0** | **100.0** | **109.0** | **118.0** | **110.0** | **-6.8** |
| *Minus:* Exports of meat | 2.0 | 2.0 | 3.0 | 2.0 | - | 1.0 | 1.0 | 0.0 |
| *Plus:* Imports of meat | 4.0 | 12.0 | 15.0 | 19.0 | 20.0 | 23.0 | 43.0 | 87.0 |
| *Minus:* Stock variations | -5.0 | -2.0 | 2.0 | 2.0 | 4.0 | 2.0 | 3.0 | |
| **Meat consumption** | **102.0** | **106.0** | **109.0** | **115.0** | **125.0** | **138.0** | **149.0** | **8.0** |
| Consumption per head *(kilogrammes per year)* | 10.1 | 10.4 | 10.7 | 11.2 | 12.1 | 13.4 | 14.4 | 7.6 |

## VEAL / VIANDE DE VEAU

|  | 1984 | 1985 | 1986 | 1987 | 1988 | 1989 | 1990 | 1989/90 % change |
|---|---|---|---|---|---|---|---|---|
| Number of animals slaughtered *(thousands)* | 45.0 | 45.0 | 70.0 [b] | 61.0 | 54.0 | 71.0 | 66.0 | -7.0 |
| Average dressed carcass weight *(kilogrammes)* | 175.0 | 160.0 | 96.0 [b] | 98.0 | 98.0 | 97.0 | 99.0 | 2.1 |
| **Gross indigenous production** | **8.0** | **9.0** | **7.0** | **4.0** | **6.0** | **6.0** | **7.0** | **16.7** |
| *Minus:* Meat equivalent of exported live animals | - | - | - | - | - | - | - | .. |
| *Plus:* Meat from slaughterings of imported live animals | - | - | - | 1.0 | - | - | - | .. |
| **Total meat production from slaughtered animals** | **8.0** | **9.0** | **7.0** | **5.0** | **6.0** | **6.0** | **7.0** | **16.7** |
| *Minus:* Exports of meat | - | - | - | - | - | - | - | .. |
| *Plus:* Imports of meat | 1.0 | 1.0 | 2.0 | 4.0 | 6.0 | 1.0 | 3.0 | 200.0 |
| *Minus:* Stock variations | - | - | - | - | - | - | 1.0 | |
| **Meat consumption** | **9.0** | **10.0** | **9.0** | **9.0** | **12.0** | **7.0** | **9.0** | **28.6** |
| Consumption per head *(kilogrammes per year)* | 0.9 | 1.0 | 0.9 | 0.9 | 1.2 | 0.7 | 0.9 | 28.2 |

## BEEF AND VEAL / TOTAL VIANDE BOVINE

|  | 1984 | 1985 | 1986 | 1987 | 1988 | 1989 | 1990 | 1989/90 % change |
|---|---|---|---|---|---|---|---|---|
| Number of animals slaughtered *(thousands)* | 317.0 | 317.0 | 484.0 [b] | 477.0 | 475.0 | 573.0 | 501.0 | -12.6 |
| Average dressed carcass weight *(kilogrammes)* | 324.9 | 324.9 | 219.0 [b] | 220.1 | 242.1 | 216.4 | 233.5 | 7.9 |
| **Gross indigenous production** | **101.0** | **98.0** | **102.0** | **99.0** | **112.0** | **120.0** | **112.0** | **-6.7** |
| *Minus:* Meat equivalent of exported live animals | - | - | - | - | - | - | - | .. |
| *Plus:* Meat from slaughterings of imported live animals | 2.0 | 5.0 | 4.0 | 6.0 | 3.0 | 4.0 | 5.0 | 25.0 |
| **Total meat production from slaughtered animals** | **103.0** | **103.0** | **106.0** | **105.0** | **115.0** | **124.0** | **117.0** | **-5.6** |
| *Minus:* Exports of meat | 2.0 | 2.0 | 3.0 | 2.0 | - | 1.0 | 1.0 | 0.0 |
| *Plus:* Imports of meat | 5.0 | 13.0 | 17.0 | 23.0 | 26.0 | 24.0 | 46.0 | 91.7 |
| *Minus:* Stock variations | -5.0 | -2.0 | 2.0 | 2.0 | 4.0 | 2.0 | 4.0 | |
| **Meat consumption** | **111.0** | **116.0** | **118.0** | **124.0** | **137.0** | **145.0** | **158.0** | **9.0** |
| Consumption per head *(kilogrammes per year)* | 11.0 | 11.4 | 11.5 | 12.1 | 13.3 | 14.0 | 15.2 | 8.6 |

# PORTUGAL

*Milliers de tonnes métriques - Poids en carcasse parée*

## VIANDE DE PORC / PIG MEAT

| | 1984 | 1985 | 1986 | 1987 | 1988 | 1989 | 1990 | 1989/90 % var. |
|---|---|---|---|---|---|---|---|---|
| Nombre d'animaux abattus *(milliers)* | 2273.0 | 2145.0 | 2424.0 | 2759.0 | 2688.0 | 3118.0 | 3510.0 | 12.6 |
| Poids moyen en carcasse parée *(kilogrammes)* | 72.0 | 70.0 | 70.0 | 69.0 | 68.0 | 67.0 | 71.0 | 6.0 |
| Production indigène brute | 208.0 | 197.0 | 223.0 | 259.0 | 226.0 | 261.0 | 278.0 | 6.5 |
| *Moins:* Équivalent en viande des animaux exportés vivants | - | - | - | - | - | - | - | .. |
| *Plus:* Viande provenant des abbattages d'animaux importés vivants | - | - | - | - | 2.0 | 3.0 | 1.0 | -66.7 |
| Production totale de viande provenant des abattages | 208.0 | 197.0 | 223.0 | 259.0 | 228.0 | 264.0 | 279.0 | 5.7 |
| *Moins:* Exportations de viande | 4.0 | 4.0 | 4.0 | 4.0 | 5.0 | 6.0 | 5.0 | -16.7 |
| *Plus:* Importations de viande | 2.0 | 21.0 | 15.0 | 10.0 | 24.0 | 31.0 | 23.0 | -25.8 |
| *Moins:* Variations des stocks | - | - | 4.0 | 5.0 | -3.0 | 4.0 | 1.0 | |
| Consommation de viande | 206.0 | 214.0 | 230.0 | 260.0 | 250.0 | 285.0 | 296.0 | 3.9 |
| Consommation par tête *(kilogrammes par an)* | 20.3 | 21.0 | 22.5 | 25.3 | 24.3 | 27.6 | 28.5 | 3.5 |

## VIANDE DE VOLAILLE / POULTRY MEAT

| | 1984 | 1985 | 1986 | 1987 | 1988 | 1989 | 1990 | 1989/90 % var. |
|---|---|---|---|---|---|---|---|---|
| Nombre d'animaux abattus *(milliers)* | | | | | | | | |
| Poids moyen en carcasse parée *(kilogrammes)* | | | | | | | | |
| Production indigène brute | 140.0 | 137.0 | 157.0 | 171.0 | 175.0 | 183.0 | 185.0 | 1.1 |
| *Moins:* Équivalent en viande des animaux exportés vivants | - | - | - | - | - | - | 1.0 | .. |
| *Plus:* Viande provenant des abbattages d'animaux importés vivants | - | - | - | - | - | - | - | .. |
| Production totale de viande provenant des abattages | 140.0 | 137.0 | 157.0 | 171.0 | 175.0 | 183.0 | 184.0 | 0.5 |
| *Moins:* Exportations de viande | - | - | - | - | - | - | 1.0 | .. |
| *Plus:* Importations de viande | - | - | - | - | - | 3.0 | 5.0 | 66.7 |
| *Moins:* Variations des stocks | - | - | - | - | - | - | - | |
| Consommation de viande | 140.0 | 137.0 | 157.0 | 171.0 | 175.0 | 186.0 | 188.0 | 1.1 |
| Consommation par tête *(kilogrammes par an)* | 13.8 | 13.5 | 15.3 | 16.7 | 17.0 | 18.0 | 18.1 | 0.8 |

## VIANDE DE MOUTON ET DE CHÈVRE / MUTTON, LAMB AND GOAT MEAT

| | 1984 | 1985 | 1986 | 1987 | 1988 | 1989 | 1990 | 1989/90 % var. |
|---|---|---|---|---|---|---|---|---|
| Nombre d'animaux abattus *(milliers)* | 2078.0 | 1910.0 | 1272.0 | 1291.0 | 1502.0 | 1519.0 | 1454.0 | -4.3 |
| Poids moyen en carcasse parée *(kilogrammes)* | 12.0 | 11.0 | 10.0 | 10.0 | 10.0 | 10.0 | 10.0 | 0.0 |
| Production indigène brute | 26.0 | 25.0 | 25.0 | 27.0 | 28.0 | 28.0 | 28.0 | 0.0 |
| *Moins:* Équivalent en viande des animaux exportés vivants | - | - | - | - | - | 1.0 | 1.0 | 0.0 |
| *Plus:* Viande provenant des abbattages d'animaux importés vivants | - | - | - | - | - | - | 1.0 | .. |
| Production totale de viande provenant des abattages | 26.0 | 25.0 | 25.0 | 27.0 | 28.0 | 27.0 | 28.0 | 3.7 |
| *Moins:* Exportations de viande | - | - | - | - | - | - | - | .. |
| *Plus:* Importations de viande | - | - | - | 4.0 | 4.0 | 6.0 | 10.0 | 66.7 |
| *Moins:* Variations des stocks | - | - | - | 1.0 | - | - | 3.0 | |
| Consommation de viande | 26.0 | 25.0 | 25.0 | 30.0 | 32.0 | 33.0 | 35.0 | 6.1 |
| Consommation par tête *(kilogrammes par an)* | 2.6 | 2.5 | 2.4 | 2.9 | 3.1 | 3.2 | 3.4 | 5.7 |

# PORTUGAL

|  | 1984 | 1985 | 1986 | 1987 | 1988 | 1989 | 1990 | 1989/90 % change |
|---|---|---|---|---|---|---|---|---|
| **Number of animals slaughtered** _(thousands)_ | 6.0 | 6.0 | 8.0 | 8.0 | 7.0 | 7.0 | 6.0 | -14.3 |
| **Average dressed carcass weight** _(kilogrammes)_ | 170.0 | 170.0 | 163.0 | 158.0 | 173.0 | 155.0 | 160.0 | 3.2 |
| **Gross indigenous production** | 2.0 | 1.0 | 1.0 | 1.0 | 1.0 | 1.0 | 1.0 | 0.0 |
| _Minus:_ Meat equivalent of exported live animals | - | - | - | - | - | - | - | .. |
| _Plus:_ Meat from slaughterings of imported live animals | - | - | - | - | - | - | - | .. |
| **Total meat production from slaughtered animals** | 2.0 | 1.0 | 1.0 | 1.0 | 1.0 | 1.0 | 1.0 | 0.0 |
| _Minus:_ Exports of meat | - | - | - | - | - | - | - | .. |
| _Plus:_ Imports of meat | - | - | - | - | - | - | - | .. |
| _Minus:_ Stock variations | - | - | - | - | - | - | - | |
| **Meat consumption** | 2.0 | 1.0 | 1.0 | 1.0 | 1.0 | 1.0 | 1.0 | 0.0 |
| **Consumption per head** _(kilogrammes per year)_ | 0.2 | 0.1 | 0.1 | 0.1 | 0.1 | 0.1 | 0.1 | -0.3 |

## _OTHER MEAT / AUTRES VIANDES_

|  | 1984 | 1985 | 1986 | 1987 | 1988 | 1989 | 1990 | 1989/90 % change |
|---|---|---|---|---|---|---|---|---|
| **Number of animals slaughtered** _(thousands)_ | | | | | | | | |
| **Average dressed carcass weight** _(kilogrammes)_ | | | | | | | | |
| **Gross indigenous production** | 16.0 | 16.0 | 16.0 | 16.0 | 17.0 | 22.0 | 23.0 | 4.5 |
| _Minus:_ Meat equivalent of exported live animals | - | - | - | - | - | - | - | .. |
| _Plus:_ Meat from slaughterings of imported live animals | - | - | - | - | - | - | - | .. |
| **Total meat production from slaughtered animals** | 16.0 | 16.0 | 16.0 | 16.0 | 17.0 | 22.0 | 23.0 | 4.5 |
| _Minus:_ Exports of meat | - | - | - | - | - | - | - | .. |
| _Plus:_ Imports of meat | - | - | - | - | 1.0 | - | 1.0 | .. |
| _Minus:_ Stock variations | - | - | - | - | - | - | - | |
| **Meat consumption** | 16.0 | 16.0 | 16.0 | 16.0 | 18.0 | 22.0 | 24.0 | 9.1 |
| **Consumption per head** _(kilogrammes per year)_ | 1.6 | 1.6 | 1.6 | 1.6 | 1.7 | 2.1 | 2.3 | 8.8 |

## _EDIBLE OFFALS / ABATS COMESTIBLES_

|  | 1984 | 1985 | 1986 | 1987 | 1988 | 1989 | 1990 | 1989/90 % change |
|---|---|---|---|---|---|---|---|---|
| **Number of animals slaughtered** _(thousands)_ | | | | | | | | |
| **Average dressed carcass weight** _(kilogrammes)_ | | | | | | | | |
| **Gross indigenous production** | 47.0 | 46.0 | 49.0 | 51.0 | 53.0 | 56.0 | 56.0 | 0.0 |
| _Minus:_ Meat equivalent of exported live animals | - | - | - | - | - | - | - | .. |
| _Plus:_ Meat from slaughterings of imported live animals | - | - | - | - | - | - | - | .. |
| **Total meat production from slaughtered animals** | 47.0 | 46.0 | 49.0 | 51.0 | 53.0 | 56.0 | 56.0 | 0.0 |
| _Minus:_ Exports of meat | 3.0 | 4.0 | 3.0 | 4.0 | - | 1.0 | 1.0 | 0.0 |
| _Plus:_ Imports of meat | 6.0 | 7.0 | 9.0 | 10.0 | 7.0 | 5.0 | 5.0 | 0.0 |
| _Minus:_ Stock variations | - | - | 2.0 | - | - | - | - | |
| **Meat consumption** | 50.0 | 49.0 | 53.0 | 57.0 | 60.0 | 60.0 | 60.0 | 0.0 |
| **Consumption per head** _(kilogrammes per year)_ | 4.9 | 4.8 | 5.2 | 5.6 | 5.8 | 5.8 | 5.8 | -0.3 |

# PORTUGAL

*Milliers de tonnes métriques - Poids en carcasse parée*

*TOTAL VIANDE / TOTAL MEAT*

| | 1984 | 1985 | 1986 | 1987 | 1988 | 1989 | 1990 | 1989/90 % var. |
|---|---|---|---|---|---|---|---|---|
| **Nombre d'animaux abattus** *(milliers)* | | | | | | | | |
| **Poids moyen en carcasse parée** *(kilogrammes)* | | | | | | | | |
| **Production indigène brute** | 540.0 | 520.0 | 573.0 | 624.0 | 612.0 | 671.0 | 683.0 | 1.8 |
| *Moins:* Équivalent en viande des animaux exportés vivants | - | - | - | - | - | 1.0 | 2.0 | 100.0 |
| *Plus:* Viande provenant des abbattages d'animaux importés vivants | 2.0 | 5.0 | 4.0 | 6.0 | 5.0 | 7.0 | 7.0 | 0.0 |
| **Production totale de viande provenant des abattages** | 542.0 | 525.0 | 577.0 | 630.0 | 617.0 | 677.0 | 688.0 | 1.6 |
| *Moins:* Exportations de viande | 9.0 | 10.0 | 10.0 | 10.0 | 5.0 | 8.0 | 8.0 | 0.0 |
| *Plus:* Importations de viande | 13.0 | 41.0 | 41.0 | 47.0 | 62.0 | 69.0 | 90.0 | 30.4 |
| *Moins:* Variations des stocks | -5.0 | -2.0 | 8.0 | 8.0 | 1.0 | 6.0 | 8.0 | |
| **Consommation de viande** | 551.0 | 558.0 | 600.0 | 659.0 | 673.0 | 732.0 | 762.0 | 4.1 |
| **Consommation par tête** *(kilogrammes par an)* | 54.4 | 54.8 | 58.7 | 64.2 | 65.3 | 70.8 | 73.5 | 3.8 |

## PRODUCTION INDIGENE BRUTE DE VIANDE
## MEAT GROSS INDIGENOUS PRODUCTION

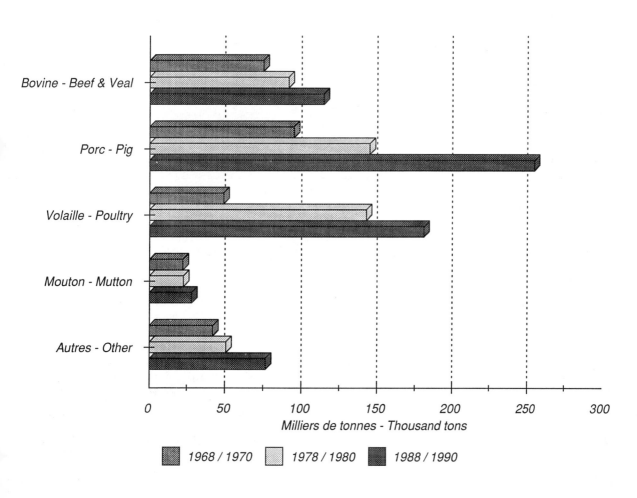

Milliers de tonnes - Thousand tons

1968 / 1970      1978 / 1980      1988 / 1990

109

# SPAIN

## BEEF / VIANDE DE BŒUF

*Thousand metric tons - Dressed carcass weight*

| | 1984 | 1985 | 1986 | 1987 | 1988 | 1989 | 1990 | 1989/90 % change |
|---|---|---|---|---|---|---|---|---|
| Number of animals slaughtered *(thousands)* | 1126.0 | 1159.0 | 1812.0 [b] | 1844.0 | 1788.0 | 1722.0 | 1955.0 | 13.5 |
| Average dressed carcass weight *(kilogrammes)* | 249.0 | 251.0 | 233.0 [b] | 234.0 | 240.0 | 255.0 | 252.0 | -1.2 |
| Gross indigenous production | 279.0 | 274.0 | 411.0 [b] | 424.0 | 412.0 | 423.0 | 492.0 | 16.3 |
| *Minus:* Meat equivalent of exported live animals | - | - | - [b] | 2.0 | 1.0 | 1.0 | 2.0 | 100.0 |
| *Plus:* Meat from slaughterings of imported live animals | 9.0 | 17.0 | 12.0 [b] | 8.0 | 17.0 | 23.0 | 13.0 | -43.5 |
| Total meat production from slaughtered animals | 288.0 | 291.0 | 423.0 [b] | 430.0 | 428.0 | 445.0 | 503.0 | 13.0 |
| *Minus:* Exports of meat | 14.0 | 1.0 | 1.0 [b] | 11.0 | 19.0 | 27.0 | 32.0 | 18.5 |
| *Plus:* Imports of meat | 30.0 | 38.0 | 7.0 [b] | 7.0 | 11.0 | 14.0 | 17.0 | 21.4 |
| *Minus:* Stock variations | -28.0 | -5.0 | 12.0 [b] | - | -8.0 | -8.0 | 10.0 | |
| Meat consumption | 332.0 | 333.0 | 417.0 [b] | 426.0 | 428.0 | 440.0 | 478.0 | 8.6 |
| Consumption per head *(kilogrammes per year)* | 8.7 | 8.7 | 10.8 [b] | 11.0 | 11.0 | 11.3 | 12.3 | 8.4 |

## VEAL / VIANDE DE VEAU

| | 1984 | 1985 | 1986 | 1987 | 1988 | 1989 | 1990 | 1989/90 % change |
|---|---|---|---|---|---|---|---|---|
| Number of animals slaughtered *(thousands)* | 640.0 | 653.0 | 105.0 [b] | 118.0 | 133.0 | 111.0 | 86.0 | -22.5 |
| Average dressed carcass weight *(kilogrammes)* | 169.0 | 168.0 | 114.0 [b] | 118.0 | 125.0 | 126.0 | 123.0 | -2.4 |
| Gross indigenous production | 111.0 | 110.0 | 12.0 [b] | 14.0 | 15.0 | 12.0 | 7.0 | -41.7 |
| *Minus:* Meat equivalent of exported live animals | - | - | - [b] | - | - | - | - | .. |
| *Plus:* Meat from slaughterings of imported live animals | - | - | - [b] | - | 1.0 | 2.0 | 4.0 | 100.0 |
| Total meat production from slaughtered animals | 111.0 | 110.0 | 12.0 [b] | 14.0 | 16.0 | 14.0 | 11.0 | -21.4 |
| *Minus:* Exports of meat | - | - | - [b] | 1.0 | 4.0 | 3.0 | 4.0 | 33.3 |
| *Plus:* Imports of meat | 1.0 | 1.0 | 1.0 [b] | 1.0 | 3.0 | 2.0 | 3.0 | 50.0 |
| *Minus:* Stock variations | - | - | - [b] | - | - | - | - | |
| Meat consumption | 112.0 | 111.0 | 13.0 [b] | 14.0 | 15.0 | 13.0 | 10.0 | -23.1 |
| Consumption per head *(kilogrammes per year)* | 2.9 | 2.9 | 0.3 [b] | 0.4 | 0.4 | 0.3 | 0.3 | -23.2 |

## BEEF AND VEAL / TOTAL VIANDE BOVINE

| | 1984 | 1985 | 1986 | 1987 | 1988 | 1989 | 1990 | 1989/90 % change |
|---|---|---|---|---|---|---|---|---|
| Number of animals slaughtered *(thousands)* | 1766.0 | 1812.0 | 1917.0 | 1962.0 | 1921.0 | 1833.0 | 2041.0 | 11.3 |
| Average dressed carcass weight *(kilogrammes)* | 225.9 | 221.3 | 226.9 | 226.3 | 231.1 | 250.4 | 251.8 | 0.6 |
| Gross indigenous production | 390.0 | 384.0 | 423.0 | 438.0 | 427.0 | 435.0 | 499.0 | 14.7 |
| *Minus:* Meat equivalent of exported live animals | - | - | - | 2.0 | 1.0 | 1.0 | 2.0 | 100.0 |
| *Plus:* Meat from slaughterings of imported live animals | 9.0 | 17.0 | 12.0 | 8.0 | 18.0 | 25.0 | 17.0 | -32.0 |
| Total meat production from slaughtered animals | 399.0 | 401.0 | 435.0 | 444.0 | 444.0 | 459.0 | 514.0 | 12.0 |
| *Minus:* Exports of meat | 14.0 | 1.0 | 1.0 | 12.0 | 23.0 | 30.0 | 36.0 | 20.0 |
| *Plus:* Imports of meat | 31.0 | 39.0 | 8.0 | 8.0 | 14.0 | 16.0 | 20.0 | 25.0 |
| *Minus:* Stock variations | -28.0 | -5.0 | 12.0 | - | -8.0 | -8.0 | 10.0 | |
| Meat consumption | 444.0 | 444.0 | 430.0 | 440.0 | 443.0 | 453.0 | 488.0 | 7.7 |
| Consumption per head *(kilogrammes per year)* | 11.6 | 11.6 | 11.1 | 11.4 | 11.4 | 11.6 | 12.5 | 7.5 |

# ESPAGNE

## VIANDE DE PORC / PIG MEAT

| | 1984 | 1985 | 1986 | 1987 | 1988 | 1989 | 1990 | 1989/90 % var. |
|---|---|---|---|---|---|---|---|---|
| Nombre d'animaux abattus *(milliers)* | 19580.0 [e] | 18950.0 [e] | 18978.0 | 19978.0 | 22710.0 | 22359.0 | 23529.0 | 5.2 |
| Poids moyen en carcasse parée *(kilogrammes)* | 73.0 | 73.0 | 73.0 | 74.0 | 75.0 | 76.0 | 76.0 | 0.0 |
| Production indigène brute | 1429.0 | 1388.0 | 1342.0 | 1448.0 | 1702.0 | 1674.0 | 1772.0 | 5.9 |
| *Moins:* Équivalent en viande des animaux exportés vivants | - | - | - | - | - | - | 6.0 | .. |
| *Plus:* Viande provenant des abbattages d'animaux importés vivants | - | - | 52.0 | 33.0 | 12.0 | 30.0 | 23.0 | -23.3 |
| Production totale de viande provenant des abattages | 1429.0 | 1388.0 | 1394.0 | 1481.0 | 1714.0 | 1704.0 | 1789.0 | 5.0 |
| *Moins:* Exportations de viande | 3.0 | 4.0 | 4.0 | 3.0 | 4.0 | 6.0 | 10.0 | 66.7 |
| *Plus:* Importations de viande | 21.0 | 19.0 | 49.0 | 37.0 | 28.0 | 55.0 | 54.0 | -1.8 |
| *Moins:* Variations des stocks | 4.0 | 1.0 | -4.0 | - | - | - | - | |
| Consommation de viande | 1443.0 | 1402.0 | 1443.0 | 1515.0 | 1738.0 | 1753.0 | 1833.0 | 4.6 |
| Consommation par tête *(kilogrammes par an)* | 37.7 | 36.5 | 37.3 | 39.1 | 44.8 | 45.1 | 47.0 | 4.4 |

## VIANDE DE VOLAILLE / POULTRY MEAT

| | 1984 | 1985 | 1986 | 1987 | 1988 | 1989 | 1990 | 1989/90 % var. |
|---|---|---|---|---|---|---|---|---|
| Nombre d'animaux abattus *(milliers)* | | | | | | | | |
| Poids moyen en carcasse parée *(kilogrammes)* | | | | | | | | |
| Production indigène brute | 790.0 | 815.0 | 754.0 | 786.0 | 819.0 | 828.0 | 834.0 | 0.7 |
| *Moins:* Équivalent en viande des animaux exportés vivants | - | - | 1.0 | 2.0 | 1.0 | 2.0 | 1.0 | -50.0 |
| *Plus:* Viande provenant des abbattages d'animaux importés vivants | - | - | 1.0 | 3.0 | 3.0 | 4.0 | 4.0 | 0.0 |
| Production totale de viande provenant des abattages | 790.0 | 815.0 | 754.0 | 787.0 | 821.0 | 830.0 | 837.0 | 0.8 |
| *Moins:* Exportations de viande | 4.0 | 2.0 | 5.0 | 9.0 | 8.0 | 7.0 | 6.0 | -14.3 |
| *Plus:* Importations de viande | 20.0 | 27.0 | 15.0 | 27.0 | 40.0 | 47.0 | 49.0 | 4.3 |
| *Moins:* Variations des stocks | - | - | - | - | - | - | - | |
| Consommation de viande | 806.0 | 840.0 | 764.0 | 805.0 | 853.0 | 870.0 | 880.0 | 1.1 |
| Consommation par tête *(kilogrammes par an)* | 21.1 | 21.9 | 19.8 | 20.8 | 22.0 | 22.4 | 22.6 | 0.9 |

## VIANDE DE MOUTON ET DE CHÈVRE / MUTTON, LAMB AND GOAT MEAT

| | 1984 | 1985 | 1986 | 1987 | 1988 | 1989 | 1990 | 1989/90 % var. |
|---|---|---|---|---|---|---|---|---|
| Nombre d'animaux abattus *(milliers)* | 18850.0 [e] | 19100.0 | 18379.0 | 19610.0 | 21030.0 | 20148.0 | 21006.0 | 4.3 |
| Poids moyen en carcasse parée *(kilogrammes)* | 11.0 | 11.0 | 11.0 | 11.0 | 11.0 | 11.0 | 11.0 | 0.0 |
| Production indigène brute | 207.0 | 210.0 | 210.0 | 225.0 | 232.0 | 218.0 | 223.0 | 2.3 |
| *Moins:* Équivalent en viande des animaux exportés vivants | - | - | 1.0 | 3.0 | 8.0 | 2.0 | 2.0 | 0.0 |
| *Plus:* Viande provenant des abbattages d'animaux importés vivants | - | - | 2.0 | 2.0 | 6.0 | 6.0 | 12.0 | 100.0 |
| Production totale de viande provenant des abattages | 207.0 | 210.0 | 211.0 | 224.0 | 230.0 | 222.0 | 233.0 | 5.0 |
| *Moins:* Exportations de viande | 1.0 | 1.0 | 5.0 | 8.0 | 20.0 | 10.0 | 4.0 | -60.0 |
| *Plus:* Importations de viande | 1.0 | 1.0 | 7.0 | 11.0 | 14.0 | 16.0 | 19.0 | 18.8 |
| *Moins:* Variations des stocks | - | - | - | - | - | - | - | |
| Consommation de viande | 207.0 | 210.0 | 213.0 | 227.0 | 224.0 | 228.0 | 248.0 | 8.8 |
| Consommation par tête *(kilogrammes par an)* | 5.4 | 5.5 | 5.5 | 5.9 | 5.8 | 5.9 | 6.4 | 8.6 |

# SPAIN

## HORSE MEAT / VIANDE D'ÉQUIDÉS

| | 1984 | 1985 | 1986 | 1987 | 1988 | 1989 | 1990 | 1989/90 % change |
|---|---|---|---|---|---|---|---|---|
| Number of animals slaughtered *(thousands)* | 53.0 | 57.0 | 49.0 | 49.0 | 44.0 | 44.0 | 44.0 | 0.0 |
| Average dressed carcass weight *(kilogrammes)* | 145.0 | 145.0 | 138.0 | 148.0 | 153.0 | 151.0 | 161.0 | 6.6 |
| Gross indigenous production | 8.0 | 8.0 | 7.0 | 7.0 | 6.0 | 6.0 | 7.0 | 16.7 |
| Minus: Meat equivalent of exported live animals | 1.0 | - | - | - | - | - | - | .. |
| Plus: Meat from slaughterings of imported live animals | - | - | - | - | - | - | - | .. |
| Total meat production from slaughtered animals | 7.0 | 8.0 | 7.0 | 7.0 | 6.0 | 6.0 | 7.0 | 16.7 |
| Minus: Exports of meat | - | - | - | - | - | - | - | .. |
| Plus: Imports of meat | - | - | - | - | - | - | - | .. |
| Minus: Stock variations | - | - | - | - | - | - | - | |
| Meat consumption | 7.0 | 8.0 | 7.0 | 7.0 | 6.0 | 6.0 | 7.0 | 16.7 |
| Consumption per head *(kilogrammes per year)* | 0.2 | 0.2 | 0.2 | 0.2 | 0.2 | 0.2 | 0.2 | 16.4 |

## OTHER MEAT / AUTRES VIANDES

| | 1984 | 1985 | 1986 | 1987 | 1988 | 1989 | 1990 | 1989/90 % change |
|---|---|---|---|---|---|---|---|---|
| Number of animals slaughtered *(thousands)* | | | | | | | | |
| Average dressed carcass weight *(kilogrammes)* | | | | | | | | |
| Gross indigenous production | 99.0 | 100.0 | 94.0 | 97.0 | 98.0 | 85.0 | 87.0 | 2.4 |
| Minus: Meat equivalent of exported live animals | - | - | - | - | - | - | - | .. |
| Plus: Meat from slaughterings of imported live animals | - | - | - | - | - | - | - | .. |
| Total meat production from slaughtered animals | 99.0 | 100.0 | 94.0 | 97.0 | 98.0 | 85.0 | 87.0 | 2.4 |
| Minus: Exports of meat | 4.0 | 3.0 | 1.0 | 2.0 | 2.0 | 2.0 | 1.0 | -50.0 |
| Plus: Imports of meat | 1.0 | - | - | - | 1.0 | 1.0 | 1.0 | 0.0 |
| Minus: Stock variations | - | - | - | - | - | - | - | |
| Meat consumption | 96.0 | 97.0 | 93.0 | 95.0 | 97.0 | 84.0 | 87.0 | 3.6 |
| Consumption per head *(kilogrammes per year)* | 2.5 | 2.5 | 2.4 | 2.5 | 2.5 | 2.2 | 2.2 | 3.4 |

## EDIBLE OFFALS / ABATS COMESTIBLES

| | 1984 | 1985 | 1986 | 1987 | 1988 | 1989 | 1990 | 1989/90 % change |
|---|---|---|---|---|---|---|---|---|
| Number of animals slaughtered *(thousands)* | | | | | | | | |
| Average dressed carcass weight *(kilogrammes)* | | | | | | | | |
| Gross indigenous production | 211.0 | 209.0 | 215.0 | 225.0 | 244.0 | 244.0 | 261.0 | 7.0 |
| Minus: Meat equivalent of exported live animals | - | - | - | - | - | - | - | .. |
| Plus: Meat from slaughterings of imported live animals | - | - | - | - | - | - | - | .. |
| Total meat production from slaughtered animals | 211.0 | 209.0 | 215.0 | 225.0 | 244.0 | 244.0 | 261.0 | 7.0 |
| Minus: Exports of meat | 7.0 | 8.0 | 8.0 | 6.0 | 4.0 | 5.0 | 5.0 | 0.0 |
| Plus: Imports of meat | 19.0 | 25.0 | 25.0 | 31.0 | 15.0 | 15.0 | 13.0 | -13.3 |
| Minus: Stock variations | - | - | - | - | - | - | - | |
| Meat consumption | 223.0 | 226.0 | 232.0 | 250.0 | 255.0 | 254.0 | 269.0 | 5.9 |
| Consumption per head *(kilogrammes per year)* | 5.8 | 5.9 | 6.0 | 6.5 | 6.6 | 6.5 | 6.9 | 5.7 |

# ESPAGNE

*Milliers de tonnes métriques - Poids en carcasse parée*

**TOTAL VIANDE / TOTAL MEAT**

|  | 1984 | 1985 | 1986 | 1987 | 1988 | 1989 | 1990 | 1989/90 % var. |
|---|---|---|---|---|---|---|---|---|
| **Nombre d'animaux abattus** *(milliers)* |  |  |  |  |  |  |  |  |
| **Poids moyen en carcasse parée** *(kilogrammes)* |  |  |  |  |  |  |  |  |
| **Production indigène brute** | 3134.0 | 3114.0 | 3045.0 | 3226.0 | 3528.0 | 3490.0 | 3683.0 | 5.5 |
| *Moins:* Équivalent en viande des animaux exportés vivants | 1.0 | - | 2.0 | 7.0 | 10.0 | 5.0 | 11.0 | 120.0 |
| *Plus:* Viande provenant des abbattages d'animaux importés vivants | 9.0 | 17.0 | 67.0 | 46.0 | 39.0 | 65.0 | 56.0 | -13.8 |
| **Production totale de viande provenant des abattages** | 3142.0 | 3131.0 | 3110.0 | 3265.0 | 3557.0 | 3550.0 | 3728.0 | 5.0 |
| *Moins:* Exportations de viande | 33.0 | 19.0 | 24.0 | 40.0 | 61.0 | 60.0 | 62.0 | 3.3 |
| *Plus:* Importations de viande | 93.0 | 111.0 | 104.0 | 114.0 | 112.0 | 150.0 | 156.0 | 4.0 |
| *Moins:* Variations des stocks | -24.0 | -4.0 | 8.0 | - | -8.0 | -8.0 | 10.0 |  |
| **Consommation de viande** | 3226.0 | 3227.0 | 3182.0 | 3339.0 | 3616.0 | 3648.0 | 3812.0 | 4.5 |
| **Consommation par tête** *(kilogrammes par an)* | 84.3 | 84.0 | 82.3 | 86.2 | 93.2 | 93.8 | 97.8 | 4.3 |

## PRODUCTION INDIGENE BRUTE DE VIANDE
## MEAT GROSS INDIGENOUS PRODUCTION

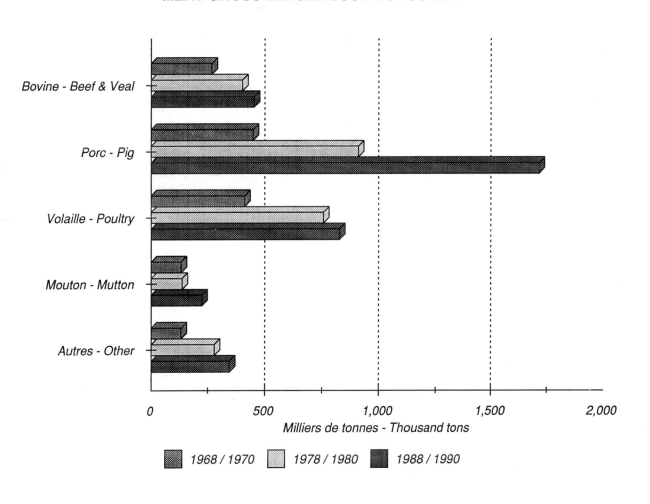

*Milliers de tonnes - Thousand tons*

■ *1968 / 1970* □ *1978 / 1980* ■ *1988 / 1990*

# UNITED KINGDOM

## BEEF / VIANDE DE BŒUF

*Thousand metric tons - Dressed carcass weight*

| | 1984 | 1985 | 1986 | 1987 | 1988 | 1989 | 1990 | 1989/90 % change |
|---|---|---|---|---|---|---|---|---|
| Number of animals slaughtered *(thousands)* | 4180.0 | 4156.0 | 3827.0 | 4007.0 | 3343.0 | 3414.0 | 3478.0 | 1.9 |
| Average dressed carcass weight *(kilogrammes)* | 274.0 | 275.0 | 272.0 | 272.0 | 283.0 | 286.0 | 287.0 | 0.3 |
| Gross indigenous production | 1091.0 | 1087.0 | 1009.0 | 1088.0 | 916.0 | 946.0 | 973.0 | 2.9 |
| *Minus:* Meat equivalent of exported live animals | 6.0 | 5.0 | 27.0 | 24.0 | 15.0 | 5.0 | 6.0 | 20.0 |
| *Plus:* Meat from slaughterings of imported live animals | 56.0 | 57.0 | 61.0 | 38.0 | 49.0 | 35.0 | 32.0 | -8.6 |
| Total meat production from slaughtered animals | 1141.0 | 1139.0 | 1043.0 | 1102.0 | 950.0 | 976.0 | 999.0 | 2.4 |
| *Minus:* Exports of meat | 214.0 | 190.0 | 191.0 | 194.0 | 135.0 | 154.0 | 125.0 | -18.8 |
| *Plus:* Imports of meat | 312.0 | 324.0 | 376.0 | 390.0 | 386.0 | 335.0 | 282.0 | -15.8 |
| *Minus:* Stock variations | 44.0 | 46.0 | -30.0 | -7.0 | -22.0 | 63.0 | 74.0 | |
| Meat consumption | 1195.0 | 1227.0 | 1258.0 | 1305.0 | 1223.0 | 1094.0 | 1082.0 | -1.1 |
| Consumption per head *(kilogrammes per year)* | 21.2 | 21.7 | 22.2 | 22.9 | 21.4 | 19.1 | 18.8 | -1.4 |

## VEAL / VIANDE DE VEAU

| | 1984 | 1985 | 1986 | 1987 | 1988 | 1989 | 1990 | 1989/90 % change |
|---|---|---|---|---|---|---|---|---|
| Number of animals slaughtered *(thousands)* | 133.0 | 99.0 | 78.0 | 65.0 | 35.0 | 28.0 | 46.0 | 64.3 |
| Average dressed carcass weight *(kilogrammes)* | 48.0 | 54.0 | 49.0 | 50.0 | 55.0 | 53.0 | 41.0 | -22.6 |
| Gross indigenous production | 13.0 | 10.0 | 11.0 | 17.0 | 11.0 | 12.0 | 13.0 | 8.3 |
| *Minus:* Meat equivalent of exported live animals | 7.0 | 5.0 | 7.0 | 14.0 | 9.0 | 11.0 | 11.0 | 0.0 |
| *Plus:* Meat from slaughterings of imported live animals | - | - | - | - | - | - | - | .. |
| Total meat production from slaughtered animals | 6.0 | 5.0 | 4.0 | 3.0 | 2.0 | 1.0 | 2.0 | 100.0 |
| *Minus:* Exports of meat | 1.0 | 1.0 | 2.0 | 3.0 | 1.0 | 1.0 | - | -100.0 |
| *Plus:* Imports of meat | 3.0 | 3.0 | 5.0 | 4.0 | 2.0 | 1.0 | 1.0 | 0.0 |
| *Minus:* Stock variations | - | - | - | - | - | - | - | |
| Meat consumption | 8.0 | 7.0 | 7.0 | 4.0 | 3.0 | 1.0 | 3.0 | 200.0 |
| Consumption per head *(kilogrammes per year)* | 0.1 | 0.1 | 0.1 | 0.1 | 0.1 | - | 0.1 | 199.1 |

## BEEF AND VEAL / TOTAL VIANDE BOVINE

| | 1984 | 1985 | 1986 | 1987 | 1988 | 1989 | 1990 | 1989/90 % change |
|---|---|---|---|---|---|---|---|---|
| Number of animals slaughtered *(thousands)* | 4313.0 | 4255.0 | 3905.0 | 4072.0 | 3378.0 | 3442.0 | 3524.0 | 2.4 |
| Average dressed carcass weight *(kilogrammes)* | 265.9 | 268.9 | 268.1 | 271.4 | 281.8 | 283.8 | 284.1 | 0.1 |
| Gross indigenous production | 1104.0 | 1097.0 | 1020.0 | 1105.0 | 927.0 | 958.0 | 986.0 | 2.9 |
| *Minus:* Meat equivalent of exported live animals | 13.0 | 10.0 | 34.0 | 38.0 | 24.0 | 16.0 | 17.0 | 6.3 |
| *Plus:* Meat from slaughterings of imported live animals | 56.0 | 57.0 | 61.0 | 38.0 | 49.0 | 35.0 | 32.0 | -8.6 |
| Total meat production from slaughtered animals | 1147.0 | 1144.0 | 1047.0 | 1105.0 | 952.0 | 977.0 | 1001.0 | 2.5 |
| *Minus:* Exports of meat | 215.0 | 191.0 | 193.0 | 197.0 | 136.0 | 155.0 | 125.0 | -19.4 |
| *Plus:* Imports of meat | 315.0 | 327.0 | 381.0 | 394.0 | 388.0 | 336.0 | 283.0 | -15.8 |
| *Minus:* Stock variations | 44.0 | 46.0 | -30.0 | -7.0 | -22.0 | 63.0 | 74.0 | |
| Meat consumption | 1203.0 | 1234.0 | 1265.0 | 1309.0 | 1226.0 | 1095.0 | 1085.0 | -0.9 |
| Consumption per head *(kilogrammes per year)* | 21.3 | 21.8 | 22.3 | 23.0 | 21.5 | 19.1 | 18.9 | -1.2 |

# ROYAUME - UNI

*Milliers de tonnes métriques - Poids en carcasse parée*

## VIANDE DE PORC / PIG MEAT

| | 1984 | 1985 | 1986 | 1987 | 1988 | 1989 | 1990 | 1989/90 % var. |
|---|---|---|---|---|---|---|---|---|
| Nombre d'animaux abattus *(milliers)* | 14938.0 | 15260.0 | 15577.0 | 15959.0 | 15787.0 | 14514.0 | 14203.0 | -2.1 |
| Poids moyen en carcasse parée *(kilogrammes)* | 63.0 | 63.0 | 64.0 | 64.0 | 64.0 | 65.0 | 67.0 | 3.1 |
| Production indigène brute | 948.0 | 976.0 | 993.0 | 1015.0 | 1021.0 | 945.0 | 960.0 | 1.6 |
| *Moins:* Équivalent en viande des animaux exportés vivants | 6.0 | 14.0 | 8.0 | 8.0 | 8.0 | 9.0 | 11.0 | 22.2 |
| *Plus:* Viande provenant des abbattages d'animaux importés vivants | 3.0 | 4.0 | 4.0 | 4.0 | 3.0 | 4.0 | 4.0 | 0.0 |
| Production totale de viande provenant des abattages | 945.0 | 966.0 | 989.0 | 1011.0 | 1016.0 | 940.0 | 953.0 | 1.4 |
| *Moins:* Exportations de viande | 49.0 | 54.0 | 61.0 | 52.0 | 63.0 | 62.0 | 59.0 | -4.8 |
| *Plus:* Importations de viande | 478.0 | 468.0 | 455.0 | 477.0 | 469.0 | 512.0 | 499.0 | -2.5 |
| *Moins:* Variations des stocks | 1.0 | - | 1.0 | 3.0 | - | 4.0 | 1.0 | |
| Consommation de viande | 1373.0 | 1380.0 | 1382.0 | 1433.0 | 1422.0 | 1386.0 | 1392.0 | 0.4 |
| Consommation par tête *(kilogrammes par an)* | 24.3 | 24.4 | 24.3 | 25.2 | 24.9 | 24.2 | 24.2 | 0.1 |

## VIANDE DE VOLAILLE / POULTRY MEAT

| | 1984 | 1985 | 1986 | 1987 | 1988 | 1989 | 1990 | 1989/90 % var. |
|---|---|---|---|---|---|---|---|---|
| Nombre d'animaux abattus *(milliers)* | | | | | | | | |
| Poids moyen en carcasse parée *(kilogrammes)* | | | | | | | | |
| Production indigène brute | 858.0 | 876.0 | 930.0 | 1029.0 | 1085.0 | 1033.0 | 1043.0 | 1.0 |
| *Moins:* Équivalent en viande des animaux exportés vivants | 3.0 | 3.0 | 3.0 | 4.0 | 4.0 | 4.0 | 5.0 | 25.0 |
| *Plus:* Viande provenant des abbattages d'animaux importés vivants | 1.0 | 1.0 | 2.0 | 2.0 | 1.0 | 1.0 | 1.0 | 0.0 |
| Production totale de viande provenant des abattages | 856.0 | 874.0 | 929.0 | 1027.0 | 1082.0 | 1030.0 | 1039.0 | 0.9 |
| *Moins:* Exportations de viande | 29.0 | 34.0 | 42.0 | 56.0 | 69.0 | 76.0 | 71.0 | -6.6 |
| *Plus:* Importations de viande | 60.0 | 70.0 | 97.0 | 92.0 | 94.0 | 102.0 | 157.0 | 53.9 |
| *Moins:* Variations des stocks | 2.0 | -6.0 | 5.0 | 15.0 | 1.0 | -25.0 | 8.0 | |
| Consommation de viande | 885.0 | 916.0 | 979.0 | 1048.0 | 1106.0 | 1081.0 | 1117.0 | 3.3 |
| Consommation par tête *(kilogrammes par an)* | 15.7 | 16.2 | 17.2 | 18.4 | 19.4 | 18.9 | 19.5 | 3.0 |

## VIANDE DE MOUTON ET DE CHÈVRE / MUTTON, LAMB AND GOAT MEAT

| | 1984 | 1985 | 1986 | 1987 | 1988 | 1989 | 1990 | 1989/90 % var. |
|---|---|---|---|---|---|---|---|---|
| Nombre d'animaux abattus *(milliers)* | 14959.0 | 15765.0 | 15385.0 | 15782.0 | 17104.0 | 19616.0 | 20012.0 | 2.0 |
| Poids moyen en carcasse parée *(kilogrammes)* | 19.0 | 19.0 | 19.0 | 19.0 | 19.0 | 19.0 | 19.0 | 0.0 |
| Production indigène brute | 295.0 | 308.0 | 301.0 | 320.0 | 342.0 | 385.0 | 391.0 | 1.6 |
| *Moins:* Équivalent en viande des animaux exportés vivants | 10.0 | 10.0 | 11.0 | 19.0 | 22.0 | 20.0 | 23.0 | 15.0 |
| *Plus:* Viande provenant des abbattages d'animaux importés vivants | 1.0 | 2.0 | 1.0 | 2.0 | 1.0 | 2.0 | 2.0 | 0.0 |
| Production totale de viande provenant des abattages | 286.0 | 300.0 | 291.0 | 303.0 | 321.0 | 367.0 | 370.0 | 0.8 |
| *Moins:* Exportations de viande | 53.0 | 49.0 | 60.0 | 72.0 | 77.0 | 91.0 | 82.0 | -9.9 |
| *Plus:* Importations de viande | 153.0 | 168.0 | 137.0 | 147.0 | 132.0 | 137.0 | 155.0 | 13.1 |
| *Moins:* Variations des stocks | -15.0 | 11.0 | -15.0 | -5.0 | -6.0 | -2.0 | 6.0 | |
| Consommation de viande | 401.0 | 408.0 | 383.0 | 383.0 | 382.0 | 415.0 | 437.0 | 5.3 |
| Consommation par tête *(kilogrammes par an)* | 7.1 | 7.2 | 6.7 | 6.7 | 6.7 | 7.3 | 7.6 | 5.0 |

# UNITED KINGDOM

## HORSE MEAT / VIANDE D'ÉQUIDÉS

*Thousand metric tons - Dressed carcass weight*

| | 1984 | 1985 | 1986 | 1987 | 1988 | 1989 | 1990 | 1989/90 % change |
|---|---|---|---|---|---|---|---|---|
| Number of animals slaughtered *(thousands)* | 26.0 | 24.0 [e] | 16.0 [e] | 12.0 [e] | 8.0 [e] | 8.0 [e] | 8.0 [e] | 0.0 |
| Average dressed carcass weight *(kilogrammes)* | 250.0 | 250.0 | 250.0 | 250.0 | 250.0 | 250.0 | 250.0 | 0.0 |
| **Gross indigenous production** | **6.0** | **6.0** | **4.0** | **4.0** | **2.0** | **1.0** | **1.0** | 0.0 |
| *Minus:* Meat equivalent of exported live animals | 2.0 | 2.0 | 2.0 | 2.0 | 2.0 | 2.0 | 2.0 | 0.0 |
| *Plus:* Meat from slaughterings of imported live animals | 2.0 | 2.0 | 2.0 | 1.0 | 2.0 | 3.0 | 2.0 | -33.3 |
| **Total meat production from slaughtered animals** | **6.0** | **6.0** | **4.0** | **3.0** | **2.0** | **2.0** | **1.0** | -50.0 |
| *Minus:* Exports of meat | 7.0 | 6.0 | 4.0 | 4.0 | 3.0 | 2.0 | 2.0 | 0.0 |
| *Plus:* Imports of meat | 1.0 | 1.0 | 1.0 | - | - | - | 1.0 | .. |
| *Minus:* Stock variations | - | - | - | -1.0 | -1.0 | - | - | |
| **Meat consumption** | **-** | **1.0** | **1.0** | **-** | **-** | **-** | **-** | .. |
| Consumption per head *(kilogrammes per year)* | - | - | - | - | - | - | - | .. |

## OTHER MEAT / AUTRES VIANDES

| | 1984 | 1985 | 1986 | 1987 | 1988 | 1989 | 1990 | 1989/90 % change |
|---|---|---|---|---|---|---|---|---|
| Number of animals slaughtered *(thousands)* | | | | | | | | |
| Average dressed carcass weight *(kilogrammes)* | | | | | | | | |
| **Gross indigenous production** | **8.0** | **8.0** | **7.0** | **8.0** | **8.0** | **9.0** | **10.0** | 11.1 |
| *Minus:* Meat equivalent of exported live animals | - | - | - | - | - | - | - | .. |
| *Plus:* Meat from slaughterings of imported live animals | - | - | - | - | - | - | - | .. |
| **Total meat production from slaughtered animals** | **8.0** | **8.0** | **7.0** | **8.0** | **8.0** | **9.0** | **10.0** | 11.1 |
| *Minus:* Exports of meat | 3.0 | 3.0 | 2.0 | 2.0 | 3.0 | 3.0 | 3.0 | 0.0 |
| *Plus:* Imports of meat | 6.0 | 3.0 | 3.0 | 3.0 | 2.0 | 2.0 | 2.0 | 0.0 |
| *Minus:* Stock variations | - | - | - | - | - | - | - | |
| **Meat consumption** | **11.0** | **8.0** | **8.0** | **9.0** | **7.0** | **8.0** | **9.0** | 12.5 |
| Consumption per head *(kilogrammes per year)* | 0.2 | 0.1 | 0.1 | 0.2 | 0.1 | 0.1 | 0.2 | 12.2 |

## EDIBLE OFFALS / ABATS COMESTIBLES

| | 1984 | 1985 | 1986 | 1987 | 1988 | 1989 | 1990 | 1989/90 % change |
|---|---|---|---|---|---|---|---|---|
| Number of animals slaughtered *(thousands)* | | | | | | | | |
| Average dressed carcass weight *(kilogrammes)* | | | | | | | | |
| **Gross indigenous production** | **166.0** | **168.0** | **160.0** | **172.0** | **158.0** | **164.0** | **168.0** | 2.4 |
| *Minus:* Meat equivalent of exported live animals | 3.0 | 3.0 | 5.0 | 7.0 | 6.0 | 6.0 | 6.0 | 0.0 |
| *Plus:* Meat from slaughterings of imported live animals | 5.0 | 6.0 | 6.0 | 4.0 | 5.0 | 4.0 | 4.0 | 0.0 |
| **Total meat production from slaughtered animals** | **168.0** | **171.0** | **161.0** | **169.0** | **157.0** | **162.0** | **166.0** | 2.5 |
| *Minus:* Exports of meat | 13.0 | 13.0 | 12.0 | 13.0 | 12.0 | 16.0 | 16.0 | 0.0 |
| *Plus:* Imports of meat | 114.0 | 130.0 | 107.0 | 102.0 | 101.0 | 85.0 | 74.0 | -12.9 |
| *Minus:* Stock variations | -3.0 | 3.0 | 1.0 | 2.0 | 1.0 | -6.0 | - | |
| **Meat consumption** | **272.0** | **285.0** | **255.0** | **256.0** | **245.0** | **237.0** | **224.0** | -5.5 |
| Consumption per head *(kilogrammes per year)* | 4.8 | 5.0 | 4.5 | 4.5 | 4.3 | 4.1 | 3.9 | -5.8 |

# ROYAUME - UNI

*Milliers de tonnes métriques - Poids en carcasse parée*

| | 1984 | 1985 | 1986 | 1987 | 1988 | 1989 | 1990 | 1989/90 % var. |
|---|---|---|---|---|---|---|---|---|
| **Nombre d'animaux abattus** *(milliers)* | | | | | | | | |
| **Poids moyen en carcasse parée** *(kilogrammes)* | | | | | | | | |
| **Production indigène brute** | 3385.0 | 3439.0 | 3415.0 | 3653.0 | 3543.0 | 3495.0 | 3559.0 | 1.8 |
| *Moins:* Équivalent en viande des animaux exportés vivants | 37.0 | 42.0 | 63.0 | 78.0 | 66.0 | 57.0 | 64.0 | 12.3 |
| *Plus:* Viande provenant des abbattages d'animaux importés vivants | 68.0 | 72.0 | 76.0 | 51.0 | 61.0 | 49.0 | 45.0 | -8.2 |
| **Production totale de viande provenant des abattages** | 3416.0 | 3469.0 | 3428.0 | 3626.0 | 3538.0 | 3487.0 | 3540.0 | 1.5 |
| *Moins:* Exportations de viande | 369.0 | 350.0 | 374.0 | 396.0 | 363.0 | 405.0 | 358.0 | -11.6 |
| *Plus:* Importations de viande | 1127.0 | 1167.0 | 1181.0 | 1215.0 | 1186.0 | 1174.0 | 1171.0 | -0.3 |
| *Moins:* Variations des stocks | 29.0 | 54.0 | -38.0 | 7.0 | -27.0 | 34.0 | 89.0 | |
| **Consommation de viande** | 4145.0 | 4232.0 | 4273.0 | 4438.0 | 4388.0 | 4222.0 | 4264.0 | 1.0 |
| **Consommation par tête** *(kilogrammes par an)* | 73.4 | 74.7 | 75.3 | 78.0 | 76.9 | 73.8 | 74.3 | 0.7 |

## PRODUCTION INDIGENE BRUTE DE VIANDE
## *MEAT GROSS INDIGENOUS PRODUCTION*

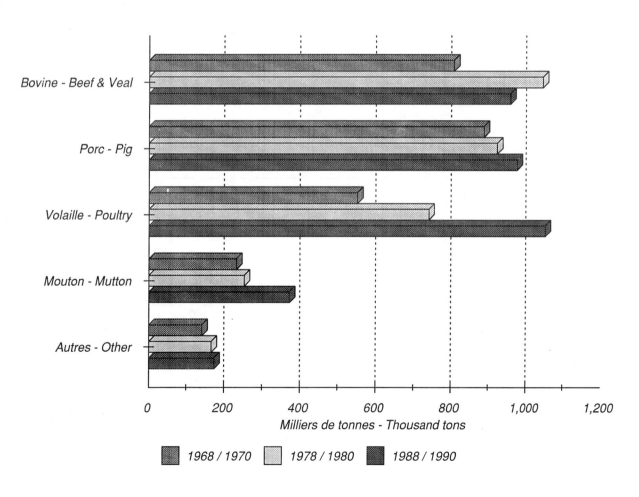

Milliers de tonnes - Thousand tons

1968 / 1970      1978 / 1980      1988 / 1990

# AUSTRIA

*Thousand metric tons - Dressed carcass weight*

## BEEF / VIANDE DE BŒUF

| | 1984 | 1985 | 1986 | 1987 | 1988 | 1989 | 1990 | 1989/90 % change |
|---|---|---|---|---|---|---|---|---|
| Number of animals slaughtered *(thousands)* | 572.0 | 595.0 | 605.0 | 603.0 | 575.0 | 551.0 | 577.0 | 4.7 |
| Average dressed carcass weight *(kilogrammes)* | 355.0 | 350.0 | 349.0 | 325.0 | 330.0 | 343.0 | 383.0 | 11.7 |
| Gross indigenous production | 210.0 | 225.0 | 230.0 | 215.0 | 207.0 | 195.0 | 222.0 | 13.8 |
| Minus: Meat equivalent of exported live animals | 7.0 | 17.0 | 19.0 | 19.0 | 17.0 | 7.0 | 2.0 | -71.4 |
| Plus: Meat from slaughterings of imported live animals | - | - | - | - | - | 1.0 | 1.0 | 0.0 |
| Total meat production from slaughtered animals | 203.0 | 208.0 | 211.0 | 196.0 | 190.0 | 189.0 | 221.0 | 16.9 |
| Minus: Exports of meat | 43.0 | 56.0 | 60.0 | 48.0 | 42.0 | 40.0 | 70.0 | 75.0 |
| Plus: Imports of meat | 3.0 | 2.0 | 1.0 | 2.0 | 2.0 | 2.0 | 1.0 | -50.0 |
| Minus: Stock variations | - | -1.0 | - | -1.0 | 1.0 | - | 1.0 | |
| Meat consumption | 163.0 | 155.0 | 152.0 | 151.0 | 149.0 | 151.0 | 151.0 | 0.0 |
| Consumption per head *(kilogrammes per year)* | 21.6 | 20.5 | 20.1 | 19.9 | 19.6 | 19.8 | 19.6 | -1.1 |

## VEAL / VIANDE DE VEAU

| | 1984 | 1985 | 1986 | 1987 | 1988 | 1989 | 1990 | 1989/90 % change |
|---|---|---|---|---|---|---|---|---|
| Number of animals slaughtered *(thousands)* | 244.0 | 257.0 | 265.0 | 264.0 | 251.0 | 230.0 | 249.0 | 8.3 |
| Average dressed carcass weight *(kilogrammes)* | 70.0 | 58.0 | 57.0 | 49.0 | 64.0 | 70.0 | 64.0 | -8.6 |
| Gross indigenous production | 17.0 | 17.0 | 17.0 | 16.0 | 16.0 | 15.0 | 17.0 | 13.3 |
| Minus: Meat equivalent of exported live animals | - | 2.0 | 2.0 | 4.0 | 2.0 | 2.0 | - | -100.0 |
| Plus: Meat from slaughterings of imported live animals | - | - | - | 1.0 | 2.0 | 3.0 | 1.0 | -66.7 |
| Total meat production from slaughtered animals | 17.0 | 15.0 | 15.0 | 13.0 | 16.0 | 16.0 | 18.0 | 12.5 |
| Minus: Exports of meat | - | - | - | - | - | - | - | .. |
| Plus: Imports of meat | 1.0 | - | 1.0 | - | - | - | - | .. |
| Minus: Stock variations | - | - | - | - | - | - | - | |
| Meat consumption | 18.0 | 15.0 | 16.0 | 13.0 | 16.0 | 16.0 | 18.0 | 12.5 |
| Consumption per head *(kilogrammes per year)* | 2.4 | 2.0 | 2.1 | 1.7 | 2.1 | 2.1 | 2.3 | 11.2 |

## BEEF AND VEAL / TOTAL VIANDE BOVINE

| | 1984 | 1985 | 1986 | 1987 | 1988 | 1989 | 1990 | 1989/90 % change |
|---|---|---|---|---|---|---|---|---|
| Number of animals slaughtered *(thousands)* | 816.0 | 852.0 | 870.0 | 867.0 | 826.0 | 781.0 | 826.0 | 5.8 |
| Average dressed carcass weight *(kilogrammes)* | 269.6 | 261.7 | 259.8 | 241.1 | 249.4 | 262.5 | 289.3 | 10.2 |
| Gross indigenous production | 227.0 | 242.0 | 247.0 | 231.0 | 223.0 | 210.0 | 239.0 | 13.8 |
| Minus: Meat equivalent of exported live animals | 7.0 | 19.0 | 21.0 | 23.0 | 19.0 | 9.0 | 2.0 | -77.8 |
| Plus: Meat from slaughterings of imported live animals | - | - | - | 1.0 | 2.0 | 4.0 | 2.0 | -50.0 |
| Total meat production from slaughtered animals | 220.0 | 223.0 | 226.0 | 209.0 | 206.0 | 205.0 | 239.0 | 16.6 |
| Minus: Exports of meat | 43.0 | 56.0 | 60.0 | 48.0 | 42.0 | 40.0 | 70.0 | 75.0 |
| Plus: Imports of meat | 4.0 | 2.0 | 2.0 | 2.0 | 2.0 | 2.0 | 1.0 | -50.0 |
| Minus: Stock variations | - | -1.0 | - | -1.0 | 1.0 | - | 1.0 | |
| Meat consumption | 181.0 | 170.0 | 168.0 | 164.0 | 165.0 | 167.0 | 169.0 | 1.2 |
| Consumption per head *(kilogrammes per year)* | 24.0 | 22.5 | 22.2 | 21.7 | 21.7 | 21.9 | 21.9 | 0.0 |

# AUTRICHE

*Milliers de tonnes métriques - Poids en carcasse parée*

## VIANDE DE PORC / PIG MEAT

| | 1984 | 1985 | 1986 | 1987 | 1988 | 1989 | 1990 | 1989/90 % var. |
|---|---|---|---|---|---|---|---|---|
| Nombre d'animaux abattus (milliers) | 5049.0 | 5260.0 | 5141.0 | 5126.0 | 5264.0 | 5294.0 | 5305.0 | 0.2 |
| Poids moyen en carcasse parée (kilogrammes) | 71.0 | 71.0 | 70.0 | 71.0 | 77.0 | 76.0 | 76.0 | 0.0 |
| Production indigène brute | 355.0 | 374.0 | 360.0 | 366.0 | 404.0 | 400.0 | 401.0 | 0.3 |
| Moins: Équivalent en viande des animaux exportés vivants | - | - | - | - | - | - | - | .. |
| Plus: Viande provenant des abbattages d'animaux importés vivants | 2.0 | - | - | - | - | - | - | .. |
| Production totale de viande provenant des abattages | 357.0 | 374.0 | 360.0 | 366.0 | 404.0 | 400.0 | 401.0 | 0.3 |
| Moins: Exportations de viande | 2.0 | 8.0 | 1.0 | 3.0 | 8.0 | 4.0 | 2.0 | -50.0 |
| Plus: Importations de viande | 5.0 | 1.0 | 1.0 | 1.0 | 1.0 | 2.0 | 2.0 | 0.0 |
| Moins: Variations des stocks | - | - | -1.0 | - | 2.0 | 1.0 | -1.0 | |
| Consommation de viande | 360.0 | 367.0 | 361.0 | 364.0 | 395.0 | 397.0 | 402.0 | 1.3 |
| Consommation par tête (kilogrammes par an) | 47.7 | 48.6 | 47.7 | 48.1 | 52.0 | 52.1 | 52.1 | 0.1 |

## VIANDE DE VOLAILLE / POULTRY MEAT

| | 1984 | 1985 | 1986 | 1987 | 1988 | 1989 | 1990 | 1989/90 % var. |
|---|---|---|---|---|---|---|---|---|
| Nombre d'animaux abattus (milliers) | | | | | | | | |
| Poids moyen en carcasse parée (kilogrammes) | | | | | | | | |
| Production indigène brute | 80.0 | 79.0 | 83.0 | 86.0 | 82.0 | 89.0 | 90.0 | 1.1 |
| Moins: Équivalent en viande des animaux exportés vivants | - | - | - | - | - | - | - | .. |
| Plus: Viande provenant des abbattages d'animaux importés vivants | - | - | - | - | - | - | - | .. |
| Production totale de viande provenant des abattages | 80.0 | 79.0 | 83.0 | 86.0 | 82.0 | 89.0 | 90.0 | 1.1 |
| Moins: Exportations de viande | 1.0 | 1.0 | 1.0 | 1.0 | 1.0 | 1.0 | 1.0 | 0.0 |
| Plus: Importations de viande | 11.0 | 11.0 | 15.0 | 16.0 | 20.0 | 21.0 | 20.0 | -4.8 |
| Moins: Variations des stocks | - | - | - | - | - | - | - | |
| Consommation de viande | 90.0 | 89.0 | 97.0 | 101.0 | 101.0 | 109.0 | 109.0 | 0.0 |
| Consommation par tête (kilogrammes par an) | 11.9 | 11.8 | 12.8 | 13.3 | 13.3 | 14.3 | 14.1 | -1.1 |

## VIANDE DE MOUTON ET DE CHÈVRE / MUTTON, LAMB AND GOAT MEAT

| | 1984 | 1985 | 1986 | 1987 | 1988 | 1989 | 1990 | 1989/90 % var. |
|---|---|---|---|---|---|---|---|---|
| Nombre d'animaux abattus (milliers) | 226.0 | 205.0 | 225.0 | 208.0 | 241.0 | 220.0 | 223.0 | 1.4 |
| Poids moyen en carcasse parée (kilogrammes) | 17.0 | 17.0 | 18.0 | 24.0 | 21.0 | 23.0 | 27.0 | 17.4 |
| Production indigène brute | 4.0 | 4.0 | 4.0 | 5.0 | 5.0 | 5.0 | 6.0 | 20.0 |
| Moins: Équivalent en viande des animaux exportés vivants | - | - | - | - | - | - | - | .. |
| Plus: Viande provenant des abbattages d'animaux importés vivants | - | - | - | - | - | - | - | .. |
| Production totale de viande provenant des abattages | 4.0 | 4.0 | 4.0 | 5.0 | 5.0 | 5.0 | 6.0 | 20.0 |
| Moins: Exportations de viande | - | - | - | - | - | - | - | .. |
| Plus: Importations de viande | 1.0 | 1.0 | 1.0 | 2.0 | 2.0 | 3.0 | 3.0 | 0.0 |
| Moins: Variations des stocks | - | - | - | - | - | - | - | |
| Consommation de viande | 5.0 | 5.0 | 5.0 | 7.0 | 7.0 | 8.0 | 9.0 | 12.5 |
| Consommation par tête (kilogrammes par an) | 0.7 | 0.7 | 0.7 | 0.9 | 0.9 | 1.0 | 1.2 | 11.2 |

# AUSTRIA

## HORSE MEAT / VIANDE D'ÉQUIDÉS

*Thousand metric tons - Dressed carcass weight*

| | 1984 | 1985 | 1986 | 1987 | 1988 | 1989 | 1990 | 1989/90 % change |
|---|---|---|---|---|---|---|---|---|
| Number of animals slaughtered *(thousands)* | 2.0 | 2.0 | 2.0 | 2.0 | 2.0 | 2.0 | 2.0 | 0.0 |
| Average dressed carcass weight *(kilogrammes)* | 211.0 | 206.0 | 209.0 | 209.0 | 209.0 | 209.0 | 209.0 | 0.0 |
| Gross indigenous production | - | - | - | - | 1.0 | 1.0 | 1.0 | 0.0 |
| *Minus:* Meat equivalent of exported live animals | - | - | - | - | - | - | - | .. |
| *Plus:* Meat from slaughterings of imported live animals | - | - | - | - | - | - | - | .. |
| Total meat production from slaughtered animals | - | - | - | - | 1.0 | 1.0 | 1.0 | 0.0 |
| *Minus:* Exports of meat | - | - | - | - | - | - | - | .. |
| *Plus:* Imports of meat | 1.0 | 1.0 | 1.0 | 1.0 | 1.0 | 1.0 | 1.0 | 0.0 |
| *Minus:* Stock variations | - | - | - | - | - | - | - | |
| Meat consumption | 1.0 | 1.0 | 1.0 | 1.0 | 2.0 | 2.0 | 2.0 | 0.0 |
| Consumption per head *(kilogrammes per year)* | 0.1 | 0.1 | 0.1 | 0.1 | 0.3 | 0.3 | 0.3 | -1.1 |

## OTHER MEAT / AUTRES VIANDES

| | 1984 | 1985 | 1986 | 1987 | 1988 | 1989 | 1990 | 1989/90 % change |
|---|---|---|---|---|---|---|---|---|
| Number of animals slaughtered *(thousands)* | | | | | | | | |
| Average dressed carcass weight *(kilogrammes)* | | | | | | | | |
| Gross indigenous production | 7.0 | 7.0 | 5.0 | 6.0 | 6.0 | 7.0 | 7.0 | 0.0 |
| *Minus:* Meat equivalent of exported live animals | - | - | - | - | - | - | - | .. |
| *Plus:* Meat from slaughterings of imported live animals | - | - | - | - | - | - | - | .. |
| Total meat production from slaughtered animals | 7.0 | 7.0 | 5.0 | 6.0 | 6.0 | 7.0 | 7.0 | 0.0 |
| *Minus:* Exports of meat | 3.0 | 3.0 | 3.0 | 4.0 | 4.0 | 3.0 | 3.0 | 0.0 |
| *Plus:* Imports of meat | 3.0 | 3.0 | 3.0 | 2.0 | 3.0 | 3.0 | 2.0 | -33.3 |
| *Minus:* Stock variations | - | - | - | - | - | - | - | |
| Meat consumption | 7.0 | 7.0 | 5.0 | 4.0 | 5.0 | 7.0 | 6.0 | -14.3 |
| Consumption per head *(kilogrammes per year)* | 0.9 | 0.9 | 0.7 | 0.5 | 0.7 | 0.9 | 0.8 | -15.3 |

## EDIBLE OFFALS / ABATS COMESTIBLES

| | 1984 | 1985 | 1986 | 1987 | 1988 | 1989 | 1990 | 1989/90 % change |
|---|---|---|---|---|---|---|---|---|
| Number of animals slaughtered *(thousands)* | | | | | | | | |
| Average dressed carcass weight *(kilogrammes)* | | | | | | | | |
| Gross indigenous production | 34.0 | 35.0 | 35.0 | 35.0 | 30.0 | 29.0 | 30.0 | 3.4 |
| *Minus:* Meat equivalent of exported live animals | - | - | - | - | - | - | - | .. |
| *Plus:* Meat from slaughterings of imported live animals | - | - | - | - | - | - | - | .. |
| Total meat production from slaughtered animals | 34.0 | 35.0 | 35.0 | 35.0 | 30.0 | 29.0 | 30.0 | 3.4 |
| *Minus:* Exports of meat | 1.0 | 1.0 | 1.0 | 1.0 | 1.0 | 1.0 | 1.0 | 0.0 |
| *Plus:* Imports of meat | 2.0 | 1.0 | 1.0 | 1.0 | - | 1.0 | 1.0 | 0.0 |
| *Minus:* Stock variations | - | - | - | - | - | - | 1.0 | |
| Meat consumption | 35.0 | 35.0 | 35.0 | 35.0 | 29.0 | 29.0 | 29.0 | 0.0 |
| Consumption per head *(kilogrammes per year)* | 4.6 | 4.6 | 4.6 | 4.6 | 3.8 | 3.8 | 3.8 | -1.1 |

# AUTRICHE

*Milliers de tonnes métriques - Poids en carcasse parée*

*TOTAL VIANDE / TOTAL MEAT*

| | 1984 | 1985 | 1986 | 1987 | 1988 | 1989 | 1990 | 1989/90 % var. |
|---|---|---|---|---|---|---|---|---|
| **Nombre d'animaux abattus** *(milliers)* | | | | | | | | |
| **Poids moyen en carcasse parée** *(kilogrammes)* | | | | | | | | |
| **Production indigène brute** | **707.0** | **741.0** | **734.0** | **729.0** | **751.0** | **741.0** | **774.0** | 4.5 |
| *Moins:* Équivalent en viande des animaux exportés vivants | 7.0 | 19.0 | 21.0 | 23.0 | 19.0 | 9.0 | 2.0 | -77.8 |
| *Plus:* Viande provenant des abbattages d'animaux importés vivants | 2.0 | - | - | 1.0 | 2.0 | 4.0 | 2.0 | -50.0 |
| **Production totale de viande provenant des abattages** | **702.0** | **722.0** | **713.0** | **707.0** | **734.0** | **736.0** | **774.0** | 5.2 |
| *Moins:* Exportations de viande | 50.0 | 69.0 | 66.0 | 57.0 | 56.0 | 49.0 | 77.0 | 57.1 |
| *Plus:* Importations de viande | 27.0 | 20.0 | 24.0 | 25.0 | 29.0 | 33.0 | 30.0 | -9.1 |
| *Moins:* Variations des stocks | - | -1.0 | -1.0 | -1.0 | 3.0 | 1.0 | 1.0 | |
| **Consommation de viande** | **679.0** | **674.0** | **672.0** | **676.0** | **704.0** | **719.0** | **726.0** | 1.0 |
| **Consommation par tête** *(kilogrammes par an)* | 89.9 | 89.2 | 88.8 | 89.2 | 92.7 | 94.3 | 94.1 | -0.2 |

## PRODUCTION INDIGENE BRUTE DE VIANDE
## MEAT GROSS INDIGENOUS PRODUCTION

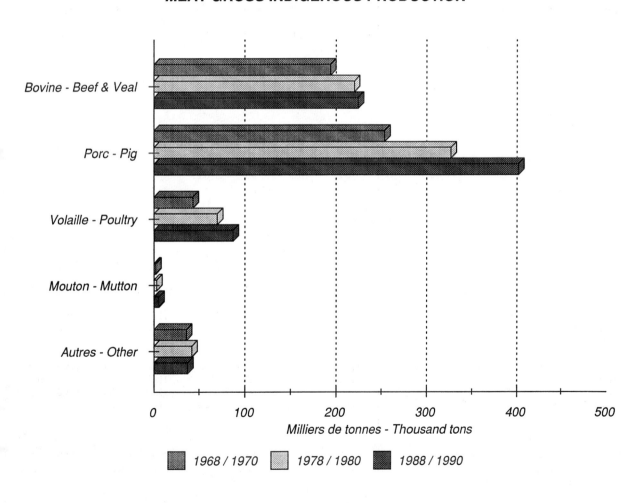

Milliers de tonnes - Thousand tons

■ 1968 / 1970　□ 1978 / 1980　■ 1988 / 1990

# FINLAND

## BEEF / VIANDE DE BŒUF

*Thousand metric tons - Dressed carcass weight*

|  | 1984 | 1985 | 1986 | 1987 | 1988 | 1989 | 1990 | 1989/90 % change |
|---|---|---|---|---|---|---|---|---|
| Number of animals slaughtered *(thousands)* | 606.0 | 614.0 | 609.0 | 603.0 | 534.0 | 488.0 | 500.0 | 2.5 |
| Average dressed carcass weight *(kilogrammes)* | 203.0 | 204.0 | 204.0 | 204.0 | 208.0 | 219.0 | 236.0 | 7.8 |
| **Gross indigenous production** | **123.0** | **125.0** | **124.0** | **123.0** | **111.0** | **107.0** | **118.0** | **10.3** |
| *Minus:* Meat equivalent of exported live animals | - | - | - | - | - | - | - | .. |
| *Plus:* Meat from slaughterings of imported live animals | - | - | - | - | - | - | - | .. |
| **Total meat production from slaughtered animals** | **123.0** | **125.0** | **124.0** | **123.0** | **111.0** | **107.0** | **118.0** | **10.3** |
| *Minus:* Exports of meat | 19.0 | 22.0 | 21.0 | 22.0 | 11.0 | 5.0 | 10.0 | 100.0 |
| *Plus:* Imports of meat | - | - | - | - | 3.0 | 2.0 | 1.0 | -50.0 |
| *Minus:* Stock variations | -1.0 | - | - | -2.0 | - | 1.0 | - |  |
| **Meat consumption** | **105.0** | **103.0** | **103.0** | **103.0** | **103.0** | **103.0** | **109.0** | **5.8** |
| Consumption per head *(kilogrammes per year)* | 21.5 | 21.0 | 20.9 | 20.9 | 20.8 | 20.7 | 21.9 | 5.4 |

## VEAL / VIANDE DE VEAU

|  | 1984 | 1985 | 1986 | 1987 | 1988 | 1989 | 1990 | 1989/90 % change |
|---|---|---|---|---|---|---|---|---|
| Number of animals slaughtered *(thousands)* | 22.0 | 18.0 | 15.0 | 18.0 | 9.0 | 7.0 | 7.0 | 0.0 |
| Average dressed carcass weight *(kilogrammes)* | 40.0 | 40.0 | 40.0 | 40.0 | 50.0 | 51.0 | 48.0 | -5.9 |
| **Gross indigenous production** | **1.0** | **1.0** | **1.0** | **1.0** | - | - | - | .. |
| *Minus:* Meat equivalent of exported live animals | - | - | - | - | - | - | - | .. |
| *Plus:* Meat from slaughterings of imported live animals | - | - | - | - | - | - | - | .. |
| **Total meat production from slaughtered animals** | **1.0** | **1.0** | **1.0** | **1.0** | - | - | - | .. |
| *Minus:* Exports of meat | - | - | - | - | - | - | - | .. |
| *Plus:* Imports of meat | - | - | - | - | - | - | - | .. |
| *Minus:* Stock variations | - | - | - | - | - | - | - |  |
| **Meat consumption** | **1.0** | **1.0** | **1.0** | **1.0** | - | - | - | .. |
| Consumption per head *(kilogrammes per year)* | 0.2 | 0.2 | 0.2 | 0.2 | - | - | - | .. |

## BEEF AND VEAL / TOTAL VIANDE BOVINE

|  | 1984 | 1985 | 1986 | 1987 | 1988 | 1989 | 1990 | 1989/90 % change |
|---|---|---|---|---|---|---|---|---|
| Number of animals slaughtered *(thousands)* | 628.0 | 632.0 | 624.0 | 621.0 | 543.0 | 495.0 | 507.0 | 2.4 |
| Average dressed carcass weight *(kilogrammes)* | 197.5 | 199.4 | 200.3 | 199.7 | 204.4 | 216.2 | 232.7 | 7.7 |
| **Gross indigenous production** | **124.0** | **126.0** | **125.0** | **124.0** | **111.0** | **107.0** | **118.0** | **10.3** |
| *Minus:* Meat equivalent of exported live animals | - | - | - | - | - | - | - | .. |
| *Plus:* Meat from slaughterings of imported live animals | - | - | - | - | - | - | - | .. |
| **Total meat production from slaughtered animals** | **124.0** | **126.0** | **125.0** | **124.0** | **111.0** | **107.0** | **118.0** | **10.3** |
| *Minus:* Exports of meat | 19.0 | 22.0 | 21.0 | 22.0 | 11.0 | 5.0 | 10.0 | 100.0 |
| *Plus:* Imports of meat | - | - | - | - | 3.0 | 2.0 | 1.0 | -50.0 |
| *Minus:* Stock variations | -1.0 | - | - | -2.0 | - | 1.0 | - |  |
| **Meat consumption** | **106.0** | **104.0** | **104.0** | **104.0** | **103.0** | **103.0** | **109.0** | **5.8** |
| Consumption per head *(kilogrammes per year)* | 21.7 | 21.2 | 21.1 | 21.1 | 20.8 | 20.7 | 21.9 | 5.4 |

# FINLANDE

*Milliers de tonnes métriques - Poids en carcasse parée*

## VIANDE DE PORC / PIG MEAT

| | 1984 | 1985 | 1986 | 1987 | 1988 | 1989 | 1990 | 1989/90 % var. |
|---|---|---|---|---|---|---|---|---|
| Nombre d'animaux abattus *(milliers)* | 2291.0 | 2284.0 | 2275.0 | 2279.0 | 2174.0 | 2183.0 | 2351.0 | 7.7 |
| Poids moyen en carcasse parée *(kilogrammes)* | 74.0 | 75.0 | 76.0 | 77.0 | 78.0 | 80.0 | 77.0 | -3.8 |
| **Production indigène brute** | **170.0** | **172.0** | **174.0** | **176.0** | **169.0** | **174.0** | **187.0** | 7.5 |
| *Moins:* Équivalent en viande des animaux exportés vivants | - | - | - | - | - | - | - | .. |
| *Plus:* Viande provenant des abbattages d'animaux importés vivants | - | - | - | - | - | - | - | .. |
| **Production totale de viande provenant des abattages** | **170.0** | **172.0** | **174.0** | **176.0** | **169.0** | **174.0** | **187.0** | 7.5 |
| *Moins:* Exportations de viande | 20.0 | 18.0 | 10.0 | 17.0 | 9.0 | 14.0 | 23.0 | 64.3 |
| *Plus:* Importations de viande | - | - | - | - | 1.0 | - | - | .. |
| *Moins:* Variations des stocks | -2.0 | -2.0 | 3.0 | -2.0 | -1.0 | 3.0 | - | |
| **Consommation de viande** | **152.0** | **156.0** | **161.0** | **161.0** | **162.0** | **157.0** | **164.0** | 4.5 |
| **Consommation par tête** *(kilogrammes par an)* | 31.1 | 31.8 | 32.7 | 32.6 | 32.8 | 31.6 | 32.9 | 4.1 |

## VIANDE DE VOLAILLE / POULTRY MEAT

| | 1984 | 1985 | 1986 | 1987 | 1988 | 1989 | 1990 | 1989/90 % var. |
|---|---|---|---|---|---|---|---|---|
| Nombre d'animaux abattus *(milliers)* | | | | | | | | |
| Poids moyen en carcasse parée *(kilogrammes)* | | | | | | | | |
| **Production indigène brute** | **20.0** | **21.0** | **22.0** | **27.0** | **28.0** | **30.0** | **33.0** | 10.0 |
| *Moins:* Équivalent en viande des animaux exportés vivants | - | - | - | - | - | - | - | .. |
| *Plus:* Viande provenant des abbattages d'animaux importés vivants | - | - | - | - | - | - | - | .. |
| **Production totale de viande provenant des abattages** | **20.0** | **21.0** | **22.0** | **27.0** | **28.0** | **30.0** | **33.0** | 10.0 |
| *Moins:* Exportations de viande | - | - | - | - | - | - | - | .. |
| *Plus:* Importations de viande | - | - | - | - | - | - | - | |
| *Moins:* Variations des stocks | - | - | - | 1.0 | - | - | - | |
| **Consommation de viande** | **20.0** | **21.0** | **22.0** | **26.0** | **28.0** | **30.0** | **33.0** | 10.0 |
| **Consommation par tête** *(kilogrammes par an)* | 4.1 | 4.3 | 4.5 | 5.3 | 5.7 | 6.0 | 6.6 | 9.6 |

## VIANDE DE MOUTON ET DE CHÈVRE / MUTTON, LAMB AND GOAT MEAT

| | 1984 | 1985 | 1986 | 1987 | 1988 | 1989 | 1990 | 1989/90 % var. |
|---|---|---|---|---|---|---|---|---|
| Nombre d'animaux abattus *(milliers)* | 84.0 | 93.0 | 83.0 | 80.0 | 54.0 | 52.0 | 53.0 | 1.9 |
| Poids moyen en carcasse parée *(kilogrammes)* | 15.0 | 16.0 | 17.0 | 17.0 | 17.0 | 18.0 | 19.0 | 5.6 |
| **Production indigène brute** | **1.0** | **1.0** | **1.0** | **1.0** | **1.0** | **1.0** | **1.0** | 0.0 |
| *Moins:* Équivalent en viande des animaux exportés vivants | - | - | - | - | - | - | - | .. |
| *Plus:* Viande provenant des abbattages d'animaux importés vivants | - | - | - | - | - | - | - | .. |
| **Production totale de viande provenant des abattages** | **1.0** | **1.0** | **1.0** | **1.0** | **1.0** | **1.0** | **1.0** | 0.0 |
| *Moins:* Exportations de viande | - | - | - | - | - | - | - | .. |
| *Plus:* Importations de viande | - | - | - | - | - | - | - | |
| *Moins:* Variations des stocks | - | - | - | - | - | - | - | |
| **Consommation de viande** | **1.0** | **1.0** | **1.0** | **1.0** | **1.0** | **1.0** | **1.0** | 0.0 |
| **Consommation par tête** *(kilogrammes par an)* | 0.2 | 0.2 | 0.2 | 0.2 | 0.2 | 0.2 | 0.2 | -0.4 |

# FINLAND

## HORSE MEAT / VIANDE D'ÉQUIDÉS

*Thousand metric tons - Dressed carcass weight*

|  | 1984 | 1985 | 1986 | 1987 | 1988 | 1989 | 1990 | 1989/90 % change |
|---|---|---|---|---|---|---|---|---|
| Number of animals slaughtered *(thousands)* | 3.0 | 3.0 | 3.0 | 3.0 | 2.0 | 3.0 | 3.0 | 0.0 |
| Average dressed carcass weight *(kilogrammes)* | 279.0 | 284.0 | 286.0 | 293.0 | 264.0 | 271.0 | 276.0 | 1.8 |
| Gross indigenous production | 1.0 | 1.0 | 1.0 | 1.0 | 1.0 | 1.0 | 1.0 | 0.0 |
| *Minus:* Meat equivalent of exported live animals | - | - | - | - | - | - | - | .. |
| *Plus:* Meat from slaughterings of imported live animals | - | - | - | - | - | - | - | .. |
| Total meat production from slaughtered animals | 1.0 | 1.0 | 1.0 | 1.0 | 1.0 | 1.0 | 1.0 | 0.0 |
| *Minus:* Exports of meat | - | - | - | - | - | - | - | .. |
| *Plus:* Imports of meat | - | - | - | - | - | - | - | .. |
| *Minus:* Stock variations | - | - | - | - | - | - | - |  |
| Meat consumption | 1.0 | 1.0 | 1.0 | 1.0 | 1.0 | 1.0 | 1.0 | 0.0 |
| Consumption per head *(kilogrammes per year)* | 0.2 | 0.2 | 0.2 | 0.2 | 0.2 | 0.2 | 0.2 | -0.4 |

## OTHER MEAT / AUTRES VIANDES

|  | 1984 | 1985 | 1986 | 1987 | 1988 | 1989 | 1990 | 1989/90 % change |
|---|---|---|---|---|---|---|---|---|
| Number of animals slaughtered *(thousands)* |  |  |  |  |  |  |  |  |
| Average dressed carcass weight *(kilogrammes)* |  |  |  |  |  |  |  |  |
| Gross indigenous production | 13.0 | 11.0 | 11.0 | 11.0 | 11.0 | 12.0 | 11.0 | -8.3 |
| *Minus:* Meat equivalent of exported live animals | - | - | - | - | - | - | - | .. |
| *Plus:* Meat from slaughterings of imported live animals | - | - | - | - | - | - | - | .. |
| Total meat production from slaughtered animals | 13.0 | 11.0 | 11.0 | 11.0 | 11.0 | 12.0 | 11.0 | -8.3 |
| *Minus:* Exports of meat | - | - | - | - | - | - | - | .. |
| *Plus:* Imports of meat | - | - | - | - | - | - | - | .. |
| *Minus:* Stock variations | - | - | - | - | - | - | - |  |
| Meat consumption | 13.0 | 11.0 | 11.0 | 11.0 | 11.0 | 12.0 | 11.0 | -8.3 |
| Consumption per head *(kilogrammes per year)* | 2.7 | 2.2 | 2.2 | 2.2 | 2.2 | 2.4 | 2.2 | -8.7 |

## EDIBLE OFFALS / ABATS COMESTIBLES

|  | 1984 | 1985 | 1986 | 1987 | 1988 | 1989 | 1990 | 1989/90 % change |
|---|---|---|---|---|---|---|---|---|
| Number of animals slaughtered *(thousands)* |  |  |  |  |  |  |  |  |
| Average dressed carcass weight *(kilogrammes)* |  |  |  |  |  |  |  |  |
| Gross indigenous production | 37.0 | 37.0 | 37.0 | 37.0 | 35.0 | 13.0 | 14.0 | 7.7 |
| *Minus:* Meat equivalent of exported live animals | - | - | - | - | - | - | - | .. |
| *Plus:* Meat from slaughterings of imported live animals | - | - | - | - | - | - | - | .. |
| Total meat production from slaughtered animals | 37.0 | 37.0 | 37.0 | 37.0 | 35.0 | 13.0 | 14.0 | 7.7 |
| *Minus:* Exports of meat | - | - | - | - | - | - | 1.0 | .. |
| *Plus:* Imports of meat | - | - | - | - | 1.0 | - | - | .. |
| *Minus:* Stock variations | - | - | - | - | - | - | - |  |
| Meat consumption | 37.0 | 37.0 | 37.0 | 37.0 | 36.0 | 13.0 | 13.0 | 0.0 |
| Consumption per head *(kilogrammes per year)* | 7.6 | 7.5 | 7.5 | 7.5 | 7.3 | 2.6 | 2.6 | -0.4 |

# FINLANDE

*Milliers de tonnes métriques - Poids en carcasse parée*

| | 1984 | 1985 | 1986 | 1987 | 1988 | 1989 | 1990 | 1989/90 % var. |
|---|---|---|---|---|---|---|---|---|
| **Nombre d'animaux abattus** *(milliers)* | | | | | | | | |
| **Poids moyen en carcasse parée** *(kilogrammes)* | | | | | | | | |
| **Production indigène brute** | 366.0 | 369.0 | 371.0 | 377.0 | 356.0 | 338.0 | 365.0 | 8.0 |
| *Moins:* Équivalent en viande des animaux exportés vivants | - | - | - | - | - | - | - | .. |
| *Plus:* Viande provenant des abbattages d'animaux importés vivants | - | - | - | - | - | - | - | .. |
| **Production totale de viande provenant des abattages** | 366.0 | 369.0 | 371.0 | 377.0 | 356.0 | 338.0 | 365.0 | 8.0 |
| *Moins:* Exportations de viande | 39.0 | 40.0 | 31.0 | 39.0 | 20.0 | 19.0 | 34.0 | 78.9 |
| *Plus:* Importations de viande | - | - | - | - | 5.0 | 2.0 | 1.0 | -50.0 |
| *Moins:* Variations des stocks | -3.0 | -2.0 | 3.0 | -3.0 | -1.0 | 4.0 | - | |
| **Consommation de viande** | 330.0 | 331.0 | 337.0 | 341.0 | 342.0 | 317.0 | 332.0 | 4.7 |
| **Consommation par tête** *(kilogrammes par an)* | 67.6 | 67.5 | 68.5 | 69.1 | 69.1 | 63.9 | 66.6 | 4.4 |

## PRODUCTION INDIGENE BRUTE DE VIANDE
## MEAT GROSS INDIGENOUS PRODUCTION

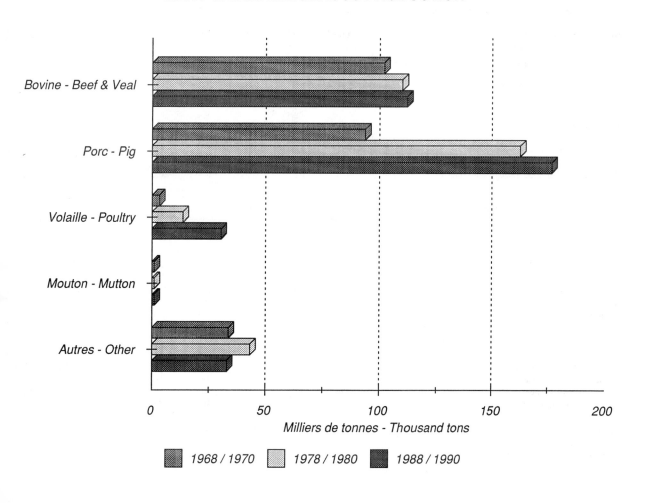

*Milliers de tonnes - Thousand tons*

■ 1968 / 1970　　□ 1978 / 1980　　■ 1988 / 1990

## BEEF / VIANDE DE BŒUF

*Thousand metric tons - Dressed carcass weight*

| | 1984 | 1985 | 1986 | 1987 | 1988 | 1989 | 1990 | 1989/90 % change |
|---|---|---|---|---|---|---|---|---|
| Number of animals slaughtered *(thousands)* | 311.0 | 325.0 | 329.0 | 327.0 | 316.0 | 311.0 | 334.0 | 7.4 |
| Average dressed carcass weight *(kilogrammes)* | 215.0 | 218.0 | 219.0 | 226.0 | 234.0 | 238.0 | 243.0 | 2.1 |
| Gross indigenous production | 67.0 | 71.0 | 72.0 | 74.0 | 74.0 | 75.0 | 81.0 | 8.0 |
| *Minus:* Meat equivalent of exported live animals | - | - | - | - | - | - | - | .. |
| *Plus:* Meat from slaughterings of imported live animals | - | - | - | - | - | - | - | .. |
| Total meat production from slaughtered animals | 67.0 | 71.0 | 72.0 | 74.0 | 74.0 | 75.0 | 81.0 | 8.0 |
| *Minus:* Exports of meat | 3.0 | 1.0 | 1.0 | 1.0 | - | 1.0 | 8.0 | 700.0 |
| *Plus:* Imports of meat | 2.0 | 2.0 | 4.0 | 2.0 | 2.0 | 2.0 | 2.0 | 0.0 |
| *Minus:* Stock variations | 2.0 | - | -1.0 | 1.0 | -2.0 | 3.0 | -1.0 | |
| Meat consumption | 64.0 | 72.0 | 76.0 | 74.0 | 78.0 | 73.0 | 76.0 | 4.1 |
| Consumption per head *(kilogrammes per year)* | 15.5 | 17.3 | 18.2 | 17.7 | 18.5 | 17.3 | 17.9 | 3.7 |

## VEAL / VIANDE DE VEAU

| | 1984 | 1985 | 1986 | 1987 | 1988 | 1989 | 1990 | 1989/90 % change |
|---|---|---|---|---|---|---|---|---|
| Number of animals slaughtered *(thousands)* | 57.0 | 57.0 | 37.0 | 41.0 | 27.0 | 19.0 | 18.0 | -5.3 |
| Average dressed carcass weight *(kilogrammes)* | 38.0 | 39.0 | 55.0 | 59.0 | 66.0 | 70.0 | 71.0 | 1.4 |
| Gross indigenous production | 2.0 | 2.0 | 2.0 | 2.0 | 2.0 | 1.0 | 1.0 | 0.0 |
| *Minus:* Meat equivalent of exported live animals | - | - | - | - | - | - | - | .. |
| *Plus:* Meat from slaughterings of imported live animals | - | - | - | - | - | - | - | .. |
| Total meat production from slaughtered animals | 2.0 | 2.0 | 2.0 | 2.0 | 2.0 | 1.0 | 1.0 | 0.0 |
| *Minus:* Exports of meat | - | - | - | - | - | - | - | .. |
| *Plus:* Imports of meat | - | - | - | - | - | - | - | .. |
| *Minus:* Stock variations | - | - | - | - | - | - | - | |
| Meat consumption | 2.0 | 2.0 | 2.0 | 2.0 | 2.0 | 1.0 | 1.0 | 0.0 |
| Consumption per head *(kilogrammes per year)* | 0.5 | 0.5 | 0.5 | 0.5 | 0.5 | 0.2 | 0.2 | -0.4 |

## BEEF AND VEAL / TOTAL VIANDE BOVINE

| | 1984 | 1985 | 1986 | 1987 | 1988 | 1989 | 1990 | 1989/90 % change |
|---|---|---|---|---|---|---|---|---|
| Number of animals slaughtered *(thousands)* | 368.0 | 382.0 | 366.0 | 368.0 | 343.0 | 330.0 | 352.0 | 6.7 |
| Average dressed carcass weight *(kilogrammes)* | 187.5 | 191.1 | 202.2 | 206.5 | 221.6 | 230.3 | 233.0 | 1.2 |
| Gross indigenous production | 69.0 | 73.0 | 74.0 | 76.0 | 76.0 | 76.0 | 82.0 | 7.9 |
| *Minus:* Meat equivalent of exported live animals | - | - | - | - | - | - | - | .. |
| *Plus:* Meat from slaughterings of imported live animals | - | - | - | - | - | - | - | .. |
| Total meat production from slaughtered animals | 69.0 | 73.0 | 74.0 | 76.0 | 76.0 | 76.0 | 82.0 | 7.9 |
| *Minus:* Exports of meat | 3.0 | 1.0 | 1.0 | 1.0 | - | 1.0 | 8.0 | 700.0 |
| *Plus:* Imports of meat | 2.0 | 2.0 | 4.0 | 2.0 | 2.0 | 2.0 | 2.0 | 0.0 |
| *Minus:* Stock variations | 2.0 | - | -1.0 | 1.0 | -2.0 | 3.0 | -1.0 | |
| Meat consumption | 66.0 | 74.0 | 78.0 | 76.0 | 80.0 | 74.0 | 77.0 | 4.1 |
| Consumption per head *(kilogrammes per year)* | 15.9 | 17.8 | 18.7 | 18.2 | 19.0 | 17.5 | 18.2 | 3.7 |

# NORVÈGE

*Milliers de tonnes métriques - Poids en carcasse parée*

## VIANDE DE PORC / PIG MEAT

| | 1984 | 1985 | 1986 | 1987 | 1988 | 1989 | 1990 | 1989/90 % var. |
|---|---|---|---|---|---|---|---|---|
| Nombre d'animaux abattus (milliers) | 1105.0 | 1088.0 | 1103.0 | 1189.0 | 1201.0 | 1126.0 | 1118.0 | -0.7 |
| Poids moyen en carcasse parée (kilogrammes) | 77.0 | 77.0 | 78.0 | 78.0 | 75.0 | 75.0 | 75.0 | 0.0 |
| Production indigène brute | 84.0 | 84.0 | 85.0 | 92.0 | 90.0 | 84.0 | 83.0 | -1.2 |
| Moins: Équivalent en viande des animaux exportés vivants | - | - | - | - | - | - | - | .. |
| Plus: Viande provenant des abbattages d'animaux importés vivants | - | - | - | - | - | - | - | .. |
| Production totale de viande provenant des abattages | 84.0 | 84.0 | 85.0 | 92.0 | 90.0 | 84.0 | 83.0 | -1.2 |
| Moins: Exportations de viande | 6.0 | 6.0 | 1.0 | 4.0 | 10.0 | 6.0 | 8.0 | 33.3 |
| Plus: Importations de viande | 2.0 | 4.0 | 2.0 | 2.0 | 2.0 | 2.0 | 1.0 | -50.0 |
| Moins: Variations des stocks | -1.0 | -2.0 | 1.0 | 3.0 | -3.0 | -1.0 | -1.0 | |
| Consommation de viande | 81.0 | 84.0 | 85.0 | 87.0 | 85.0 | 81.0 | 77.0 | -4.9 |
| Consommation par tête (kilogrammes par an) | 19.6 | 20.2 | 20.4 | 20.8 | 20.2 | 19.2 | 18.2 | -5.3 |

## VIANDE DE VOLAILLE / POULTRY MEAT

| | 1984 | 1985 | 1986 | 1987 | 1988 | 1989 | 1990 | 1989/90 % var. |
|---|---|---|---|---|---|---|---|---|
| Nombre d'animaux abattus (milliers) | | | | | | | | |
| Poids moyen en carcasse parée (kilogrammes) | | | | | | | | |
| Production indigène brute | 11.0 | 12.0 | 13.0 | 15.0 | 18.0 | 20.0 | 20.0 | 0.0 |
| Moins: Équivalent en viande des animaux exportés vivants | - | - | - | - | - | - | - | .. |
| Plus: Viande provenant des abbattages d'animaux importés vivants | - | - | - | - | - | - | - | .. |
| Production totale de viande provenant des abattages | 11.0 | 12.0 | 13.0 | 15.0 | 18.0 | 20.0 | 20.0 | 0.0 |
| Moins: Exportations de viande | - | - | - | 1.0 | - | - | - | .. |
| Plus: Importations de viande | 1.0 | 1.0 | 2.0 | 2.0 | 1.0 | - | - | .. |
| Moins: Variations des stocks | 1.0 | - | - | - | 1.0 | 2.0 | - | |
| Consommation de viande | 11.0 | 13.0 | 15.0 | 16.0 | 18.0 | 18.0 | 20.0 | 11.1 |
| Consommation par tête (kilogrammes par an) | 2.7 | 3.1 | 3.6 | 3.8 | 4.3 | 4.3 | 4.7 | 10.7 |

## VIANDE DE MOUTON ET DE CHÈVRE / MUTTON, LAMB AND GOAT MEAT

| | 1984 | 1985 | 1986 | 1987 | 1988 | 1989 | 1990 | 1989/90 % var. |
|---|---|---|---|---|---|---|---|---|
| Nombre d'animaux abattus (milliers) | 1276.0 | 1385.0 | 1371.0 | 1391.0 | 1335.0 | 1321.0 | 1340.0 | 1.4 |
| Poids moyen en carcasse parée (kilogrammes) | 19.0 | 19.0 | 19.0 | 19.0 | 19.0 | 18.0 | 19.0 | 5.6 |
| Production indigène brute | 25.0 | 25.0 | 26.0 | 26.0 | 25.0 | 24.0 | 25.0 | 4.2 |
| Moins: Équivalent en viande des animaux exportés vivants | - | - | - | - | - | - | - | .. |
| Plus: Viande provenant des abbattages d'animaux importés vivants | - | - | - | - | - | - | - | .. |
| Production totale de viande provenant des abattages | 25.0 | 25.0 | 26.0 | 26.0 | 25.0 | 24.0 | 25.0 | 4.2 |
| Moins: Exportations de viande | - | - | - | - | - | 2.0 | 2.0 | 0.0 |
| Plus: Importations de viande | 1.0 | - | 1.0 | - | - | - | - | .. |
| Moins: Variations des stocks | -1.0 | - | 1.0 | 1.0 | 2.0 | -3.0 | -2.0 | |
| Consommation de viande | 27.0 | 25.0 | 26.0 | 25.0 | 23.0 | 25.0 | 25.0 | 0.0 |
| Consommation par tête (kilogrammes par an) | 6.5 | 6.0 | 6.2 | 6.0 | 5.5 | 5.9 | 5.9 | -0.4 |

# NORWAY

|  | 1984 | 1985 | 1986 | 1987 | 1988 | 1989 | 1990 | 1989/90 % change |
|---|---|---|---|---|---|---|---|---|
| **Number of animals slaughtered** *(thousands)* | 3.0 | 3.0 | 3.0 | 3.0 | 3.0 | 3.0 | 3.0 | 0.0 |
| **Average dressed carcass weight** *(kilogrammes)* | 248.0 | 248.0 | 248.0 | 248.0 | 248.0 | 248.0 | 248.0 | 0.0 |
| **Gross indigenous production** | 1.0 | 1.0 | 1.0 | 1.0 | 1.0 | 1.0 | 1.0 | 0.0 |
| *Minus:* Meat equivalent of exported live animals | - | - | - | - | - | - | - | .. |
| *Plus:* Meat from slaughterings of imported live animals | - | - | - | - | - | - | - | .. |
| **Total meat production from slaughtered animals** | 1.0 | 1.0 | 1.0 | 1.0 | 1.0 | 1.0 | 1.0 | 0.0 |
| *Minus:* Exports of meat | - | - | - | - | - | - | - | .. |
| *Plus:* Imports of meat | - | - | - | - | - | - | - | .. |
| *Minus:* Stock variations | - | - | - | - | - | - | - | |
| **Meat consumption** | 1.0 | 1.0 | 1.0 | 1.0 | 1.0 | 1.0 | 1.0 | 0.0 |
| **Consumption per head** *(kilogrammes per year)* | 0.2 | 0.2 | 0.2 | 0.2 | 0.2 | 0.2 | 0.2 | -0.4 |

## OTHER MEAT / AUTRES VIANDES

|  | 1984 | 1985 | 1986 | 1987 | 1988 | 1989 | 1990 | 1989/90 % change |
|---|---|---|---|---|---|---|---|---|
| **Number of animals slaughtered** *(thousands)* | | | | | | | | |
| **Average dressed carcass weight** *(kilogrammes)* | | | | | | | | |
| **Gross indigenous production** | 8.0 | 10.0 | 9.0 | 9.0 | 9.0 | 9.0 | 10.0 | 11.1 |
| *Minus:* Meat equivalent of exported live animals | - | - | - | - | - | - | - | .. |
| *Plus:* Meat from slaughterings of imported live animals | - | - | - | - | - | - | - | .. |
| **Total meat production from slaughtered animals** | 8.0 | 10.0 | 9.0 | 9.0 | 9.0 | 9.0 | 10.0 | 11.1 |
| *Minus:* Exports of meat | - | - | - | - | - | - | - | .. |
| *Plus:* Imports of meat | - | - | - | - | - | - | - | .. |
| *Minus:* Stock variations | - | - | - | - | - | - | - | |
| **Meat consumption** | 8.0 | 10.0 | 9.0 | 9.0 | 9.0 | 9.0 | 10.0 | 11.1 |
| **Consumption per head** *(kilogrammes per year)* | 1.9 | 2.4 | 2.2 | 2.1 | 2.1 | 2.1 | 2.4 | 10.7 |

## EDIBLE OFFALS / ABATS COMESTIBLES

|  | 1984 | 1985 | 1986 | 1987 | 1988 | 1989 | 1990 | 1989/90 % change |
|---|---|---|---|---|---|---|---|---|
| **Number of animals slaughtered** *(thousands)* | | | | | | | | |
| **Average dressed carcass weight** *(kilogrammes)* | | | | | | | | |
| **Gross indigenous production** | 13.0 | 13.0 | 13.0 | 14.0 | 13.0 | 14.0 | 14.0 | 0.0 |
| *Minus:* Meat equivalent of exported live animals | - | - | - | - | - | - | - | .. |
| *Plus:* Meat from slaughterings of imported live animals | - | - | - | - | - | - | - | .. |
| **Total meat production from slaughtered animals** | 13.0 | 13.0 | 13.0 | 14.0 | 13.0 | 14.0 | 14.0 | 0.0 |
| *Minus:* Exports of meat | - | - | - | - | - | - | 1.0 | .. |
| *Plus:* Imports of meat | 2.0 | 2.0 | 2.0 | 1.0 | 2.0 | - | 1.0 | .. |
| *Minus:* Stock variations | - | - | - | - | 1.0 | - | - | |
| **Meat consumption** | 15.0 | 15.0 | 15.0 | 15.0 | 14.0 | 14.0 | 14.0 | 0.0 |
| **Consumption per head** *(kilogrammes per year)* | 3.6 | 3.6 | 3.6 | 3.6 | 3.3 | 3.3 | 3.3 | -0.4 |

# NORVÈGE

*Milliers de tonnes métriques - Poids en carcasse parée*

**TOTAL VIANDE / TOTAL MEAT**

| | 1984 | 1985 | 1986 | 1987 | 1988 | 1989 | 1990 | 1989/90 % var. |
|---|---|---|---|---|---|---|---|---|
| **Nombre d'animaux abattus** *(milliers)* | | | | | | | | |
| **Poids moyen en carcasse parée** *(kilogrammes)* | | | | | | | | |
| **Production indigène brute** | 211.0 | 218.0 | 221.0 | 233.0 | 232.0 | 228.0 | 235.0 | 3.1 |
| *Moins:* Équivalent en viande des animaux exportés vivants | - | - | - | - | - | - | - | .. |
| *Plus:* Viande provenant des abbattages d'animaux importés vivants | - | - | - | - | - | - | - | .. |
| **Production totale de viande provenant des abattages** | 211.0 | 218.0 | 221.0 | 233.0 | 232.0 | 228.0 | 235.0 | 3.1 |
| *Moins:* Exportations de viande | 9.0 | 7.0 | 2.0 | 6.0 | 10.0 | 9.0 | 19.0 | 111.1 |
| *Plus:* Importations de viande | 8.0 | 9.0 | 11.0 | 7.0 | 7.0 | 4.0 | 4.0 | 0.0 |
| *Moins:* Variations des stocks | 1.0 | -2.0 | 1.0 | 5.0 | -1.0 | 1.0 | -4.0 | |
| **Consommation de viande** | 209.0 | 222.0 | 229.0 | 229.0 | 230.0 | 222.0 | 224.0 | 0.9 |
| **Consommation par tête** *(kilogrammes par an)* | 50.5 | 53.5 | 54.9 | 54.7 | 54.6 | 52.5 | 52.8 | 0.5 |

## PRODUCTION INDIGENE BRUTE DE VIANDE
## MEAT GROSS INDIGENOUS PRODUCTION

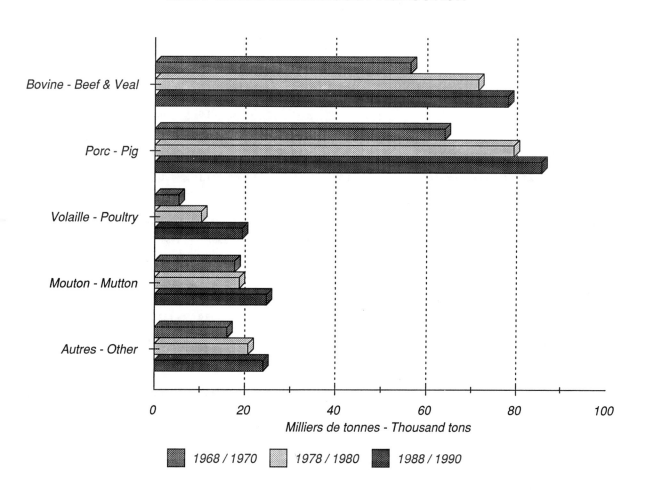

*Milliers de tonnes - Thousand tons*

■ 1968 / 1970    □ 1978 / 1980    ■ 1988 / 1990

# SWEDEN

## BEEF / VIANDE DE BŒUF

*Thousand metric tons - Dressed carcass weight*

| | 1984 | 1985 | 1986 | 1987 | 1988 | 1989 | 1990 | 1989/90 % change |
|---|---|---|---|---|---|---|---|---|
| Number of animals slaughtered *(thousands)* | 577.0 | 584.0 | 547.0 | 503.0 | 470.0 | 503.0 | 523.0 | 4.0 |
| Average dressed carcass weight *(kilogrammes)* | 250.0 | 248.0 | 249.0 | 253.0 | 257.0 | 260.0 | 268.0 | 3.1 |
| Gross indigenous production | 144.0 | 145.0 | 136.0 | 127.0 | 121.0 | 131.0 | 140.0 | 6.9 |
| *Minus:* Meat equivalent of exported live animals | - | - | - | - | - | - | - | .. |
| *Plus:* Meat from slaughterings of imported live animals | - | - | - | - | - | - | - | .. |
| Total meat production from slaughtered animals | 144.0 | 145.0 | 136.0 | 127.0 | 121.0 | 131.0 | 140.0 | 6.9 |
| *Minus:* Exports of meat | 23.0 | 33.0 | 21.0 | 7.0 | 5.0 | 7.0 | 12.0 | 71.4 |
| *Plus:* Imports of meat | 5.0 | 7.0 | 8.0 | 15.0 | 19.0 | 13.0 | 12.0 | -7.7 |
| *Minus:* Stock variations | 5.0 | 2.0 | -1.0 | -1.0 | 1.0 | 1.0 | -2.0 | |
| Meat consumption | 121.0 | 117.0 | 124.0 | 136.0 | 134.0 | 136.0 | 142.0 | 4.4 |
| Consumption per head *(kilogrammes per year)* | 14.5 | 14.0 | 14.8 | 16.2 | 15.9 | 16.0 | 16.6 | 3.5 |

## VEAL / VIANDE DE VEAU

| | 1984 | 1985 | 1986 | 1987 | 1988 | 1989 | 1990 | 1989/90 % change |
|---|---|---|---|---|---|---|---|---|
| Number of animals slaughtered *(thousands)* | 123.0 | 138.0 | 127.0 | 79.0 | 55.0 | 59.0 | 54.0 | -8.5 |
| Average dressed carcass weight *(kilogrammes)* | 89.0 | 94.0 | 87.0 | 101.0 | 109.0 | 119.0 | 130.0 | 9.2 |
| Gross indigenous production | 11.0 | 13.0 | 11.0 | 8.0 | 6.0 | 7.0 | 7.0 | 0.0 |
| *Minus:* Meat equivalent of exported live animals | - | - | - | - | - | - | - | .. |
| *Plus:* Meat from slaughterings of imported live animals | - | - | - | - | - | - | - | .. |
| Total meat production from slaughtered animals | 11.0 | 13.0 | 11.0 | 8.0 | 6.0 | 7.0 | 7.0 | 0.0 |
| *Minus:* Exports of meat | - | - | 2.0 | - | - | - | - | .. |
| *Plus:* Imports of meat | - | - | - | 1.0 | 1.0 | 1.0 | - | -100.0 |
| *Minus:* Stock variations | - | - | -2.0 | - | - | - | - | |
| Meat consumption | 11.0 | 13.0 | 11.0 | 9.0 | 7.0 | 8.0 | 7.0 | -12.5 |
| Consumption per head *(kilogrammes per year)* | 1.3 | 1.6 | 1.3 | 1.1 | 0.8 | 0.9 | 0.8 | -13.2 |

## BEEF AND VEAL / TOTAL VIANDE BOVINE

| | 1984 | 1985 | 1986 | 1987 | 1988 | 1989 | 1990 | 1989/90 % change |
|---|---|---|---|---|---|---|---|---|
| Number of animals slaughtered *(thousands)* | 700.0 | 722.0 | 674.0 | 582.0 | 525.0 | 562.0 | 577.0 | 2.7 |
| Average dressed carcass weight *(kilogrammes)* | 221.4 | 218.8 | 218.1 | 232.0 | 241.9 | 245.6 | 254.8 | 3.8 |
| Gross indigenous production | 155.0 | 158.0 | 147.0 | 135.0 | 127.0 | 138.0 | 147.0 | 6.5 |
| *Minus:* Meat equivalent of exported live animals | - | - | - | - | - | - | - | .. |
| *Plus:* Meat from slaughterings of imported live animals | - | - | - | - | - | - | - | .. |
| Total meat production from slaughtered animals | 155.0 | 158.0 | 147.0 | 135.0 | 127.0 | 138.0 | 147.0 | 6.5 |
| *Minus:* Exports of meat | 23.0 | 33.0 | 23.0 | 7.0 | 5.0 | 7.0 | 12.0 | 71.4 |
| *Plus:* Imports of meat | 5.0 | 7.0 | 8.0 | 16.0 | 20.0 | 14.0 | 12.0 | -14.3 |
| *Minus:* Stock variations | 5.0 | 2.0 | -3.0 | -1.0 | 1.0 | 1.0 | -2.0 | |
| Meat consumption | 132.0 | 130.0 | 135.0 | 145.0 | 141.0 | 144.0 | 149.0 | 3.5 |
| Consumption per head *(kilogrammes per year)* | 15.8 | 15.6 | 16.1 | 17.3 | 16.7 | 17.0 | 17.4 | 2.6 |

# SUÈDE

       *VIANDE DE PORC / PIG MEAT*

|  | 1984 | 1985 | 1986 | 1987 | 1988 | 1989 | 1990 | 1989/90 % var. |
|---|---|---|---|---|---|---|---|---|
| Nombre d'animaux abattus *(milliers)* | 4175.0 | 4250.0 | 3879.0 | 3595.0 | 3691.0 | 3804.0 | 3632.0 | -4.5 |
| Poids moyen en carcasse parée *(kilogrammes)* | 77.0 | 78.0 | 80.0 | 80.0 | 81.0 | 81.0 | 81.0 | 0.0 |
| Production indigène brute | 323.0 | 332.0 | 309.0 | 288.0 | 299.0 | 307.0 | 293.0 | -4.6 |
| *Moins:* Équivalent en viande des animaux exportés vivants | - | - | - | - | - | - | - | .. |
| *Plus:* Viande provenant des abbattages d'animaux importés vivants | - | - | - | - | - | - | - | .. |
| Production totale de viande provenant des abattages | 323.0 | 332.0 | 309.0 | 288.0 | 299.0 | 307.0 | 293.0 | -4.6 |
| *Moins:* Exportations de viande | 75.0 | 75.0 | 51.0 | 46.0 | 45.0 | 53.0 | 47.0 | -11.3 |
| *Plus:* Importations de viande | 6.0 | 6.0 | 7.0 | 13.0 | 15.0 | 15.0 | 16.0 | 6.7 |
| *Moins:* Variations des stocks | -4.0 | 1.0 | 5.0 | -2.0 | -1.0 | - | -2.0 | |
| Consommation de viande | 258.0 | 262.0 | 260.0 | 257.0 | 270.0 | 269.0 | 264.0 | -1.9 |
| Consommation par tête *(kilogrammes par an)* | 30.9 | 31.4 | 31.1 | 30.6 | 32.0 | 31.7 | 30.8 | -2.7 |

*VIANDE DE VOLAILLE / POULTRY MEAT*

|  | 1984 | 1985 | 1986 | 1987 | 1988 | 1989 | 1990 | 1989/90 % var. |
|---|---|---|---|---|---|---|---|---|
| Nombre d'animaux abattus *(milliers)* | | | | | | | | |
| Poids moyen en carcasse parée *(kilogrammes)* | | | | | | | | |
| Production indigène brute | 46.0 | 46.0 | 45.0 | 43.0 | 41.0 | 45.0 | 51.0 | 13.3 |
| *Moins:* Équivalent en viande des animaux exportés vivants | - | - | - | - | - | - | - | .. |
| *Plus:* Viande provenant des abbattages d'animaux importés vivants | - | - | - | - | - | - | - | .. |
| Production totale de viande provenant des abattages | 46.0 | 46.0 | 45.0 | 43.0 | 41.0 | 45.0 | 51.0 | 13.3 |
| *Moins:* Exportations de viande | 4.0 | 1.0 | 1.0 | 2.0 | - | - | - | .. |
| *Plus:* Importations de viande | - | - | - | - | 1.0 | 1.0 | 1.0 | 0.0 |
| *Moins:* Variations des stocks | -2.0 | - | - | 3.0 | -2.0 | - | - | |
| Consommation de viande | 44.0 | 45.0 | 44.0 | 38.0 | 44.0 | 46.0 | 52.0 | 13.0 |
| Consommation par tête *(kilogrammes par an)* | 5.3 | 5.4 | 5.3 | 4.5 | 5.2 | 5.4 | 6.1 | 12.1 |

*VIANDE DE MOUTON ET DE CHÈVRE / MUTTON, LAMB AND GOAT MEAT*

|  | 1984 | 1985 | 1986 | 1987 | 1988 | 1989 | 1990 | 1989/90 % var. |
|---|---|---|---|---|---|---|---|---|
| Nombre d'animaux abattus *(milliers)* | 321.0 | 318.0 | 299.0 | 278.0 | 272.0 | 292.0 | 274.0 | -6.2 |
| Poids moyen en carcasse parée *(kilogrammes)* | 16.0 | 16.0 | 17.0 | 18.0 | 18.0 | 17.0 | 18.0 | 5.9 |
| Production indigène brute | 5.0 | 5.0 | 5.0 | 5.0 | 5.0 | 5.0 | 5.0 | 0.0 |
| *Moins:* Équivalent en viande des animaux exportés vivants | - | - | - | - | - | - | - | .. |
| *Plus:* Viande provenant des abbattages d'animaux importés vivants | - | - | - | - | - | - | - | .. |
| Production totale de viande provenant des abattages | 5.0 | 5.0 | 5.0 | 5.0 | 5.0 | 5.0 | 5.0 | 0.0 |
| *Moins:* Exportations de viande | - | - | - | - | - | - | - | .. |
| *Plus:* Importations de viande | 1.0 | 1.0 | 1.0 | 2.0 | 2.0 | 2.0 | 2.0 | 0.0 |
| *Moins:* Variations des stocks | - | - | -1.0 | - | 1.0 | 1.0 | - | |
| Consommation de viande | 6.0 | 6.0 | 7.0 | 7.0 | 6.0 | 6.0 | 7.0 | 16.7 |
| Consommation par tête *(kilogrammes par an)* | 0.7 | 0.7 | 0.8 | 0.8 | 0.7 | 0.7 | 0.8 | 15.7 |

# SWEDEN

*Thousand metric tons - Dressed carcass weight*

| | 1984 | 1985 | 1986 | 1987 | 1988 | 1989 | 1990 | 1989/90 % change |
|---|---|---|---|---|---|---|---|---|
| Number of animals slaughtered *(thousands)* | 10.0 | 11.0 | 9.0 | 9.0 | 8.0 | 8.0 | 8.0 | 0.0 |
| Average dressed carcass weight *(kilogrammes)* | 248.0 | 251.0 | 254.0 | 257.0 | 257.0 | 258.0 | 250.0 | -3.1 |
| **Gross indigenous production** | **2.0** | **3.0** | **2.0** | **2.0** | **2.0** | **2.0** | **2.0** | 0.0 |
| *Minus:* Meat equivalent of exported live animals | - | - | - | - | - | - | - | .. |
| *Plus:* Meat from slaughterings of imported live animals | - | - | - | - | - | - | - | .. |
| **Total meat production from slaughtered animals** | **2.0** | **3.0** | **2.0** | **2.0** | **2.0** | **2.0** | **2.0** | 0.0 |
| *Minus:* Exports of meat | - | - | - | - | - | - | - | .. |
| *Plus:* Imports of meat | - | - | 1.0 | 2.0 | 1.0 | 1.0 | 1.0 | 0.0 |
| *Minus:* Stock variations | - | - | - | - | - | - | - | |
| **Meat consumption** | **2.0** | **3.0** | **3.0** | **4.0** | **3.0** | **3.0** | **3.0** | 0.0 |
| Consumption per head *(kilogrammes per year)* | 0.2 | 0.4 | 0.4 | 0.5 | 0.4 | 0.4 | 0.4 | -0.9 |

## OTHER MEAT / AUTRES VIANDES

| | 1984 | 1985 | 1986 | 1987 | 1988 | 1989 | 1990 | 1989/90 % change |
|---|---|---|---|---|---|---|---|---|
| Number of animals slaughtered *(thousands)* | | | | | | | | |
| Average dressed carcass weight *(kilogrammes)* | | | | | | | | |
| **Gross indigenous production** | **23.0** | **25.0** | **19.0** | **20.0** | **21.0** | **22.0** | **21.0** | -4.5 |
| *Minus:* Meat equivalent of exported live animals | - | - | - | - | - | - | - | .. |
| *Plus:* Meat from slaughterings of imported live animals | - | - | - | - | - | - | - | .. |
| **Total meat production from slaughtered animals** | **23.0** | **25.0** | **19.0** | **20.0** | **21.0** | **22.0** | **21.0** | -4.5 |
| *Minus:* Exports of meat | - | - | - | - | - | - | - | .. |
| *Plus:* Imports of meat | 2.0 | 2.0 | 2.0 | 2.0 | 2.0 | 2.0 | 2.0 | 0.0 |
| *Minus:* Stock variations | - | - | - | - | - | - | - | |
| **Meat consumption** | **25.0** | **27.0** | **21.0** | **22.0** | **23.0** | **24.0** | **23.0** | -4.2 |
| Consumption per head *(kilogrammes per year)* | 3.0 | 3.2 | 2.5 | 2.6 | 2.7 | 2.8 | 2.7 | -5.0 |

## EDIBLE OFFALS / ABATS COMESTIBLES

| | 1984 | 1985 | 1986 | 1987 | 1988 | 1989 | 1990 | 1989/90 % change |
|---|---|---|---|---|---|---|---|---|
| Number of animals slaughtered *(thousands)* | | | | | | | | |
| Average dressed carcass weight *(kilogrammes)* | | | | | | | | |
| **Gross indigenous production** | **24.0** | **24.0** | **23.0** | **21.0** | **20.0** | **21.0** | **21.0** | 0.0 |
| *Minus:* Meat equivalent of exported live animals | - | - | - | - | - | - | - | .. |
| *Plus:* Meat from slaughterings of imported live animals | - | - | - | - | - | - | - | .. |
| **Total meat production from slaughtered animals** | **24.0** | **24.0** | **23.0** | **21.0** | **20.0** | **21.0** | **21.0** | 0.0 |
| *Minus:* Exports of meat | 4.0 | 5.0 | 4.0 | 3.0 | 2.0 | 4.0 | 3.0 | -25.0 |
| *Plus:* Imports of meat | - | - | - | 1.0 | 1.0 | 1.0 | - | -100.0 |
| *Minus:* Stock variations | - | - | - | - | - | - | - | |
| **Meat consumption** | **20.0** | **19.0** | **19.0** | **19.0** | **19.0** | **18.0** | **18.0** | 0.0 |
| Consumption per head *(kilogrammes per year)* | 2.4 | 2.3 | 2.3 | 2.3 | 2.3 | 2.1 | 2.1 | -0.9 |

# SUÈDE

*Milliers de tonnes métriques - Poids en carcasse parée*

**TOTAL VIANDE / TOTAL MEAT**

|  | 1984 | 1985 | 1986 | 1987 | 1988 | 1989 | 1990 | 1989/90 % var. |
|---|---|---|---|---|---|---|---|---|
| **Nombre d'animaux abattus** *(milliers)* | | | | | | | | |
| **Poids moyen en carcasse parée** *(kilogrammes)* | | | | | | | | |
| **Production indigène brute** | 578.0 | 593.0 | 550.0 | 514.0 | 515.0 | 540.0 | 540.0 | 0.0 |
| *Moins:* Équivalent en viande des animaux exportés vivants | - | - | - | - | - | - | - | .. |
| *Plus:* Viande provenant des abbattages d'animaux importés vivants | - | - | - | - | - | - | - | .. |
| **Production totale de viande provenant des abattages** | 578.0 | 593.0 | 550.0 | 514.0 | 515.0 | 540.0 | 540.0 | 0.0 |
| *Moins:* Exportations de viande | 106.0 | 114.0 | 79.0 | 58.0 | 52.0 | 64.0 | 62.0 | -3.1 |
| *Plus:* Importations de viande | 14.0 | 16.0 | 19.0 | 36.0 | 42.0 | 36.0 | 34.0 | -5.6 |
| *Moins:* Variations des stocks | -1.0 | 3.0 | 1.0 | - | -1.0 | 2.0 | -4.0 | |
| **Consommation de viande** | 487.0 | 492.0 | 489.0 | 492.0 | 506.0 | 510.0 | 516.0 | 1.2 |
| **Consommation par tête** *(kilogrammes par an)* | 58.4 | 58.9 | 58.4 | 58.6 | 60.0 | 60.0 | 60.2 | 0.3 |

## PRODUCTION INDIGENE BRUTE DE VIANDE
## MEAT GROSS INDIGENOUS PRODUCTION

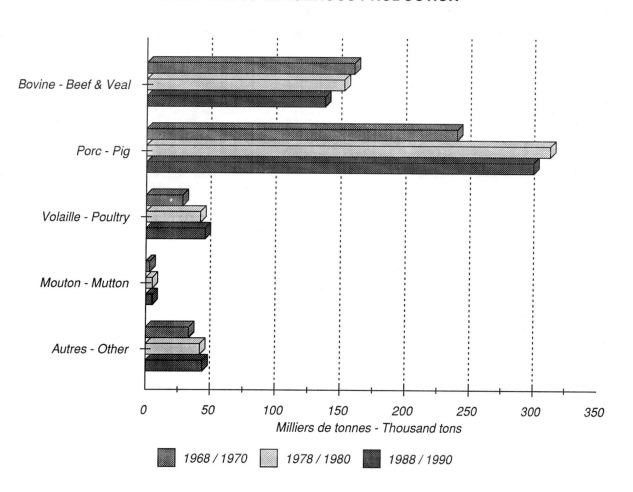

*Milliers de tonnes - Thousand tons*

1968 / 1970    1978 / 1980    1988 / 1990

133

# SWITZERLAND

## BEEF / VIANDE DE BŒUF

*Thousand metric tons - Dressed carcass weight*

|  | 1984 | 1985 | 1986 | 1987 | 1988 | 1989 | 1990 | 1989/90 % change |
|---|---|---|---|---|---|---|---|---|
| Number of animals slaughtered *(thousands)* | 476.0 | 491.0 | 495.0 | 496.0 | 450.0 | 450.0 | 471.0 | 4.7 |
| Average dressed carcass weight *(kilogrammes)* | 271.0 | 270.0 | 271.0 | 268.0 | 275.0 | 270.0 | 274.0 | 1.5 |
| Gross indigenous production | 128.0 | 133.0 | 134.0 | 133.0 | 121.0 | 121.0 | 129.0 | 6.6 |
| *Minus:* Meat equivalent of exported live animals | - | - | - | - | - | - | - | .. |
| *Plus:* Meat from slaughterings of imported live animals | 1.0 | - | - | - | 3.0 | - | - | .. |
| Total meat production from slaughtered animals | 129.0 | 133.0 | 134.0 | 133.0 | 124.0 | 121.0 | 129.0 | 6.6 |
| *Minus:* Exports of meat | - | 2.0 | 3.0 | 5.0 | - | - | - | .. |
| *Plus:* Imports of meat | 11.0 | 7.0 | 8.0 | 11.0 | 13.0 | 11.0 | 11.0 | 0.0 |
| *Minus:* Stock variations | 8.0 | -3.0 | 1.0 | -4.0 | -1.0 | - | 3.0 | |
| Meat consumption | 132.0 | 141.0 | 138.0 | 143.0 | 138.0 | 132.0 | 137.0 | 3.8 |
| Consumption per head *(kilogrammes per year)* | 20.3 | 21.6 | 21.0 | 21.6 | 20.7 | 19.6 | 20.2 | 2.7 |

## VEAL / VIANDE DE VEAU

|  | 1984 | 1985 | 1986 | 1987 | 1988 | 1989 | 1990 | 1989/90 % change |
|---|---|---|---|---|---|---|---|---|
| Number of animals slaughtered *(thousands)* | 361.0 | 354.0 | 348.0 | 370.0 | 337.0 | 325.0 | 323.0 | -0.6 |
| Average dressed carcass weight *(kilogrammes)* | 105.0 | 107.0 | 104.0 | 107.0 | 108.0 | 111.0 | 112.0 | 0.9 |
| Gross indigenous production | 38.0 | 38.0 | 36.0 | 40.0 | 36.0 | 36.0 | 36.0 | 0.0 |
| *Minus:* Meat equivalent of exported live animals | - | - | - | - | - | - | - | .. |
| *Plus:* Meat from slaughterings of imported live animals | - | - | - | - | - | - | - | .. |
| Total meat production from slaughtered animals | 38.0 | 38.0 | 36.0 | 40.0 | 36.0 | 36.0 | 36.0 | 0.0 |
| *Minus:* Exports of meat | - | - | - | - | - | - | - | .. |
| *Plus:* Imports of meat | 1.0 | 1.0 | 1.0 | 1.0 | 2.0 | 2.0 | 1.0 | -50.0 |
| *Minus:* Stock variations | - | 1.0 | - | - | - | - | - | |
| Meat consumption | 39.0 | 38.0 | 37.0 | 41.0 | 38.0 | 38.0 | 37.0 | -2.6 |
| Consumption per head *(kilogrammes per year)* | 6.0 | 5.8 | 5.6 | 6.2 | 5.7 | 5.7 | 5.4 | -3.7 |

## BEEF AND VEAL / TOTAL VIANDE BOVINE

|  | 1984 | 1985 | 1986 | 1987 | 1988 | 1989 | 1990 | 1989/90 % change |
|---|---|---|---|---|---|---|---|---|
| Number of animals slaughtered *(thousands)* | 837.0 | 845.0 | 843.0 | 866.0 | 787.0 | 775.0 | 794.0 | 2.5 |
| Average dressed carcass weight *(kilogrammes)* | 198.3 | 202.4 | 201.7 | 199.8 | 199.5 | 202.6 | 207.8 | 2.6 |
| Gross indigenous production | 166.0 | 171.0 | 170.0 | 173.0 | 157.0 | 157.0 | 165.0 | 5.1 |
| *Minus:* Meat equivalent of exported live animals | - | - | - | - | - | - | - | .. |
| *Plus:* Meat from slaughterings of imported live animals | 1.0 | - | - | - | 3.0 | - | - | .. |
| Total meat production from slaughtered animals | 167.0 | 171.0 | 170.0 | 173.0 | 160.0 | 157.0 | 165.0 | 5.1 |
| *Minus:* Exports of meat | - | 2.0 | 3.0 | 5.0 | - | - | - | .. |
| *Plus:* Imports of meat | 12.0 | 8.0 | 9.0 | 12.0 | 15.0 | 13.0 | 12.0 | -7.7 |
| *Minus:* Stock variations | 8.0 | -2.0 | 1.0 | -4.0 | -1.0 | - | 3.0 | |
| Meat consumption | 171.0 | 179.0 | 175.0 | 184.0 | 176.0 | 170.0 | 174.0 | 2.4 |
| Consumption per head *(kilogrammes per year)* | 26.3 | 27.4 | 26.6 | 27.8 | 26.4 | 25.3 | 25.6 | 1.3 |

# SUISSE

*Milliers de tonnes métriques - Poids en carcasse parée*

## VIANDE DE PORC / PIG MEAT

| | 1984 | 1985 | 1986 | 1987 | 1988 | 1989 | 1990 | 1989/90 % var. |
|---|---|---|---|---|---|---|---|---|
| Nombre d'animaux abattus *(milliers)* | 3368.0 | 3428.0 | 3435.0 | 3386.0 | 3354.0 | 3415.0 | 3285.0 | -3.8 |
| Poids moyen en carcasse parée *(kilogrammes)* | 82.0 | 83.0 | 83.0 | 82.0 | 83.0 | 82.0 | 82.0 | 0.0 |
| Production indigène brute | 276.0 | 285.0 | 286.0 | 278.0 | 279.0 | 280.0 | 270.0 | -3.6 |
| *Moins:* Équivalent en viande des animaux exportés vivants | - | - | - | - | - | - | - | .. |
| *Plus:* Viande provenant des abbattages d'animaux importés vivants | - | - | - | - | - | - | - | .. |
| Production totale de viande provenant des abattages | 276.0 | 285.0 | 286.0 | 278.0 | 279.0 | 280.0 | 270.0 | -3.6 |
| *Moins:* Exportations de viande | 1.0 | 1.0 | - | 3.0 | 1.0 | 1.0 | 2.0 | 100.0 |
| *Plus:* Importations de viande | 1.0 | - | 1.0 | 7.0 | 5.0 | 4.0 | 6.0 | 50.0 |
| *Moins:* Variations des stocks | - | - | 2.0 | -2.0 | - | - | - | |
| Consommation de viande | 276.0 | 284.0 | 285.0 | 284.0 | 283.0 | 283.0 | 274.0 | -3.2 |
| Consommation par tête *(kilogrammes par an)* | 42.4 | 43.5 | 43.4 | 42.9 | 42.4 | 42.1 | 40.3 | -4.2 |

## VIANDE DE VOLAILLE / POULTRY MEAT

| | 1984 | 1985 | 1986 | 1987 | 1988 | 1989 | 1990 | 1989/90 % var. |
|---|---|---|---|---|---|---|---|---|
| Nombre d'animaux abattus *(milliers)* | | | | | | | | |
| Poids moyen en carcasse parée *(kilogrammes)* | | | | | | | | |
| Production indigène brute | 26.0 | 27.0 | 27.0 | 26.0 | 31.0 | 33.0 | 33.0 | 0.0 |
| *Moins:* Équivalent en viande des animaux exportés vivants | - | - | - | - | - | - | - | .. |
| *Plus:* Viande provenant des abbattages d'animaux importés vivants | - | - | - | - | - | - | - | .. |
| Production totale de viande provenant des abattages | 26.0 | 27.0 | 27.0 | 26.0 | 31.0 | 33.0 | 33.0 | 0.0 |
| *Moins:* Exportations de viande | - | - | - | - | 1.0 | - | - | .. |
| *Plus:* Importations de viande | 33.0 | 32.0 | 36.0 | 40.0 | 45.0 | 43.0 | 40.0 | -7.0 |
| *Moins:* Variations des stocks | - | - | - | - | - | - | - | |
| Consommation de viande | 59.0 | 59.0 | 63.0 | 66.0 | 75.0 | 76.0 | 73.0 | -3.9 |
| Consommation par tête *(kilogrammes par an)* | 9.1 | 9.0 | 9.6 | 10.0 | 11.2 | 11.3 | 10.7 | -5.0 |

## VIANDE DE MOUTON ET DE CHÈVRE / MUTTON, LAMB AND GOAT MEAT

| | 1984 | 1985 | 1986 | 1987 | 1988 | 1989 | 1990 | 1989/90 % var. |
|---|---|---|---|---|---|---|---|---|
| Nombre d'animaux abattus *(milliers)* | 232.0 | 241.0 | 246.0 | 251.0 | 261.0 | 250.0 | 270.0 | 8.0 |
| Poids moyen en carcasse parée *(kilogrammes)* | 18.0 | 19.0 | 19.0 | 19.0 | 18.0 | 19.0 | 19.0 | 0.0 |
| Production indigène brute | 4.0 | 5.0 | 5.0 | 5.0 | 5.0 | 5.0 | 5.0 | 0.0 |
| *Moins:* Équivalent en viande des animaux exportés vivants | - | - | - | - | - | - | - | .. |
| *Plus:* Viande provenant des abbattages d'animaux importés vivants | - | - | - | - | - | - | - | .. |
| Production totale de viande provenant des abattages | 4.0 | 5.0 | 5.0 | 5.0 | 5.0 | 5.0 | 5.0 | 0.0 |
| *Moins:* Exportations de viande | - | - | - | - | - | - | - | .. |
| *Plus:* Importations de viande | 6.0 | 7.0 | 6.0 | 5.0 | 6.0 | 7.0 | 7.0 | 0.0 |
| *Moins:* Variations des stocks | - | 1.0 | - | - | - | - | - | |
| Consommation de viande | 10.0 | 11.0 | 11.0 | 10.0 | 11.0 | 12.0 | 12.0 | 0.0 |
| Consommation par tête *(kilogrammes par an)* | 1.5 | 1.7 | 1.7 | 1.5 | 1.6 | 1.8 | 1.8 | -1.1 |

## HORSE MEAT / VIANDE D'ÉQUIDÉS

*Thousand metric tons - Dressed carcass weight*

| | 1984 | 1985 | 1986 | 1987 | 1988 | 1989 | 1990 | 1989/90 % change |
|---|---|---|---|---|---|---|---|---|
| Number of animals slaughtered *(thousands)* | 6.0 | 6.0 | 5.0 | 5.0 | 5.0 | 5.0 | 4.0 | -20.0 |
| Average dressed carcass weight *(kilogrammes)* | 268.0 | 242.0 | 257.0 | 251.0 | 282.0 | 269.0 | 283.0 | 5.2 |
| Gross indigenous production | 2.0 | 1.0 | 1.0 | 2.0 | 2.0 | 1.0 | 1.0 | 0.0 |
| *Minus:* Meat equivalent of exported live animals | - | - | - | - | - | - | - | .. |
| *Plus:* Meat from slaughterings of imported live animals | - | - | - | - | - | - | - | .. |
| Total meat production from slaughtered animals | 2.0 | 1.0 | 1.0 | 2.0 | 2.0 | 1.0 | 1.0 | 0.0 |
| *Minus:* Exports of meat | - | - | - | - | - | - | - | .. |
| *Plus:* Imports of meat | 3.0 | 3.0 | 3.0 | 3.0 | 4.0 | 4.0 | 5.0 | 25.0 |
| *Minus:* Stock variations | - | - | - | - | - | - | - | |
| Meat consumption | 5.0 | 4.0 | 4.0 | 5.0 | 6.0 | 5.0 | 6.0 | 20.0 |
| Consumption per head *(kilogrammes per year)* | 0.8 | 0.6 | 0.6 | 0.8 | 0.9 | 0.7 | 0.9 | 18.7 |

## OTHER MEAT / AUTRES VIANDES

| | 1984 | 1985 | 1986 | 1987 | 1988 | 1989 | 1990 | 1989/90 % change |
|---|---|---|---|---|---|---|---|---|
| Number of animals slaughtered *(thousands)* | | | | | | | | |
| Average dressed carcass weight *(kilogrammes)* | | | | | | | | |
| Gross indigenous production | 4.0 | 4.0 | 4.0 | 4.0 | 3.0 | 3.0 | 3.0 | 0.0 |
| *Minus:* Meat equivalent of exported live animals | - | - | - | - | - | - | - | .. |
| *Plus:* Meat from slaughterings of imported live animals | - | - | - | - | - | - | - | .. |
| Total meat production from slaughtered animals | 4.0 | 4.0 | 4.0 | 4.0 | 3.0 | 3.0 | 3.0 | 0.0 |
| *Minus:* Exports of meat | - | - | - | - | - | - | - | .. |
| *Plus:* Imports of meat | 6.0 | 6.0 | 6.0 | 7.0 | 7.0 | 7.0 | 8.0 | 14.3 |
| *Minus:* Stock variations | - | - | - | - | - | - | - | |
| Meat consumption | 10.0 | 10.0 | 10.0 | 11.0 | 10.0 | 10.0 | 11.0 | 10.0 |
| Consumption per head *(kilogrammes per year)* | 1.5 | 1.5 | 1.5 | 1.7 | 1.5 | 1.5 | 1.6 | 8.8 |

## EDIBLE OFFALS / ABATS COMESTIBLES

| | 1984 | 1985 | 1986 | 1987 | 1988 | 1989 | 1990 | 1989/90 % change |
|---|---|---|---|---|---|---|---|---|
| Number of animals slaughtered *(thousands)* | | | | | | | | |
| Average dressed carcass weight *(kilogrammes)* | | | | | | | | |
| Gross indigenous production | 20.0 | 19.0 | 21.0 | 21.0 | 19.0 | 21.0 | 19.0 | -9.5 |
| *Minus:* Meat equivalent of exported live animals | - | - | - | - | - | - | - | .. |
| *Plus:* Meat from slaughterings of imported live animals | - | - | - | - | - | - | - | .. |
| Total meat production from slaughtered animals | 20.0 | 19.0 | 21.0 | 21.0 | 19.0 | 21.0 | 19.0 | -9.5 |
| *Minus:* Exports of meat | 1.0 | 1.0 | 1.0 | 6.0 | - | - | - | .. |
| *Plus:* Imports of meat | 2.0 | 2.0 | 2.0 | 2.0 | 2.0 | 2.0 | 2.0 | 0.0 |
| *Minus:* Stock variations | - | - | - | - | - | - | - | |
| Meat consumption | 21.0 | 20.0 | 22.0 | 17.0 | 21.0 | 23.0 | 21.0 | -8.7 |
| Consumption per head *(kilogrammes per year)* | 3.2 | 3.1 | 3.3 | 2.6 | 3.1 | 3.4 | 3.1 | -9.7 |

# SUISSE

*Milliers de tonnes métriques - Poids en carcasse parée*

*TOTAL VIANDE / TOTAL MEAT*

| | 1984 | 1985 | 1986 | 1987 | 1988 | 1989 | 1990 | 1989/90 % var. |
|---|---|---|---|---|---|---|---|---|
| **Nombre d'animaux abattus** *(milliers)* | | | | | | | | |
| **Poids moyen en carcasse parée** *(kilogrammes)* | | | | | | | | |
| **Production indigène brute** | 498.0 | 512.0 | 514.0 | 509.0 | 496.0 | 500.0 | 496.0 | -0.8 |
| *Moins:* Équivalent en viande des animaux exportés vivants | - | - | - | - | - | - | - | .. |
| *Plus:* Viande provenant des abbattages d'animaux importés vivants | 1.0 | - | - | - | 3.0 | - | - | .. |
| **Production totale de viande provenant des abattages** | 499.0 | 512.0 | 514.0 | 509.0 | 499.0 | 500.0 | 496.0 | -0.8 |
| *Moins:* Exportations de viande | 2.0 | 4.0 | 4.0 | 14.0 | 2.0 | 1.0 | 2.0 | 100.0 |
| *Plus:* Importations de viande | 63.0 | 58.0 | 63.0 | 76.0 | 84.0 | 80.0 | 80.0 | 0.0 |
| *Moins:* Variations des stocks | 8.0 | -1.0 | 3.0 | -6.0 | -1.0 | - | 3.0 | |
| **Consommation de viande** | 552.0 | 567.0 | 570.0 | 577.0 | 582.0 | 579.0 | 571.0 | -1.4 |
| **Consommation par tête** *(kilogrammes par an)* | 84.9 | 86.8 | 86.7 | 87.2 | 87.2 | 86.1 | 84.0 | -2.4 |

## PRODUCTION INDIGENE BRUTE DE VIANDE
## MEAT GROSS INDIGENOUS PRODUCTION

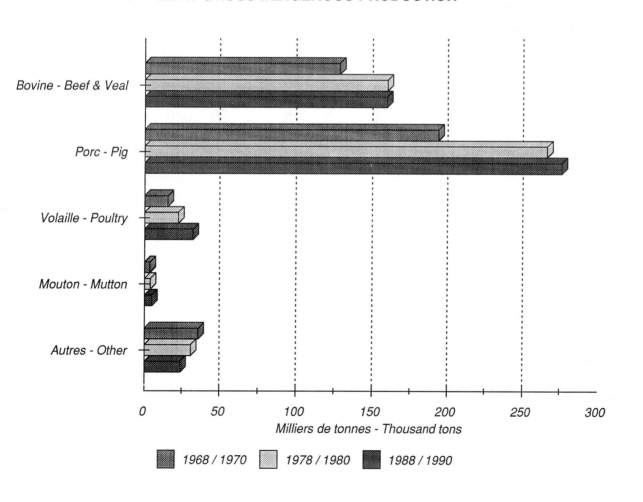

*Milliers de tonnes - Thousand tons*

1968 / 1970     1978 / 1980     1988 / 1990

# TURKEY

*Thousand metric tons - Dressed carcass weight*

|  | 1984 | 1985 | 1986 | 1987 | 1988 | 1989 | 1990 | 1989/90 % change |
|---|---|---|---|---|---|---|---|---|
| **Number of animals slaughtered** *(thousands)* | .. | .. | .. | .. | .. | .. | .. | .. |
| **Average dressed carcass weight** *(kilogrammes)* | .. | .. | .. | .. | .. | .. | .. | .. |
| **Gross indigenous production** | 491.0 | 510.0 | 444.0 | 358.0 | 461.0 | 506.0 | 413.0 | -18.4 |
| *Minus:* Meat equivalent of exported live animals | - | - | - | - | - | - | - | .. |
| *Plus:* Meat from slaughterings of imported live animals | - | - | - | - | - | - | - | .. |
| **Total meat production from slaughtered animals** | 491.0 | 510.0 | 444.0 | 358.0 | 461.0 | 506.0 | 413.0 | -18.4 |
| *Minus:* Exports of meat | 13.0 | 6.0 | 1.0 | 1.0 | - | - | - | .. |
| *Plus:* Imports of meat | - | 37.0 | 24.0 | 23.0 | 10.0 | 7.0 | 10.0 | 42.9 |
| *Minus:* Stock variations | - | - | - | - | - | - | - | |
| **Meat consumption** | 478.0 | 541.0 | 467.0 | 380.0 | 471.0 | 513.0 | 423.0 | -17.5 |
| **Consumption per head** *(kilogrammes per year)* | 9.7 | 10.7 | 9.0 | 7.2 | 8.7 | 9.3 | 7.4 | -20.3 |

## VEAL / VIANDE DE VEAU

|  | 1984 | 1985 | 1986 | 1987 | 1988 | 1989 | 1990 | 1989/90 % change |
|---|---|---|---|---|---|---|---|---|
| **Number of animals slaughtered** *(thousands)* | .. | .. | .. | .. | .. | .. | .. | .. |
| **Average dressed carcass weight** *(kilogrammes)* | .. | .. | .. | .. | .. | .. | .. | .. |
| **Gross indigenous production** | . | . | . | . | . | . | . | .. |
| *Minus:* Meat equivalent of exported live animals | . | . | . | . | . | . | . | .. |
| *Plus:* Meat from slaughterings of imported live animals | . | . | . | . | . | . | . | .. |
| **Total meat production from slaughtered animals** | . | . | . | . | . | . | . | .. |
| *Minus:* Exports of meat | . | . | . | . | . | . | . | .. |
| *Plus:* Imports of meat | . | . | . | . | . | . | . | .. |
| *Minus:* Stock variations | . | . | . | . | . | . | . | |
| **Meat consumption** | . | . | . | . | . | . | . | |
| **Consumption per head** *(kilogrammes per year)* | . | . | . | . | . | . | . | .. |

## BEEF AND VEAL / TOTAL VIANDE BOVINE

|  | 1984 | 1985 | 1986 | 1987 | 1988 | 1989 | 1990 | 1989/90 % change |
|---|---|---|---|---|---|---|---|---|
| **Number of animals slaughtered** *(thousands)* | .. | .. | .. | .. | .. | .. | .. | .. |
| **Average dressed carcass weight** *(kilogrammes)* | .. | .. | .. | .. | .. | .. | .. | .. |
| **Gross indigenous production** | 491.0 | 510.0 | 444.0 | 358.0 | 461.0 | 506.0 | 413.0 | -18.4 |
| *Minus:* Meat equivalent of exported live animals | - | - | - | - | - | - | - | .. |
| *Plus:* Meat from slaughterings of imported live animals | - | - | - | - | - | - | - | .. |
| **Total meat production from slaughtered animals** | 491.0 | 510.0 | 444.0 | 358.0 | 461.0 | 506.0 | 413.0 | -18.4 |
| *Minus:* Exports of meat | 13.0 | 6.0 | 1.0 | 1.0 | - | - | - | .. |
| *Plus:* Imports of meat | - | 37.0 | 24.0 | 23.0 | 10.0 | 7.0 | 10.0 | 42.9 |
| *Minus:* Stock variations | - | - | - | - | - | - | - | |
| **Meat consumption** | 478.0 | 541.0 | 467.0 | 380.0 | 471.0 | 513.0 | 423.0 | -17.5 |
| **Consumption per head** *(kilogrammes per year)* | 9.7 | 10.7 | 9.0 | 7.2 | 8.7 | 9.3 | 7.4 | -20.3 |

(1) Including veal / Y compris la viande de veau

# TURQUIE

## VIANDE DE PORC / PIG MEAT

| | 1984 | 1985 | 1986 | 1987 | 1988 | 1989 | 1990 | 1989/90 % var. |
|---|---|---|---|---|---|---|---|---|
| Nombre d'animaux abattus *(milliers)* | - | - | - | - | - | - | - | .. |
| Poids moyen en carcasse parée *(kilogrammes)* | - | - | - | - | - | - | - | .. |
| Production indigène brute | • | • | • | • | • | • | • | .. |
| *Moins:* Équivalent en viande des animaux exportés vivants | - | - | - | - | - | - | - | .. |
| *Plus:* Viande provenant des abbattages d'animaux importés vivants | - | - | - | - | - | - | - | .. |
| Production totale de viande provenant des abattages | • | • | • | • | • | • | • | .. |
| *Moins:* Exportations de viande | - | - | - | - | - | - | - | .. |
| *Plus:* Importations de viande | - | - | - | - | - | - | - | .. |
| *Moins:* Variations des stocks | - | - | - | - | - | - | - | |
| Consommation de viande | • | • | • | • | • | • | • | .. |
| Consommation par tête *(kilogrammes par an)* | - | - | - | - | - | - | - | .. |

## VIANDE DE VOLAILLE / POULTRY MEAT

| | 1984 | 1985 | 1986 | 1987 | 1988 | 1989 | 1990 | 1989/90 % var. |
|---|---|---|---|---|---|---|---|---|
| Nombre d'animaux abattus *(milliers)* | | | | | | | | |
| Poids moyen en carcasse parée *(kilogrammes)* | | | | | | | | |
| Production indigène brute | 286.0 | 285.0 | 315.0 | 350.0 | 380.0 | 390.0 | 415.0 | 6.4 |
| *Moins:* Équivalent en viande des animaux exportés vivants | - | - | - | - | - | - | - | .. |
| *Plus:* Viande provenant des abbattages d'animaux importés vivants | - | - | - | - | - | - | - | .. |
| Production totale de viande provenant des abattages | 286.0 | 285.0 | 315.0 | 350.0 | 380.0 | 390.0 | 415.0 | 6.4 |
| *Moins:* Exportations de viande | - | 5.0 | 4.0 | 5.0 | 2.0 | 1.0 | 1.0 | 0.0 |
| *Plus:* Importations de viande | - | - | - | - | - | - | - | .. |
| *Moins:* Variations des stocks | - | - | - | - | - | - | - | |
| Consommation de viande | 286.0 | 280.0 | 311.0 | 345.0 | 378.0 | 389.0 | 414.0 | 6.4 |
| Consommation par tête *(kilogrammes par an)* | 5.8 | 5.5 | 6.0 | 6.5 | 7.0 | 7.0 | 7.2 | 2.9 |

## VIANDE DE MOUTON ET DE CHÈVRE / MUTTON, LAMB AND GOAT MEAT

| | 1984 | 1985 | 1986 | 1987 | 1988 | 1989 | 1990 | 1989/90 % var. |
|---|---|---|---|---|---|---|---|---|
| Nombre d'animaux abattus *(milliers)* | - | - | - | - | - | - | - | .. |
| Poids moyen en carcasse parée *(kilogrammes)* | - | - | - | - | - | - | - | .. |
| Production indigène brute | 458.0 | 487.0 | 423.0 | 416.0 | 512.0 | 463.0 | 327.0 | -29.4 |
| *Moins:* Équivalent en viande des animaux exportés vivants | - | - | - | - | - | - | - | .. |
| *Plus:* Viande provenant des abbattages d'animaux importés vivants | - | - | - | - | - | - | - | .. |
| Production totale de viande provenant des abattages | 458.0 | 487.0 | 423.0 | 416.0 | 512.0 | 463.0 | 327.0 | -29.4 |
| *Moins:* Exportations de viande | 67.0 | 35.0 | 35.0 | 22.0 | 99.0 | 98.0 | 70.0 | -28.6 |
| *Plus:* Importations de viande | - | - | - | - | - | - | - | .. |
| *Moins:* Variations des stocks | - | - | - | - | - | - | - | |
| Consommation de viande | 391.0 | 452.0 | 388.0 | 394.0 | 413.0 | 365.0 | 257.0 | -29.6 |
| Consommation par tête *(kilogrammes par an)* | 7.9 | 8.9 | 7.5 | 7.5 | 7.7 | 6.6 | 4.5 | -31.9 |

# TURKEY

## HORSE MEAT / VIANDE D'ÉQUIDÉS

*Thousand metric tons - Dressed carcass weight*

| | 1984 | 1985 | 1986 | 1987 | 1988 | 1989 | 1990 | 1989/90 % change |
|---|---|---|---|---|---|---|---|---|
| **Number of animals slaughtered** *(thousands)* | - | - | - | - | - | - | - | .. |
| **Average dressed carcass weight** *(kilogrammes)* | - | - | - | - | - | - | - | .. |
| **Gross indigenous production** | 2.0 | 1.0 | 1.0 | 1.0 | 1.0 | 1.0 | 1.0 | 0.0 |
| *Minus:* Meat equivalent of exported live animals | 2.0 | 1.0 | 1.0 | 1.0 | 1.0 | 1.0 | 1.0 | 0.0 |
| *Plus:* Meat from slaughterings of imported live animals | - | - | - | - | - | - | - | .. |
| **Total meat production from slaughtered animals** | - | - | - | - | - | - | - | .. |
| *Minus:* Exports of meat | - | - | - | - | - | - | - | .. |
| *Plus:* Imports of meat | - | - | - | - | - | - | - | .. |
| *Minus:* Stock variations | - | - | - | - | - | - | - | |
| **Meat consumption** | - | - | - | - | - | - | - | .. |
| **Consumption per head** *(kilogrammes per year)* | - | - | - | - | - | - | - | .. |

## OTHER MEAT / AUTRES VIANDES

| | 1984 | 1985 | 1986 | 1987 | 1988 | 1989 | 1990 | 1989/90 % change |
|---|---|---|---|---|---|---|---|---|
| **Number of animals slaughtered** *(thousands)* | | | | | | | | |
| **Average dressed carcass weight** *(kilogrammes)* | | | | | | | | |
| **Gross indigenous production** | - | - | - | - | - | - | - | .. |
| *Minus:* Meat equivalent of exported live animals | - | - | - | - | - | - | - | .. |
| *Plus:* Meat from slaughterings of imported live animals | - | - | - | - | - | - | - | .. |
| **Total meat production from slaughtered animals** | - | - | - | - | - | - | - | .. |
| *Minus:* Exports of meat | - | - | - | - | - | - | - | .. |
| *Plus:* Imports of meat | - | - | - | - | - | - | - | .. |
| *Minus:* Stock variations | - | - | - | - | - | - | - | |
| **Meat consumption** | - | - | - | - | - | - | - | .. |
| **Consumption per head** *(kilogrammes per year)* | - | - | - | - | - | - | - | .. |

## EDIBLE OFFALS / ABATS COMESTIBLES

| | 1984 | 1985 | 1986 | 1987 | 1988 | 1989 | 1990 | 1989/90 % change |
|---|---|---|---|---|---|---|---|---|
| **Number of animals slaughtered** *(thousands)* | | | | | | | | |
| **Average dressed carcass weight** *(kilogrammes)* | | | | | | | | |
| **Gross indigenous production** | 105.0 | 100.0 | 86.0 | 78.0 | 78.0 | 81.0 [e] | 80.0 [e] | -1.2 |
| *Minus:* Meat equivalent of exported live animals | - | - | - | - | - | - | - | .. |
| *Plus:* Meat from slaughterings of imported live animals | - | - | - | - | - | - | - | .. |
| **Total meat production from slaughtered animals** | 105.0 | 100.0 | 86.0 | 78.0 | 78.0 | 81.0 [e] | 80.0 [e] | -1.2 |
| *Minus:* Exports of meat | - | - | - | - | - | - | - | .. |
| *Plus:* Imports of meat | - | - | - | - | - | - | - | .. |
| *Minus:* Stock variations | - | - | - | - | - | - | - | |
| **Meat consumption** | 105.0 | 100.0 | 86.0 | 78.0 | 78.0 | 81.0 [e] | 80.0 [e] | -1.2 |
| **Consumption per head** *(kilogrammes per year)* | 2.1 | 2.0 | 1.7 | 1.5 | 1.4 | 1.5 [e] | 1.4 [e] | -4.5 |

# TURQUIE

*Milliers de tonnes métriques - Poids en carcasse parée*

| | 1984 | 1985 | 1986 | 1987 | 1988 | 1989 | 1990 | 1989/90 % var. |
|---|---|---|---|---|---|---|---|---|
| **Nombre d'animaux abattus** *(milliers)* | | | | | | | | |
| **Poids moyen en carcasse parée** *(kilogrammes)* | | | | | | | | |
| **Production indigène brute** | 1342.0 | 1383.0 | 1269.0 | 1203.0 | 1432.0 | 1441.0 e | 1236.0 e | -14.2 |
| *Moins:* Équivalent en viande des animaux exportés vivants | 2.0 | 1.0 | 1.0 | 1.0 | 1.0 | 1.0 | 1.0 | 0.0 |
| *Plus:* Viande provenant des abbattages d'animaux importés vivants | - | - | - | - | - | - | - | .. |
| **Production totale de viande provenant des abattages** | 1340.0 | 1382.0 | 1268.0 | 1202.0 | 1431.0 | 1440.0 e | 1235.0 e | -14.2 |
| *Moins:* Exportations de viande | 80.0 | 46.0 | 40.0 | 28.0 | 101.0 | 99.0 | 71.0 | -28.3 |
| *Plus:* Importations de viande | - | 37.0 | 24.0 | 23.0 | 10.0 | 7.0 | 10.0 | 42.9 |
| *Moins:* Variations des stocks | - | - | - | - | - | - | - | |
| **Consommation de viande** | 1260.0 | 1373.0 | 1252.0 | 1197.0 | 1340.0 | 1348.0 e | 1174.0 e | -12.9 |
| **Consommation par tête** *(kilogrammes par an)* | 25.5 | 27.1 | 24.2 | 22.7 | 24.8 | 24.4 e | 20.5 e | -15.8 |

## PRODUCTION INDIGENE BRUTE DE VIANDE
## MEAT GROSS INDIGENOUS PRODUCTION

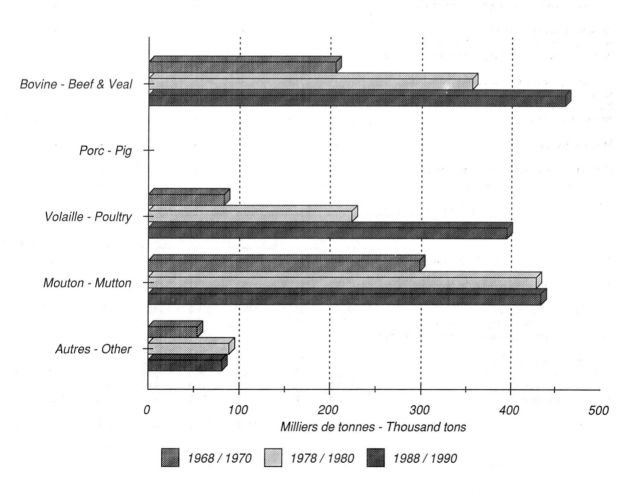

*Milliers de tonnes - Thousand tons*

- 1968 / 1970
- 1978 / 1980
- 1988 / 1990

# YUGOSLAVIA

## BEEF / VIANDE DE BŒUF

*Thousand metric tons - Dressed carcass weight*

|  | 1984 | 1985 | 1986 | 1987 | 1988 | 1989 | 1990 | 1989/90 % change |
|---|---|---|---|---|---|---|---|---|
| Number of animals slaughtered *(thousands)* | 2402.0 | 2386.0 | 2175.0 | 2185.0 | 2207.0 | 2168.0 | 2212.0 | 2.0 |
| Average dressed carcass weight *(kilogrammes)* | 146.0 | 132.0 | 136.0 | 145.0 | 136.0 | 143.0 | 137.0 | -4.2 |
| Gross indigenous production | 371.0 | 333.0 | 317.0 | 359.0 | 346.0 | 357.0 ᵉ | 356.0 ᵉ | -0.3 |
| *Minus:* Meat equivalent of exported live animals | 21.0 | 19.0 | 22.0 | 42.0 | 45.0 | 48.0 ᵉ | 4.0 ᵉ | -91.7 |
| *Plus:* Meat from slaughterings of imported live animals | - | - | - | - | - | - | - | .. |
| Total meat production from slaughtered animals | 350.0 | 314.0 | 295.0 | 317.0 | 301.0 | 309.0 | 352.0 | 13.9 |
| *Minus:* Exports of meat | 44.0 | 59.0 | 30.0 | 29.0 | 39.0 | 28.0 | 23.0 | -17.9 |
| *Plus:* Imports of meat | 24.0 | 18.0 | 32.0 | 45.0 | 53.0 | 81.0 | 74.0 | -8.6 |
| *Minus:* Stock variations | -3.0 | -42.0 | -4.0 | 12.0 | -1.0 | -7.0 | 12.0 | |
| Meat consumption | 333.0 | 315.0 | 301.0 | 321.0 | 316.0 | 369.0 | 391.0 | 6.0 |
| Consumption per head *(kilogrammes per year)* | 14.5 | 13.6 | 12.9 | 13.7 | 13.4 | 15.6 | 16.4 | 5.5 |

## VEAL / VIANDE DE VEAU

|  | 1984 | 1985 | 1986 | 1987 | 1988 | 1989 | 1990 | 1989/90 % change |
|---|---|---|---|---|---|---|---|---|
| Number of animals slaughtered *(thousands)* | - | - | - | - | - | - | - | .. |
| Average dressed carcass weight *(kilogrammes)* | - | - | - | - | - | - | - | .. |
| Gross indigenous production | . | . | . | . | . | . | . | .. |
| *Minus:* Meat equivalent of exported live animals | - | - | - | - | - | - | - | .. |
| *Plus:* Meat from slaughterings of imported live animals | - | - | - | - | - | - | - | .. |
| Total meat production from slaughtered animals | . | . | . | . | . | . | . | .. |
| *Minus:* Exports of meat | - | - | - | - | - | - | - | .. |
| *Plus:* Imports of meat | - | - | - | - | - | - | - | .. |
| *Minus:* Stock variations | - | - | - | - | - | - | - | .. |
| Meat consumption | . | . | . | . | . | . | . | .. |
| Consumption per head *(kilogrammes per year)* | - | - | - | - | - | - | - | .. |

## BEEF AND VEAL / TOTAL VIANDE BOVINE

|  | 1984 | 1985 | 1986 | 1987 | 1988 | 1989 | 1990 | 1989/90 % change |
|---|---|---|---|---|---|---|---|---|
| Number of animals slaughtered *(thousands)* | 2402.0 | 2386.0 | 2175.0 | 2185.0 | 2207.0 | 2168.0 | 2212.0 | 2.0 |
| Average dressed carcass weight *(kilogrammes)* | 145.7 | 131.6 | 135.6 | 145.1 | 136.4 | 142.5 | 159.1 | 11.6 |
| Gross indigenous production | 371.0 | 333.0 | 317.0 | 359.0 | 346.0 | 357.0 ᵉ | 356.0 ᵉ | -0.3 |
| *Minus:* Meat equivalent of exported live animals | 21.0 | 19.0 | 22.0 | 42.0 | 45.0 | 48.0 ᵉ | 4.0 ᵉ | -91.7 |
| *Plus:* Meat from slaughterings of imported live animals | - | - | - | - | - | - | - | .. |
| Total meat production from slaughtered animals | 350.0 | 314.0 | 295.0 | 317.0 | 301.0 | 309.0 | 352.0 | 13.9 |
| *Minus:* Exports of meat | 44.0 | 59.0 | 30.0 | 29.0 | 39.0 | 28.0 | 23.0 | -17.9 |
| *Plus:* Imports of meat | 24.0 | 18.0 | 32.0 | 45.0 | 53.0 | 81.0 | 74.0 | -8.6 |
| *Minus:* Stock variations | -3.0 | -42.0 | -4.0 | 12.0 | -1.0 | -7.0 | 12.0 | |
| Meat consumption | 333.0 | 315.0 | 301.0 | 321.0 | 316.0 | 369.0 | 391.0 | 6.0 |
| Consumption per head *(kilogrammes per year)* | 14.5 | 13.6 | 12.9 | 13.7 | 13.4 | 15.6 | 16.4 | 5.5 |

# YOUGOSLAVIE

*Milliers de tonnes métriques - Poids en carcasse parée*                     *VIANDE DE PORC / PIG MEAT*

|  | 1984 | 1985 | 1986 | 1987 | 1988 | 1989 | 1990 | 1989/90 % var. |
|---|---|---|---|---|---|---|---|---|
| Nombre d'animaux abattus *(milliers)* | 14418.0 | 13805.0 | 13358.0 | 14128.0 | 14156.0 | 13758.0 | 13630.0 | -0.9 |
| Poids moyen en carcasse parée *(kilogrammes)* | 61.0 | 60.0 | 60.0 | 62.0 | 60.0 | 60.0 | 61.0 | 1.7 |
| Production indigène brute | 876.0 | 833.0 | 795.0 | 871.0 | 853.0 | 789.0 | 781.0 | -1.0 |
| *Moins:* Équivalent en viande des animaux exportés vivants | - | - | - | - | - | - | - | .. |
| *Plus:* Viande provenant des abbattages d'animaux importés vivants | - | - | - | - | - | - | - | .. |
| Production totale de viande provenant des abattages | 876.0 | 833.0 | 795.0 | 871.0 | 853.0 | 789.0 | 781.0 | -1.0 |
| *Moins:* Exportations de viande | 53.0 | 62.0 | 28.0 | 36.0 | 42.0 | 25.0 | 24.0 | -4.0 |
| *Plus:* Importations de viande | 4.0 | 14.0 | 61.0 | 31.0 | 42.0 | 89.0 | 90.0 | 1.1 |
| *Moins:* Variations des stocks | 92.0 | 51.0 | -20.0 | 8.0 | 14.0 | -8.0 | -34.0 | |
| Consommation de viande | 735.0 | 734.0 | 848.0 | 858.0 | 839.0 | 861.0 | 881.0 | 2.3 |
| Consommation par tête *(kilogrammes par an)* | 32.0 | 31.7 | 36.4 | 36.7 | 35.6 | 36.3 | 37.0 | 1.9 |

*VIANDE DE VOLAILLE / POULTRY MEAT*

|  | 1984 | 1985 | 1986 | 1987 | 1988 | 1989 | 1990 | 1989/90 % var. |
|---|---|---|---|---|---|---|---|---|
| Nombre d'animaux abattus *(milliers)* | | | | | | | | |
| Poids moyen en carcasse parée *(kilogrammes)* | | | | | | | | |
| Production indigène brute | 313.0 | 297.0 | 328.0 | 323.0 | 351.0 | 310.0 | 295.0 | -4.8 |
| *Moins:* Équivalent en viande des animaux exportés vivants | - | - | - | - | - | - | - | .. |
| *Plus:* Viande provenant des abbattages d'animaux importés vivants | - | - | - | - | - | - | - | .. |
| Production totale de viande provenant des abattages | 313.0 | 297.0 | 328.0 | 323.0 | 351.0 | 310.0 | 295.0 | -4.8 |
| *Moins:* Exportations de viande | 30.0 | 24.0 | 11.0 | 17.0 | 17.0 | 16.0 | 10.0 | -37.5 |
| *Plus:* Importations de viande | 1.0 | 1.0 | 3.0 | 3.0 | 2.0 | 3.0 | 2.0 | -33.3 |
| *Moins:* Variations des stocks | - | 2.0 | 12.0 | -1.0 | -9.0 | - | -3.0 | |
| Consommation de viande | 284.0 | 272.0 | 308.0 | 310.0 | 345.0 | 297.0 | 290.0 | -2.4 |
| Consommation par tête *(kilogrammes par an)* | 12.4 | 11.8 | 13.2 | 13.2 | 14.6 | 12.5 | 12.2 | -2.8 |

*VIANDE DE MOUTON ET DE CHÈVRE / MUTTON, LAMB AND GOAT MEAT*

|  | 1984 | 1985 | 1986 | 1987 | 1988 | 1989 | 1990 | 1989/90 % var. |
|---|---|---|---|---|---|---|---|---|
| Nombre d'animaux abattus *(milliers)* | 4778.0 | 4948.0 | 5053.0 | 5238.0 | 5476.0 | 5285.0 | 5320.0 | 0.7 |
| Poids moyen en carcasse parée *(kilogrammes)* | 12.0 | 12.0 | 12.0 | 12.0 | 13.0 | 13.0 | 13.0 | 0.0 |
| Production indigène brute | 59.0 | 62.0 | 63.0 | 65.0 | 70.0 | 69.0 | 67.0 | -2.9 |
| *Moins:* Équivalent en viande des animaux exportés vivants | - | 1.0 | - | - | - | - | - | .. |
| *Plus:* Viande provenant des abbattages d'animaux importés vivants | - | - | - | - | - | - | - | .. |
| Production totale de viande provenant des abattages | 59.0 | 61.0 | 63.0 | 65.0 | 70.0 | 69.0 | 67.0 | -2.9 |
| *Moins:* Exportations de viande | 26.0 | 5.0 | 4.0 | 7.0 | 5.0 | 5.0 | 3.0 | -40.0 |
| *Plus:* Importations de viande | - | - | - | - | - | - | 3.0 | .. |
| *Moins:* Variations des stocks | -4.0 | 3.0 | 2.0 | -1.0 | 2.0 | -2.0 | -1.0 | |
| Consommation de viande | 37.0 | 53.0 | 57.0 | 59.0 | 63.0 | 66.0 | 68.0 | 3.0 |
| Consommation par tête *(kilogrammes par an)* | 1.6 | 2.3 | 2.4 | 2.5 | 2.7 | 2.8 | 2.9 | 2.6 |

# YUGOSLAVIA

## HORSE MEAT / VIANDE D'ÉQUIDÉS

| | 1984 | 1985 | 1986 | 1987 | 1988 | 1989 | 1990 | 1989/90 % change |
|---|---|---|---|---|---|---|---|---|
| Number of animals slaughtered *(thousands)* | 1.0 | 2.0 | 1.0 | 1.0 | 2.0 | 1.0 | 1.0 | 0.0 |
| Average dressed carcass weight *(kilogrammes)* | - | - | - | - | - | - | - | .. |
| Gross indigenous production | 7.0 | 10.0 | 6.0 | 21.0 | 10.0 | 8.0 | 3.0 | -62.5 |
| *Minus:* Meat equivalent of exported live animals | 7.0 | 10.0 | 6.0 | 21.0 | 10.0 | 8.0 | 3.0 | -62.5 |
| *Plus:* Meat from slaughterings of imported live animals | - | - | - | - | - | - | - | .. |
| Total meat production from slaughtered animals | • | • | • | • | • | • | • | .. |
| *Minus:* Exports of meat | - | - | - | - | - | - | - | .. |
| *Plus:* Imports of meat | - | - | - | - | - | - | - | .. |
| *Minus:* Stock variations | - | - | - | - | - | - | - | |
| Meat consumption | • | • | • | • | • | • | • | .. |
| Consumption per head *(kilogrammes per year)* | - | - | - | - | - | - | - | .. |

## OTHER MEAT / AUTRES VIANDES

| | 1984 | 1985 | 1986 | 1987 | 1988 | 1989 | 1990 | 1989/90 % change |
|---|---|---|---|---|---|---|---|---|
| Number of animals slaughtered *(thousands)* | | | | | | | | |
| Average dressed carcass weight *(kilogrammes)* | | | | | | | | |
| Gross indigenous production | 8.0 | 8.0 | 8.0 | 8.0 | 8.0 | 7.0 | 7.0 | 0.0 |
| *Minus:* Meat equivalent of exported live animals | - | - | - | - | - | - | - | .. |
| *Plus:* Meat from slaughterings of imported live animals | - | - | - | - | - | - | - | .. |
| Total meat production from slaughtered animals | 8.0 | 8.0 | 8.0 | 8.0 | 8.0 | 7.0 | 7.0 | 0.0 |
| *Minus:* Exports of meat | 1.0 | - | - | 2.0 | - | - | - | .. |
| *Plus:* Imports of meat | - | - | - | - | - | - | - | .. |
| *Minus:* Stock variations | - | - | - | - | - | - | - | |
| Meat consumption | 7.0 | 8.0 | 8.0 | 6.0 | 8.0 | 7.0 | 7.0 | 0.0 |
| Consumption per head *(kilogrammes per year)* | 0.3 | 0.3 | 0.3 | 0.3 | 0.3 | 0.3 | 0.3 | -0.5 |

## EDIBLE OFFALS / ABATS COMESTIBLES

| | 1984 | 1985 | 1986 | 1987 | 1988 | 1989 | 1990 | 1989/90 % change |
|---|---|---|---|---|---|---|---|---|
| Number of animals slaughtered *(thousands)* | | | | | | | | |
| Average dressed carcass weight *(kilogrammes)* | | | | | | | | |
| Gross indigenous production | 82.0 | 74.0 | 70.0 | 73.0 | 72.0 | 71.0 | 72.0 | 1.4 |
| *Minus:* Meat equivalent of exported live animals | - | - | - | 4.0 | - | - | - | .. |
| *Plus:* Meat from slaughterings of imported live animals | - | - | - | - | - | - | - | .. |
| Total meat production from slaughtered animals | 82.0 | 74.0 | 70.0 | 69.0 | 72.0 | 71.0 | 72.0 | 1.4 |
| *Minus:* Exports of meat | 1.0 | 5.0 | 14.0 | 4.0 | 2.0 | - | 2.0 | .. |
| *Plus:* Imports of meat | 3.0 | 2.0 | 2.0 | 1.0 | 3.0 | 1.0 | 7.0 | 600.0 |
| *Minus:* Stock variations | -2.0 | - | - | 2.0 | -1.0 | 1.0 | - | |
| Meat consumption | 86.0 | 71.0 | 58.0 | 64.0 | 74.0 | 71.0 | 77.0 | 8.5 |
| Consumption per head *(kilogrammes per year)* | 3.7 | 3.1 | 2.5 | 2.7 | 3.1 | 3.0 | 3.2 | 8.0 |

# YOUGOSLAVIE

*Milliers de tonnes métriques - Poids en carcasse parée*

*TOTAL VIANDE / TOTAL MEAT*

| | 1984 | 1985 | 1986 | 1987 | 1988 | 1989 | 1990 | 1989/90 % var. |
|---|---|---|---|---|---|---|---|---|
| **Nombre d'animaux abattus** *(milliers)* | | | | | | | | |
| **Poids moyen en carcasse parée** *(kilogrammes)* | | | | | | | | |
| **Production indigène brute** | 1716.0 | 1617.0 | 1587.0 | 1720.0 | 1710.0 | 1611.0 <sup>e</sup> | 1581.0 <sup>e</sup> | -1.9 |
| *Moins:* Équivalent en viande des animaux exportés vivants | 28.0 | 30.0 | 28.0 | 67.0 | 55.0 | 56.0 <sup>e</sup> | 7.0 <sup>e</sup> | -87.5 |
| *Plus:* Viande provenant des abbattages d'animaux importés vivants | - | - | - | - | - | - | - | .. |
| **Production totale de viande provenant des abattages** | 1688.0 | 1587.0 | 1559.0 | 1653.0 | 1655.0 | 1555.0 | 1574.0 | 1.2 |
| *Moins:* Exportations de viande | 155.0 | 155.0 | 87.0 | 95.0 | 105.0 | 74.0 | 62.0 | -16.2 |
| *Plus:* Importations de viande | 32.0 | 35.0 | 98.0 | 80.0 | 100.0 | 174.0 | 176.0 | 1.1 |
| *Moins:* Variations des stocks | 83.0 | 14.0 | -10.0 | 20.0 | 5.0 | -16.0 | -26.0 | |
| **Consommation de viande** | 1482.0 | 1453.0 | 1580.0 | 1618.0 | 1645.0 | 1671.0 | 1714.0 | 2.6 |
| **Consommation par tête** *(kilogrammes par an)* | 64.5 | 62.8 | 67.9 | 69.1 | 69.8 | 70.5 | 72.0 | 2.1 |

## PRODUCTION INDIGENE BRUTE DE VIANDE
## MEAT GROSS INDIGENOUS PRODUCTION

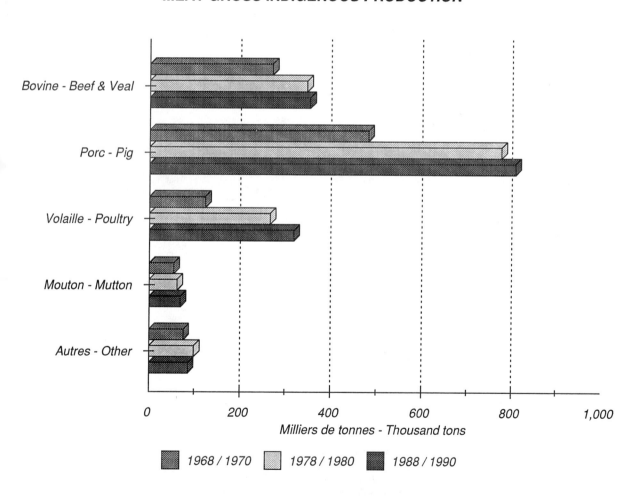

*Milliers de tonnes - Thousand tons*

1968 / 1970      1978 / 1980      1988 / 1990

# ALSO AVAILABLE

*Agricultural Policies, Markets and Trade*
**Monitoring and Outlook 1991** (1991)
(51 91 03 1) ISBN 92-64-13490-5                                      FF190    £25.00    US$46.00    DM74
**Economic Accounts for Agriculture: 1976-1989** (1991)
(51 91 07 3) ISBN 92-64-03521-4                                      FF170    £23.00    US$40.00    DM70
**Food Consumption Statistics: 1979-1988** (1991)
(51 91 02 3) ISBN 92-64-03513-3                                      FF425    £60.00    US$100.00    DM175

# ÉGALEMENT DISPONIBLES

**Comptes économiques de l'agriculture : 1976-1989** (1991)
(51 91 07 3) ISBN 92-64-03521-4                                        FF170    £23.00    US$40.00    DM70

*Politiques, marchés et échanges agricoles*

**Suivi et perspectives 1991** (1991)
(51 91 03 2) ISBN 92-64-23490-X                                        FF190    £25.00    US$46.00    DM74

**Statistiques de la consommation des denrées alimentaires : 1979-1988** (1991)
(51 91 02 3) ISBN 92-64-03513-3                                        FF425    £60.00    US$100.00   DM175

*Prix de vente au public dans la librairie du siège de l'OCDE.*

*LE CATALOGUE DES PUBLICATIONS de l'OCDE et ses suppléments seront envoyés*
*gratuitement sur demande adressée soit à l'OCDE, Service des Publications,*
*soit au distributeur des publications de l'OCDE de votre pays.*

# MAIN SALES OUTLETS OF OECD PUBLICATIONS – PRINCIPAUX POINTS DE VENTE DES PUBLICATIONS DE L'OCDE

**Argentina – Argentine**
Carlos Hirsch S.R.L.
Galería Güemes, Florida 165, 4° Piso
1333 Buenos Aires          Tel. (1) 331.1787 y 331.2391
                           Telefax: (1) 331.1787

**Australia – Australie**
D.A. Book (Aust.) Pty. Ltd.
648 Whitehorse Road, P.O.B 163
Mitcham, Victoria 3132          Tel. (03) 873.4411
                                Telefax: (03) 873.5679

**Austria – Autriche**
OECD Publications and Information Centre
Schedestrasse 7
D-W 5300 Bonn 1 (Germany)   Tel. (49.228) 21.60.45
                            Telefax: (49.228) 26.11.04

Gerold & Co.
Graben 31
Wien I                      Tel. (0222) 533.50.14

**Belgium – Belgique**
Jean De Lannoy
Avenue du Roi 202
B-1060 Bruxelles      Tel. (02) 538.51.69/538.08.41
                      Telefax: (02) 538.08.41

**Canada**
Renouf Publishing Company Ltd.
1294 Algoma Road
Ottawa, ON K1B 3W8          Tel. (613) 741.4333
                            Telefax: (613) 741.5439
Stores:
61 Sparks Street
Ottawa, ON K1P 5R1          Tel. (613) 238.8985
211 Yonge Street
Toronto, ON M5B 1M4          Tel. (416) 363.3171
Federal Publications
165 University Avenue
Toronto, ON M5H 3B8          Tel. (416) 581.1552
                            Telefax: (416)581.1743
Les Éditions La Liberté Inc.
3020 Chemin Sainte-Foy
Sainte-Foy, PQ G1X 3V6          Tel. (418) 658.3763
                                Telefax: (418) 658.3763

**China – Chine**
China National Publications Import
 Export Corporation (CNPIEC)
P.O. Box 88
Beijing                     Tel. 44.0731
                            Telefax: 401.5661

**Denmark – Danemark**
Munksgaard Export and Subscription Service
35, Nørre Søgade, P.O. Box 2148
DK-1016 København K          Tel. (33) 12.85.70
                            Telefax: (33) 12.93.87

**Finland – Finlande**
Akateeminen Kirjakauppa
Keskuskatu 1, P.O. Box 128
00100 Helsinki          Tel. (358 0) 12141
                        Telefax: (358 0) 121.4441

**France**
OECD/OCDE
Mail Orders/Commandes par correspondance:
2, rue André-Pascal
75775 Paris Cédex 16          Tel. (33-1) 45.24.82.00
                             Telefax: (33-1) 45.24.85.00
                              or (33-1) 45.24.81.76
                             Telex: 620 160 OCDE
Bookshop/Librairie:
33, rue Octave-Feuillet
75016 Paris          Tel. (33-1) 45.24.81.67
                          (33-1) 45.24.81.81
Librairie de l'Université
12a, rue Nazareth
13100 Aix-en-Provence          Tel. 42.26.18.08
                               Telefax: 42.26.63.26

**Germany – Allemagne**
OECD Publications and Information Centre
Schedestrasse 7
D-W 5300 Bonn 1          Tel. (0228) 21.60.45
                         Telefax: (0228) 26.11.04

**Greece – Grèce**
Librairie Kauffmann
Mavrokordatou 9
106 78 Athens          Tel. 322.21.60
                       Telefax: 363.39.67

**Hong Kong**
Swindon Book Co. Ltd.
13 - 15 Lock Road
Kowloon, Hong Kong          Tel. 366.80.31
                            Telefax: 739.49.75

**Iceland – Islande**
Mál Mog Menning
Laugavegi 18, Pósthólf 392
121 Reykjavik          Tel. 162.35.23

**India – Inde**
Oxford Book and Stationery Co.
Scindia House
New Delhi 110001          Tel.(11) 331.5896/5308
                          Telefax: (11) 332.5993
17 Park Street
Calcutta 700016          Tel. 240832

**Indonesia – Indonésie**
Pdii-Lipi
P.O. Box 269/JKSMG/88
Jakarta 12790          Tel. 583467
                       Telex: 62 875

**Ireland – Irlande**
TDC Publishers – Library Suppliers
12 North Frederick Street
Dublin 1          Tel. 74.48.35/74.96.77
                  Telefax: 74.84.16

**Israel**
Electronic Publications only
Publications électroniques seulement
Sophist Systems Ltd.
71 Allenby Street
Tel-Aviv 65134          Tel. 3-29.00.21
                        Telefax: 3-29.92.39

**Italy – Italie**
Libreria Commissionaria Sansoni
Via Duca di Calabria 1/1
50125 Firenze          Tel. (055) 64.54.15
                       Telefax: (055) 64.12.57
Via Bartolini 29
20155 Milano          Tel. (02) 36.50.83
Editrice e Libreria Herder
Piazza Montecitorio 120
00186 Roma          Tel. 679.46.28
                    Telex: NATEL I 621427
Libreria Hoepli
Via Hoepli 5
20121 Milano          Tel. (02) 86.54.46
                      Telefax: (02) 805.28.86
Libreria Scientifica
Dott. Lucio de Biasio 'Aeiou'
Via Meravigli 16
20123 Milano          Tel. (02) 805.68.98
                      Telefax: (02) 80.01.75

**Japan – Japon**
OECD Publications and Information Centre
Landic Akasaka Building
2-3-4 Akasaka, Minato-ku
Tokyo 107          Tel. (81.3) 3586.2016
                   Telefax: (81.3) 3584.7929

**Korea – Corée**
Kyobo Book Centre Co. Ltd.
P.O. Box 1658, Kwang Hwa Moon
Seoul          Tel. 730.78.91
               Telefax: 735.00.30

**Malaysia – Malaisie**
Co-operative Bookshop Ltd.
University of Malaya
P.O. Box 1127, Jalan Pantai Baru
59700 Kuala Lumpur
Malaysia          Tel. 756.5000/756.5425
                  Telefax: 757.3661

**Netherlands – Pays-Bas**
SDU Uitgeverij
Christoffel Plantijnstraat 2
Postbus 20014
2500 EA's-Gravenhage          Tel. (070 3) 78.99.11
Voor bestellingen:            Tel. (070 3) 78.98.80
                              Telefax: (070 3) 47.63.51

**New Zealand – Nouvelle-Zélande**
GP Publications Ltd.
Customer Services
33 The Esplanade - P.O. Box 38-900
Petone, Wellington          Tel. (04) 5685.555
                            Telefax: (04) 5685.333

**Norway – Norvège**
Narvesen Info Center - NIC
Bertrand Narvesens vei 2
P.O. Box 6125 Etterstad
0602 Oslo 6          Tel. (02) 57.33.00
                     Telefax: (02) 68.19.01

**Pakistan**
Mirza Book Agency
65 Shahrah Quaid-E-Azam
Lahore 3          Tel. 66.839
                  Telex: 44886 UBL PK. Attn: MIRZA BK

**Portugal**
Livraria Portugal
Rua do Carmo 70-74
Apart. 2681
1117 Lisboa Codex          Tel.: (01) 347.49.82/3/4/5
                           Telefax: (01) 347.02.64

**Singapore – Singapour**
Information Publications Pte. Ltd.
Pei-Fu Industrial Building
24 New Industrial Road No. 02-06
Singapore 1953          Tel. 283.1786/283.1798
                        Telefax: 284.8875

**Spain – Espagne**
Mundi-Prensa Libros S.A.
Castelló 37, Apartado 1223
Madrid 28001          Tel. (91) 431.33.99
                      Telefax: (91) 575.39.98
Libreria Internacional AEDOS
Consejo de Ciento 391
08009 - Barcelona          Tel. (93) 488.34.92
                           Telefax: (93) 487.76.59
Llibreria de la Generalitat
Palau Moja
Rambla dels Estudis, 118
08002 - Barcelona   Tel. (93) 318.80.12 (Subscripcions)
                         (93) 302.67.23 (Publicacions)
                    Telefax: (93) 412.18.54

**Sri Lanka**
Centre for Policy Research
c/o Colombo Agencies Ltd.
No. 300-304, Galle Road
Colombo 3          Tel. (1) 574240, 573551-2
                   Telefax: (1) 575394, 510711

**Sweden – Suède**
Fritzes Fackboksföretaget
Box 16356
Regeringsgatan 12
103 27 Stockholm          Tel. (08) 23.89.00
                          Telefax: (08) 20.50.21
Subscription Agency/Abonnements:
Wennergren-Williams AB
Nordenflychtsvägen 74
Box 30004
104 25 Stockholm          Tel. (08) 13.67.00
                          Telefax: (08) 618.62.32

**Switzerland – Suisse**
OECD Publications and Information Centre
Schedestrasse 7
D-W 5300 Bonn 1 (Germany)   Tel. (49.228) 21.60.45
                            Telefax: (49.228) 26.11.04
Suisse romande
Maditec S.A.
Chemin des Palettes 4
1020 Renens/Lausanne          Tel. (021) 635.08.65
                              Telefax: (021) 635.07.80
Librairie Payot
6 rue Grenus
1211 Genève 11          Tel. (022) 731.89.50
                        Telex: 28356
Subscription Agency – Service des Abonnements
Naville S.A.
7, rue Lévrier
1201 Genève          Tél.: (022) 732.24.00
                     Telefax: (022) 738.87.13

**Taiwan – Formose**
Good Faith Worldwide Int'l. Co. Ltd.
9th Floor, No. 118, Sec. 2
Chung Hsiao E. Road
Taipei          Tel. (02) 391.7396/391.7397
                Telefax: (02) 394.9176

**Thailand – Thaïlande**
Suksit Siam Co. Ltd.
113, 115 Fuang Nakhon Rd.
Opp. Wat Rajbopith
Bangkok 10200          Tel. (662) 251.1630
                       Telefax: (662) 236.7783

**Turkey – Turquie**
Kültur Yayinlari Is-Türk Ltd. Sti.
Atatürk Bulvari No. 191/Kat. 21
Kavaklidere/Ankara          Tel. 25.07.60
Dolmabahce Cad. No. 29
Besiktas/Istanbul          Tel. 160.71.88
                           Telex: 43482B

**United Kingdom – Royaume-Uni**
HMSO
Gen. enquiries          Tel. (071) 873 0011
Postal orders only:
P.O. Box 276, London SW8 5DT
Personal Callers HMSO Bookshop
49 High Holborn, London WC1V 6HB
                        Telefax: 071 873 2000
     Branches at: Belfast, Birmingham, Bristol, Edinburgh,
                                              Manchester

**United States – États-Unis**
OECD Publications and Information Centre
2001 L Street N.W., Suite 700
Washington, D.C. 20036-4910          Tel. (202) 785.6323
                                     Telefax: (202) 785.0350

**Venezuela**
Libreria del Este
Avda F. Miranda 52, Aptdo. 60337
Edificio Galipán
Caracas 106          Tel. 951.1705/951.2307/951.1297
                     Telegram: Libreste Caracas

**Yugoslavia – Yougoslavie**
Jugoslovenska Knjiga
Knez Mihajlova 2, P.O. Box 36
Beograd          Tel. (011) 621.992
                 Telefax: (011) 625.970

Orders and inquiries from countries where Distributors have
not yet been appointed should be sent to: OECD Publications Service, 2 rue André-Pascal, 75775 Paris Cédex 16,
France.

Les commandes provenant de pays où l'OCDE n'a pas
encore désigné de distributeur devraient être adressées à
OCDE, Service des Publications, 2, rue André-Pascal, 75775
Paris Cédex 16, France.

OECD PUBLICATIONS, 2 rue André-Pascal, 75775 PARIS CEDEX 16
PRINTED IN FRANCE
(51 92 06 3) ISBN 92-64-03538-9 - No. 46058 1992